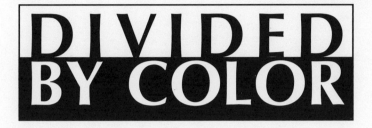

AMERICAN POLITICS AND POLITICAL ECONOMY

A series edited by Benjamin I. Page

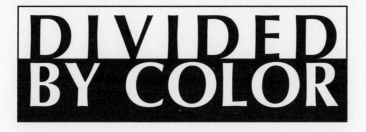

RACIAL POLITICS AND DEMOCRATIC IDEALS

Donald R. Kinder

and

Lynn M. Sanders

THE UNIVERSITY OF CHICAGO PRESS
Chicago & London

DONALD R. KINDER is professor of political science and of psychology at the University of Michigan and the coauthor of *News That Matters*. Lynn M. Sanders is assistant professor of political science at the University of Chicago.

THE UNIVERSITY OF CHICAGO PRESS, CHICAGO 60637
THE UNIVERSITY OF CHICAGO PRESS, LTD., LONDON

© 1996 by The University of Chicago
All rights reserved. Published 1996
Printed in the United States of America
05 04 03 02 01 00 99 98 97 96   1 2 3 4 5

ISBN: 0-226-43573-3 (cloth)
      0-226-43574-1 (paper)

Library of Congress Cataloging-in-Publication Data

Kinder, Donald R.
      Divided by color : racial politics and democtatic ideals / Donald R. Kinder and Lynn
M. Sanders.
            p.   cm. —(American politics and political economy)
      Includes bibliographical references and index.
      1. United States—Race relations—Political aspects.   I. Sanders, Lynn M.   II. Series.
E184.615.K483   1996
323.1'73—dc20   95-42651
                                                                                          CIP

To Janet,
for everything

CONTENTS

ACKNOWLEDGMENTS

When do books begin? Hard to say. This one got its start, perhaps, in the fall of 1969 when I wandered into graduate school and had the good fortune to meet up with David Sears. Sears was about to embark on an analysis of the just-completed contest for the mayor's office of Los Angeles. The race had matched Tom Bradley, then a city councilman, against Sam Yorty, the incumbent mayor. Bradley was black, Yorty was white, and the people of Los Angeles were angry and apprehensive, preoccupied with memories of their city burning. Trying to understand this one episode, I fell into the study of race and politics, from which I have not yet recovered. The problem of race in America, as Gunnar Myrdal put it, "is difficult to settle and equally difficult to leave alone" (1944, p. lxvii).

If I am foggy about when the book began, I am clear about the many debts Sanders and I incurred along the way to its completion, and I am pleased to record our appreciation here. For starters, I am grateful to David Sears for introducing me, by inspired example, to the scientific study of social problems; to colleagues Michael Dawson (now at the University of Chicago) and Tali Mendelberg (now at Princeton), who collaborated with us in our examination of the 1988 American presidential campaign; to Christopher Achen, who provided statistical advice at a few key points; to Tom Nelson (now at Ohio State University), who contributed to our development of the idea of opinion frames; to Mary Breijak and Julie Weatherbee, who helped prepare parts of the manuscript for publication; and to a succession of remarkable graduate students who assisted in the computing, among them Lisa D'Ambrosio, Karin Tamerius, Margaret Petralla, and especially Kimberly Gross. Late in the game, when things looked bleak, Gross stepped in and saved us. We owe her a lot. We are grateful also to Cecilia Bartoli and Wolfgang Amadeus Mozart, whose collaboration made the final stages of writing almost bearable.

Ah, yes: money and time. At the earliest stage of the project, before this book was even a gleam in our eye, we received a Research Partnership Grant from the Rackham Graduate School at the University of Michigan. This support was crucial: it gave Sanders time to switch fields of specialization, from political theory to American politics. We thank John D'Arms, then dean of Rackham, for creating this program, and we thank him as well for the wit, warmth, and wisdom he gave the university in his tenure as dean. The Rackham grant, and a sabbatical year I spent in that best of all possible worlds, the Center for Advanced Study in the Behavioral Sciences, got us started. I spent the tag end of my Center year reading American history, after Gardner Lindzey, then director of the Center, said that it was OK to do so, that I could follow my interests wherever they carried me. I thank Gardner, Bob Scott, associate director, and the Center staff, for making my stay so enjoyable and stimulating (I would be delighted to do it again). Then, midway through the project (though we thought we were nearly finished), I was awarded a Guggenheim Fellowship. Along with support generously provided by the College of Literature Arts and Sciences at Michigan, the Guggenheim allowed me a full year of writing, unencumbered by duties of administration or teaching (well, mostly unencumbered). I am deeply grateful to the Guggenheim Foundation and to the college for this beneficence. Finally, there would have been no evidence to analyze, no National Election Study, no General Social Survey, and so no book to write, without the support of the National Science Foundation.

We are pleased to be associated with the University of Chicago Press, and not just because of the fine books it publishes. The Press is also people, and for us, especially, it is one person, our editor, John Tryneski. Tryneski is the perfect editor; he comes fully equipped: excellent sense of humor, great talker, shrewd judgment, and not least, epic patience, We thank him for believing that someday there would be a book.

Before we were done, we presented pieces of our argument and portions of our evidence to a variety of audiences: at annual meetings of the American Political Science Association, and at seminars at Princeton, Cal Tech, Michigan, Stanford, Harvard, Ohio State, and Yale. On these occasions we received many stimulating questions. Our interrogators may have forgotten their questions by now, but we have not, and though it has taken us a while we finally have come up with some answers. For their penetrating questions, we would like to thank Roger Brown, Robert Dahl, Michael Dawson, Don Green, Jennifer Hochschild, Mary Jackman, Morgan Kousser, David Mayhew, Doug Rivers, Ian Shapiro, Paul Starr, and Donald Stokes.

Several people read some of what we had written and told us what they thought. For their good advice and helpful comments, we are grateful to Stanley Feldman, Steve Rosenstone, Jim Stimson, and especially Mo Fiorina, who really told us what he thought, and on more than one occasion. A few people went so far as to read the whole manuscript. One such person served as a reader for the Press, and though anonymous, he or she is a real person to us (the book is certainly different and perhaps even better for his or her efforts). Another dutiful reader is Ben Page, who gave us a detailed and perceptive assessment, one that we returned to often as we prepared the book for publication. Then there is Don Herzog, good friend and esteemed colleague. Herzog owns the quickest mind and the fastest fingers on the planet; in incredibly short order, he read the entire manuscript and provided us with some thirty pages of (single-spaced) advice. We certainly didn't take it all, but we took a lot of it, and thinking about what Herzog wrote was as interesting an intellectual experience as anyone could hope for.

For all this support and care and advice, we are amazed and most grateful. Of course, and unfortunately, nobody named above can be blamed for what we have written here (though it will surprise no one if we try).

Finally, Janet Weiss slogged through the whole book once and fragments of it many times. She offered advice, insisted on clarity, refused to give in when she thought we were wrong, and supplied praise and support in the dark days. Without all these contributions, the book would never have been completed. It is dedicated to her—but not because of the help she gave the book, as essential as it was. The book is dedicated to her for something more important: for her many and astonishing gifts that, for reasons that remain mysterious, she has chosen to bestow on me.

The most precious of these gifts are the Kinder-Weiss boys. During the life of this project, our children grew alarmingly. Benjamin, the eldest, now teeters on the edge of dreaded adolescence. Jacob, the youngest, is no longer a baby (he can identify a hexagon and does a passable imitation of a donkey, drawn from *Pinocchio*). Samuel, the middle son, eyebrows arched, mischievous smile crossing his otherwise angelic face, gave this project its family name. Sam called it "Dad's ten-year book." He was impressed with its length and bewildered that it took so long to complete. My feelings exactly.

PART I

DIVIDED BY RACE

CHAPTER ONE

Race and Democratic Aspirations in America

One late afternoon in December 1955 in Montgomery, Alabama, Mrs. Rosa Parks left work at the Fair Department Store. She boarded a bus, found a seat, and settled in for the ride home. The bus was soon full, whites in the front, blacks in the back, in accordance with the segregation codes then in effect in Montgomery, as in much of the South. When the bus stopped to pick up an additional white passenger, the driver, J. P. Blake, told the four blacks sitting in the forwardmost row to get up and move to the rear. Mrs. Parks was among them, and while the others gathered their belongings and moved to the back of the bus, she remained, saying she was not in the white section and didn't think she ought to move. Blake threatened Parks with arrest; Parks replied, softly but firmly, that he should do what he had to do; she was not moving. Mrs. Parks didn't move, and she was of course arrested. Her arrest and incarceration are famous, for they set in motion the Montgomery bus boycott, a turning point in the black struggle for civil rights in the twentieth century. Rosa Parks had found not just a seat, but a place in American history.[1]

Forty years passed, and Mrs. Parks was back in the news. This time the story was ordinary, all-too familiar; but because of who Rosa Parks was and what she had done, it drew national attention and wide comment. In the fall of 1994 Mrs. Parks was living quietly on modest means in Detroit. A young black man from the neighborhood, reeking of alcohol, broke into her home, beat her until she gave up what money she had, and fled. "I had never been hit in that manner in my life," Mrs. Parks said later. "I was screaming and trying to ask him not to hit me. . . . we still have a long way to go, and so many of our children are going astray." Questioned after his quick arrest, Mrs. Parks's assailant said he had never heard of Rosa Parks, had no idea of the role she had played in the previous generation's fight for civil rights.[2]

Mrs. Parks's two stories, and the arc of history that connects them, are precisely where our analysis begins. In 1955 the country was entering a period of enormous social change, marked in the early stages by high hopes and moral certainties. Came the full flowering of the noble and heroic struggle for civil rights; historic Supreme Court decisions finding segregation unconstitutional; and landmark federal legislation declaring discrimination a crime. But came also George Wallace and his stunningly successful and racially reactionary third-party movement; the assassinations of Medgar Evers, Malcolm X, and Martin Luther King; and in cities in all parts of the country, catastrophic riots, grinding poverty, and explosions of crime. The moral certainties are gone now; the high hopes have given way to cynicism and, not infrequently, despair.[3]

Where are we now, four decades after Rosa Parks's quiet defiance? In 1995 slavery is a dim and fading memory; segregation backed by the force of law dismantled; discrimination on account of race or color illegal. Compared with the past, American society has come a long way, surely. Race relations must be judged not only against the nightmare of slavery and Jim Crow, however, but also against reasonable constructions of what American democracy could and should be. And with democratic aspirations in mind, we are inclined to agree with Rosa Parks: "We still have a long way to go."

Consider segregation as one test. The Jim Crow statutes are gone, but segregation by race continues. American cities are now more segregated by race than they were at the turn of the century.[4] In the public schools of the nation's large cities today, segregation prevails and may even be increasing.[5] Racial segregation creates and amplifies economic inequalities, and it makes democratic projects more difficult to carry out.[6] Genuine democracy, according to a prominent strand of contemporary American political theory, requires real deliberation: citizens joining together to discuss public issues in their neighborhoods, at city council meetings, or in some other comparable forum.[7] But because American society is deeply segregated by race, such democratic assemblies seldom cross racial lines. Citizens who do not live in the same neighborhoods cannot easily come together, not to mention that the more citizens are drawn apart, the fewer shared concerns they have to discuss.

Like segregation, discrimination has not disappeared either. Since the 1964 Civil Rights Act, discrimination by race has been illegal, and surely it is neither as flagrant nor as pervasive today as it once was. But it continues. Blacks still face discrimination on the job. Blacks looking to purchase homes are still steered away from white neighborhoods. Blacks still endure racist epithets on the streets, harassment by police officers as they make their way through public spaces, rudeness and excessive surveillance while they shop, coolness from their teachers and bosses, and racist jokes from their co-workers. Whereas whites tend to believe that discrimination is a problem of the past, blacks see it as pervasive in society and a demoralizing presence in their own lives.[8]

What about participation in the political life of the nation, perhaps the most fundamental of democratic requirements? Progress here has been a long time coming. The Fifteenth Amendment to the United States Constitution, ratified in 1870, was designed to ensure that former black slaves, freed by the Thirteenth Amendment and made citizens by the Fourteenth, would not be denied the right to vote "on account of race, color, or previous condition of servitude."[9] And for the brief moment of Reconstruction, it was true.[10] In the South as a whole, as many as two-thirds of the eligible blacks voted in national and state elections, and scores of blacks were elected to statehouses and to Congress.[11] As Reconstruction came to an end, however, blacks quickly disappeared from political life. Across the South, white-dominated legislatures implemented an assortment of ingenious contrivances to banish blacks from politics, erasing the Fifteenth Amendment's bold promise. These included literacy requirements, property tests, grandfather clauses, the poll tax, the understanding clause, and, later, the white primary: all in all, as V. O. Key Jr. once put it, "the most impressive systems of obstacles between the voter and the ballot box known to the democratic world."[12] As late as 1940, only about 3% of southern blacks were registered to vote. Disqualified from politics, the rest were, as Judith Shklar would say, "dishonored" and "scorned by their fellow citizens."[13]

The obstacles are gone now, of course, swept away by hundreds of local struggles, by Supreme Court decisions, by the Voting Rights Act of 1965, and by the threat of federal enforcement. As a consequence, black participation in elections towers over what it was a generation ago, and the number of black elected officials has risen dramatically. This is progress to be sure, but blacks still vote less faithfully than whites do, and they lag further behind on forms of democratic participation that go beyond voting.[14] Moreover, despite recent gains, black citizens remain substantially underrepresented: all together, fewer than 2% of elected officials in the United States are black.[15] This condition violates the democratic standard that the composition of elected assemblies should resemble the population as a whole, and it is likely to worsen in the future, not improve.[16] Recent increases in black representation have been due in large measure to the creation of favorable districts through reapportionment or court order, since it remains today not quite impossible, but very difficult, for black candidates to succeed outside black majority districts.[17] And such districts are currently under challenge in the courts, attacked as extreme and discriminatory, not at all what the 1965 Voting Rights Act was meant to do.

Democracy also depends on material conditions that go beyond matters of formal rights. Vast differences in wealth or income distort the degree to which all citizens have an equal say in politics. Viewed from this perspective, the racial record in the United States is mixed. On the one hand, over the last forty years or so, black Americans have made significant inroads into the middle class, sharing in the economic prosperity and educational opportunities that came to most of American society following World War II.[18] On the other, imposing racial differences in employment, income, and wealth remain. Blacks are twice as likely as whites to be unemployed; they are substantially overrepresented among "discouraged workers," those who have given up looking for work and so do not appear in official unemployment figures; and when they are employed, they earn less. These differences are large, but they are dwarfed by racial differences in wealth: according to the most recent figures, the average white household commands more than *ten times* the financial assets of the average black household. Furthermore, the growth of the black middle class needs to be placed against the collapse of the core of many large American cities, where most poor blacks live. There, epidemics of idleness, theft, violence, drugs, and welfare dependence have transformed many inner-city communities into "deadly neighborhoods."[19]

Perhaps the most complicated aspect of race relations in America today concerns attitude. Reviewing the results of dozens of public opinion surveys spread across several decades, Smith and Sheatsley conclude, quite correctly, we think, that "a massive and wide-ranging liberalization of racial attitudes has swept America over the last forty years. . . . Whites have steadily abandoned beliefs in the desirability of segregation and the notion that blacks are and should be second-class citizens."[20] Not so long ago white Americans defended racial segregation and supported racial discrimination as matters of principle; now, majorities say that blacks and whites should attend school together, that blacks should have an equal chance to compete for jobs, that they have a right to live wherever they wish.

If democratic politics is to succeed, citizens must believe that everyone should have a chance to participate; they must value each others' comments and contributions; they must treat each other with respect. From this perspective, the dramatic increases in white Americans' support for racially egalitarian principles are clearly welcome; they indicate a greater willingness on the part of whites to treat blacks democratically, at least in principle.

But what Americans think about racial equality as a matter of principle must be distinguished from what they think about efforts to *apply* racial equality. For political analysis, the difference is crucial. Douglas Rae and his colleagues put this point well:

> Our fascination with equality lies . . . with the repeated moment of transition from theory into practice. The importance of this moment is obvious, since it forces an abstraction's sterile form to accommodate life. Trying to make laws or families or universities live up to the doctrine of equality is the point at which we discover egalitarianism as a living conception.[21]

As it happens, white Americans express considerably more enthusiasm for the principle of racial equality than they do for policies that are designed to bring the principle to life—for "egalitarianism as a living conception." By the late 1970s, for example, most whites endorsed the idea that black and white children should attend school together, but only one in four said that the federal government should see to it that this actually happens, and scarcely anyone favored the specific remedy of busing. The "massive and wide-ranging liberalization of racial attitudes," while real enough, applies only to principles, not to policies. White opinion on government efforts to desegregate schools or federal programs to assist blacks shows nothing like the dramatic increase in support we see for egalitarian principles. Most opinion trends on policies are flat; some policies to promote racial equality are actually less popular now than they were a decade or two ago.[22]

And it is public opinion on policy that we aim to illuminate here. Our purpose is to undertake an exploration of the terrain of current American racial politics by examining public opinion toward policies on race. In light of our turbulent past, and on the eve of a new century, what do Americans think about issues of race? What are their views on affirmative action, school desegregation, federal aid to cities, and welfare reform? Our first objective is to describe the contours of public opinion across a range of issues that captures the diverse political manifestations of racial conflict today.

We do this for white *and* black Americans. By paying attention to both sides of the color line, we depart from what has become a standard and unwelcome practice in research on public opinion. Sometimes studies simply ignore race, on the idea that the political differences between blacks and whites are either negligible or uninteresting. Or blacks are set aside entirely, on the idea that there are differences, but ones that would confuse analysis of the public as a whole. Both procedures deprive us of any understanding of the ways that black Americans think about matters of race; they also prevent us from hearing the dialogue that takes place between white and black Americans over their common future—however intermittent and halting such a conversation might be. Our investigation insists that there are two sides to the color line: both white and black voices are represented here.

We hope to offer an accurate and detailed description of public opinion, but our main purpose is to explain the views white and black Americans hold on matters of race. Why do Americans believe what they do about school desegregation or affirmative action or Food Stamps? Perhaps public opinion on matters of race reflects the familiar politics of self-interest: then opinions would depend on whether the policy appeared to pose an economic threat or promise an economic benefit. Or perhaps public opinion on such matters as affirmative action and Food Stamps is explained by group animosities and solidarities: whites oppose such policies because they feel resentment toward blacks, while blacks support such policies because they feel identified with their race. Perhaps public opinion over race is really a matter of principle, a clash of competing values: affirmative action might be rejected on the grounds that it violates the idea of individualism, or embraced because it advances the idea of equality. Or perhaps public opinion depends primarily on how the issues are raised and defined: then opinion would hinge on the energies and activities of elites who seek to frame issues to their own political advantage.

Answers to these questions are important. They tell us not just what public opinion is, but what it means. If political conflict over matters of race takes the form of a clash of interests, that is one thing. Interest politics are a familiar story, one that lies at the center of pluralist accounts of the American political process. If instead the divisions over racial issues reflect social hatreds and cherished principles, that is quite another. Then the pluralist language of bargaining and compromise seems much less pertinent, and optimism about the democratic resolution of racial conflict much less secure. If conflict over matters of race can be reduced or exacerbated by how the issue is framed, then that is yet another thing. Such a result would mean that responsibility for how (and whether) racial conflict is confronted and resolved lies importantly in the hands of elites. Of course, the politics of race might well be all these things: a stew of interests, social attachments, and animosities, as well as principles, cooked up according to elite recipes. Our main business here is to determine what is important and what is not among the plausible ingredients of public opinion on matters of race.

As we do so, we will use public opinion on race as a window on American democracy, much as Gunnar Myrdal did fifty years ago in *An American Dilemma*.[23] Examining public opinion on affirmative action and welfare reform becomes a way for us to gauge the extent to which America lives up to its democratic aspirations. Half a century after Myrdal, we hope our investigation will clarify an important aspect of American political life that seems today, if anything, increasingly difficult and inaccessible to analysis.

To carry this project out, we have gone directly to the source, to American citizens themselves: black and white, young and old, rich and poor, men and women. Our analysis draws primarily upon recent national surveys carried out by the Center for Political Studies of the Institute for Social Research, located at the University of Michigan, as part of the Center's ongoing series of National Election Studies. Given our interest in public opinion, it is fitting that our evidence should come from sample surveys. And not just any surveys: the National Election Studies possess many advantages for the investigation we undertake here, not least that they were designed in part with our purposes expressly in mind (more on this in Chapter 2). Our project focuses on contem-

porary opinion on racial matters and depends upon the analysis of recent national surveys, but we try to place our results in a broader context, one informed
by a variety of perspectives: by historical descriptions of American race relations, by detailed accounts of racial conflicts in particular American communities, and by philosophical treatments of the ideas of equality, liberty, and
democracy itself that current debates over race engage.

A LOOK AHEAD

The next chapter introduces the surveys and questions that serve as our
main source of evidence. There, as an empirical point of departure, we demonstrate that blacks and whites are deeply divided over racial policy. The racial
divide is most pronounced on policies such as affirmative action that bear unambiguously and differentially on the fortunes of blacks and whites. But it is
also apparent on issues like federal support for Food Stamps, where the racial
implications are unstated and covert. The differences are enormous, quite unlike any other social cleavage, and cannot be explained by black-white differences in income or educational attainment or indeed anything else. The racial
divide in political aspirations and demands is really racial.

Of course, not all blacks take the same position on affirmative action, just
as all whites do not express the same view on welfare. In Chapter 3 we set out
a general framework for understanding the views Americans hold on matters
of race. We argue that American public opinion—in general and on matters of
race—is an expression of a small set of primary *ingredients:* the material interests that citizens see at stake in the issue; the sympathies and resentments that
citizens feel toward those social groups implicated in the dispute, especially
those groups that the policy appears to benefit or victimize; and commitment
to the political principles that the policy seems to honor or repudiate. We argue
further that how citizens understand a particular issue and, as a consequence,
which ingredients they weigh heavily and which they ignore as they form their
views depend on how the issue is *framed* by political elites. We develop this
general perspective in Chapter 3, translate it into testable claims, and argue
why the results of our empirical tests should be taken seriously.

With these preliminary matters concluded, the second part of the book then
presents empirical results, organized by theoretical claim, one to a chapter. In
Chapter 4 we examine the claim of self-interest: that in their role as citizens,
Americans are single-minded seekers of advantage. According to this view,
high-minded reference to the public interest or the good society is just so much
idle talk; underneath all the uplifting words is the relentless press for personal
advantage. Chapter 5 examines the importance of social animosity to contemporary public opinion on matters of race. A major question there is whether

race prejudice has diminished or even disappeared or whether, instead, it continues as a major force in American politics, taking a more subtle form than the cruder racism of bygone days. In Chapter 6 we consider the place of American principles in public opinion on race. We take up three ideas in particular, each central to the American political experience: equality, economic individualism, and limited government. To what extent is public opinion on affirmative action or welfare reform really a debate about the relative importance of competing principles?

Part Three takes us from ordinary citizens to political elites. Here we argue that American opinion on matters of race depends not only on the sentiments of individual citizens—their interests, social attachments and animosities, and their principles—but also on the nature of the ongoing debate among political elites. Elites are constantly bombarding citizens with suggestions about how issues should be understood or, as we will say, about how issues should be framed. Which frames prevail in elite discourse influence how citizens understand issues and, in the end, what their opinions turn out to be. So we will argue and hope to show in Chapter 7.

Chapters 8 and 9 carry this line of argument forward by taking up how racial issues have been insinuated into the modern American presidential campaign. In Chapter 8 we argue that Democratic and Republican presidential candidates have confronted, since 1964, an electoral predicament that centers on race. The strategic problem for Democratic candidates is to maintain the loyalty and enthusiasm of black voters without alienating conservative whites: for Democratic presidential campaigns, the temptation on matters of race is silence and evasion. The strategic problem of Republican candidates is to draw the support of white conservatives without appearing to make racist appeals: the Republican temptation is racial codewords. We illustrate this analysis in Chapter 9, treating the 1988 presidential campaign as an excellent and dispiriting case in point. We provide a detailed examination of the 1988 presidential campaign itself, as well as an analysis of the difference the campaign made to white and black voters who witnessed it.

In the book's final chapter, we draw out the implications of our results for the performance and promise of American democracy. Because the framework we offer for understanding public opinion is general, some of what we say will transcend the specifics of race itself. Among other long-standing themes in democratic politics, we take up the role of interests in public opinion, the vulnerability of citizens to manipulation by elites, and the recovery of ideas in the study of American political life. But much of what we say pertains directly to racial politics today: we wrestle with the meaning and place of prejudice in our politics, we speculate on the future of code words and neglect in our campaigns, and we suggest how political discussion on matters of race might be improved.

RUNNING THROUGH MUCH POPULAR COMMENTARY on race and politics in America today is a kind of weariness and pessimism, a reflection, perhaps, of the complexity and enormity of the problems facing the country that are bundled together under the heading of race. Such sentiments may have a contemporary feel, but they are not new. Tocqueville, we may remember, regarded the presence of blacks on North American soil as "the most formidable of all the ills that threaten the future of the Union." He believed that slavery would eventually crumble under the weight of civilized world opinion, but that emancipation would lead to a war between the races.[24] At least as pessimistic was Thomas Jefferson, who became persuaded that a future society in which blacks and whites lived side by side in harmony and equality was inconceivable. Jefferson's forecast ran instead to "convulsions which will probably never end but in the extermination of one or the other race."[25] And Abraham Lincoln, even as he saw the necessity for emancipation, remained convinced that the best solution for the problem of race was to establish black colonies outside the borders of the United States, in Central America or in the Caribbean. Colonization, Lincoln reasoned, reconciled the "self-interest" and "moral sense" of the whites. More important, it took account of the sheer physical differences between blacks and whites that Lincoln believed would "forever forbid the two races living together."[26]

Such bleak predictions run squarely counter to the usual American outlook on progress and perpetual improvement. Race has been and remains still our nation's most difficult subject. Slavery, Jim Crow, and even Rosa Parks belong to the history books now, but racial inequalities persist, and they are difficult to talk about. Too often, our discussions degenerate into angry and choreographed exchanges; worse yet, we have no discussion at all, only tense and uneasy silence. Without expecting that we can alter this condition by ourselves, we proceed here with the conviction that on so central an issue as race, discussion is better than silence, and discussion informed by evidence and theory better still. We offer our analysis in the hope that it might contribute to a keener understanding of the nature of racial politics and American democracy at the end of the twentieth century, and with the wish that it might help us find our way to a future that not Jefferson, Tocqueville, or Lincoln could imagine in their time.[27]

CHAPTER TWO

The Racial Divide in Public Opinion

In this chapter we begin our investigation of American public opinion on matters of race. Should the federal government step in to ensure that black and white children attend integrated schools? Is the government obliged to provide special assistance to black citizens? Are affirmative action programs required now to compensate for the injustices of the past? Such questions are central to the continuing political struggle over racial equality, and on such questions, as we will see shortly, blacks and whites are deeply divided. Before we get to the racial divide itself, however, and to the surveys that we rely upon to assess American opinion on racial questions, we should first say a bit about the nature of public opinion, in more general terms, as a way of providing a context for the analysis and results to come.

Nonattitudes and Real Opinions

Few concepts are more central to the analysis and evaluation of politics than public opinion. The concept looms especially large in discussions of democratic politics, since it is to the public's aspirations and demands that democratic governments are supposed to respond. Indeed, the invention and development of the very idea of public opinion are intimately connected to the spread of democracy in the modern world.

Today the concept of public opinion is utterly commonplace, a completely familiar idea. We are daily bombarded with reports on what Americans think about welfare reform, the president's performance, the latest shenanigans in Washington, or some other topical issue. Media coverage of campaigns is obsessed with late-breaking poll results. We are even beginning to learn about what other publics, in faraway places, think about this or that aspect of their society. Public opinion is the atmosphere of American politics; it is the air we citizens breathe.

All the more reason to stop for a moment to say what we think public opinion is. In matters of definition, we follow V. O. Key. In the introduction to his magisterial *Public Opinion and American Democracy*, Key took public opinion to be "those opinions held by private citizens which governments find it prudent to heed."[1] Note that Key is not making the claim that public opinion determines government action. Under Key's definition, government may look to public opinion for guidance, but it may also ignore the public's interests and aspirations; it may try to inform and educate public opinion; it may attempt to pacify or subvert it. Key's definition also leaves aside the question of virtue. In debates over democracy, public opinion has been characterized as the dangerous and deranged ravings of the mob or, on the other side, as the prudent expression of the people's calm and thoughtful reflection. Key's definition allows for both; as he put it, "Opinion may be shared by many or a few people. It may be the veriest whim, or it may be a settled conviction. The opinion may represent a general agreement formed after the widest discussion; it may be far less firmly founded."[2]

A large fraction of the empirical research on American public opinion over the past forty years has been devoted to just this issue: to ascertaining the extent to which public opinion is whim or conviction. With this in mind, the first full encounters with scientific samplings of American opinion in the 1950s were sobering exercises, for they portrayed the public as indifferent to the full and vibrant participation in political life that democracy would seem to require. In the most forceful and influential presentation of this case, Philip Converse concluded that most Americans glance at public life bewildered by ideological concepts, without a consistent outlook on government policy, in possession of genuine opinions on only a few issues, and knowing precious little.[3]

With one exception, these general conclusions have stood up quite well, both to a torrent of criticism and reanalysis, and to the events that have transformed American politics since the 1950s.[4] The exception concerns the nonattitude thesis, the most devastating element in Converse's original indictment. Converse discovered that when Americans were questioned over a succession of interviews, their opinions wobbled back and forth in seemingly random fashion, liberal on one occasion, conservative on the next. Some citizens appeared to possess genuine opinions and hold on to them tenaciously, but they were substantially outnumbered, in Converse's analysis, by those who either confessed their ignorance outright or, when gently prodded by the interviewers, invented a "nonattitude" on the spot. This result makes big trouble for the wide-ranging political discussion that democracy requires, since so many citizens seem unable to take part, disqualified by their own indifference.

Fortunately for democratic prospects, the nonattitude thesis now seems less persuasive. For one thing, we have come to appreciate that unstable opinions are a reflection not only of vague and confused citizens, as Converse would have it, but of vague and confused questions as well. Opinion instability is partly a product of the imperfect way survey questions are formulated and put to citizens.[5] For another, the political controversies of the last thirty years have made plain that real opinions need not be confined to tiny fractions of the public. Conspicuous among such cases were those involving race: the national debate over civil rights that culminated in landmark federal legislation in 1964 and 1965; the impassioned reaction to the urban uprisings of the late 1960s; later still, the controversies surrounding busing as a remedy for school segregation; and affirmative action and reverse discrimination today.

Thus when policies become entangled with race, nonattitudes tend to disappear, replaced by the real thing. Compared with opinion on other matters, opinions on race are more coherent, more tenaciously held, and more difficult to alter.[6] Not all Americans have carefully worked out, deeply felt opinions on all questions of racial policy. And as we will see, even those opinions that are carefully worked out and deeply felt are not immovable. But for the most part— and for better or for worse—Americans know what they think on matters of race. Our subject here is real opinions, not nonattitudes.[7]

Sources of Evidence

To find out what Americans want government to do on racial matters, what they want government not to do, and why, we analyze a series of recent national surveys. Each was carried out by the Center for Political Studies of the Institute for Social Research, located at the University of Michigan, as part of the center's ongoing sequence of National Election Studies. The series began in 1952 and has continued in an unbroken line to the present, covering every presidential and midterm election in between.

The National Election Study (NES) surveys that we analyze have many virtues. They are based on carefully drawn probability samples of the entire American voting-age population. Individual survey questions are tested and refined. The survey questionnaires as a whole are thoroughly examined and revised in pretest interviews. Interviews are conducted by well-trained professionals. Reluctant respondents are pursued doggedly. And responses are meticulously checked and coded before analysis. NES data are hardly free of error and ambiguity, but it is no extravagance to say that in the survey research world, NES (along with the General Social Survey and the Panel Study of Income Dynamics) sets the scientific standard, and that the standard is high.[8]

Our analysis concentrates in the first instance on the NES carried out in the fall of 1986. Immediately following the national midterm elections, a seventy-minute, face-to-face interview was completed with a national sample of 2,176 American citizens of voting age. In order for the demand for new questions to be accommodated, the 1986 questionnaire was divided into two versions, each administered to one-half of the full sample. The unique portion of the first version contained an extensive set of questions on race, while the second version carried many questions on Ronald Reagan's performance as president. For obvious reasons, our analysis will be confined, for the most part, to the first. This move reduces the effective sample size of the 1986 NES to 1,090—still comfortably large for most of our purposes.

The 1986 sample was selected through a multistage area probability design, which ensured that every household in the (continental) United States had an equal probability of falling into the sample. As a result, those black and white Americans interviewed in 1986 should constitute a faithful sample of blacks and whites in the nation as a whole—and they do. On measures of income, region, marital status, and more, the samples we analyze closely resemble the national population. Thus we can proceed on the assumption that our results are representative of black and white Americans generally.[9]

We focus on the 1986 study for the simple reason that it was devoted, in significant measure, to an assessment of the American public's views on matters of race. In the mid-1980s, the governing board of the National Election Studies decided that it was time to review and improve the measurement of American racial opinion on NES, and appointed one of us to oversee the project. With board approval, we developed a large battery of survey questions relevant to the politics of race, guided by two major priorities.

First, we wanted to ensure that NES would carry questions that faithfully represented the complexity of American opinion on public policy. We operated under the assumption that public opinion is studied most profitably in the messy, complicated settings of political application, where "racial attitudes and democratic principles are tested on an everyday basis."[10] Thus our first task was to identify pressing policy issues on race and to specify how such issues should be put to citizens.

A second priority was to develop questions that would help analysts explain public opinion on race policy. With this goal in mind, we first identified theories that have something plausible to say about public opinion on race, and then did our best to develop reliable ways to measure the core explanatory variables nominated by those theories, often by appropriating instrumentation devised by others.

Questions of both types—those that attempt to elicit opinion on race policy and those that attempt to elicit the plausible underpinnings of opinion on race policy—were included in the 1985 NES pilot study (more about pilot studies below). Questions that survived various empirical tests eventually made their way on to the 1986 NES and are a primary basis for our empirical investigation here. In their careful development and comprehensive coverage, these questions have few rivals. They provide the best evidence we know of to describe what Americans think about race policy, and more important, why Americans think what they do about race policy.[11]

In addition to the 1986 NES survey, we also draw upon a pair of smaller national studies, one undertaken in the winter of 1985, the other in the summer of 1989. In NES parlance, these are pilot studies, carried out as part of an ongoing effort to test new instrumentation for possible incorporation into future National Election Studies. For our purpose, the special feature of both studies is that they enabled us to carry out experiments. In such experiments, we ask comparable groups of citizens for their opinions on the identical policy, with the policy framed in alternative ways. Our analysis of the consequences of different frames, for how the public understands the issue, and for what public opinion on the issue turns out to be, forms the empirical centerpiece of Chapter 7.

Our analysis also makes use of the 1988 and 1992 National Election Studies. Because the 1988 study was conducted at the climax of a presidential campaign that spotlighted race—thanks to the early success and visibility of Jesse Jackson on the Democratic side and to the racially coded references to crime on the Republican side—the 1988 study allows us to investigate how political settings influence the dynamics of racial opinion. Too often studies of public opinion ignore the political setting, pretending that the data were collected in some sanitized laboratory. Since identical questions appear in the 1988 and 1992 NES, we can see what difference a racially charged setting makes. (As we will see in Chapter 9, it makes a difference.)

Finally, in more limited fashion, we exploit relevant evidence from virtually every major study carried out by NES from 1970 to 1992. For good measure, we also analyze the 1990 General Social Survey. Our attitude toward such studies is opportunistic: our primary purpose is to replicate analysis carried out first on the 1986 NES. In order to avoid cluttering up the text and burying the reader under an avalanche of findings, we will tuck most of these results away in footnotes and appendices. We do this for aesthetic reasons, not because we think replication is unimportant. Replication is terribly important and all too rare in social science research. That we have at our disposal several studies, not just one, gives us a tremendous advantage. On the one hand, the studies are fundamentally alike, making parallel analysis possible. On the other hand, they differ from one another in several, perhaps important ways: they are carried out in different political settings, they are based on independent samples, they are conducted sometimes in person and sometimes over the telephone, and they include a somewhat different mix of questions on the politics of race. This variety means that to the degree we find convergence across the studies—as, for the most part, we do—we can be that much more confident in our results.

THE RACIAL DIVIDE

On then to public opinion. The six race policy questions taken from the 1986 NES that will be the focus of our investigation here and over the next several chapters are presented in table 2.1. The questions come in three pairs, each exploring a related, but distinctive, aspect of contention in American racial politics: the first pair takes up guarantees of equal opportunity; the second, the general role of the federal government in providing assistance to blacks; and the third, affirmative action programs in employment and schooling.[12]

As reported in table 2.1, differences in opinion between blacks and whites

Table 2.1 Opinions on Race Policy among White and Black Americans, 1986

Issue	Whites	Blacks
Equal opportunity		
FAIR EMPLOYMENT		
Government should ensure fair treatment of blacks	46.2%	89.8%
Other, depends	3.9	2.9
Not the government's business	49.9	7.3
SCHOOL DESEGREGATION		
Government should see to school integration	35.6	82.9
Other, depends	9.3	6.0
Government should stay out of it	55.2	11.1
Federal programs		
FEDERAL SPENDING ON PROGRAMS THAT ASSIST BLACKS		
Increased	17.6	74.6
Kept the same	62.3	21.9
Decreased	20.0	3.2
GOVERNMENT EFFORT TO IMPROVE THE POSITION OF BLACKS		
Government should make special efforts	4.8	33.6
*	7.1	6.3
*	13.8	7.0
* } Intermediate positions	31.3	28.7
*	19.9	9.8
*	13.0	9.1
Blacks should help themselves	10.1	5.6
Affirmative action		
PREFERENTIAL HIRING AND PROMOTION OF BLACKS		
Favor strongly	4.9	49.3
Favor	10.5	18.4
Oppose	21.7	12.5
Oppose strongly	62.9	19.7
COLLEGE QUOTAS FOR BLACKS		
Favor strongly	11.3	62.1
Favor	18.4	17.6
Oppose	21.7	7.2
Oppose strongly	48.6	13.1

Source: 1986 National Election Study.

on these questions are simply staggering. No one should be surprised that racial differences emerge on matters of policy that engage racial interests so directly. It is the magnitude of the difference that is surprising. The racial difference is a racial *divide,* and it demands a closer look.[13]

EQUAL OPPORTUNITY

The first pair of race policy questions presented in table 2.1 goes directly to the theme of equality of opportunity—what Rae and his colleagues call "the most distinctive and compelling element of our national ideology."[14] The questions ask not whether equal opportunity is desirable in principle, but whether the government should bring equal opportunity about, first in employment and second in education:

> *Some people feel that if black people are not getting fair treatment in jobs, the government in Washington should see to it that they do. Others feel that this is not the government's business. Have you been interested enough in this question to favor one side over the other?*
> *[If yes] How do you feel? Should the government in Washington see to it that black people get fair treatment in jobs or is this not the government's business?*
>
> *Some people say that the government in Washington should see to it that white and black children go to the same schools. Others claim that this is not the government's business. Have you been interested enough in this question to favor one side over the other?*
> *[If yes] Do you think the government in Washington should see to it that white and black children go to the same schools or stay out of this area as it is not the government's business?*

Formulated in this fashion, both issues have a history intertwined with the civil rights movement. The struggle to enlist the federal government to enforce equal opportunity in employment began during the Depression, though success in legislation did not come until the tumultuous and racially preoccupied year of 1964. As the civil rights movement continued to press its case, as peaceful demonstrators were set upon by angry mobs and local police, and as white opinion was shifting toward equal opportunity as an ideal, Congress passed the historic Civil Rights Bill of 1964. Title VII of the bill made it unlawful for an employer "to fail or refuse to hire or to discharge any individual, or discriminate against any individual with respect to his compensation, terms, conditions, or privileges of employment, because of such individual's race, color, religion, sex, or national origin." To accompany Title VII, Congress established the Equal Employment Opportunity Commission and charged it with monitoring and enforcing compliance. Amended and strengthened in 1972, Title VII now covers employment agencies, labor unions, and governments, as well as private employers.[15]

Despite its legislative successes, the policy of equal employment opportunity remains quite unpopular among whites. In 1986, according to the figures presented in table 2.1, more white Americans opposed equal employment opportunity than supported it: Title VII would have failed as a referendum among white Americans in 1986. There is nothing new in this. White opinion has been shaded against a federal policy of equal employment opportunity for as long as the question has been asked.[16] Opposition among whites is evidently not to equal employment opportunity as a principle, but to its implementation. By 1972, the last time the question was asked, 97% of white Americans subscribed to the view that blacks and whites should have an equal chance at any kind of job. But federal policy to ensure equal employment opportunity is evidently quite another matter, one that sharply divides the white public. More dramatically, the issue separates whites from blacks, as table 2.1 also shows. The 50% of the white public that signs on to the proposition that guaranteeing fair employment practices is really not the government's business dwindles to a barely visible 7% among black Americans.

The history of equal opportunity in education, the object of our second policy question, lies more in the courts than in the legislative or executive branch of government. Through the middle of the twentieth century, segregation of the public schools in the United States was virtually complete. Then, on May 17, 1954, in *Brown v. Board of Education,* Chief Justice Earl Warren concluded for a unanimous Supreme Court that "in the field of public education the doctrine of 'separate but equal' has no place. Separate educational facilities are inherently unequal."[17] But while the NAACP pressed desegregation suits in hundreds of local school districts, and lower courts began to order prompt compliance, the forces of white supremacy reacted with impressive ingenuity. White Citizens Councils formed throughout the South; violence and intimidation met those who spoke in favor of integration; private educational academies sprung up; state legislatures both promised to withhold funds from schools that complied with court orders and transferred responsibility for the assignment of pupils to local authorities, thereby complicating and delaying desegregation enormously; mobs greeted black students attempting to attend school with whites; and throughout the South, senators, governors, members of Congress, and local officials pledged to "resist forced integration by any lawful means."[18] By 1963, almost a full decade after the Supreme Court had commanded that the public schools desegregate "with all deliberate speed," fewer than 13,000 black students in the South—roughly one-half of one percent of the total black student population—were attending school with whites.

Things finally began to change, thanks to unwavering federal efforts at enforcement and a series of additional Supreme Court decisions. After the Civil Rights Bill of 1964, the U.S. Department of Health, Education, and Welfare (HEW) began to insist that local school districts comply with federal desegregation guidelines if they were to receive federal funds. Then in 1967, the Supreme Court declared that freedom-of-choice plans that had sprung up in the South as a way to circumvent *Brown* were unconstitutional if they left blacks and whites in separate schools (*Green v. New Kent Co.*). In a case decided in 1969 (*Alexander v. Holmes*), the court concluded that desegregation of the public schools must begin immediately, without regard for local extenuating circumstances. In 1971 (*Swann v. Charlotte-Mecklenburg*), the court authorized busing as a remedy for race segregation in the public schools. As a consequence of HEW initiatives and these court decisions, and perhaps a growing weariness among those carrying on the struggle, desegregation in the South finally began in earnest. Whereas virtually no blacks attended desegregated schools in 1954, and just 2% did so a decade later, by 1968 the figure had grown to 18%, reaching 46% in 1973.

Since 1973, however, the pace of desegregation has slowed within the South, and outside the South it was never very impressive to begin with. Especially in large cities, segregation of the public schools prevails. Moreover, in a 1974 decision (*Milliken v. Bradley*), the Supreme Court concluded that busing for the purposes of racial integration across school district boundaries was unacceptable unless all districts were found guilty of deliberate segregation. In theory, such a finding was possible, but as a practical matter, *Milliken v. Bradley* effectively disallowed metropolitan desegregation. By the late 1970s, school desegregation ground to a halt and now appears, if anything, to be reversing.[19]

Rather like the Supreme Court these days, the white public shows little enthusiasm for school desegregation. According to table 2.1, only about one-third (35.6%) of whites interviewed in the fall of 1986 agreed that the government in Washington should see to it that white and black children attend the same schools. Like equal employment opportunity, school integration exposes a huge racial rift: 83% of black Americans believed government was obliged to ensure that black and white children attend school together. And while black support for a federal policy of school desegregation has been essentially steadfast over the last two decades, white support has declined sharply as the problem of school desegregation became national in scope and as mandatory busing became the only practical—and wildly unpopular—remedy.[20] Just as we saw on employment, finally, Americans are ambivalent not over the principle of equal opportunity but over its implementation. By the early 1980s, 90% of whites agreed with the idea that white and black students should attend the same schools. But as the decade came to a close, only about one white in three was willing to recommend that the federal government should step in to make school desegregation actually happen.[21]

To some degree, both school desegregation and equal employment opportunity are issues of the past. As the civil rights movement faded, and the landmark federal legislation of the 1960s became the law of the land, school integration and workplace discrimination retreated from public discussion and consciousness. The two problems seem to be in the final stage, the twilight realm, of the "issue-attention cycle" described by Anthony Downs. According to Downs,

> American public attention rarely remains sharply focused upon any one domestic issue for very long—even if it involves a continuing problem of crucial importance to society. Instead, a systematic "issue-attention cycle" seems strongly to influence public attitudes and behavior concerning most key domestic problems. Each of these problems suddenly leaps into prominence, remains there for a short time, and then—though still largely unsolved—gradually fades from the center of public attention.[22]

So it has been, we think, for school segregation and workplace discrimination. Evidence on this point comes not from shifts in opinion but from downward trends in the likelihood that citizens express any opinion at all. It turns out that on both the equal employment and school desegregation questions, the proportion of the public admitting that they have no interest in the issue has more than doubled over the last quarter-century, for whites and blacks alike. For white Americans, on equal employment opportunity, the proportion declaring no interest has climbed upward from just 13% in 1964 to 33% in 1986; on school segregation, from 11% in 1966 to 30% in 1986. For black Americans, the corresponding increases are just as impressive: from 4% to 14% on employment, and from 12% to 27% on school segregation. Of course, neither school segregation nor workplace discrimination has disappeared as a social problem; the evidence suggests quite the contrary.[23] Nor, as we have just seen, do governmental efforts to reduce segregation in schools or discrimination at work generate majority support among white Americans. Nevertheless, the public's attention has moved on to other things—another instance, perhaps, of Valrey's observation that "works are not finished, they are abandoned."

Federal Programs

The second pair of questions displayed in table 2.1 takes up the role the federal government should play in providing assistance to blacks. The first refers to federal spending on programs that help blacks; the second calls attention to the government in Washington and the efforts it should make to improve the social and economic position of black Americans:

> *If you had a say in making up the federal budget this year, on which of these programs would you like to see spending increased and which decreased? Should federal spending on programs that assist blacks be increased, decreased, or kept about the same?*

> *Some people feel that the government in Washington should make every effort to improve the social and economic position of blacks. Suppose these people are at one end of the scale at point number 1. Others feel that the government should not make any special effort to help blacks because they should help themselves. Suppose these people are at the other end, at point 7. And, of course, some other people have opinions somewhere in between at points 2, 3, 4, 5, or 6. Where would you place yourself on this scale, or haven't you thought much about it?*

Neither question mentions specific programs or policies. Nevertheless, citizens might well have had specific programs and policies in mind when they answered them. They might have been thinking about Aid to Families with Dependent Children (AFDC), Head Start, Food Stamps, job training, the School Lunch program, Legal Services, or even Medicaid. Or perhaps they were thinking about presidential appointments, Supreme Court decisions, the presence or absence of blacks at official occasions, the volume and direction of Justice Department litigation, and more. We have no way of knowing with certainty exactly what signal citizens are attempting to send when they say, in response to these questions, that the government should be doing more, or less, for blacks.

Such ambiguity could be thought of as a defect in our questions. Without claiming that our measures are perfect, we prefer to think of ambiguity as inherent in public opinion in any large, complex society. In such settings, few citizens are equipped for micromanaging public policy; nor are they much interested in providing detailed instruction. At best, citizens provide general guidance on the broad direction of government policy.

Pitched at this level, the advice that whites and blacks offer is diametrically opposed. In 1986, an overwhelming majority of white Americans either favored a decrease in federal spending for programs that assist blacks or would leave current levels of support unchanged. At the same time, nearly three-quarters of black Americans supported an increase in federal spending. (As before, the percentages are set out in table 2.1.) The reluctance on the part of whites to provide additional resources to blacks reflects more than a general distaste for federal spending. Citizens were asked about a variety of programs in the 1986 survey, and all but one attracted more support among whites than did programs to assist blacks. Social Security, protecting the environment, financial aid to college students, space and scientific research, and assistance to the unemployed all enjoyed much more support among white Americans than did federal spending on blacks. In the fall of 1986, only the Nicaraguan Contras were less popular.

Our second question in this pair frames the issue of the federal role as a choice between the needs of blacks and the virtue of self-reliance. When the issue is formulated in this fashion, white support for government assistance to blacks seems, if anything, weaker. More whites said that blacks should help themselves (about 23%) than said that the government should make a special effort (about 12%). These percentages reverse among black Americans. More than twice as many blacks came down on the side of special federal efforts (40%) than endorsed the view that government should leave blacks to their own devices (15%).

This question has also appeared in each NES presidential election study since 1972, in the identical form, except for 1980. In that year alone, for reasons that we cannot reconstruct, a phrase was added to the core question: the issue was presented as whether the government in Washington should make every effort to improve the social and economic position of blacks *even if it means giving them preferential treatment*. With the federal role defined in this way, white support for governmental efforts sharply declined. This can be seen in figure 2.1, which charts the proportion of whites supporting government assis-

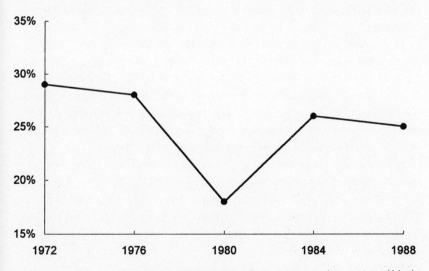

FIGURE 2.1 White support for special government efforts to improve the position of blacks, 1972–1988. *Source:* 1972–1988 National Election Studies.

tance to blacks in each presidential year from 1972 to 1988. Over the years the trend line is essentially flat, except in 1980, when support suddenly falls by more than one-third.

This result contains several important lessons. First of all, the collapse of white support for government action in 1980 should make us skeptical of authoritative claims about exactly what Americans think about federal assistance to blacks, or equal opportunity, or, indeed, anything else. What public opinion is on any particular issue depends in part on how, exactly, the issue is defined. Acknowledging this point does not make the answers Americans have given to our questions meaningless. That answers must be interpreted within the particular context of the wording of the questions does not mean that anything goes. That would be like saying, as the economist Robert Solow once remarked, that as a perfectly aseptic environment is impossible, one might as well conduct surgery in a sewer.

We composed our questions with the expectation not that they would reveal some immaculate picture of American opinion on race, but that they would yield interpretable opinions. Our questions were written to avoid fine detail (on the assumption that hardly any citizen has such details in mind) and to be faithful to the terms of the ongoing public debate. Perhaps most important, our investigation depends upon *multiple* questions. We pose the complex issue of racial inequality and exclusion in a variety of ways. We hope thereby "to escape the confines of any single question" and to provide "a richer context of inquiry."[24] But as figure 2.1 reminds us, had we formulated our questions somewhat differently, the American public no doubt would have answered somewhat differently.[25]

In any event, we are less interested in being able to say precisely how many Americans take one position or another on a particular issue—an enterprise that cannot succeed in any case—than in understanding why Americans line up on different sides of an issue, in uncovering the underpinnings of opinion. For that purpose, the undeniable connection between how questions are formulated and how answers are expressed is less troublesome. Indeed, in Chapter 7, we will show that the "problem" is actually an opportunity.

A final lesson suggested by figure 2.1 is how completely white Americans reject preferential treatment. Support for federal efforts to improve the social and economic position of black Americans is not very strong to begin with. But when the policy is defined to include special breaks for blacks, as in the revised version of the question asked in 1980, white support crumbles. This result reveals the wall of white disapproval greeting policies of affirmative action, our next topic.

Affirmative Action

According to Nathan Glazer, affirmative action has become "familiar to tens of millions of Americans, tens of thousands of businesses, thousands of lawyers and hundreds of judges, affecting in some way the livelihood and educational choices of all Americans. It is disputed at national conventions, argued over in newspaper editorials and law review articles, debated in philosophical journals and weekly news magazines."[26] Glazer is an ardent critic of the policy—his phrase is affirmative *discrimination*—and he exaggerates, but only a bit. Perhaps he was merely slightly ahead of his time: affirmative action is surely the most visible outcropping of racial conflict today. To some, affirmative action is an entrenched abomination; to others, a fragile lifeline.

The phrase "affirmative action" first appeared in American law in Title VII of the 1964 Civil Rights Act, in a section dealing with discrimination in employment: "If the court finds that the respondent has intentionally engaged in or is intentionally engaging in an unlawful employment practice . . . the court may . . . order such affirmative action as may be appropriate, which may include, but is not limited to, reinstatement or hiring of employees, with or without back pay . . . or any other equitable relief as the court deems appropriate." It appeared also in an executive order issued by President Johnson the following year, which imposed "affirmative action" on federal contractors. The order required those doing business with the federal government to undertake special efforts to make employment and promotion opportunities accessible to minority applicants.

From these relatively modest beginnings, affirmative action has come in the last three decades to mean something rather more. Through judicial interpretations and administrative guidelines, affirmative action now refers, variously, to goals, timetables, and quotas as remedies for discrimination. Critics like Glazer regard this transformation as a perverse distortion of the Civil Rights Act; supporters insist that such remedies are required to bring real equality about.[27]

Both sides of this debate imply that when putting questions about affirmative action to the American public, it is appropriate to refer to preferential treatment. Both our questions do so. The first refers to racial preference in hiring and promotion; the second, to quotas in college admissions:

Some people say that because of past discrimination against blacks, preference in hiring and promotion should be given to blacks. Others say preferential hiring and promotion of blacks is wrong because it gives blacks advantages they haven't earned. What about your opinion—are you for or against preferential hiring and promotion of blacks?

Some people say that because of past discrimination, it is sometimes necessary for colleges and universities to reserve openings for black students. Others oppose quotas because they say quotas give blacks advantages they haven't earned. What about your opinion—are you for or against quotas to admit black students?

Notice that both questions suggest that affirmative action can be justified on the grounds of remedial action: that race-conscious programs are required now in order to offset the continuing consequences of racial discrimination. This is presumably what Lyndon Johnson had in mind in his famous speech at Howard University in 1965, when he declared that "freedom is not enough. You do not take a person who for years has been hobbled by chains . . . bring him to the starting line of a race and then say, 'you're free to compete' and justly believe that you have been completely fair." Notice, too, that both questions suggest that affirmative action might be opposed because such programs give to blacks advantages they do not deserve. This argument was commonly advanced by public figures who opposed affirmative action in the late 1960s, and although it has since faded from elite discourse, it remains a prominent justification in the thinking and conversation of ordinary citizens.[28]

Formulated in this fashion—pinned between remedial action and undeserved advantage—affirmative action turns out to be thoroughly unpopular among whites. As table 2.1 shows, favoring blacks in hiring and promotion decisions was opposed by more than eight in ten white Americans; not quite as many, but still a one-sided majority, opposed setting aside openings for black students in college admissions. Strong supporters of affirmative action were few and far between, greatly outnumbered by the policy's strong opponents: by a margin of twelve to one in the case of affirmative action in the workplace and by more than four to one in the case of affirmative action in college admissions. Little wonder that, early in 1995, the declared contenders for the Republican presidential nomination were busy elbowing each other out of the way to claim their adamant opposition to affirmative action; and why President Clinton, while defending the need for affirmative action in particular cases, promised to review all affirmative action policies in the federal government and to cancel those no longer serving a useful purpose.[29]

Meanwhile, on the other side of the racial divide, most black Americans were supporting affirmative action. More than two-thirds of blacks interviewed in 1986 favored preferential hiring and promotion; nearly 80% supported quotas in college admissions. By the usual standards, these figures would signify overwhelming approval—and they do—but comparatively speaking, affirmative action generates less support from blacks than does fair employment, school desegregation, or the federal government's obligation to provide help. Of all the various policies we consider, affirmative action is the least popular, among blacks and whites alike.

A DIVIDE WITHOUT PEER

In each of three domains of race policy—equal opportunity, federal assistance, and affirmative action—differences between blacks and whites are extraordinary. The racial divide in opinion is summarized in figure 2.2, which presents the distribution of opinion for blacks and whites on a composite measure of race policy, based on answers given to the six policy questions. On the left-hand side of the figure is the proportion of blacks and whites who support equal opportunity, federal assistance, and affirmative action; on the right hand side are those who oppose all three.[30] As we would anticipate, the figure depicts two utterly dissimilar publics: most blacks pile up on the left; most whites on the right. More precisely, the three left-most categories of opinion collect 63% of blacks and just 9% of the whites; meanwhile, the three right-most categories collect 36% of whites and just 2% of blacks.

Differences as drastic as these simply have no counterpart in studies of public opinion. In particular, differences associated with class or gender pale by comparison. We examined class differences over class issues, those matters of public policy where the interests of the middle class and working class most conflict, and gender differences over gender issues, where the political interests of men and women collide most directly. In order to sharpen whatever class

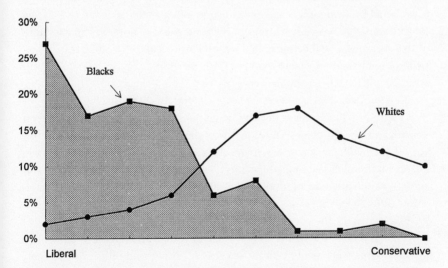

FIGURE 2.2 Opinion on race policy, separately for blacks and whites. *Source:* 1986 National Election Study.

differences there might be, we defined our measure of class restrictively, to include only those Americans who said that they did indeed think of themselves in class terms and who then went on to claim identification with either the working class or the middle class. Defined in this way, class is associated with views on social welfare policies, but the associations are in every case modest. For example, working-class Americans are more likely to support an expansion of government services, more inclined to favor increases in assistance to the unemployed, and more likely to say that the federal government is obliged to provide a good standard of living for its citizens than are middle-class Americans (the relevant percentages are 53% versus 39% on government services, 47% versus 32% on unemployment, and 32% versus 21% on standard of living). Such differences should not be dismissed, but they are slender when set next to the race differences we have been examining.

The contrast is even more striking with gender. No difference at all can be detected between men and women on the issue of abortion. In the 1986 NES, 40% of the women and 38% of the men agreed that a woman should always be able to obtain an abortion as a matter of choice. Not only in absolute terms, then, but also by comparison with class and gender differences, the racial divide is extraordinary.[31]

WITHIN THE VEIL

The gap revealed so vividly in figure 2.2 may actually understate the real differences that divide blacks from whites. In the 1986 NES, some blacks were questioned by white interviewers, and some whites were questioned by black interviewers.[32] In a society as thoroughly segregated as our own, an encounter of this sort might well be infiltrated by the tensions and discomforts that seem to accompany many racial exchanges. If so, we should see indications of this in what people have to say on matters of race.

As it happens, blacks did express more liberal positions on race policy when interviewed by blacks than they did when questioned by whites. Thus in conversations between blacks, those that take place "within the veil" as Du Bois would have said, blacks present themselves as more forceful advocates of racial change. In parallel fashion, whites interviewed by whites appeared more conservative on matters of race policy than they did when interviewed by blacks. These differences show up on every policy question, and they are substantial: for black citizens, the average race-of-interviewer difference is nearly thirteen percentage points; for whites, the average effect is about eighteen percentage points.[33] Thus were we to redraw figure 2.2, setting aside those blacks questioned by whites, along with those whites questioned by blacks, the racial gap would widen. Of course, whoever is doing the asking, the opinion divide between black and white Americans remains enormous.[34]

BEYOND RACIAL POLICY

Is the racial divide confined to matters of policy that bear unambiguously and uniquely on race? Table 2.2 provides a panoramic answer to this question. For the sake of comparison, we have included, in the top panel of the table, our set of six race policy questions, which show the now-familiar huge racial gap: across these questions, blacks are more supportive than whites by an average of forty-six percentage points. But blacks and whites also differ sharply over what we call "implicit" or "covert" racial issues. Such policies do not explicitly mention race but may be widely understood to have a racial implication. Table 2.2 includes five: federal support for the Food Stamps program, sanctions against South Africa, increased support for welfare, remedies for urban unrest, and capital punishment. On each, sharp differences emerge between blacks and whites. For example, while just 18% of whites favored increases in federal support for Food Stamps, 51% of blacks did so. If somewhat less pronounced than on policy issues where the racial connection is explicit, where nothing is left to the imagination, the racial gap on implicit race issues is nevertheless impressive.

Race differences are nearly as substantial on domestic social spending, the next category in table 2.2. When asked whether they would rather see an expansion of government services or cuts in federal spending, 42% of white Americans chose more services; 72% of black Americans did so. Differences of roughly equal magnitude also show up over Social Security, Medicare, federal aid to education, and government assistance to the poor. The modern American welfare state enjoys much more support among blacks than among whites.

On other kinds of policy debates, however, race differences are less impressive. When it comes to social issues, for example, blacks and whites, take on average roughly the same position. Table 2.2 shows that black Americans are noticeably more liberal on gay rights, but somewhat more conservative on school prayer. Social questions do not seem to produce a consistent racial divide. Nor do the new issues that have arisen over the recent arrival of huge numbers of immigrants from Latin and South America and the Pacific rim. White Americans are not particularly generous in their views toward this "clamor at the gates"—they are not much interested in easing restrictions governing the flow of immigrants into the country or in expanding benefits for the immigrants already here, but neither are black Americans. Nor does a racial gap invariably show up on foreign policy. Table 2.2 shows that blacks are less

Table 2.2 A Panoramic View of the Racial Divide in Public Opinion, 1986–1992

Issue	Whites	Blacks
Race policy		
Government should ensure equal employment opportunity	46.2%	89.8%
Government should see to school desegregation	35.6	82.9
Increase federal spending on programs that assist blacks	17.6	74.6
Government should make special effort to help blacks	11.9	39.9
Preferential hiring	15.4	67.7
College quotas	29.7	79.7
Implicit racial issues		
Increase support for Food Stamps	18.0	50.9
Sanctions against South Africa	26.5	45.8
More assistance for welfare	14.7	32.3
Solve underlying problems that give rise to urban unrest	48.3	71.7
Oppose capital punishment	14.4	36.9
Social spending		
Expand government services	41.5	72.0
Increase Social Security	60.2	82.0
Federal support for education	61.0	81.0
Increase support for Medicare	83.2	93.9
Government assistance to the poor	50.5	81.0
Social issues		
Protect gays from job discrimination	50.8	65.2
Oppose school prayer	53.1	47.9
Abortion is women's right	39.7	36.7
Protect against sexual harassment	54.3	74.3
Immigration		
Ease immigration restrictions	7.0	13.0
Increase benefits to immigrants	19.5	31.0
Oppose English as official language	26.3	38.5
Foreign affairs		
Cooperate with the Soviet Union	28.0	27.3
Oppose limits on foreign imports	22.0	7.6
Keep out of Central America	48.1	47.1
Cut defense spending	33.6	37.2
Oppose Persian Gulf War	15.8	45.5
Alienation from government		
People like me have no say	13.3	28.3
Public officials don't care	15.3	29.0
Distrust government	56.1	74.4
Government run by big interests	66.0	73.3

Source: 1986, 1988, and 1992 National Election Studies.

willing to impose limits on foreign imports, slightly more interested in cutting defense spending, and a good bit more opposed to the Persian Gulf War. But there are no differences at all between blacks and whites on cooperation with the Soviet Union or on U.S. involvement in Central America. One conspicuous exception to this pattern is completely unmysterious: U.S. policy toward South Africa, nominally a matter of foreign policy, though we included it for obvious reasons among the implicit race issues in table 2.2. This case and the Gulf War aside, blacks and whites differ little on questions of foreign policy.

The racial divide opens up again on matters of political distrust, the final category in table 2.2. Blacks are twice as likely as whites to believe that they have no say in government and that public officials don't care what they think. They are also more likely to endorse the idea that government is run by big interests, and that public officials simply cannot be trusted.

Taken all around, then, differences between blacks and whites are not restricted to matters of race. To be sure, the racial divide is most pronounced over policies that bear unambiguously and differentially on the fortunes of black and white. But the divide is also apparent on issues where the racial implications are unstated and covert, on the desirability of the American version of the modern welfare state and on distrust in government. Such differences recall the Kerner Commission's warning of a quarter-century ago, issued in the midst of the urban riots of the 1960s, that the United States was drifting towards two societies, one white, the other black. On many matters of public policy, black and white Americans do seem to live in different worlds.

RACE, NOT CLASS

But is the racial divide really racial? Perhaps the differences we see between black and white on matters of race policy are really differences of class. From a Marxist perspective, race is a distraction: the real divide in industrial society is between owners and workers, or between those who command and those who obey, or between the bourgeoisie and the proletariat, not between black and white.[35]

Perhaps, then, the racial divide in opinion is due to the fact that whites and blacks find themselves in such different locations in society. On average, whites possess more education, more income, and more occupational prestige than do blacks, and so may have different political interests in mind. Put another way, if we control for class, by comparing middle-class whites with middle-class blacks, poor whites with poor blacks, and so on, the racial divide should diminish. Perhaps it will disappear entirely.

It does not. The race differences that we see in table 2.1 and figure 2.2 really are race differences. Controlling for class does nothing to diminish their magnitude. It is race, not class, that divides contemporary American society over racial policy.[36]

OPINION AMONG THE INFLUENTIAL

Democratic governments are supposed to be responsive to the aspirations and interests of their citizens. Although the evidence is not airtight, and there are many local exceptions, the democratic requirement of harmony between public desires and government action appears to hold up reasonably well in the American case, both as a general proposition and with reference to recent civil rights legislation in particular. As democratic theory insists, the national government does seem responsive to what citizens want—even if sluggishly, incompletely, and on the direction of policy, not its details.[37]

But to which citizens does government respond? V. O. Key's sensible answer was, politically active ones: "In the operations of government those who make themselves heard, those who argue their case, and those who take a hand enjoy an advantage."[38] If Key is right, then a natural question for us is whether politically influential citizens hold distinctive ideas about what the government should do about race.

They do not. The politically influential, defined by affluence, superior educational attainment, and deep engagement in public affairs, take positions on race that are virtually indistinguishable from those expressed by the public as a whole.[39] This conclusion, which applies to blacks and whites alike, demolishes the hope that the political manifestations of racial conflict might become more tractable among those citizens most likely to have a voice in how things turn out. We find instead that the racial divide is every bit as wide among the influential—another indication of how deeply race divides Americans.

IS THE RACIAL DIVIDE WIDENING?

Political agendas change, issues come and go. While such turbulence makes for interesting politics, it frustrates efforts to assess whether the opinion gap between blacks and whites is expanding. And there are practical impediments as well. Not until the late 1950s did questions on racial matters begin to make regular appearances on national surveys, and not until 1964 was it thought sufficiently interesting or important to solicit the views of blacks as well as those of whites on such questions.[40]

What we can say is that the divide between black and white on those race polices most central to the politics of the times seems if anything greater today than in any other period for which we have data. To be sure, differences between black and white on segregated accommodations in 1964, the centerpiece of the historic Civil Rights Act of that year, were substantial. So, too, were racial differences over school busing in 1972, a major bone of contention in the Nixon-McGovern campaign. But these differences are not quite as large as the current racial divide over affirmative action. In 1964, 44% of whites and 89% of blacks endorsed the idea that the federal government should see to it that black people were free to enter hotels and restaurants (a racial gap of forty-five percentage points). In 1972, 13% of whites and 46% of blacks supported busing children to

THE RACIAL DIVIDE IN PUBLIC OPINION

achieve school desegregation (a gap of thirty-three percentage points). In 1986, 15% of whites and 68% of blacks favored giving preferences to blacks in hiring and promotion decisions (a gap of fifty-three percentage points). Although we cannot say for sure, the racial divide appears, if anything, to be growing.

CONCLUSIONS

Bryce's 1921 indictment of public opinion in *Modern Democracies* as "confused, incoherent, amorphous, varying from day to day and week to week" has a contemporary ring.[41] Many recent observers, some armed with evidence, have questioned whether ordinary citizens are up to the burdens of democracy, given the inconsistency and instability of their political views. Whatever the general merits of this contention, it looks to be misplaced when it comes to race. On racial matters, Americans, both black and white, are in possession of real opinions: they know what they want their government to do, and they know what they want their government not to do.

That the American public appears reasonably well informed and strongly opinionated on matters of race does not mean the news for democracy is uniformly good, however. No doubt the most striking feature of public opinion on race is how emphatically black and white Americans disagree with each other. On the obligation of government to ensure equal opportunity, on federal efforts to help blacks, and on affirmative action, a huge racial divide opens up. Blacks and whites also disagree sharply over policy questions that are racial only by implication, over how generous the American welfare state should be, and over the integrity of American political institutions. The racial divide in opinion widens when whites talk with whites and blacks talk with blacks, itself a sign of the difference race makes to our social and political lives. It is as apparent among ordinary citizens as it is among elites. It is not a mask for class differences: it is rooted in race, in differences of history and circumstance that define the black and white experiences. And if differences by race are nothing new to American politics, they are, if anything, more dramatic now than a generation ago.[42]

Many contemporary theorists of democracy urge communal dialogues designed to uncover or create consensus among Americans on matters of public concern. Racial matters obviously qualify as pressing public concerns, but the evidence presented here of a deep and perhaps widening racial divide makes the discovery of commonality and agreement between the races a dim prospect. When it comes to questions of race policy in the United States, this particular vision of contemporary democratic theorists looks to be more a distant aspiration than a realistic immediate goal.[43]

The huge and evidently persistent racial divide in opinion also amounts to a dramatic disconfirmation of the "liberal expectancy" so confidently issued from so many quarters not so long ago. From this perspective, racial and ethnic categories were about to become obsolete, irrelevant to any serious political analysis. The clear expectation was that "the kinds of features that divide one group from another would inevitably lose their weight and sharpness in modern and modernizing societies."[44] It hasn't happened, of course, not in the United States, and not around the world, where we have seen a murderous eruption of conflict organized by ethnicity.[45]

The racial divide also makes trouble for pluralist conceptions of American society, which portray citizens as pushed and pulled by many social forces, such that no single division has any special or lasting claim.[46] Pluralists remind us that Americans are divided from one another by more than just race: by religion, ethnicity, class, region, the organizations they join, and much more. In such social diversity lies enormous political significance. In the pluralist view, social factors, taken all together, "form a great web of crosscutting axes that divide and redivide the public," thereby inhibiting "the emergence of any single profound line of cleavage."[47] Blacks and whites are socially diverse; they are subject to various crosscutting pressures—but this is not enough, evidently, to prevent race from emerging as a "single profound line of cleavage."

That blacks and whites disagree so sharply, and that such disagreements appear to be rooted in race itself, should not be taken to mean that all whites believe one thing and that all blacks believe another. The racial divide is imposing, but there are serious disagreements within each group as well. Among blacks and whites alike, opinion is very far from monolithic. How such disagreements should be interpreted is the main business of this book, which we begin in earnest in the next chapter.

No Single Sovereign Theory Will Do: Multiple Interpretations of Public Opinion on Race

The extraordinary effort that has been invested in the measurement, description, and interpretation of American public opinion over the last four decades has produced at least one stunning result: the discovery of the virtual absence, among the American public, of fully developed ideological points of view. One searches the public in vain for the articulation of a comprehensive program, for the expression of a grand idea on the relationship between society and government. Most Americans are bewildered by ideological concepts; they have little use for terms like "libertarian" or "neoconservative"; public appeals enunciated through ideological abstractions fall largely on deaf ears. All in all, Americans appear to be, as McClosky once put it, quite innocent of ideology.[1]

Ideological innocence is an important discovery, but it leaves us without anything to say about how Americans think about political life—how they think about racial matters in particular. The great debate over ideology, the consuming preoccupation of public opinion studies for more than a generation, has taught us more about how Americans do not think about politics than about how they do.[2]

Our purpose here is to introduce a positive theoretical perspective for understanding the opinions black and white Americans hold on matters of race. The racial divide in public opinion that was the centerpiece of the preceding chapter cannot be understood, evidently, as the expression of a deep ideological difference between blacks and whites. If we take ideological innocence for granted, then how should the racial divide be understood? More generally, how should we make sense of the views blacks and whites take on racial issues in the contemporary United States?

In the first part of this chapter, we sketch a general framework for answering such questions and then translate that framework into more specific claims about the determinants of public opinion on race. The second part then argues that the extensive social science literature on racial attitudes, though valuable for some purposes, cannot supply us with the evidence we need to sort these claims out. To assess the adequacy of our framework, and to illuminate public opinion on racial issues, we must supply our own evidence. In the last part of the chapter, as a gateway to the empirical analysis shortly to follow, we describe how we will test the various claims and suggest why the results of these tests should be taken seriously.

OPINION INGREDIENTS

Our first and perhaps primary task in creating a general framework is to identify the various theoretical claims about the determinants of public opinion that deserve to be taken seriously. Here we assert that American public opinion—in general and on matters of race—is an expression of a small number of *primary ingredients:* the material interests that citizens see at stake in the issue; the sympathies and resentments that citizens feel toward those social groups implicated in the dispute, especially those groups that the policy appears to benefit or victimize; and commitment to the political principles that the policy seems to honor or repudiate. Interests, attitudes toward social groups, and political principles are the core ingredients of public opinion.[3]

Material Interests

The notion that citizens seek to advance their own material interests is hardly original with us—it crops up prominently in the writings of Thomas Hobbes, David Hume, Adam Smith, and James Madison, among others. Self-interest also enjoys a special prominence in contemporary analysis of American political life, much of it animated by what Brian Barry has called the "economic approach" to democratic theory.[4] From this theoretical position, citizens are little more than single-minded seekers of self-interest: they support policies and candidates that advance their own material interests, and they oppose policies and candidates that threaten them. Politics, like commerce, emerges out of citizens' avidly pursuing their own interests. Only the "granite of self-interest" can supply a sturdy foundation for a theory of political life.[5]

If the self-interested citizen is a familiar figure in much empirical analysis these days, the concept of self-interest itself is notoriously slippery. We will accordingly spend some time in Chapter 4 specifying what self-interest means in the context of racial politics. In a departure from conventional practice, we will examine self-interest at work among white Americans *and* among black Americans: we will be as curious about the impact on public opinion of the material advantages that many black Americans see in race policies as we are in the material threats that worry many white Americans. With a defensible conception of self-interest established and a reliable set of measures developed, we can then assess the extent to which public opinion on matters of race is an expression, as David Hume once put it, of the "perpetual" and "universal" appetite for personal advantage.[6]

Sympathy and Resentment toward Social Groups

Citizens propelled entirely by calculations of self-interest would be, in Amartya Sen's memorable phrase, "social morons."[7] On the radical idea that citizens are not, in fact, social morons, our framework includes, as a second general category of opinion ingredients, attitudes toward social groups. From this perspective, opinions on public policy are to be read as expressions of sentiments toward those groups whose interests and status are thought to be most affected. Public opinion is, in a phrase, *group centric:* shaped in powerful ways by the feelings citizens harbor toward the social groups they see as the principal beneficiaries (or victims) of the policy.

In some ways the claim of group centrism is little more than an amplification of a point buried in Converse's famous analysis of belief systems. Remembered best for its demolition of the proposition that citizens derive their views on topical political issues from abstract ideological principles, Converse's analysis hinted at a positive argument as well. If ideological abstractions were beyond most citizens, perhaps they instead organized their political thinking around "visible social groupings." Perhaps, Converse suggested, citizens converted questions on policy into judgments on the moral qualifications of the groups involved.[8]

In this way, public opinion seems to be an expression principally of what Robert Lane once called "social identity": "a sense of group placement, of allies, of 'people like me,' in contrast to strangers and enemies." Social identity requires boundaries, lines of separation between us and them. According to Lane, the foundations of social identity can be situated in various differences: "language, customs, rituals, codes, histories, and myths," all can do the trick. Such differences "help provide demarcations and, equally important, rationales for these boundary lines."[9]

Missing from Lane's list of demarcating features is precisely that aspect of social life that occupies center stage here: the separation provided by race. First and foremost for our analysis, the social categories of white and black define the "us" and the "them," the two visible social groupings most essential to understanding public opinion on race.

Attitudes toward social groups that we suspect provide one foundation for public opinion on race can be negative as well as positive, reflecting resentment as well as sympathy. We need not agree with Henry Adams's claim that "politics, as a practice, whatever its professions, had always been the systematic organization of hatreds" to recognize that the social dimension to politics may entail both attraction and hostility. Indeed, our analysis of this ingredient of public opinion, set out in detail in Chapter 5, attends exclusively to the negative side of the social dimension. In Chapter 5, we assess the extent to which white Americans' opposition to various policy initiatives designed to promote racial equality hinges on their feelings of racial resentment.

Matters of Principle

Opinions on affirmative action or welfare reform might also have a principled base, our third opinion ingredient. From this perspective, policies are supported or opposed to the degree they are seen as enhancing or violating valued principles.

An emphasis upon principles is nothing new in the study of American politics. A long line of distinguished analysts—including, most notably, Tocqueville, Hartz, Hofstadter, Lipset, and Myrdal—have favored an approach that defines what is distinctive about American public opinion in terms of certain basic values or principles. Appeals to the American Creed are common not only in the academic literature but in political rhetoric as well. With a handful of exceptions, however, principles have received rather little attention in quantitative studies of American public opinion.[10] Here we examine three principles in particular, selected because they are regularly and prominently featured in influential descriptions of the American political tradition: equality, economic individualism, and limited government.[11]

These three bear some resemblance to the ideological frameworks that public opinion researchers have searched for and not found. But the principles of equality, economic individualism, and limited government are less sweeping, more local in scope, than the kind of "master ideas" or "crowning postures" that have been the target of public opinion researchers' quest. Such principles are arguably more available to ordinary citizens. Their acquisition and use require neither sophisticated reasoning nor deep interest in political matters. Equality, economic individualism, and limited government, it is said, are ingrained in American society, woven into the fabric of American social and political relations. However true this may be, in Chapter 6 we will see the extent to which public disputes over such issues as affirmative action and school integration should be interpreted as clashes of principle.

OPINION FRAMES

American opinion on race depends not only on what goes on inside the minds of individual citizens—the jumble of interests, group feelings, and principles relevant to an issue—but also on the nature of the ongoing debate among political elites. The president, the Justice Department, the NAACP, CBS News, "Hard Copy," the *New York Times*, and more are continually bombarding Americans with suggestions about how issues should be understood. The questions taken up by government are always complex, always subject to alternative interpretations. What is affirmative action? Is it reverse discrimination? Remedial compensation for injustices of the past? A handout to the undeserving? Which of these interpretations prevails in elite discourse may substantially affect what ordinary citizens take affirmative action to mean and, in the end, what their opinions on affirmative action turn out to be.

More specifically, how citizens understand a debate, which features of it are central and which are peripheral, is reflected in how an issue is *framed*. We claim that frames lead a double life: they are internal structures of the mind that help individuals order and give meaning to the parade of events they witness in public life; they are also interpretive structures that are a part of political discourse, invented and employed by political elites to advance their interests. In Chapter 7, we will see whether, as we claim, public opinion depends in a systematic and intelligible way on how issues are framed.

LIMITATIONS OF PREVIOUS EVIDENCE

Social science already has a lot to say about the underpinnings of public opinion on race—especially about the underpinnings of white opinion. We have drawn upon this literature already and will do so again before we are done. We have culled from it a number of plausible claims, rehearsed in the preceding section of the chapter: that public opinion on race is a reflection of material interests, group sympathies and resentments, and various political principles, all organized and assembled with the assistance of elite frames. Each of these claims has its advocates and at least a smattering of supporting evidence. So why do we need another study? Why do we need this study?

The crippling problem with the available evidence, as we read it, is this: with few exceptions, the evidence is supplied by research *that takes up just one explanation at a time*. Study by study, Americans are portrayed in single-minded ways, their views governed by a simple sovereign doctrine. Sometimes they are depicted exclusively as pursuers of self-interest, preoccupied entirely with calculating the consequences a policy is likely to have for them. Other times they are portrayed exclusively as repositories of primordial racial hatreds, reacting reflexively to the conflicts and symbols of the day. On still other occasions, Americans are assumed to be amateur moral philosophers, wrestling with the proper balance to strike between the principles of equality and liberty.[12]

This parochialism is intellectually disheartening, and it undermines the project we wish to advance. It encourages the view that all explanations are equal, that each must have something to say about the views Americans express on race. It leaves us helpless in deciding which explanations are powerful and which are weak. The problem is not just one of somehow adding up results across different studies that happen to focus on different explanations. (That would be difficult enough.) The problem is worse: because each study tends to concentrate on a single explanation, ignoring the rest, and because the key variables associated with the various explanations are very likely correlated with each other, the results produced by any single exercise, no matter how immaculately executed, are necessarily indeterminate.

To illustrate this point, consider the following example. It is hypothetical but may seem familiar. Suppose it is true that those white Americans who are most resentful toward black Americans also tend to be the most enthusiastic advocates of economic individualism, the idea that success goes to those who apply themselves diligently. (As we will see later, it is true.) Enter Smith and Jones, social scientists with excellent credentials and superior training. Smith develops reliable and valid measures of racial resentment, administers them to a carefully drawn probability sample of white Americans, and discovers that resentment is strongly (and negatively) associated with views on equal opportunity and affirmative action. Smith concludes that the major force behind white opposition to government-led efforts to diminish racial inequalities is racial resentment.

In the meantime, Jones develops reliable and valid measures of individualism, administers them to a carefully drawn probability sample of white Americans, and discovers that individualism is strongly (and positively) associated with views on equal opportunity and affirmative action. Jones concludes that behind white opposition to racial equality is the American commitment to individualism. Both Smith and Jones are wrong—or at least, both are probably wrong. Because each neglects a plausible rival explanation ("omitted variable bias" in the technical vocabulary of model specification), it is impossible to know from their results what's really going on—whether and in what proportion multiple forces might be at work in shaping American opinion on race.

Put more generally, the single-mindedness of the literature on racial attitudes has produced, inevitably, something of an epistemological mess: a literature replete with misspecified models, biased estimates, and questionable conclusions. From this perspective, social science research devoted to racial attitudes amounts to little more than a encyclopedia, in which each explanation has its own page. Which explanations are powerful and which are weak? We cannot say.[13]

Nor is the available evidence instructive on the power and influence of opinion frames. At one level, the public opinion literature is positively preoccupied with frames: that is, with precisely how survey questions are formulated. We know, all too well, that shifts in opinion can be produced by ostensibly innocuous alterations in how survey questions are worded, exactly how they are formatted, even where they are placed in the course of the overall interview.[14] But widespread appreciation that alternative formulations of the same question inside a survey may yield different results is not our point. Our point is that the same process goes on outside the survey, as various elites seek to formulate political questions to their own advantage. And on these frames constantly at work in political debate, the public opinion literature is virtually silent.[15]

Taken all around, the present state of affairs is not satisfactory and, more to the point, not what it could be. What we need, and what we try to supply here, is a pluralistic and empirically grounded approach to understanding public opinion. Our approach is pluralistic in that it recognizes the potential merit in a variety of theoretical points of view. Material interests, attitudes toward social groups, political principles, and opinion frames are all given their due here. Our approach is also empirically grounded. In the chapters to come, the various rival explanations are subjected to a sustained series of empirical tests. That all the explanations are plausible does not mean that they are all equally important. Indeed, as we will see, some explanations survive these empirical tests in much better shape than do others.

EMPIRICAL TESTS

We take our results seriously, and believe that you should, in part because of the care we have given to measurement. In this respect, we have tried to follow the good example set by our neighbors in the natural and life sciences, who seem, to their credit, positively obsessed with measurement. We share Gerald Kramer's observation that:

> In every science I know anything about, researchers worry a lot about error, and the quality of their measurements. They spend a lot of time calibrating their instruments, discovering their characteristics, and finding out what kinds of tasks they can do and what they can't. Awareness of the fallibility of their measurements, and of the possibility—indeed, the probability—of error, is really a major preoccupation.[16]

Kramer offered these remarks as part of an essay he entitled, perhaps wistfully, "Political Science as Science." If we have fallen short of the scientific ideal that Kramer had in mind, it is still fair to say that we have worried about measurement, too, and that we have done something about it. In the first place, our results are based on analysis carried out on NES data, the virtues of which we recited in the last chapter and will not repeat here except to say that most of the measures we use have survived elaborate and rigorous pretesting. Moreover, as a general practice, our analysis will rely not on individual survey items, but on composite scales based on answers combined across a number of related questions.

A scale is always preferred to a single item. A single item cannot represent complex concepts of the sort we examine here; it necessarily lacks precision, it cannot discriminate well between levels of a variable; and it is inevitably unreliable. Measurement problems do not magically disappear when answers to multiple questions are combined into composite scales, of course, but they do diminish. Scales stand a better chance of representing complex concepts faithfully; they generally provide more precision, finer discriminations, and all around more reliable measurement.

Moreover, using multiple-item scales enables us to assess how reliably we have measured such complicated concepts as equal opportunity, and then to take such reliability into account in our analysis. Relying on single items would blind us to whatever imperfections blemish our measures. Such a practice would leave us in the dark about whether the various theoretical claims advanced here have been fairly tested. In short, knowing that without adequate measurement our empirical project never lifts off the ground, we have tried our best to develop reliable and valid measures of key variables.

Measurement is crucial to the success of our endeavor, but it is not enough. Just as important are the interrelated matters of specification and estimation. By specification we mean the formal representation of the theoretical claims regarding the determinants of public opinion on race; by estimation we mean the statistical procedures for estimating the formal representation given by a particular specification.

The first business in developing a specification is to designate the variables that we believe, on theoretical grounds, determine public opinion on race. Our claim here, to repeat, is that the essential determinants of American opinion on racial questions include, for blacks and whites alike, the material interests citizens see at stake for themselves and their families, feelings of hostility or solidarity citizens direct toward social groups, and citizens' commitments to the principles of equality, economic individualism, and limited government. We are interested in assessing the independent effect of each such element on public opinion, taking into account the effects due to all others. This calls in the first place for a multivariate specification: we need to consider the effects of all variables simultaneously.

What assumptions do we make about how citizens combine the various ingredients into an overall opinion? Here we are in pursuit of what Stanley Kelley has called, in his analysis of the act of voting, *the rule:* a mental program that describes how people combine diverse considerations. In Kelley's view, "To know both the considerations [ingredients, in our vocabulary] and the rule is to explain the choice."[17] Consistent with an extensive experimental literature on judgment and choice in psychology, we claim that the "cognitive algebra" implicated in such combination processes is relatively simple. For the most part, people seem to follow an additive rule, generally foregoing more complicated formulas. They behave, as Robert Abelson once put it, like "ragged statistical processors."[18] Americans assemble their opinions on race as if they had added together the primary ingredients, each ingredient weighted by its subjective importance. As a first approximation, our specification assumes a simple linear rule of combination.

All along we have said specification when we should have said *specifications*. Rather than presume that the one true model has been revealed to us, we will instead develop and test a set of plausible models: those specifications that seem to us reasonable representations of the process by which public opinion on matters of race is determined. Their purpose will be to help us in the knotty problem of estimating the effects on public opinion on race due to interests, attitudes toward social groups, political principles, and elite frames. Our practice will be to estimate the causal effect of a particular variable—say commitment to the idea of equality—over a set of plausible specifications. Insofar as the effects of equality are robust across alternative specifications, we can have greater confidence in our conclusions about the power of equality to shape opinion on racial questions.[19]

This leaves the special problem of how to test our claim that elite discourse frames public understanding and, ultimately, public opinion. Our solution is provided by experiments: we ask equivalent samples of Americans for their views on racial policy questions with the questions posed—or *framed*—in alternative ways. Our argument, developed in more detail in Chapter 7, is that by examining the kinds of alterations in opinions that are induced by variations in question wording that mimic the rival frames that prevail in elite discourse, we can learn about how changes in public opinion are induced by changes in the setting beyond the survey, in the ongoing, everyday process of political debate.

Finally, as we have presented it so far, our framework refers to "the average American"—or better, it takes the average American for granted. But of course there really is no such creature: Americans are amazingly diverse, and they may be diverse in ways that make a difference in their views on race. Are the opinion ingredients that matter most to a school teacher living in a small town in Montana likely to be the same as those that dominate the views of an unemployed assembly line worker in Detroit? Will the promotion of alternative frames on affirmative action be as consequential for a political activist as for someone who pays no attention to the public debate? In the end, our understanding of public opinion must take such diversity into account.

As a general matter, the public opinion literature takes rather little notice of American diversity. Or, more precisely, while individual diversity is nearly always acknowledged in principle, it is as frequently ignored in practice. A very large share of published analysis presumes that Americans think about interests, or social groups, or principles in just the same way.[20] This inclination, which is of great convenience for empirical estimation, is dangerous. Average results, as Douglas Rivers once put it, may disguise "population heterogeneity in much the same way census averages describing the 'average' family as having 2.5 children do: one has trouble finding an average family."[21]

Conceding the point of individual diversity can make a lot of trouble. In the extreme, diversity could render our project impossible to carry out. Americans might be so different from one another in ways that are consequential for their views on race that the systematic examination of public opinion requires biographical analysis, one citizen at a time. Or Americans might be so different from one another that all we can do is close our eyes and proceed, operating under the false but analytically convenient assumption that Americans are interchangeable.

Fortunately, there is a useful middle ground between these two extremes. Americans are amazingly diverse, but such diversity can be incorporated, at least in broad strokes, in the kind of quantitative analysis we provide. And when we do so—when we reestimate our plausible models within various segments of the full public—we generally find modest differences. That is, men and women, working class and middle class, southern and northern, old and young, and more seem to follow roughly the same rule in putting their opinions together. When we run across occasional exceptions to this broad conclusion, we will report the results in the relevant chapters ahead. In the meantime we can say that while Americans certainly are not identical and interchangeable, neither are they endlessly idiosyncratic and eccentric when it comes to opinions on race. The diversity that we do uncover, moreover, appears both circumscribed and intelligible—a welcome result for those who hope for a science of public opinion.

MOVING ON

The pursuit of a single sovereign theory to explain public opinion on race—or on any other topic—is misguided. Public opinion is a complex expression of various core ingredients: the material interests that citizens see at stake in the issue; the sympathies and resentments that citizens feel toward those social groups implicated in the dispute, especially those groups that the policy appears to benefit; and commitment to the political principles that the policy seems to honor or repudiate. At the same time, public opinion also reflects and follows political debate. Elites are constantly engaged in symbolic warfare over how complex issues are to be framed. Frames are opinion recipes: they are suggestions to citizens regarding which ingredients, in what proportion, should be combined to make a good opinion.

Perhaps all this seems distressingly abstract and general. In compensation, the next several chapters get concrete and specific. We begin, in Chapter 4, with the political effect of material interests.

PART II

PRIMARY INGREDIENTS OF OPINION

CHAPTER FOUR

Threat and Advantage

According to one long and distinguished line of argument, citizens are little more than single-minded seekers of self-interest. In forming political opinions, they fasten their attention securely on what is in it for themselves, supporting policies that advance their own material interests while standing against policies that threaten them. In this view, "Men always act from self-interest. . . . when we see the actions of a man, we know with certainty what he thinks his interest to be."[1]

As self-interest is regarded as a perfectly general motive, it should motivate public opinion on racial matters in particular—and perhaps it does. Our purpose in this chapter is to subject the claim of self-interest to a series of pointed empirical tests. We begin by noting its privileged place both in philosophic writing on human nature and politics and in much contemporary analysis of public opinion. Then we set out a conception of self-interest that is sufficiently broad to encompass the range of meanings attached to it in various influential writings yet sufficiently circumscribed to be useful empirically. After introducing the various measures available to us in the NES surveys, we then proceed, in the heart of the chapter, to estimate the impact of self-interest on public opinion on matters of race. To what extent is political conflict over racial issues reducible to the "universal passion" for personal advantage?[2]

THE PRIVILEGED PLACE OF SELF-INTEREST

In Hobbes's world, individuals were driven by a "perpetual and restless desire of Power after power, that ceaseth only in Death."[3] Given this reality, a peaceful and commodious life could be attained only when all subjects surrendered their right to self-government to a higher authority, the sovereign. Writing at a time of social disintegration and disorder, against the background of the English Civil War, Hobbes believed that without submission to the sovereign, society would dissolve into the "Warre of every one against every one."

Leviathan's self-interest was a regrettable, if rational, response to the state of nature. In the analyses of politics that followed, self-interest was no less prominent, but its reputation improved dramatically: self-interest became a virtue, a quality to be admired and cultivated. Albert Hirschman's *The Passions and the Interests* traces this transformation. Hirschman points out that various notable thinkers, including David Hume, promoted self-interest as superior to the motives of glory and honor, which had left Europe soaked in blood. Interests held out the hope that they might, as Hirschman put it, *tame* the passions. The central contrast here was between, on the one hand, "the favorable effects that follow when men are guided by their interests" and, on the other, "the calamitous state of affairs that prevails when men give free rein to their passions."[4]

Self-interest was also prominent in political writings on the American continent. Most famous was the series of remarkable *Federalist* essays written by James Madison. Madison, like Hobbes, accepted that politics was based on self-interest. The relentless pursuit for preeminence, power, and profit was inescapable; it was "sown in the nature of man." Conflicts among distinct interests, or factions, were a fundamental and ineradicable feature of social life and have constantly "divided mankind . . . inflamed them with mutual animosity, and rendered them much more disposed to vex and oppress each other than to cooperate for their common good."[5] To Madison's way of thinking, the management of faction rooted in opposed interests was *the* problem of politics.

Self-interested citizens thrive in contemporary renditions of democratic theory as well. This is apparent in pluralist accounts of American politics, where citizens organize around common interests and then effectively press their claims on government.[6] Citizens moved by self-interest are even more conspicuous in the explosion of recent work that advances the economic approach to political analysis. In *An Economic Theory of Democracy*, Anthony Downs made self-interest the foundation stone of his deductive analysis. The revelatory way that Downs reworked ancient questions of democratic politics encouraged scores of others to take up political analysis from an economic perspective. In this approach, citizens (not to mention leaders) are portrayed as completely absorbed in their selfish interests.[7]

Prominently positioned as it is in various strands of political theory, the assumption of self-interest also occupies a privileged place in much contemporary empirical analysis. Take, as one example, Kramer's influential study of the electoral consequences of economic performance. Kramer began with the premise that citizens cast their vote for the party they expect will provide them with more benefits than any other. And to calculate such expectations, Kramer presumed that voters simply review their own circumstances.[8] Kramer's analysis, and the explosion of empirical activity that it touched off, have established clear connections between economic conditions and electoral outcomes: parties in power do best under conditions of economic prosperity.[9] This aggregate result is compatible with any number of conceptions of how individual citizens come to their political choices. Nevertheless, it is for the self-interested voter that analysts reach in speculating about individual citizens wrestling with economic problems. And why not? It seems entirely reasonable to suppose that voters who run into economic difficulties in their own lives will march to the polls to throw the rascals out.

To take another high profile example, in *The American Voter,* Angus Campbell and his colleagues concluded that the underpinnings of public support for government policy are to be found in what they called "primitive self-interest." This is self-interest unencumbered by any ideological pretensions, self-interest "simple and naked." Working-class citizens support social welfare policies because the benefits of such policies fall to them, while the middle-class line up in opposition because they must shoulder the costs.[10]

It would be easy enough to drag out additional examples, but the general point should now be established. Self-interest figures heavily—and until quite recently, rather uncritically—in our comprehension of politics.[11]

SELF-INTEREST DEFINED

Self-interest is important, evidently, but what is it exactly? By itself, "interest" is an elusive concept, the hyphenated concept "self-interest" more so. We need to be clear at the outset what we mean when we say that citizens have formed opinions that reflect their interests.

Our definition is drawn from several sources, but most immediately from Brian Barry's useful discussion spelled out in *Political Argument.* Barry maintains that "an action or policy is in a man's interests if it increases his opportunities to get what he wants."[12] Such opportunities are best defined in terms of wealth and power, assets that are potential means to any imaginable end. Following Barry, our definition also emphasizes material assets. Self-interest is at stake whenever politics threatens to redistribute wealth or power.

Self-interested citizens, it could be said further, pursue their own wealth and power in political life, and no one else's. It is the accumulation of personal assets that drives them. Self-interested citizens are indifferent to others; they have only their own wealth and power in mind, not those of their community or group, or their nation as a whole.

There is merit in defining self-interest strictly, but this is a bit too strict for our taste. We want self-interest to include not just the material interests of the self, but also the material interests of the immediate family. This expansion of self-interest reflects the special place accorded the family in modern Western society. It is the family, not the community and certainly not politics, that occupies the energy and attention of most Americans. When citizens are portrayed as privately preoccupied, it is with family matters first and foremost.

Relations among family members are uniquely intimate and durable; members of families care for one another, are responsible for one another, in ways that are seldom duplicated in the wider world. Thus we will say that self-interest is at issue among parents contemplating the prospect that their children might be transported across town for purposes of racial desegregation. Likewise, we will allow as a case of self-interest the views of a husband whose wife is employed outside the home and likely to be affected, one way or another, by affirmative action guidelines. Self-interest encompasses the material interests of the family as well as the material interests of the self.

We focus here mainly on self-interest in the short run: the immediate threats or advantages that policies seem to offer. It is of course entirely possible that citizens may be willing to forego short-term benefits or endure pain in the short run in the expectation that policies will benefit them handsomely later on. That in the long run, as Keynes reminds us, we are all dead is no justification for insisting that for interests to matter, citizens must be utterly preoccupied with the here and now. Granting Keynes his point, we assume nevertheless that citizens motivated by self-interest have mostly the near future in mind.

Are self-interested citizens rational? Not necessarily. If citizens pursue their own interests, they may do so having calculated their interests well and having chosen their options wisely—or they may have made a mess of it. In symmetric fashion, rational citizens might have their own interests in mind, but their calculations might involve benefits and harms that have nothing to do with their own or their family's well-being: the theory of rational choice cares nothing for tastes. In short, the finding that citizens are, or are not, self-interested has nothing to say about whether citizens are, or are not, rational.

Nor, finally, should self-interest be set in opposition to altruism, as if these two exhausted the possibilities. The diversity of human motivation is an inescapable lesson of modern psychology. It is apparent as well in the psychological writings of the seventeenth and eighteenth centuries, including, most notably, the works of David Hume and Adam Smith. Reviewing such writings, Stephen Holmes provides a catalog of twenty-four motives that were typically contrasted with self-interest, including relish of conflict, hatred of uncertainty, and pity for undeserved misfortune.[13] If self-interest turns out to be irrelevant to the views black and white Americans develop on policies of race, we cannot conclude that Americans must therefore be altruistic.

In sum, self-interest should neither be confused with rationality nor opposed to altruism. Self-interested citizens pursue material benefits and harms in politics, and they have in mind only themselves and their immediate families. Communities, groups, the nation, humankind as a whole: all drift to the periphery for citizens driven by self-interest. For the self-interested citizen, the question is always and relentlessly: What's in it for me (and mine)?

THE MEASUREMENT OF SELF-INTEREST

To measure self-interest, defined in this way, we make use of both subjective and objective measures of interest, oriented to both the short and the somewhat longer term. By making use of a variety of measures, we hope to gain a clearer and more comprehensive picture of self-interest in operation in racial politics.

The advantage of the subjective measures is that we need not indulge in the tricky business of imputing interests. Rather, citizens tell us what they take the personal threats and advantages of racial policies to be. We also make use of extensive batteries of objective questions that are a regular feature of NES surveys. Such questions provide a thorough mapping of each citizen's social location: their income, employment status, age, gender, marital status, and much more. As we will argue in detail shortly, some of these characteristics are relevant to the interests arising in racial policies. For example, blacks who are active participants in the labor market have the greatest personal stake in employment policies. Black Americans who are currently working, or who are unemployed or temporarily laid off, should, all other things equal, favor government efforts to ensure that blacks do not suffer discrimination at work and should support affirmative action in hiring and promotion decisions more than those blacks who are out of the labor market. Our general point is that demographic characteristics, when used judiciously and selectively, index the likely personal effect of particular racial policies and so can be used to test the claim of self-interest.[14]

To identify self-interest precisely, we use demographic characteristics selectively and in combination. We control statistically on other considerations. And to sustain the claim of self-interest, we expect—indeed, we require—specificity of effects. Whether or not citizens are participants in the labor market, for example, should, according to self-interest theory, influence their opinions on affirmative action policies at work, but not their views on school policy. Developing this argument about specificity of effects requires us to identify our particular measures of self-interest, which we do next.

Perceived Threat and Advantage

Our first two measures of self-interest are subjective. One refers to employment, the other to education. Both questions focus on affirmative action policies, and both ask people to consider the consequences of such policies for their families. The questions deal in potential harms when asked of white Americans and potential benefits when put to black Americans. For whites, the two questions read this way:

> *What do you think the chances are these days that you or anyone in your family won't get a job or a promotion while an equally or less qualified black employee receives one instead?*

> *What do you think the chances are these days that you or anyone in your family won't get admitted to a school while an equally or less qualified black person gets admitted instead?* [15]

As revealed in table 4.1, many whites experienced affirmative action policies as a clear and present danger. More than 40% of whites thought it likely that they or a member of their family would be passed over for a job or promotion; slightly more believed that family members would be denied admission to a school. Thus many whites appear convinced that in vital domains of life—at work, in school—policies and procedures operate against their own interests and for the interests of blacks.

Table 4.1 Self-Interest among Whites and Blacks

	Whites	Blacks
Personal threat/personal advantage of racial policies		
WORKPLACE		
Very unlikely	30.3%	47.0%
Somewhat unlikely	28.2	23.5
Somewhat likely	29.0	20.8
Very likely	12.6	8.7
COLLEGE ADMISSIONS		
Very unlikely	28.2%	45.3%
Somewhat unlikely	28.7	30.7
Somewhat likely	30.4	22.0
Very likely	12.6	2.0
Class		
FAMILY INCOME ($)		
<5K	5.6%	18.4%
5–10K	10.9	18.4
10–15K	12.1	19.5
15–20K	8.6	10.3
20–25K	10.9	8.5
25–35K	17.4	11.3
35–50K	19.4	6.0
50K+	15.2	7.4

continues

Table 4.1 *Continued*

	Whites	Blacks
Head of household occupation		
Unskilled worker	10.9%	14.3%
Service	8.3	21.2
Skilled worker	27.6	28.7
Sales	18.2	15.4
Manager	15.2	3.1
Professional	16.2	13.3
Respondent education		
11 years or less	18.9%	34.0%
High school	35.7	35.8
Some college	24.0	19.2
College degree	14.1	7.5
Advanced degree	7.2	3.5
Homeownership		
Homeowner	70.1%	43.0%
Family economic position (change over the past year)		
Much better	8.6%	8.7%
Better	32.8	24.3
Same	32.5	33.0
Worse	18.0	21.5
Much worse	8.1	12.5
Current employment status		
Out of work	5.2%	8.7%
Employment apprehensions		
Not at all	78.5%	74.4%
Some	12.5	15.8
A lot	9.0	9.8
Children in household (% yes)		
Younger than 6 years	19.2%	25.1%
6–9 years	14.4	13.9
10–13 years	14.0	12.1
14–17 years	14.6	17.3
Racial composition of neighborhood		
All white	28.8%	3.7%
Overwhelmingly white (96–99%)	62.4	5.8
Predominantly white (86–95%)	20.1	10.3
76–85%	10.3	11.6
51–75%	6.0	18.5
26–50%	1.8	18.3
16–25%	.2	7.4
6–15%	0.0	6.9
0–5%	0.1	20.3
All nonwhite	0.0	5.6
Employment status		
In labor force	68.6%	66.9%
Self-employed	15.3	5.7
Government employee	23.6	31.7

Source: 1986 National Election Study.

Black Americans were asked about the potential gains that affirmative action might bring their family. For blacks, the questions read this way:

> What do you think the chances are these days that you or anyone in your family will get a job or a promotion while an equally qualified white employee gets turned down?

> What do you think the chances are these days that you or anyone in your family will get admitted to a school while an equally qualified white person gets turned down?

According to these questions, blacks seem rather unimpressed with the personal benefits of affirmative action. When asked how likely it was that they or anyone in their family would get a job or promotion while an equally qualified white employee was turned down, more than two- thirds believed such an outcome unlikely, and two-thirds of those thought it very unlikely. Similarly, when asked to assess the chances that they or anyone in their family would get admitted to a school while an equally qualified white person was turned away, more than three-quarters of black Americans answered in the negative. In short, while many whites feel personally threatened by affirmative action policies, relatively few blacks see affirmative action providing personal benefits.

The real issue here, which we will get to shortly, is how well differences in perceptions of self-interest can account for differences in opinion. We generally expect that the perception of personal threat among whites will operate against support for policies designed to help blacks, and that the perception of personal gain among blacks will operate in favor of policies designed to help blacks. But the case for self-interest requires a more nuanced pattern of results than that. The impact of these perceptions should be greatest on views toward affirmative action, since the perceptions themselves are tied specifically to affirmative action. Further still, perceptions of threat and gain from affirmative action at work should most affect opinions on affirmative action at work; just as perceptions of threat and gain from affirmative action in school admissions should most affect opinions on affirmative action in college admissions. Self-interest requires specificity, and so we will be on the lookout for it.

Class

In class analysis, race is often treated as a social cleavage with no future. Marx believed that group differences defined by race would be overtaken in modern society by identities rooted in class. For Marx, the real divide in industrial society was between owners and workers, clearly defined groups with mutually antagonistic interests, locked in political conflict. From this perspective, race is little more than a distraction. That things didn't quite work out the way Marx imagined doesn't mean that class has nothing to say here. Diverse and distinctive interests are associated with position in the American class structure, and we will do our best to assess their consequences for public opinion on race.

The implications of class analysis for black public opinion are straightforward. Relative to the working class and the poor, middle-class blacks should oppose redistributive policies, whether they are targeted at the poor generally or at the black poor specifically. While poor blacks should continue to insist on government assistance and special treatment, middle-class blacks may be pushed by the imperative of their class interests toward the center. As more blacks make their way to the middle class, they will begin to entertain political views commensurate with their new station. Like other members of the middle class, they will come to appreciate the virtue in conservative policies. This emerging class alignment among black Americans may be attenuated or even reversed on affirmative action, however, since, it is often argued, such policies primarily benefit the black middle class.

The class argument for white public opinion is less obvious. Support for policies that are designed to narrow racial inequalities should be most generous among affluent whites, who can most easily afford to pay for them and who are most likely to be protected from their consequences. What is not so clear is where, in the class structure, opposition will be greatest. One line of argument, associated most prominently with Bonacich, is that racial conservatism will be most pronounced among working-class whites, who are in direct economic competition with blacks.[16] Such conservatism should show up especially on policies that affect the workplace. Another line of argument, articulated by Rieder, is that racial conservatism is most prominent among the marginal middle class, who believe they have the most to lose by changes in the racial status quo. In Rieder's analysis, school integration or affirmative action threatens to take away from whites what they have just managed to acquire.[17]

Following common practice, we define class with reference to three correlated, but distinct, aspects of social resources: family income, occupational status (of the head of household), and education (of the respondent). To these standard three, we add home ownership, which allows us to take into account huge racial differences in wealth that are mostly missed by indicators of current income or occupation. As table 4.1 discloses, blacks and whites differ sharply on all measures of class: 34.6% of whites report an annual family income of greater than $35,000; just 13.4% of blacks do so. 21.3% of whites report at least a college degree, compared with just 11.0% of blacks. 31.4% of whites work as professionals or managers, as against just 16.4% of blacks. And 70.1% of white Americans own their own homes, compared with just 43.0% of black Americans.

Family Economic Well-Being

With self-interest in mind, black Americans who have recently experienced economic troubles or who are worried about their economic future will, as a consequence, favor government assistance: they will support special government efforts for blacks, more federal money for programs that help blacks, and employment policies that both prohibit discrimination and take race into consideration when people are hired and promoted. Views on government assistance and affirmative action should reflect in a direct and immediate way blacks' own economic predicament.

The same should hold true for whites, but here economic adversities and apprehensions should generate opposition to such initiatives. Federal assistance and employment policies designed to help blacks should be resisted most vehemently by whites who have run into economic troubles themselves.

We measure change in family economic well-being in several ways, with questions that mix objective and subjective measures. We ask people to assess whether their family's economic condition is better or worse compared with a year ago, we find out whether the family's head of household is currently unemployed or temporarily laid off, and we determine how apprehensive the head of household is about remaining employed into the near future (or, if currently out of work, how worried he or she is about finding employment).

Consulting table 4.1, we find, as expected, that blacks are more likely than whites to say that their family's economic situation has deteriorated over the past year (34.0% versus 26.1%), more likely to be currently out of work (8.7% versus 5.2%), and somewhat more worried about finding work in the future or hanging onto the job they currently have (25.6% versus 21.5%).

Children and Schooling

Schools, as Gary Orfield reminds us, are "the largest and most visible of public institutions, directly affecting millions of families."[18] Both black and white parents want high-quality education for their children; they believe that schools are escalators of success. As the protracted and bitter struggle over school desegregation attests, the stakes could scarcely be higher.

Two of our policy questions reflect the continuing debate over race and education. The first asks whether the federal government should insure that black and white children are educated together. To assess self-interest for school desegregation, we identify people who have children and who are living in racially mixed communities. The presence of children, in the context of a racially mixed community, raises the personal stakes in desegregated schooling. The presence of young children in particular, should, other things equal, lead whites to oppose government efforts to guarantee that blacks and whites attend school together while at the same time lead blacks to support such efforts. As table 4.1 indicates, young children are a bit more common in black households than in whites (25.1% versus 19.2%). The table also shows that while racial segregation is the norm in American communities, some whites, and quite a few blacks, reside in racially mixed neighborhoods.[19]

Our policy measures also include a question on the desirability of guaranteeing slots for black students in college admissions. Self-interest in this context is indicated by the presence of older children, and the possession of sufficient resources to make college education a reasonable aspiration. White parents of teen-age children with at least roughly middle-class resources should, from the perspective of self-interest, be most opposed to college quotas for blacks. Black parents who find themselves in the identical circumstance should be the most enthusiastic supporters of reserving space for black students in college admissions. The figures in table 4.1 reveal that the proportion of blacks and whites with strong personal interests in college admission policies is far from trivial.

Employment Status

Finally, whites and blacks have different interests in various racial policies depending upon their relationship to the economy. Those who are active participants in the labor market have the greatest personal interest in employment policies, represented in our policy questions by fair employment policies and affirmative action in hiring and promotion decisions. The divide here is between those who are currently working, or who are unemployed or temporarily laid off, on the one hand, and those who are retired, homemakers, or permanently disabled, on the other.[20] Blacks in the former group (66.9% of all blacks, according to table 4.1) should, other things equal, favor government efforts to ensure that blacks do not suffer discrimination at work and should support affirmative action in hiring and promotion decisions. By the same logic, white participants in the labor market (68.6% of all whites) should oppose such policies.

Under the category of employment status we will examine two additional and more specific propositions. First, opposition to affirmative action at work will be particularly sharp among whites who are self-employed, since they may see the burden of such policies falling heavily on their shoulders (some 15.3% of all whites in the labor market). Second, support for a strong government role on behalf of blacks—more federal money, more special assistance from Washington—will be especially evident among blacks whose head of household is employed by government (31.7% of all those blacks currently at work).

THE IMPACT OF SELF-INTEREST: ANALYSIS AND RESULTS

The various and diverse interests we have just identified tend to be correlated with one another. The working class are more likely to be apprehensive of their economic futures than the middle class, those who see personal threat in affirmative action policies at work may look at affirmative action in school admissions in a similar way, and so on. Because interests are correlated, and because we wish to determine the effect due to each aspect of self-interest, we must estimate the impact of each, holding constant the effect due to all the others.

Interests tend to be correlated not only with one another, but with various aspects of social location as well: the well-to-do tend to be older, the better educated tend to live in suburban rings outside central cities, the middle class tend to be Protestant, and so on. Such characteristics may be related to opinion on race policy for reasons that have nothing to do with self-interest. In order to obtain accurate (or consistent) estimates of the impact of any single aspect of self-interest, therefore, we need to control statistically on the impact due to social position more broadly. Here we take into account age, region, religion, marital status, gender, union household, ethnicity (present only in the analysis of whites), as well as race of interviewer.[21]

To estimate the effects of self-interest, we relied on the standard solution provided by ordinary least squares (OLS) regression. We produced six sets of estimates, for whites and blacks separately, each set associated with one of the six race policies. As we argued in Chapter 2, each presents a somewhat different face of the political struggle over racial equality, and so it is proper for us to take each up separately. It is actually doubly appropriate, since we expect the impact of self-interest to vary across different policy disputes. Some questions of race policy engage certain aspects of self-interest in a particularly pointed way, and our results should reflect that.

Racial Threat and White Opinion

The results for whites are presented in table 4.2. The table is organized into six columns, one for each of the six policies, from school integration, in the far left column of the table, to affirmative action in college admissions, in the far right. The rows of the table represent the various measures of self-interest, from the perception of personal threat due to affirmative action policies in school admissions, at the top, to employed by the government, at the bottom. The numbers that fill the table are the unstandardized regression coefficients, B,

Table 4.2 Impact of Self-Interest on White Opinion

	Fair Employment	School Desegregation	Federal Spending	Government Effort	Preferential Hiring	College Quotas
Personal threat	.19	.23	.15	.09	.13	.25
education	(.10)	(.09)	(.05)	(.04)	(.05)	(.06)
Personal threat	.06	.06	.06	.03	.02	.02
employment	(.10)	(.10)	(.05)	(.04)	(.05)	(.06)
Family income						
< 10K	−.06	−.15	−.01	−.03	−.05	−.08
	(.12)	(.12)	(.06)	(.05)	(.06)	(.07)
10–17 K	.01	−.18	−.01	.03	−.02	−.10
	(.11)	(.11)	(.06)	(.05)	(.06)	(.07)
17–25 K	−.01	−.16	.03	.00	−.04	−.07
	(.12)	(.11)	(.06)	(.05)	(.06)	(.07)
25–35 K	−.08	−.16	−.00	.03	−.02	−.05
	(.11)	(.11)	(.06)	(.05)	(.06)	(.07)
35–50 K	−.06	−.20	.03	.02	−.07	−.09
	(.12)	(.12)	(.06)	(.05)	(.06)	(.07)
50–75 K	−.25	−.25	−.03	−.06	−.13	−.16
	(.13)	(.13)	(.07)	(.06)	(.06)	(.08)
> 75K	−.12	−.20	.02	−.02	−.04	−.02
	(.16)	(.16)	(.08)	(.07)	(.08)	(.10)
Household occupation						
Professional	.05	−.10	−.01	.01	−.06	−.02
	(.10)	(.10)	(.05)	(.04)	(.05)	(.06)
Manager	.06	−.14	−.03	−.00	−.02	.00
	(.09)	(.09)	(.05)	(.04)	(.04)	(.05)
Sales	.01	.01	−.00	.00	−.01	.03
	(.08)	(.08)	(.04)	(.03)	(.04)	(.05)
Service	−.00	−.13	.00	.03	−.00	−.02
	(.10)	(.10)	(.05)	(.04)	(.05)	(.06)
Farmer	.08	.07	.08	.07	.01	.10
	(.15)	(.14)	(.08)	(.06)	(.07)	(.09)
Unskilled worker	−.04	−.15	.01	−.03	−.03	−.05
	(.09)	(.09)	(.05)	(.04)	(.05)	(.06)
Education						
8 or less	−.05	−.10	−.05	−.03	−.13	−.15
	(.11)	(.11)	(.06)	(.05)	(.06)	(.07)
Some high school	.06	.02	−.03	.02	−.06	−.08
	(.09)	(.09)	(.05)	(.04)	(.04)	(.06)
Some college	.01	.03	−.03	−.02	.03	−.02
	(.07)	(.07)	(.04)	(.03)	(.03)	(.04)
BA	−.12	−.03	−.01	−.04	.02	−.03
	(.09)	(.09)	(.05)	(.04)	(.04)	(.06)
Advanced degree	−.12	−.05	−.10	−.09	−.01	−.01
	(.12)	(.12)	(.06)	(.05)	(.06)	(.07)
Homeowner	.13	.04	.05	.08	.06	.04
	(.06)	(.06)	(.03)	(.03)	(.03)	(.04)

continues

Table 4.2 *Continued*

	Fair Employment	School Desegregation	Federal Spending	Government Effort	Preferential Hiring	College Quotas
Family economic	.02	−.03	−.03	.04	−.02	−.05
situation	(.10)	(.10)	(.05)	(.04)	(.05)	(.06)
HH out of work	−.01	−.12	−.02	.04	−.14	−.10
	(.12)	(.12)	(.06)	(.05)	(.06)	(.08)
HH worried	−.13	.05	−.03	.01	.00	−.00
about work	(.09)	(.09)	(.05)	(.04)	(.04)	(.06)
Young children*						
racially mixed	−.05	−.13	.04	.04	−.05	.14
community	(.18)	(.18)	(.09)	(.08)	(.09)	(.11)
Older children*	−.02	.04	.01	.00	.02	.04
middle class	(.10)	(.09)	(.05)	(.04)	(.05)	(.06)
HH in labor force	.05	−.02	.01	−.07	.03	.02
	(.09)	(.09)	(.05)	(.04)	(.04)	(.05)
HH self-employed	.01	−.03	.03	−.02	−.02	−.07
	(.07)	(.07)	(.04)	(.03)	(.03)	(.04)
HH government						
employee	−.07	−.00	.00	−.00	−.04	−.06
	(.07)	(.07)	(.03)	(.03)	(.03)	(.04)
Constant	.42	.94	.45	.54	.80	.66
	(.18)	(.18)	(.09)	(.08)	(.09)	(.11)
R-squared	.19	.20	.12	.17	.16	.17
Standard error	.48	.47	.30	.25	.29	.35
Number of cases	371	361	544	533	544	542

Source: 1986 National Election Study.
Note: Table entry is *B*, the unstandardized ordinary least square regression coefficient, with standard errors in parentheses underneath. All variables coded 0–1. Each equation also included measures of age, region, sex, marital status, union membership, religion, and race of interviewer. HH = head of household.

with the standard errors in parentheses underneath. *B* gives our best estimate of the direct and independent effects due to self-interest, for each measure of self-interest and for each measure of racial policy. For ease in reading the table, we excluded the estimated effects due to social background characteristics; coded all variables onto the 0–1 interval, and reversed some variables so that from the perspective of self-interest, the coefficients should be positive in all instances.

From the perspective of self-interest, table 4.2 is a major disappointment. Most of the estimated effects of self-interest presented in table 4.2 are indistinguishable from no effect at all.[22] There is a hint that home ownership induces opposition to racial policies (consistent with a self-interest interpretation), and that the experience of being out of work induces support for racial policies (in contradiction to the self-interest expectation). There is, perhaps, a faint suggestion that income leads white Americans to be a bit more generous on racial questions (trouble for self-interest), and that education produces opposition to affirmative action (consistent with self-interest). None of this is worth taking too seriously, however. Our sample is reasonably large, yet the "effects" we just discussed seldom surpass conventional levels of statistical significance; even when they do, they are too small to worry over.[23]

In the entire table, only one result stands out consistently: whites who believe their family at risk from school admissions practices that favor blacks are generally more opposed to the various racial policies we examine. They are less enthusiastic about school integration, less likely to favor a policy that would ensure that blacks no longer face discrimination at work, less willing to support federal programs that help blacks, less inclined to say that the government should make special efforts to assist black Americans, less favorable toward affirmative action policies that take race into account in employment decisions, and less tolerant of racial quotas in college admissions procedures.

These effects of perceived threat are not only reliably different from zero; they are sizable. Consider the case of funding for federal programs that help blacks, where the estimated impact of racial threat is neither the biggest in the table nor the smallest. To interpret this effect, remember that all variables are coded on the 0–1 interval, including the race policy variables. Thus on the policy matter in question, whites who favor cutting back on federal programs are scored "1"; those who favor increases in federal spending are scored "0"; and those whites who wish to keep spending roughly the same are scored "0.5." An unstandardized regression coefficient of .15 (shown in the first row of table 4.2) therefore means this: among white Americans who are otherwise identical on measures of self-interest and social background, those who say that they or a member of their families is very likely to be turned away from a school while an equally or less qualified black person is admitted instead are, on average, more opposed to federal programs for blacks than are those whites who say that it is very unlikely that they or a member of their families will be turned away, the difference given by .15 on the 0–1 scale. This is a sizable difference. It is equivalent to a shift in opinion from slightly favoring *decreases* in federal spending on programs to assist blacks to slightly favoring *increases* in federal spending (a move from .58 to .43 on the 0–1 scale). Such effects, which are repeated throughout the first row of table 4.2, are well worth our attention.

Also worth our attention is that the perception of personal racial threat in school admissions, which is tied to a specific domain, appears to produce opposition to racial policy initiatives of all kinds. The effect of perceived threat in school admissions is largest where it ought to be, on opposition to college quotas. But contrary to expectation, contrary to our reading of how self-interest should operate, the effect shows up on every racial policy that we consider. That so specific a threat should produce so general an effect is puzzling.

Equally puzzling is that its close companion—the perception of racial threat at work—seems to have no effect on policy views whatsoever. The relevant coefficients, presented in the second row of table 4.2, all hover close to zero. Why should the personal threat of reverse discrimination in schooling be so powerful while the apparently comparable personal threat of reverse discrimination in employment be so weak? It is not that whites believe themselves threatened by the first but safe from the second. A glance back at table 4.1 reminds us that nearly as many whites thought it likely that they or a member of their family would be passed over for a job or promotion as believed that family members would be denied educational opportunities. Whites feel personally threatened in both domains. Perhaps we should write the difference off: the two perceptions are positively correlated; if examined separately in simple bivariate analysis, they are associated with policy views in roughly equal fashion. Perhaps we shouldn't take the multivariate results too seriously.

Perhaps, but when we estimated the same relationships, this time making use of data from the 1985 NES, we found exactly the same result: the perception of risk in schooling is associated with racial conservatism across the board, while the perception of personal risk in employment is once again utterly irrelevant. Apparently there is something especially provocative about race and schooling, the sense among white Americans that black students are being handed educational advantages that rightfully belong to their own children.

Realistic threat? This result leads us to wonder about the meaning of personal racial threat. How do people go about deciding whether or not they are at risk? Why do some whites feel that their children are likely to be discriminated against in education, while others see no threat at all? Surely some of the answer is that differences in perception reflect differences in circumstance. The rather dramatic variation we observe in whites' perception of racial threat must be at least partially grounded in the realities of their social and economic lives.

Quite another answer is provided by recent psychological research on risk perception. This work presumes that intuitive judgments of probability and risk are complicated matters, and that to cope with such complexity, people rely on simple strategies, or cognitive heuristics. Heuristics are concessions to complexity; they are, as Nisbett and Ross put it, "an inevitable feature of the cognitive apparatus of any organism that must make as many judgments, inferences, and decisions as humans have to do."[24]

Two such cognitive heuristics—availability and simulation—appear to govern judgments of risk. According to the availability heuristic, people determine risks through the retrieval of relevant instances. When asked to assess the likelihood of some possible threat, such as whether their children might be denied educational opportunities owing to racial quotas in admissions, people answer by the ease with which relevant instances can be brought to mind. Insofar as instances are easily available, the threat will seem imminent. Such instances might come from their own direct experience, from the experiences reported by others, from rumor and gossip, from vivid news accounts, and more.

According to the simulation heuristic, when asked to assess the likelihood of some possible threat, people answer by the ease with which instances can be constructed. The question prompts the running of a mental simulation. Insofar as the simulation is easy to construct and run, people will regard the threat as close at hand.[25]

Neither the availability nor the simulation heuristic implies a close correspondence between social reality and perceptions of risk. Heuristics may be useful, but they are also fallible: judgments of risk are inevitably contaminated by error and bias. One likely source of bias in the case at hand is feelings of racial hostility. Whites who distrust or fear blacks may be more likely to feel threatened. In their minds, if not in their lives, they are surrounded by danger. Translated into the vocabulary of heuristics, racially resentful whites will be more able to call up instances that they interpret as cases of racial threat, and they will have less trouble running mental simulations where their children are denied educational opportunities.

Although the 1986 NES was not designed with the purpose of determining the sources of personal threat, we can go some distance in this direction. We rely again on regression analysis, taking up the perception of personal threat in the workplace and the perception of racial personal threat in schooling separately. In each instance, we estimate the effects due to a large collection of variables, all of which are plausibly associated with actual threat, as a test of the claim of realism. We also include a measure of racial resentment, the centerpiece of our analysis in Chapter 5, on the assumption that the perception of racial threat is partly a projection of racial hostility.[26]

The results from this analysis are summarized in table 4.3. As indicated there, the perception of racial threat is grounded to some extent in life circumstances—but the grounding is shallow and frail. Such traces of realism are more visible on the perception of threat in the workplace. Whites who are affluent, professional, economically secure, largely free from economic tribulations and apprehensions, are less likely to see affirmative action posing a threat at work. On the other side, whites who are enlisted in unions, who live in racially integrated neighborhoods, and especially those whites who work in racially

Table 4.3 Sources of the Perception of Personal Racial Threat among Whites

	Threat at Work	Threat at School
Racial resentment	.55	.85
	(.25)	(.26)
Family income		
< 10K	.02	−.08
	(.07)	(.07)
10−17K	−.02	−.09
	(.07)	(.07)
17−25K	−.01	−.03
	(.07)	(.07)
25−35K	.02	−.02
	(.07)	(.07)
35−50K	.02	−.02
	(.07)	(.07)
50−75K	.00	−.02
	(.08)	(.08)
75K+	−.04	−.08
	(.09)	(.09)
HH occupation		
Farmer	−.09	−.05
	(.09)	(.09)
Unskilled	−.09	.01
	(.05)	(.06)
Service	−.05	.02
	(.06)	(.06)
Sales	−.04	−.05
	(.05)	(.05)
Manager	−.05	.01
	(.05)	(.05)
Professional	−.09	−.01
	(.05)	(.05)
Change in family economic situation	.10	−.04
	(.06)	(.06)
HH currently unemployed	−.10	−.01
	(.07)	(.07)
HH unemployed recently	−.04	.03
	(.05)	(.05)
HH in labor force	.04	—
	(.05)	
HH worried about work	.09	.11
	(.05)	(.06)
Racial composition of workplace		
Mostly black	.16	−.04
	(.10)	(.10)
Somewhat black	.07	.04
	(.05)	(.05)
Few black	.06	.04
	(.03)	(.04)

continues

Table 4.3 *Continued*

	Threat at Work	Threat at School
Racial composition of neighborhood		
>15% black	.09	.04
	(.06)	(.06)
6–15% black	.06	.04
	(.05)	(.05)
1–5% black	−.02	−.02
	(.04)	(.04)
Age		
17–29	−.04	.02
	(.05)	(.05)
30–39	−.04	.01
	(.05)	(.05)
50–59	−.02	−.02
	(.06)	(.06)
60–69	.03	.05
	(.07)	(.06)
70+	−.03	−.02
	(.08)	(.07)
Children in household		
Younger than 6 years	.01	−.06
	(.04)	(.05)
6–9 years	.07	.08
	(.05)	(.05)
10–13 years	−.03	.01
	(.07)	(.05)
14–17 years	.02	−.02
	(.05)	(.05)
Labor union	.04	—
	(.09)	
Political knowledge	−.05	−.02
	(.07)	(.07)
Constant	.02	−.05
	(.07)	(.18)
R-squared	.09	.07
Standard error	.36	.36
Number of cases	586	577

Source: 1986 National Election Study.
Note: Table entry is *B,* the unstandardized regression coefficient, with standard errors in parentheses underneath. Racial resentment is treated as endogenous; its effect is estimated with two-stage least squares. All variables coded 0–1. HH = head of household.

integrated environments are more likely to see a threat at work. These relationships are not strong—indeed, they do not always pass the minimal test of statistical significance—but they do suggest some correspondence between the perception of racial threat at work and actual circumstance. Roughly the same pattern holds for the perception of racial threat in schooling, except that the relationships are attenuated; some disappear altogether. Thus the connection between the politically potent form of personal threat and actual circumstance is weak indeed.

If most of the effects presented in table 4.3 are modest or negligible, one is not. One is enormous. Racially resentful whites are much more likely to believe themselves and their families at risk, both at work and at school. According to these results, the racial threats whites see are almost entirely a consequence of the racial sentiments that they feel.[27] This puts a sharp twist on the one apparent effect of self-interest that we have been able to turn up so far. Remember that, of the two measures, it was the perception of racial threat in school admissions rather than the perception of racial threat at work that made a difference in opinion. Now perhaps we see why. Compared with the perception of racial threat at work, the perception of racial threat in school admissions is less connected to real circumstance, and it is much more a reflection of racial resentments.

To bring this line of argument to its logical completion, we reestimated the effects of self-interest, adding in the measure of racial resentment. When we did so, we discovered that the effect of personal racial threat in schooling collapses to zero. The coefficient is generally positive, as predicted, but in no case does the estimated effect exceed its standard error. Across the six race policies, the coefficient averages .01.

In sum, our investigation of self-interest and public opinion on affairs of race among white Americans has turned up one strong result and a bushel of disconfirmations. Upon further examination, moreover, the one strong result turns out to be an illusion: the effect that we might have attributed to self-interest seems really to belong to feelings of racial resentment.

Racial Advantage and Black Opinion

But what about the impact of self-interest on the views of black Americans? As we noted earlier, this is largely uncharted territory. Black public opinion has become the topic of serious empirical work only recently, and that research has been preoccupied primarily with aspects of racial group solidarity. About black opinion and self-interest little is known.[28]

Our analysis of blacks is comparable in most every respect to that we have just reported for whites. One difference is that now we combine three elements of class—income, occupation, and education—into a single index, a concession to the demands of multivariate analysis and small sample size. Because our analysis of blacks is based on a much smaller sample than for whites, our estimates of the effect of self-interest will necessarily bounce around a bit more. In partial compensation, we employ less-stringent standards of statistical signifi-

Table 4.4 Impact of Self-Interest on Black Opinion

	Fair Em-ployment	School Deseg-regation	Federal Spending	Govern-ment Effort	Preferen-tial Hiring	College Quotas
Personal gain	.11	.20	.12	.27	−.00	−.08
education	(.15)	(.17)	(.14)	(.15)	(.20)	(.19)
Personal gain	.05	.02	.05	−.01	.07	.17
employment	(.12)	(.14)	(.11)	(.12)	(.16)	(.15)
Class	−.10	−.08	.03	.11	−.06	.03
	(.20)	(.22)	(.18)	(.20)	(.27)	(.25)
Homeownership	−.00	.03	−.02	−.06	−.00	.02
	(.09)	(.09)	(.08)	(.09)	(.11)	(.11)
Family economic	−.12	.01	.01	−.03	−.05	.05
situation	(.13)	(.15)	(.12)	(.13)	(.18)	(.16)
HH out of work	.01	.19	−.03	−.03	.04	.06
	(.14)	(.16)	(.13)	(.14)	(.19)	(.18)
HH worried	.04	.07	.01	.01	−.00	−.11
about work	(.12)	(.13)	(.11)	(.12)	(.16)	(.15)
Young children* racially	.01	.02	.05	.07	.28	.13
mixed community	(.09)	(.10)	(.09)	(.09)	(.12)	(.12)
Older children*	−.08	−.07	−.02	−.01	−.01	−.27
middle class	(.20)	(.22)	(.18)	(.20)	(.26)	(.25)
HH in labor	.07	.18	.03	.01	.09	.07
force	(.11)	(.12)	(.10)	(.10)	(.14)	(.13)
HH self-employed	.04	.01	−.03	−.15	.12	.09
	(.12)	(.13)	(.11)	(.12)	(.16)	(.15)
HH government	−.07	−.08	−.09	−.09	−.11	.07
employee	(.09)	(.09)	(.08)	(.08)	(.11)	(.11)
Constant	.26	.22	.20	.44	.28	.07
	(.23)	(.25)	(.21)	(.23)	(.31)	(.29)
R-squared	.17	.20	.17	.29	.24	.18
Standard error	.32	.36	.30	.32	.43	.40
Number of cases	93	93	93	93	93	93

Source: 1986 National Election Study.
Note: Table entry is *B*, the unstandardized ordinary least square regression coefficient, with standard errors in parentheses underneath. All variables coded 0–1. Each equation also included measures of age, region, religion, marital status, gender, union household, and race of interviewer. HH = head of household.

cance here than we did in the analysis of white public opinion. The otherwise comparable results for self-interest and public opinion for black Americans are shown in table 4.4.

All things considered, table 4.4 resembles its immediate predecessor in that it, too, is awash in tiny coefficients. Consider the virtually undetectable role of social class or, perhaps more surprising, the political irrelevance of family economic conditions. Downturns in the family's financial situation, the debilitating experience of being out of work, apprehensions about the family's economic future: none of this tells us anything about black public opinion. We find this result surprising, if not remarkable, one that makes trouble for an understanding of public opinion based on self-interest.

Only one effect appears with any consistency in table 4.4: that due to the perception of the personal gains to be realized by affirmative action policies in school admissions. As was true for whites, education rather than employment appears once again to be more potent politically. The surprise here is that the perception of personal advantage works in a direction opposite to that predicted by self-interest. Blacks who believe that they are likely to benefit from affirmative action in school policies are generally *less* supportive of policies designed to reduce racial inequalities. They support school integration less, they push less for fair employment policies, and they are less insistent that the federal government provide special help to black citizens. Putting the result the other way around, support on these matters comes most from those black Americans who say they have nothing to gain, whose families are least likely to be improved by government initiatives. This result is indigestible from the perspective of self-interest. It is not merely a failure to confirm; the result is diametrically opposed to the self-interest prediction.

One way out of this predicament is to argue that treating the perception of family advantage as a measure of self-interest is a mistake. Instead, this perception should be interpreted as part of a broader orientation toward racial change: about how much progress there has been, about the obstacles and barriers that blacks still face. Then those who say that they and their families are unlikely to be helped by affirmative action policies are really making a declaration about the state of American society: they are pessimistic about the opportunities available to themselves and perhaps to blacks in general. Such pessimism would lead quite naturally to what we see in our results: namely, the demand for more government intervention and assistance. Consistent with this interpretation, we find that blacks who see little likelihood that current policies will be of any assistance to themselves or to their families are also unimpressed with racial progress generally, more taken with the idea that whites deliberately attempt to hold blacks down, and more apt to identify with their racial group.[29]

However this single positive result should be interpreted, we must not be distracted from the main lesson here: that it is impossible to make a case for self-interest out of the meager results laid out in table 4.4. The primary motives behind black public opinion must lie elsewhere. Black Americans, like whites, do not seem to come to their opinion on racial issues by asking themselves, "What's in it for me?"

Perhaps. But especially where black public opinion is concerned, this conclusion may be premature. That black Americans in dire economic straits do not press their government for help is certainly surprising; from the perspective of self-interest, it is wholly anomalous. But our findings are based on just one study, undertaken at a particular and perhaps peculiar time, with relatively few cases, and they rely on just one set of admittedly imperfect measures. Before settling too comfortably into a final conclusion, therefore, we decided to pursue a series of additional analyses.

Self-interest and windows of political opportunity. First of all, we set about to see whether the relationship between the family's economic situation and black public opinion—or better, the lack of relationship between the two—would hold in other settings. Two key questions, one on change in family economic well-being and the other on whether the federal government is obliged to make special efforts for black citizens, have appeared on every NES since 1970. Taking advantage of this opportunity allows us to estimate the political effect of family economic well-being across a variety of contexts: at the close of presidential campaigns and following midterm elections, during economic expansions and deep recessions, when the nation is preoccupied with domestic concerns and when the nation's attention turns to international affairs, and under administrations seen as sympathetic and as hostile. Furthermore, when we combine all eleven NES surveys between 1970 and 1990, we accumulate cases: in the end, we base our analysis on data from interviews with nearly 2,000 black Americans. Thus the worry that we might have failed to find a relationship between family economic well-being and support for government programs to assist blacks in 1986 because we lacked the statistical power to detect it can be put safely to the side. Our primary purpose here is to trace the political consequences of family economic well-being, since our failure to find any such consequences in the 1986 NES data is so troublesome for self-interest. At the same time we can also look again at the effects on public opinion associated with other aspects of self-interest, notably employment status, class, and home ownership (though, alas, not the perception of family advantage, since those measures appeared on the 1985 and 1986 NES surveys alone).

These regression results, displayed in table 4.5, reveal a modest role for self-interest, consistent with our earlier findings.[30] As seen there, views on policy among black Americans are generally unconnected to whether or not they are out of work, whether they are professionals or unskilled laborers, whether they graduated from college or never made it through high school, whether or not they own their homes, and whether they are rich or poor. Coefficients occasionally approach statistical significance, but they are uniformly modest, and they run against the self-interest prediction as often as with it.

One patch of blue sky for self-interest is apparent in table 4.5, however, and it has to do with family economic well-being, really the heart of the analysis. Blacks whose family economic condition was deteriorating were more likely to

Table 4.5 Impact of Self-Interest on Black Support
for Government Assistance to Blacks

	Support for Government Assistance
Change in family economic situation	−.04
	(.02)
Respondent current unemployed	.02
	(.02)
Family income	
Poor	−.02
	(.02)
Below average	−.02
	(.02)
Above average	.02
	(.03)
Rich	.13
	(.08)
Respondent occupation	
Farmer	−.08
	(.05)
Homemaker	.01
	(.03)
Laborer	−.02
	(.04)
Clerical	−.06
	(.02)
Professional	−.05
	(.03)
Respondent education	
Grade school	−.04
	(.03)
Less than high school graduate	−.01
	(.02)
Some college	.03
	(.02)
College graduate	.02
	(.03)
Homeowner	.03
	(.02)
Constant	.35
	(.04)
R-squared	.06
Standard error	.31
Number of cases	1,749

Source: 1970–90 National Election Studies.
Note: Table entry is *B,* the unstandardized regression coefficient, with standard errors in parentheses underneath. All variables coded 0–1. The regression equation also included measures of age, region, marital status, and religion.

say that the federal government was obliged to make special efforts for blacks. The effect is modest, but it is statistically significant, and it is quite consistent over diverse circumstances, as we found out when we redid the analysis for each election year taken separately.[31] It is not any bigger in presidential years than in midterm years, for example, and it does not vary in any obvious way with fluctuations in national economic conditions.

There is one exception to this pattern, however, one political moment when the impact of self-interest is visibly stronger. This takes place in 1978, at the midterm of the Carter administration. There we estimate the impact of change in family economic well-being to be roughly three times its average size.[32] Perhaps it is coincidental that the effect of self-interest is most pronounced at the one time in the entire series that the Democratic party, the party notably sympathetic to the interests of blacks (according to blacks), controls the federal government. But perhaps not. Black Americans in economic trouble were more likely to say that the federal government was obliged to make special efforts for blacks especially when the federal government was actually predisposed to do so. Put the other way around, under Republican regimes, most blacks in economic distress may have looked elsewhere rather than to national policy and the federal government for help. The activation of self-interest in public opinion may require the expectation that government be responsive.

The broader and better-supported point here, when we take all the NES studies into account, is a modest effect of self-interest. Black Americans whose family economic condition was deteriorating were slightly, but consistently, more likely to say that the federal government should make special efforts for their racial group. This holds for the combined sample taken as a whole, for the yearly samples taken separately, and, most specifically, for the 1986 sample taken alone (this last observation is reassuring on the point that 1986, where we concentrate our analysis, is not by some malicious accident of history unrepresentative). These results generally support our interim conclusion that as a motive for black public opinion, self-interest carries little weight.

Improving the measurement of self-interest. But the frail results reported so far on the political power of family economic well-being might have to do primarily with frail measurement. Perhaps self-interest does in fact play the prominent role in black public opinion scripted for it, and we would see this if only we improved our measures.

One remedy for unreliable measurement is statistical. As before, we combined all NES surveys conducted between 1970 and 1990, and we again concentrated on the impact of family economic well-being on support for government's special obligation to black citizens. When we corrected for errors in measurement statistically (by treating assessments of change in family economic well-being as endogenous and estimating its effect on black opinion with two-stage least squares regression), we found that our estimate of the effect of self-interest actually declined. In table 4.5, before the measurement error correction, we estimated the impact of change in family economic well-being to be −.04—small, but negative, as predicted, and reliably different from zero. With measurement error removed, we estimated the impact of change in family economic well-being to be .02 (standard error = .12), essentially zero. This result works against the argument that the weak effects of self-interest that we report are due to inadequacies of measurement.[33]

A second solution to the measurement error problem takes advantage of new questions developed to measure family economic condition in a more detailed and thorough way. These new questions assume that change in family economic well-being has both behavioral and cognitive manifestations. On the behavioral side, people may cope with economic adversity by cutting back on purchases, looking for additional work, borrowing more, saving less, or by putting off creditors. The cognitive side to change in family economic well-being is reflected in the judgments people make about alterations in their family's overall economic condition, in their assessments of whether family income is running ahead or falling behind increases in the cost of living, in whether or not they have to watch their budget more closely, and the like. The full set of questions was first tried out in a small national survey carried out by NES in 1983 and then included with minor modifications in the 1984 NES. Taken collectively, the questions provide a close approximation to a comprehensive reading of change in Americans' family economic well-being.[34]

Does all the effort poured into the measurement of change in family economic well-being make a difference? Well, yes, a bit. The relevant results are shown in table 4.6, taken from our analysis of the 1984 NES. The table summarizes our estimate of the impact of change in family economic well-being on three aspects of black public opinion: on government assistance to blacks and other minorities, on federal support for programs that help blacks, and on the general trade-off between government services and cuts in federal spending. Under each of the three policies, the left-hand column presents our estimate of the impact due to change in family economic well-being when it is measured by the single item that has figured prominently in our analysis so far. The results there should look familiar. They indicate, as we have come to expect, a small effect of self-interest. The coefficients are negative, as predicted, but they are uniformly small, and in two of three cases are indistinguishable in statistical terms from no effect at all.

Compare these results with those presented in the right-hand column under each policy in table 4.6. There we present estimates of the impact of change

Table 4.6 Impact of Change in Family Economic Well-Being on Black Support for Government Assistance

	Government Assistance to Blacks		Federal Money for Black Programs		Government Services vs. Spending Cuts	
	(1)	(2)	(1)	(2)	(1)	(2)
Change in family	−.05	−.10	−.10	−.13	−.05	−.15
economic well-being	(.04)	(.11)	(.05)	(.12)	(.04)	(.10)
R-squared	.01	.01	.02	.01	.01	.01
Standard error	.27	.27	.27	.27	.25	.25
Number of cases	235	226	196	190	235	226

Source: 1984 National Election Study.
Note: Table entry is B, the unstandardized regression coefficient, giving the impact of change in family economic well-being on black support for each of three policies. In each case, we measured change in family economic well-being in one of two ways: (1) with a single item; (2) with a five-item scale that includes the single item under (1). Standard errors are shown in parentheses underneath. Variables coded 0–1.

in family economic well-being when it is measured in more comprehensive fashion. In this analysis, *retrospective assessment of family economic well-being* is a linear composite scale representing the cognitive dimension to change in family economic well-being, based on equally weighted answers to five separate questions.[35] Measured in this more reliable fashion, the impact of self-interest does indeed increase: from −.05 to −.10 in the case of government assistance to blacks, from −.10 to −.13 in the case of federal support for programs that aid blacks, and from −.05 to −.15 in the case of the expansion of government services. Self-interest matters more under the new, improved measurement regime—but we should not be swept away by the differences. For one thing, our ability to predict opinion improves not at all (as indicated by the standard error of the regression, shown toward the bottom of table 4.6). More important, the estimated effect of self-interest remains decidedly modest, even when we assess it in this more elaborate way. In short, neither these results nor those produced by our statistical solution to the measurement problem suggest that we need revise our original conclusion: that when it comes to black public opinion, self-interest plays a small part.

Politicized self-interest. Perhaps the real problem is one not of measurement but of definition. Perhaps we have defined economic well-being too broadly; what we need to do is focus on that part of economic well-being that it is tied immediately and conspicuously to government. Here we consider the possibility that change in economic well-being takes on political significance when citizens see connections between their own personal predicaments and the policies of government. The politically relevant aspects of self-interest are perhaps to be found in *government-induced* changes in economic well-being. If citizens see their economic fortunes determined by their own efforts and skills, or by impersonal market forces, or by the vagaries of weather and historical accident, then they might not look to government for help when things go sour.[36]

With this more narrowly drawn conception of self-interest in mind, we turned to the 1982 NES, carried out in the context of what many commentators took to be a conservative revolution in American domestic policy. Two years before, President Reagan had come triumphantly to office by rejecting the liberal consensus on domestic policy that had dominated both parties over the previous forty years. Early in his presidency, Reagan argued successfully with the Congress for less government and more individual enterprise in social policy. The result, according to Palmer and Sawhill of the Urban Institute: "Not since 1932 has there been such a redirection of public purposes."[37]

Among the most notable of the Reagan redirections were deep cuts in federal programs serving the poor. In his first budget the president proposed reductions of nearly 30% in real terms in such programs as Food Stamps, AFDC, child nutrition, housing assistance, and Medicaid. For the most part, Congress accepted these cuts. Reductions were accomplished by imposing tighter income eligibility limits, by offsetting benefits for other sources of income more aggressively, by directly cutting benefits, and by postponing adjustments for inflation. The result was to exclude millions of poor and near-poor Americans who had been receiving benefits, and to reduce benefits for those who continued to receive them. In combination with the deepest recession since the Depression— the unemployment rate reached nearly 11% in 1982—these cutbacks in federal programs resulted in a sharp increase in the proportion of Americans living in poverty, and occasioned a national debate over whether the safety net provided by government was still intact.[38]

The comparative advantage of the 1982 NES for our purposes is not only that it was carried out at a revealing historical moment. In addition, and not coincidentally, the 1982 study included a brace of questions to assess the extent to which respondents' families depended on government programs. For recipients of government benefits, the connection between family economic well-being and government policy should be relatively obvious. Examining dependence on government programs takes us directly and immediately to government-induced well-being, and therefore to what should be a politically potent form of self-interest.

In the 1982 survey, respondents were asked whether they or anyone in their family was currently receiving a variety of government benefits, from Social Security to disability payments. Our analysis focuses on two programs in particular: Food Stamps and AFDC, primary targets of the 1981 Reagan budget reductions. The full roster of government programs is displayed in table 4.7. As a general matter, black and white Americans were equally likely to be the bene-

Table 4.7 Black and White Beneficiaries of Government Programs

Program	Blacks (n = 152)	Whites (n = 1,246)
Food Stamps	28.0%	5.6%
AFDC	10.7	2.3
Social Security	31.8	28.3
Medicare or Medicaid	36.0	24.5
Unemployment compensation	6.7	4.4
Disability payments	2.0	1.3
Veterans benefits	2.7	5.5
Federal pensions	3.4	3.6

Source: 1982 National Election Study.

ficiaries of government programs. Roughly comparable proportions of blacks and whites were receiving Social Security, disability payments, federal pensions, and so forth. Sharp racial differences show up only on Food Stamps and on AFDC, where blacks were four to five times as likely as whites to report that their families were currently receiving benefits. When asked whether their benefits had been reduced over the previous year, twice as many blacks than whites reported cuts (20.4% versus 9.2%), and in another round of questioning, blacks were also more likely than whites to say that they expected reductions in benefits in the next year (41.2% versus 30.7%).

The question of the moment is whether we can detect self-interest at work among the recipients of these programs. Do black Americans who are themselves the direct beneficiaries of government policies support such policies the most? When government assistance is cut back, or when further cuts appear imminent, do black Americans press for more help?

Answers to these questions are spelled out in table 4.8. The results presented in the left-hand column of the table indicate that, consistent with the self-interest prediction, black Americans who in 1982 were receiving either Food Stamps or AFDC payments were more supportive of special efforts for blacks, compared with those who received no such benefits. The effect, though not large, is statistically significant. At the same time, whether such benefits were cut back in the past or were expected to be reduced in the future was irrelevant to black support for government assistance. Thus we find modest empirical support for self-interest when defined in a way that directly connects government to economic welfare.[39]

Even the one positive result is suspect, however. It would be convenient, from a statistical point of view, if AFDC and Food Stamps were distributed randomly. The regression results we have just presented assume they are. But this is most unlikely, not least because AFDC and Food Stamps are means

PRIMARY INGREDIENTS OF OPINION

Table 4.8 Impact of Receiving Food Stamps or AFDC on Black Support
for Government Assistance to Blacks

	Support for Government Assistance to Blacks	
	1 (without corrections for selection bias)	2 (with corrections)
Currently receiving benefits	.14	.01
	(.07)	(.02)
Benefits recently cut	.07	—
	(.08)	
Expect cuts in benefits	−.06	—
	(.09)	
Change in family economic situation	−.06	−.05
	(.06)	(.06)
Constant	.66	.71
	(.05)	(.05)
R-squared	.06	.01
Standard error	.27	.28
Number of cases	146	142

Source: 1982 National Election Study.
Note: Under specification (1), the impact of receiving benefits is estimated with OLS regression. Under specification (2), receiving benefits is treated as endogeneous and its effect is estimated with two-stage least squares. All variables coded 0–1.

tested. More generally, beneficiaries of these two programs are likely to be distinctive in a variety of ways that may influence how they think about government policy. This means that the estimates presented in the left-hand side of table 4.8 suffer from selection bias. To correct this problem, we follow the logic and procedures set out by Achen.[40]

The results from our revised statistical analysis are summarized in the right-hand column of table 4.8. As indicated there, when selection bias is corrected, the estimated impact of receiving government benefits on support for government assistance drops to zero.[41] Direct dependence on government programs, by itself, does not build support for government intervention, another blow against the political potency of self-interest.

Self-interest and redistributive policies. Our inability to detect much of an effect of self-interest on black opinion may have something to do with the policies that have been the focus of our analysis. Up until now we have primarily examined black support for increases in government assistance. Should the government in Washington make special efforts to improve the position of black Americans? Should federal spending on programs that assist blacks be increased? These questions are important, and so it is important that we are hard pressed to find self-interest at work in views toward them. But the policies are noteworthy also for their generality, for their application to black Americans as an entire category. If read literally, the questions have to do with providing unspecified assistance to black Americans of all sorts. Under this interpretation, it would not be all that surprising if such questions did not open up cleavages of interest among black Americans; moreover it would be instructive to see whether self-interest might become important in explaining opinion on policies that conspicuously redistribute resources within the black population.

A good specimen of a redistributive policy of just this sort is the Food Stamps program. Food Stamps are means tested: among black Americans, the benefits go primarily to the poor and are paid for primarily by the middle class. And as we just learned, even in the wake of the Reagan cuts, more than one-quarter of black Americans interviewed in 1982 reported that their family had received food stamps over the preceding year. The question here is whether self-interest figures more prominently in black opinion toward the Food Stamps program as a consequence of its redistributive quality.

Fortunately for our purposes, a relevant opinion question was introduced into the 1984 NES.[42] On this measure black support for Food Stamps turns out to be rather mixed. Combining NES surveys from 1984 to 1990, not quite a majority of black Americans—48.5%—say that federal spending on Food Stamps should be increased; another 41.2% believe that spending should remain the same; and 10.3% favor cuts in the Food Stamps program.[43] How far can self-interest take us in understanding this variation in opinion?

Quite a ways, is the answer given out in table 4.9. The regression results shown there reveal a more visible trace of self-interest than we have grown accustomed to seeing. If we are permitted generous interpretations of statistical significance, then we can say that support for increases in federal money for Food Stamps is systematically and positively related to poverty, unemployment, and declining economic fortunes, and is systematically and negatively related to professional status, college education, and home ownership. None of these effects is impressive by itself. But when taken cumulatively, they begin to add up to large differences. Consider these two hypothetical black Americans who are located at opposite ends of the American class structure. The first is poor and ill-educated. Her family's economic condition has recently deteriorated; the head of her household is out of work; when employed at all, the best the head can hope for is unskilled labor. The second is college educated, securely employed as a professional, earns a good income, and owns her own home. The results summarized in table 4.9 imply that the first will be much more likely to support increases in the Food Stamps program than will the second: the regression equation predicts that their opinions will differ by nearly .3, where the full range of opinion is 0–1. This is a real difference in political

Table 4.9 Impact of Self-Interest on Black Support for the Food Stamps Program

	Support for Food Stamps
Change in family economic situation	−.04
	(.03)
Respondent currently unemployed	.05
	(.03)
Family income	
Poor	−.16
	(.03)
Below average	−.06
	(.03)
Above average	−.07
	(.04)
Rich	−.03
	(.10)
Respondent occupation	
Farmer	.03
	(.07)
Homemaker	−.01
	(.04)
Laborer	.10
	(.05)
Clerical	−.01
	(.03)
Professional	.09
	(.04)
Respondent education	
Grade school	.00
	(.04)
Less than high school graduate	−.06
	(.03)
Some college	.06
	(.03)
College graduate	.07
	(.05)
Homeowner	.02
	(.03)
Constant	.26
	(.06)
R-squared	.16
Standard error	.31
Number of cases	868

Source: 1984–90 National Election Studies.
Note: Table entry is *B,* the unstandardized regression coefficient, with standard errors in parentheses underneath. All variables coded 0–1. The regression equation also included measures of age, region, marital status, and religion.

views, even if dramatic differences in class position and economic experience are required to produce it. The general lesson here is that when government programs are targeted specifically at the black poor, interest-based cleavages within the black community begin to open up. At long last, a role for self-interest.[44]

IF NOT SELF-INTEREST, PERHAPS GROUP INTEREST

Despite the one positive result we have finally managed to produce, the self-interest motive seems generally quite unimportant to our understanding of public opinion on race. In this section we develop and test a related, but distinct, view, one that takes seriously the proposition that policy proposals may be evaluated in terms of the implications they hold for *group* interest. In matters of public opinion, perhaps citizens are really asking themselves, in effect, "What's in it for *my group?*"

The development of the idea of group interest owes much to realistic group conflict theory, introduced in rudimentary form at the turn of the century by William Graham Sumner in his famous *Folkways*.[45] The theory begins with the assertion that antagonism between groups is rooted in actual conflict: groups have incompatible goals, and they compete for scarce resources. In this analysis, racial groups are neither vestiges of premodern society nor convenient outlets for psychological distress but rather, as Giles and Evans put it, "vehicles for the pursuit of interest in modern pluralist societies," "participants in ongoing competition for control of economic, political, and social structures."[46] Conflicts of interest cause intergroup conflict, and conflict between groups is most intense where the real conflicts of interest are greatest, where the groups have the most at stake.

The relevance of realistic group conflict theory to American race relations is supported by a line of empirical work that extends back to V. O. Key's *Southern Politics*. Key showed in fine detail that politics in the American South through the middle of the twentieth century was most reactionary in the so-called black belt: an arc that extended from the Chesapeake Bay in the northeast, through the eastern shore of the Carolinas, down through the midlands of Georgia and Alabama, along the rivers of Mississippi, Arkansas, and Louisiana, and into east Texas. It was in the black belt where the plantation system and slavery had flourished and where, as Key put it, whites possessed "the deepest and most immediate concern with the maintenance of white supremacy."[47] Racism prevailed throughout the South, of course, but it was whites in the black belt, because they had the most to lose, who acted on their racism. Inside the black belt, the threat was real and serious; outside it, "blacks were neither so central to the local economy nor so sizable a bloc of prospective voters in local elections."[48] Accordingly, it was within the black belt where support for secession and war was most adamant, where the subsequent drive for black disfranchisement came with greatest force, where the Populist revolt was crushed, and where, in the 1950s and 1960s, defense of segregation was most ferocious.[49]

Key's observations in *Southern Politics* have been corroborated by scores of more modest investigations. This work demonstrates the lingering significance of the black belt in Southern politics and establishes the more general point of the political importance of sheer numbers. As the great migration carried blacks out of the rural South into the cities, South and North, miniature black belts were created everywhere. And time and again, as the black share of the population increased, whites became more reactionary in their views on race.[50]

This evidence is certainly consistent with realistic group-conflict theory, and we have no particular quarrel with this interpretation. It is worth pointing out, however, that no study actually attempts to measure the perception of threat, the theory's pivotal concept. Threat is inferred, not directly measured.[51] This means that we cannot know for certain whether, say, whites in the black belt in fact felt threatened by large black populations. Nor can we know, if they did feel threatened, whether the threat was experienced as a danger to themselves personally, or to their group collectively.

Granted that the level of analysis for realistic group conflict theory is primarily the group, not the individual, the theory nevertheless carries "inevitable implications for psychological processes."[52] Our analysis takes such implications seriously by directly measuring the individual's perception of group threat. Again, the threat singled out here is not personal but collective, involving the welfare of whites in general. Whites resist policies promoting racial equality, in this view, out of a sense that such policies threaten their collective interests.[53]

Another limitation of the empirical literature motivated by realistic group-conflict theory is that it has been preoccupied entirely with the political response of whites. The vocabulary of realistic group-conflict theory, which we have simply appropriated here, is oriented to threat, not to advantage, and so takes the perspective of whites threatened by blacks. From the perspective of our project, however, this is just one side of the story. We are equally interested in the views of black Americans, and the possibility that their support for racial policies may be driven by the perception of group gain. Blacks who see an advantage for their racial group in a certain policy should support it, all other things equal, irrespective of the consequences they see for themselves.[54]

Our purpose here, then, is to test realistic group-conflict theory with evidence hand-tailored to the individual level, taking into account both that whites might be motivated by a sense of group threat and that blacks might be motivated by a sense of group advantage.

Group Threat and White Resistance to Racial Equality

We do so by capitalizing on questions appearing on the 1986 NES that inquire into citizens' views of the consequences of affirmative action policies for blacks and whites considered as social groups.[55] These questions, shown in table 4.10, parallel the self-interest questions we analyzed earlier in the chapter, except that references to families are replaced by references to racial groups. As table 4.10 indicates, many white Americans believe that affirmative action policies harm the interests of whites. A majority (57.4%) agreed that affirmative action programs for blacks have reduced whites' chances for jobs, promotions, and admissions to schools and training programs.[56] Three-quarters of whites (74.9%) said that it was very or somewhat likely that a white person wouldn't get a job or promotion while an equally or less qualified black person got one instead. And almost as many (69.0%) believed that it was very or somewhat likely that a white person would not get admitted to a school while an equally or less qualified black person got in instead.

Among white Americans, these perceptions of racial group threat are very consistent: those who believe that affirmative action programs for blacks have

Table 4.10 Perception of Racial Group Threat among White Americans

Affirmative action programs for blacks have reduced whites' chances for jobs, promotions, and admission to schools and training programs.	
Strongly agree	29.8%
Agree	27.6
Disagree	27.5
Strongly disagree	15.1
What do you think the chances are these days that a white person won't get admitted to a school while an equally or less qualified black person gets admitted instead?	
Very likely	27.6
Somewhat likely	41.4
Not very likely	31.1
What do you think the chances are these days that a white person won't get a job or promotion while an equally or less qualified black person gets one instead?	
Very likely	26.6
Somewhat likely	48.3
Not very likely	25.1

Source: 1986 National Election Study.

reduced whites' opportunities also are inclined to think that whites often get turned down for jobs or promotions that go instead to blacks, and they also tend to believe that white applicants are regularly turned away from schools while blacks are invited in. Indeed, the pattern here is perhaps too consistent. The correlations are so high that the perception of group threat resembles more a tidy ideology than a realistic assessment of a messy social reality.[57]

Equally worrisome is that perceptions of group threat are highly correlated with perceptions of threat to family. The correlation between responses to the two kinds of threat, one centered on the family, the other on the group, is little different, on average, from the typical correlation among the group threat questions (average Pearson $r = .46$ and $.52$, respectively). As a purely empirical matter, then, personal and group racial threats among white Americans are not as distinct as we had hoped.

These simple and preliminary results lead us immediately to question the extent to which whites' perceptions of racial group threat can be regarded as realistic. Earlier we found that the perception of personal racial threat is largely unconnected to actual circumstance but is tightly bound to feelings of racial resentment. Exactly the same suspicion arises here, since personal and collective racial threats seem so intertwined in the minds of white Americans.

Indeed, we find essentially the same pattern of results for racial group threat as we did in our previous analysis of personal racial threat. In both instances, the perception of racial threat among white Americans is connected, but weakly, to personal economic insecurities and to living and working in close proximity to blacks. And in both instances, the perception of racial threat is predicted best, far and away, by the resentments whites feel toward blacks. In theory, the sources of perceived threat are found in real conflicts of interest. Threat is supposed to be, in a word, realistic. Here again we see that it is not. Our results suggest that the perception of threat is a product not so much of the social circumstances white Americans find themselves in, but of how they look at the social world, and especially whether or not they regard blacks with suspicion and resentment.[58]

This brings us finally to the central business of determining the effects of racial group threat on public opinion. We expect these effects to be most pronounced on opinions toward affirmative action, since the group-interest questions themselves refer to the consequences of affirmative action policies. Because racial resentment is so strongly implicated in whites' perceptions of the threats that blacks appear to pose to their collective interests, our analysis of white opinion must take into account its impact as well.[59]

The regression results, summarized in table 4.11, indicate that white Americans who believe that blacks threaten their collective interests are less support-

Table 4.11 Impact of Group Interest on White Support for Racial Policy

	School Deseg- regation	Fair Em- ployment	Govern- ment Help	Federal Programs	Preferen- tial Hiring	College Quotas
Perception of racial group threat	−.17 (.06)	−.10 (.06)	−.11 (.03)	−.11 (.04)	−.20 (.04)	−.25 (.05)

Source: 1986 National Election Study.
Note: Entry is B, the unstandardized regression coefficient, with standard errors presented in parentheses underneath. All variables coded 0–1. Each regression equation also included measures of age, region, sex, marital status, union membership, religion, race of interviewer, and racial resentment.

ive of policies designed to reduce racial inequalities, consistent with theoretical expectations. The effect is statistically significant in each of the six policies we examine; it ranges in size from modest, in the case of federal programs, to sizable, in the case of affirmative action. Thus the effect is most visible just where it should be. Moreover, when we repeated this analysis, making use of the 1985 NES that carried many of the same questions, we uncovered virtually the identical pattern of results.[60] We take these findings to mean that interests matter to whites' views on matters of race. *Group* interests matter. Insofar as interests figure prominently in white opinion on race, it is through the threats blacks appear to pose to whites' collective well-being, not their personal welfare.

Group Advantage and Black Support for Racial Equality

Fashioned for black Americans, the NES group interest questions draw attention to the potential advantages presented by affirmative action. These questions are presented in full in table 4.12. They show that black Americans were very likely to endorse the general proposition that affirmative action policies increase blacks' chances in education and employment: an overwhelming majority (87.0%) agreed that affirmative action programs have increased blacks' chances for jobs, promotions, and admissions to schools and training programs. On more specific questions, however, black Americans were much less impressed with the collective benefits of affirmative action—with affirmative action as a practical remedy. Close to two-thirds (62.2%) thought it unlikely that a black person would get a job or promotion while an equally qualified white person would be turned down. More than two-thirds (68.0%) believed it unlikely that a black applicant would be admitted to a school while an equally qualified white was turned away. In short, black Americans seem quite attached to affirmative action, and believe that affirmative action programs have had beneficial consequences for their group. But they also believe that blacks continue to face discrimination in schooling and employment. One might say that in the view of many blacks, affirmative action has not yet been implemented.[61]

Table 4.12 Perception of Racial Group Advantage among Black Americans

Affirmative action programs for blacks have increased blacks' chances for jobs, promotions, and admission to schools and training programs.	
Strongly agree	61.0%
Agree	26.0
Disagree	6.8
Strongly disagree	6.2
What do you think the chances are these days that a black person will get admitted to a school while an equally qualified white person gets turned down?	
Very likely	7.8
Somewhat likely	24.2
Not very likely	68.0
What do you think the chances are these days that a black person will get a job while an equally qualified white person gets turned down?	
Very likely	8.3
Somewhat likely	29.5
Not very likely	62.2

Source: 1986 National Election Study.

This split between the widespread impression that policies of affirmative action benefit blacks and pessimism about the power of affirmative action to carry the day in concrete cases continues when we examine correlations among the items. Black Americans who believe that members of their racial group are typically disadvantaged in school admissions also believe that members of their race are usually shunted aside in hiring and promotion decisions at work (as indexed by a Pearson r of .45). But these beliefs are completely unrelated to views regarding the general consequences of affirmative action programs for blacks' opportunities (the Pearson r's are $-.06$ and $-.05$, essentially zero in both instances).[62] These results strongly suggest that we have measured not one thing—the perception of racial group advantage—but two.

The first, indexed by a single item, represents blacks' beliefs about the consequences of affirmative action programs for their racial group. This measure matches our original intent well, and so we will refer to it as *the perception of racial group advantage* (or *group advantage*, for short). The second, indexed by answers to a pair of closely related questions, represents blacks' views about the extent to which, in close decisions at work and school, blacks are the beneficiaries of affirmative action. As we read table 4.12, most blacks detect little in the way of decisions running their way. Nearly thirty years after federal legislation made racial discrimination illegal, blacks continue to believe that schools and businesses favor whites. We call such views *perceptions of racial group discrimination* (*group discrimination*, for short).

Given this interpretation, we expect that black Americans will be more likely to support government policies intended to reduce racial inequalities insofar as, first, they believe that affirmative action programs enhance opportunities for blacks (not for themselves necessarily, but for blacks as a whole) and, second, they believe that racial discrimination impedes the progress of blacks (not their own progress necessarily, but the progress of blacks as a whole). In both cases, the questions are framed in terms of collective opportunities and outcomes; both should be taken as aspects of group interest. But they are empirically distinct aspects, and our analysis, summarized in table 4.13, treats them separately.[63]

In table 4.13, we find first of all a detectable, though not overpowering, effect of the perception of racial group advantage on blacks' policy views. The effect shows up in three of six cases. It is most visible in the policy domain of affirmative action, as expected, and invisible in the domain of equal opportunity, where black support verges on the unanimous. These results lend some support to the general claim that black thinking on matters of policy is motivated by the perception of racial group interest.

Additional support for the same proposition can be found in the next row in table 4.13. There we see that opinions on matters of racial policy are consistently shaped by perceptions of racial group discrimination. If blacks believe that members of their racial group continue to face discrimination in schools and the workplace, they are consequently more likely to call for government assistance. The coefficient indexing this effect takes the right sign for each of the six policies, it surpasses statistical significance (leniently interpreted) in four, and it is strongest in the domain of affirmative action, as anticipated.

Taken together, these findings suggest a place for group interest in our understanding of black public opinion. The results we see in table 4.13 are independent of any effects due to social background or to the perception of personal

Table 4.13 Impact of Group Interest on Black Support for Racial Policy

	School Desegregation	Fair Employment	Government Help	Federal Programs	Preferential Hiring	College Quotas
Perception of racial group advantage	−.08 (.11)	−.07 (.10)	.01 (.09)	.21 (.08)	.15 (.14)	.20 (.12)
Perception of racial group discrimination	−.02 (.13)	−.15 (.11)	−.03 (.11)	−.19 (.10)	−.18 (.16)	−.23 (.14)

Source: 1986 National Election Study.
Note: Entry is B, the unstandardized regression coefficient, with standard errors presented in parentheses underneath. All variables coded 0–1. Each regression equation also included measures of age, region, sex, marital status, union membership, religion, race of interviewer, racial ideology, and perception of personal advantage in education.

advantage. Earlier in this chapter, remember, we discovered that black Americans who believed that their families were unlikely to benefit personally from affirmative action in school policies were generally more supportive of policies designed to reduce racial inequalities. They supported school integration more, they pushed harder for fair employment policies, and they were more insistent that the federal government provide special help to black citizens. This pattern is consistent with what we find here, that black Americans who believed that blacks in general were unlikely to get a break at school or at work were more likely to support government action on blacks' behalf. These group-interest effects are over and above those due to perceptions of personal interest. Indeed, when both are entered in the same equation, as they are for the purpose of producing the results summarized in table 4.13, we find that the impact due to the personal benefits of affirmative action in school admissions fades in significance; now it shows up in only a single case (that predicting opinion on government making special efforts for blacks). This result—that perceptions of personal or family interest generally disappear when perceptions of group interest are also taken into account—adds to the empirical case we are building here: namely, that the interests which enter into the formation of public opinion are collective rather than personal; they are group centered rather than self-centered.[64]

CONCLUSIONS

In a famous paper entitled "Ethnocentrism and Other Altruistic Motives," Donald Campbell complained about the inclination within some schools of psychology to reduce all of human motivation to the pursuit of self-interest—to what Campbell called "skin-surface hedonism." Campbell had especially in mind the important and influential work of Thibaut and Kelley and Homans, who set forward "a social psychology deriving group processes and structures entirely from the self-centered concern of the actors as to 'What's there in it for me?'—a mutual backscratching on the part of fundamentally selfish organisms."[65] Here we have seen that when it comes to public opinion on affairs of race, the assumption of "fundamentally selfish organisms" doesn't carry us very far. Our purpose at the end of this chapter is to recapitulate our findings on interests and place them in a broader context.

The Diminished Place of Self-Interest

Under our definition, self-interested citizens pursue material benefits and avoid material harms in politics, and as they do so, they have only themselves and their immediate families in mind. Defined this way, self-interest turns out to be largely irrelevant to public opinion on matters of race. For the most part, when faced with policy proposals on school desegregation or affirmative action, whites and blacks come to their views without calculating what's in it for them. This is a robust result: it holds for a variety of measures of threat and advantage, both subjective and objective; regardless of statistical adjustments for measurement error or improvements in the measurement of self-interest; across a range of settings and circumstances; and even for measures of politicized self-interest, where the connection between personal welfare and government policy should be most conspicuous. To be sure, self-interest is not entirely absent from our results. We detect intimations that self-interest takes on significance among black Americans when they believe the national government will be responsive to their needs and on policies that would clearly redistribute benefits within the black community. But taken all around, our analysis turns up small and usually negligible effects. And this means that self-interest cannot explain the huge differences we see between black and white Americans on matters of racial policy. Self-interest, simple and unencumbered, cannot bridge the racial divide.

These results may seem remarkable, given the entrenchment of the self-interest assumption in so much writing on human nature and politics. But in fact, our results resemble the returns from the recent flurry of empirical research directed at self-interest and public opinion in general. Summarizing scores of such studies, Citrin and Green conclude that the evidence is "devastating for the claim that self-interest, defined narrowly as the pursuit of immediate material benefits, is the central motive underlying American public opinion."[66] As a basis for public opinion, self-interest has been oversold.

The Importance of Group Interest

Our results have less to say about group interest than self-interest, but what they say is more positive. They suggest that the interests which enter into the formation of public opinion are collective rather than personal, group centered rather than self-centered. Many white Americans believe that affirmative policies threaten their collective interests, that powerful institutions cater to black Americans, and this sense of group threat and disadvantage is systematically related to their views on matters of race. Whites who believe that blacks threaten their collective interests are less supportive of policies designed to reduce racial inequalities. We also find group interest at work in black public opinion, though in a more complex way. In general, black Americans are inclined to believe that affirmative action generally works to their racial group's advantage, but they are also dubious that this actually happens very often in specific cases. Both these aspects of group interest leave their mark on opinion. Black Americans are more likely to support government policies on race insofar as they believe that such policies will help blacks, and insofar as they believe that blacks continue to face discrimination. On matters of public opinion, then, citizens both black and white seem to be asking themselves not what's in it for me, but what's in it for my group?

Threat and Reality

Contrary to realistic group-conflict theory, we detect only fragile connections between whites' sense of racial threat, on the one hand, and actual conditions, on the other. Our results thereby undermine the idea of exclusively *realistic* group conflict and suggest, as Coser does, that conflict can be induced by the false or exaggerated perception of threat.[67]

We do find that the perception of threat has a systematic foundation, but the foundation is provided not by actual conditions of conflict and competition but by feelings of racial resentment. Threat is not so much a clear-eyed perception as it is an emotion-laden attitude. Whites feel racially threatened because they are predisposed to look at the world that way; they see danger and risk when others, more sympathetic in their racial sentiments, do not. Near the beginning of this chapter we noted the hope among eighteenth-century moral philosophers that interests might tame the passions; that a politics based on the calculation of material rewards might replace one based on honor and glory. In our results, at least, this hope is annihilated. In American race relations, interests appear to be less an alternative to the passions than their instrument.

Sociological Release

To Seymour Martin Lipset, competitive elections and public opinion were to be the political "expression of the democratic class struggle."[68] Politics in modern democratic society were where class conflict would be played out. But here we see that class reveals little. For white and black Americans alike, not occupation or education or income or wealth tells us much about opinion on racial affairs.

In some respects, this result should not be too surprising. "Class struggle" is far too strong a phrase to hang on the rather anemic correlations typically reported between Americans' class position and their political views. Among postindustrial democratic societies, the United States tends to finish near the bottom on measures of class polarization. Moreover, associations between class and opinion are declining, and not only in the United States.[69]

Perhaps the fading of class as a force in politics is simply one aspect of a more general "sociological release" under way in modern society.[70] One striking aspect of this chapter's results, taken all together, is how weakly connected opinions on race policy are to social position in general. Remember that our analysis of the impact due to interests took into account the effects due to various aspects of social background. These results were not pertinent to our investigation of self-interest and so were not displayed in the tables, but they are easy to summarize: the general pattern is small, usually negligible differences. With the conspicuous exception of race itself, social background tells us next to nothing about the wide range of views that the American public expresses on race policy. Income, occupation, education, wealth, age, gender, religion, marital status—none of these characteristics reveals with much precision what Americans now think about racial inequality and public policy. Public opinion on race is no longer securely tethered (if it ever was) to social position. In politics as least, individuals now seem to be more on their own, more autonomous, more open to individual choice.

Finally, that self-interest plays a subordinate role in public opinion on matters of race is not necessarily cause for celebration. As we will see all too clearly in the next chapter, Americans can sink below self-interest as often as they rise above it.

CHAPTER FIVE

Subtle Prejudice for Modern Times

In 1936, President Roosevelt selected Marshall Shepard, a black clergyman from Mount Olivet Tabernacle Baptist Church in Philadelphia and a member of the Pennsylvania legislature, to deliver the invocation at the Democratic National Convention. When Shepard reached the podium, Senator Smith of South Carolina rose from his seat and bolted from the hall, declaring as he went that, "By God, he's black as melted midnight. Get outa my way. This mongrel meeting ain't no place for a white man." Later Smith explained his protest by saying that he was "not opposed to any Negro praying for me, but [he didn't] want any blue-gummed, slewfooted Senegambian praying for [him] politically!" Smith refused to lend his support to a Democratic party that, as he put it, "caters to [the Negro] as a political and social equal."[1]

Senator Smith's remarks, once thoroughly representative of a particular time and place, are unimaginable today. Politicians and officials simply no longer say such things. Nor, for the most part, do ordinary citizens. Whites' views on racial matters have undergone a sweeping change over the past half-century, quite unlike any other in the annals of public opinion research. Most white Americans now say that blacks and whites should attend school together, that blacks should have an equal chance to compete for jobs, that segregation of buses and restaurants is wrong, that blacks have a right to live wherever they wish. On matters of principle, whites have become dramatically more egalitarian.[2]

Against these unmistakable signs of progress, however, are clear indications of continuing racial discord. While most white Americans believe that prejudice and discrimination are problems of the past, black Americans see prejudice and discrimination everywhere.[3] And although whites' support for the principles of racial equality and integration has increased majestically over the last four decades, their backing for policies designed to bring equality and integration about has increased scarcely at all. Indeed, in some cases, white support has actually declined. Today, as we know from Chapter 2, large numbers of whites believe that the federal government is too generous with blacks, that school desegregation and equal employment opportunity are not the government's business, and that affirmative action programs for blacks should be abandoned.

By themselves, such opinions should not be taken as evidence of racial malice. To be opposed to affirmative action and simultaneously sympathetic to blacks is not schizophrenic: rejection of affirmative action may be rooted in considerations that have nothing to do with race. Whites might be convinced that affirmative action programs violate principles they care deeply about: that individuals should advance or fall back entirely on the basis of their own talents and efforts, say, or that government should keep out of matters that are essentially private. We will take such possibilities seriously as analysts, just as many white Americans may take them seriously as citizens.

At the same time, we must also consider the possibility that behind white opposition to school desegregation or affirmative action lurk considerations that have everything to do with race. Many white Americans may resist changes in the racial status quo not out of principle but out of prejudice. Such prejudice, if it exists, must take a different form from the unvarnished racism expressed by Senator Smith a generation or two ago. The purpose of this chapter is to offer a conception of subtle prejudice for modern times and to ascertain its role in contemporary white opinion.

DISTANT ORIGINS

The origins of race prejudice in America can be traced back at least to the middle of the sixteenth century, when English voyagers began to encounter the people of West Africa. At this fateful moment, "one of the fairest-skinned nations suddenly came face to face with one of the darkest peoples on earth."[4] Much more than color set the African apart from the English, of course. In the reports they carried back home, the English explorers portrayed the African as utterly different from themselves: as lecherous, apelike, radically defective in religion, and thoroughly uncivilized. Africans were, by one such account, "a people of beastly living, without a God, law, religion, or common wealth."[5] According to Winthrop Jordan, the perception of profound difference provided "the mental margin absolutely requisite for placing the European on the deck of the slave ship and the Negro in the hold."[6]

Whether Jordan was correct, chattel slavery was well established in the English colonies by 1700, justified on the ground that the African was fit for slavery and for slavery alone. The justification was racist, of course, but it was not until slavery came under direct attack by the abolitionists in the early decades of the nineteenth century that the presumption of black inferiority developed into a full-blown theory of racism.[7] Prior to the abolitionist challenge, slaveholders could defend their practice merely by referring to the fact that slavery was a legally sanctioned economic arrangement. They did not need to make the argument that blacks were inferior; that was simply taken for granted.[8]

But when Northern abolitionists charged that slavery was evil, Southern slaveholders rose to the challenge. They began to argue that slaveholding was a just and virtuous institution, and that Negroes were "destined by providence" for slavery.[9] They portrayed the African homeland as barbarous, "the scene of unmitigated savagery, cannibalism, devil worship, and licentiousness." They embraced and popularized scientific research that claimed to prove the inferiority of the African race. They introduced "miscegenation" into the American vocabulary, arguing that the abolition of slavery would lead to intermarriage and the mongrelization of the white race. And they emphasized the squalid condition of the freed black in the North: the "vice and pauperism," the "deafness, insanity, and idiocy," that Calhoun and others took as authoritative evidence of blacks' unfitness for freedom. All these arguments in defense of slavery transformed what had been an unthinking assumption of racial superiority into a self-conscious theory of racism.[10]

Slavery and the debate it touched off certainly helped to fortify race prejudice. And yet, when slavery was abolished, prejudice lived on. Discrimination, segregation, and prejudice continued to flourish—and not only in the South. In the view of Leon Litwak, "Discrimination against the Negro and a firmly held belief in the superiority of the white race .˙. . were shared by an overwhelming majority of white Americans in both the North and the South. Abraham Lincoln, in his vigorous support of both white supremacy and denial of equal rights for Negroes, simply gave expression to almost universal American convictions."[11] As momentous a transformation as it was, emancipation did not mean the eradication of prejudice.

Race prejudice survived slavery's disappearance no doubt for more than one reason, but not least was the persistence of pervasive racism among American elites. Until quite recently, prejudice was an eminently respectable idea in respectable circles. Well into the twentieth century, American institutions of all sorts, including universities, participated in legitimizing the idea of black inferiority. As late as 1921, President Harding felt free to justify his opposition to "racial amalgamation" on grounds of the "fundamental, eternal, and inescapable differences" that he believed placed whites above blacks.[12]

By emphasizing that American race prejudice has a long and durable history, we do not mean to imply that it is somehow permanent and immutable. It is not. Racial prejudice today is not what it once was; its public expression and private language are different now from what they were in the days of slavery.[13] Prejudice is not some fixed and universal prescription. Rather, like other social doctrines, it is altered by turns in intellectual currents, changes in economic arrangements, and eruptions of political crisis. Prejudice, we believe, has been transformed twice in this fashion during our own century alone: first was the decline of biological racism in scientific and popular discourse on race, which took place in the first decades of the twentieth century; second and more complex was the change set in motion by the struggle for civil rights in the middle of the century and brought to completion by the epidemic of racial violence that raced through scores of American cities in the late 1960s. We sketch these two changes next. If we want to understand the terminology and logic of racial prejudice today, we must be reminded of the forms it took in the imaginable past.[14]

THE DECLINE — NOT DEMISE — OF BIOLOGICAL RACISM

The doctrine of biological racism began as a rationale first for slavery itself and later for postemancipation forms of racial oppression. At its center is the contention that blacks are an inherently and permanently inferior race. During the nineteenth century, biological racism was refined and enriched by various intellectual trends and political causes, most notably by the triumph of social Darwinism. These various developments were mainly slight variations on a constant theme, however. Into the twentieth century, the idea persisted that blacks were inferior to whites in intelligence and character, and that such inferiorities were inherent and permanent, a reflection of inborn differences.

In a shift that Fredrickson calls "the most fundamental change that occurred in white racial thinking after the First World War," biological racism was challenged and eventually replaced by liberal environmentalism.[15] Racial environmentalists insisted that blacks and whites did not differ in any essential way; that the observed differences between blacks and whites in economic standing or artistic achievement were due to differences in environmental conditions, not genetic predispositions. Liberal environmentalists thereby challenged the conventional understanding that blacks were a permanently alien element of the American population. Remove the socially created obstacles that stood in their way, so went the argument, and blacks would take their rightful and equal place in society.

The ascendance of liberal environmentalism reflects first and foremost a tidal change in American intellectual currents, detectable in a variety of places. For one, in the social and biological sciences, the idea of separate and distinct races came under relentless attack, which weakened the popular contention that the "white race" had developed further along the path of evolution.[16] At the same time, studies began to show that differences between blacks and whites in mortality and illness could be reduced or eliminated altogether when variations in housing, nutrition, sanitation, and medical care were taken into account. As a consequence, the argument that blacks were an inferior race, "doomed to spin their brutish existence downward into extinction," relinquished some of its force.[17] Meanwhile, scores of anthropological studies were celebrating the contributions made by African and Asian societies, and were revealing huge differences in temperament and personality due, evidently, to culture. Investigations by Mead and Benedict, among others, argued that human behavior was molded less by genes and more by tradition and custom.[18] And at home came the artistic flowering of the Harlem Renaissance of the 1920s and 1930s. The conspicuous achievements of Richard Wright, Langston Hughes, Marian Anderson, Paul Robeson, Louis Armstrong, and others made it more difficult to maintain that blacks were inherently disqualified from distinguished contributions to American life.

Perhaps most striking in this broad shift from biology to culture was the revolution in the scientific study of intelligence. The superiority of the "Nordic" type was the standard early result in studies of intelligence, based on the measurement of cranial capacity in the nineteenth century and IQ in the early stages of the twentieth. But then came a series of embarrassing demonstrations that differences between racial groups in intellectual performance could be traced to differences in cultural or environmental factors. Authoritative conclusions of Nordic superiority and Negro inferiority were retracted; inquiries into the genetic foundations for racial differences in intelligence quietly disappeared.[19]

All in all, a remarkable transformation had taken place. At the turn of the century, the social scientific investigation of race was preoccupied with the pathologies of Negro life, interpreting such pathologies as evidence of the inferiority and alien nature of the Negro, condemned by heredity to a permanent low station. Two or three decades later, racial inequalities were taken as evidence of pervasive prejudice and discrimination. Under the new intellectual regime, the Negro "problem" was situated in the hearts and minds of white citizens and in the discriminatory practices of white society.

By the Second World War, liberal environmentalism had taken over American social science. We presume that its entrenchment was a reflection of a more general turn toward egalitarianism among American elites, and that the liberal environmentalists positioned in America's most prestigious universities contributed directly to a more racially egalitarian public discourse.[20] Following the war, their cause was perhaps advanced by "revulsion against the racism of the Nazis" and by American leaders' embarrassment over flagrant incidents of racial discrimination at home that undermined efforts to compete with the Soviet Union for the loyalty of the peoples of Asia and Africa.[21] Public discussions of race came to be dominated by the assumptions of liberal environmentalism, and this continues to be true, for the most part, today.

The virtual disappearance of biological racism from elite circles leaves open the question of whether it also diminished in the minds of average citizens. The answer here appears to be yes, though the evidence is fragmentary. One bit comes from a series of careful studies undertaken by Apostle and his colleagues in the early 1970s, set in the San Francisco Bay Area and recounted in *The Anatomy of Racial Attitudes*. In this research, Americans were questioned about the differences they saw between blacks and whites and, most relevant to our point here, about how they explained the differences they saw. It turns out that relatively few whites attributed racial inequalities to inborn differences: to differences in intellectual capacity, differences "in the genes," in the "makeup" of blacks and whites, to differences "in the blood." Roughly 6% of Bay Area whites were in possession of a pure version of a genetic account for racial differences, and another 16% or so incorporated such thinking partially. Biological racism was relatively unpopular, therefore, and it was least popular among younger and better-educated whites, suggesting that it might be fading away altogether.[22]

Other evidence supports this conclusion more directly. In both the 1972 and 1986 NES surveys, white Americans were asked to consider whether they thought blacks came from a less-able race. In 1972, 31% of white Americans subscribed to the view that blacks were disabled by virtue of their biological inheritance; by 1986, the percentage had fallen to 14%.[23]

Another and final example pertains to the allegation of racial differences in intelligence. Beginning with a national survey carried out by NORC in 1942, white Americans have been asked periodically whether they think blacks and whites are equal in native intelligence. In 1942, fewer than half of the whites interviewed (47%) agreed that blacks were the intellectual equal of whites; by 1956, 80% did so. This is a remarkable increase in so short a time, offering further testimony to the declining fortunes of biological racism.[24]

From several quarters, then, it seems reasonable to conclude that racial thinking underwent an important change in twentieth-century America, and not only among white elites but also within the white public generally. The notion of genetic difference, of permanent disadvantage, is now less prominent than it once was. The biological argument has not disappeared altogether, but it has diminished. Racial prejudice no longer hangs on the contention that blacks are an inferior race, incapacitated from the outset by their biological inheritance.

The decline of biological racism must not be equated with the decline of racism generally. That most white Americans no longer subscribe to the view that blacks are crippled by inferior genetic endowment is a sign of real progress, but it does not mean that white Americans are now color-blind. As biological racism has declined, a new form of racial prejudice has appeared, shaped by the racial crisis of the middle part of the century.

FROM CIVIL DISOBEDIENCE TO URBAN VIOLENCE: TRANSFORMATIONS IN THE BLACK IMAGE DURING THE KING YEARS

The assault on segregation that began in the middle of the twentieth century eventually brought a social, economic, and political transformation to the South and to the nation. In courtrooms, blacks pressed claims on an increasingly sympathetic federal judiciary. In the streets—or more precisely, on buses and streetcars, and at lunch counters and department stores—blacks challenged the statutes and customs designed to keep them in their place. And in the halls of Congress, the civil rights movement finally succeeded in securing passage of landmark legislation that made discrimination illegal. Blacks' demands for equal rights triggered a massive and violent resistance in the Deep South, provoked a white backlash in the nation as a whole, and set in motion a racial reorientation in American party politics. This tumultuous time was capped by the outbreak of armed conflict and civil disorder in scores of American cities and, in the spring of 1968, by the assassination of Martin Luther King, Jr.

Nothing like this had taken place since the debate over slavery and the Civil War more than 100 years before. What did white Americans see during this tempestuous period and, more important, what lessons were they likely to draw about black Americans as a consequence? [25]

The first public stirrings of the modern civil rights movement took place in the 1950s in a series of protests and boycotts, first in Baton Rouge, then in Montgomery, Tallahassee, and Birmingham. The most famous of these was the Montgomery bus boycott, characterized by Aldon Morris as "the watershed of the modern civil rights movement," not least because it launched the political career of Martin Luther King, Jr., recently arrived from Atlanta to assume the post of pastor for the Dexter Avenue Baptist Church.[26] The historic significance of Montgomery is beyond dispute, but from the perspective of white America at the time, the commotion in Montgomery was not all that visible, little more than a premonition.

In the meantime, the 1954 Supreme Court decision outlawing segregation in the public schools was provoking a panic in the South. By 1957, according to C. Vann Woodward,

> a fever of rebellion and a malaise of fear spread over the region. Books were banned, libraries were purged, newspapers were

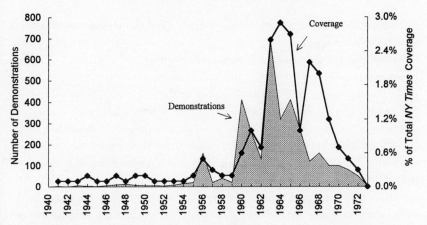

FIGURE 5.1 Civil rights demonstrations and coverage of civil rights demonstrations in the New York Times, 1940–1971. Source: Burstein 1985, pp. 74, 80.

slanted, magazines disappeared from the stands, television programs were withheld, films were excluded. Teachers, preachers, and college professors were questioned, harassed, and many were driven from their positions or fled the South. The N.A.A.C.P. was virtually driven underground in some states. Words began to shift and lose their common meaning. A "moderate" became a man who dared to open his mouth, an "extremist" one who favored eventual compliance with the law, and "compliance" took on the connotations of treason. Politicians who had once spoken for moderation began to vie with each other in defiance of government.[27]

In the face of increasing intimidation and violence, black Americans nevertheless continued to protest for their rights. Figure 5.1 shows the number of civil rights demonstrations each year from 1940 to 1972. The figure displays an initial spike of activity at the time of the Montgomery bus boycott, and then another and more sustained surge during the Kennedy years. In 1963 alone, more than 700 civil rights demonstrations took place. Most occurred in the South and were protests against local conditions, but they were intended to be witnessed by Americans all over the country, as indeed they were. Vivid accounts of the struggle for civil rights under way in such places as Oxford, Mississippi, and Birmingham, Alabama, began to creep into national news reporting. Civil rights protesters who sat in at segregated lunch counters or hotels were hauled away and jailed; marchers were flattened by high-pressure water hoses and mauled by police dogs; movement headquarters were dynamited; efforts to desegregate public schools were greeted with full-pitched riots. These melodramatic confrontations made terrific stories. Civil rights was national news (also revealed in figure 5.1).

In the meantime, President Johnson was pushing civil rights as a top legislative priority. In July 1964, in the wake of the longest legislative debate in the history of the U.S. Congress and over the fierce objection of Southern Democrats, the Civil Rights Bill became law. Discrimination on account of "race, color, religion, or national origin" was now illegal. To the British historian J. R. Pole, the Civil Rights Act represented a legislative revolution in American history: for the first time, "equality became a major object of government policy."[28]

The act also became a central part of the 1964 presidential campaign, thanks in no small measure to Senator Goldwater's success in capturing his party's presidential nomination. In his campaign, Goldwater argued against the encroachments of the federal government in private affairs in general and against the civil rights legislation sponsored by the Johnson administration in particular. Partly as a consequence, Goldwater did splendidly in the American South. Outside the Deep South, however, the Republican campaign was a disaster: Goldwater carried only his home state of Arizona and was buried under a landslide of historic proportions.

Following his overwhelming victory, President Johnson gave clear indications that government must do more than guarantee civil rights. In a major address delivered at Howard University in 1965, Johnson argued that the black community had "been twisted and battered by endless years of hatred and hopelessness." In language little different from that employed by Dr. King, the president characterized the ghetto as "a world of decay, ringed by an invisible wall," where "escape is arduous and uncertain, and the saving pressures of a more hopeful society are unknown." The president backed up his rhetoric with a flurry of new programs: VISTA, Head Start, Model Cities, the Office of Economic Opportunity, and more. Discrimination in voting was to be eliminated through the Voting Rights Bill, passed in 1965. The president established the Department of Housing and Urban Development, putting in place for the first time the capacity to develop and carry out an urban policy, and appointed Robert Weaver its secretary, the first black cabinet member in U.S. history. Johnson pressed for and eventually obtained legislation to prohibit discrimination in the housing market, through the Fair Housing Act of 1968. And he appointed Thurgood Marshall to the Supreme Court, the ninety-sixth justice and the first black, some twenty-five years after Marshall had argued the *Brown* school desegregation case.

Of all these, perhaps Johnson's most notable accomplishment was the Voting Rights Act, the long-delayed triumph of the struggle to secure the right to vote.

In the aftermath of "bloody Selma," where blacks intent on peacefully petitioning Governor Wallace for the right to vote were set upon by state troopers and local police officers, and beaten, trampled, and teargassed, President Johnson summoned a joint session of Congress.[29] In an evening address broadcast to the nation, Johnson embraced both the methods and the aspirations of the Selma demonstrators, calling for the prompt passage of a voting rights bill, insisting on "no delay, no hesitation, no compromise."[30] After some months of skirmishing, and against a backdrop of continuing violence in the South, Congress finally delivered. The president signed the Voting Rights Act into law on August 6, 1965, thereby bringing to completion a year of remarkable legislative achievements for civil rights. In the assessment of C. Vann Woodward, "Nothing comparable had ever happened before even during the high moments of the First Reconstruction."[31]

Political tempests in Washington often go unnoticed by citizens around the country, but this rule does not apply to the racial crisis of the 1960s. To an unusual degree, the struggle for civil rights caught and held the public's attention. One way to see this is by scanning figure 5.2, which summarizes the results of more than 100 national surveys conducted between 1946 and 1976. In each, Americans were asked to nominate the most important problems facing the country. The question was completely open-ended; people could say whatever they wished. Before the Montgomery bus boycott, as the figure indicates, virtually no American mentioned civil rights. But as the movement gathered momentum, civil rights made its way into the national news and eventually into public consciousness. The figure shows several sharp rises associated with

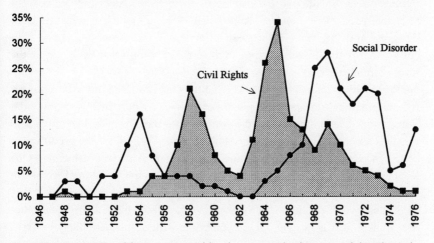

FIGURE 5.2 Percentage of the American public choosing civil rights or social disorder as the country's most important problem, 1946–1976. *Source:* Smith 1980, pp. 170, 171.

dramatic events, like the Little Rock school desegregation controversy in 1957, followed by a sustained takeoff in the latter half of 1963, stimulated, presumably, by the events taking place in Birmingham. Through most of 1964 and 1965, Americans—north and south—regarded civil rights as the nation's most important problem. For one extended moment, from the bombings in Birmingham to the march in Selma, the fight over civil rights commanded center stage.[32]

And with what consequence? Faced with this historic run of events, many white Americans appeared to come to a new conclusion: that segregation and discrimination were wrong, that black Americans should enjoy the same formal rights and opportunities as whites. On questions of broad principle of equal treatment and opportunity, a massive shift of white opinion was taking place.[33]

Presumably some of this change was a direct reflection of what whites saw. To the national audience, the sit-ins, boycotts, marches, freedom rides, and especially the outpouring of violence such protests provoked, vividly exposed the discriminatory practices and racial hatred that prevented blacks from claiming their rights as citizens. Moreover, these dramatic scenes often came accompanied by a kind of moral instruction. President Kennedy, President Johnson, and other prominent figures came to interpret massive resistance as evidence of a glaring moral defect, a failure to live up to America's historic commitment to egalitarian ideals. As one example, in the midst of the beatings and bombings taking place in Birmingham, President Kennedy began an address to the nation by asserting that "we are confronted primarily with a moral issue. It is as old as the Scriptures and it is as clear as the American Constitution. The heart of the question is whether all Americans are to be afforded equal rights and equal opportunities, whether we are going to treat our fellow Americans as we want to be treated. . . ."[34] In much the same spirit, President Johnson, in his speech to Congress and the nation calling for immediate action on voting rights, concluded that "equality depends not on the force of arms or tear gas but upon the force of moral right."[35]

What white Americans saw and what they heard turned out to be a powerful combination. In important spheres of life—education, public accommodations, employment, housing, and more—whites moved toward equality. Segregation and discrimination were losing ground. Concern for the predicament blacks faced was understood to be consistent with American principles. One legacy of the civil rights movement, we believe, was this bundling together, in public debate and private attitude, of egalitarian ideals and racial sympathy.

But as civil disobedience in the South was replaced by violence in the cities everywhere, it was not the only lesson white Americans were likely to draw. Five days after the Voting Rights Act was signed into law, the Watts riot exploded. Riots had broken out the previous summer—in Harlem, Bedford-

Stuyvesant, and Rochester in late July, and in Jersey City, Elizabeth, Paterson, and North Philadelphia in August—but they were, relatively speaking, short-lived and easily contained.[36] In Watts the violence raged unchecked for three days, and three days longer in sporadic eruptions. Blacks looted stores, set fires, burned cars, and shot at policemen and firemen. Before the violence was halted, 14,000 National Guard troops, 1,000 police officers, and more than 700 sheriff's deputies were pressed into service. More than 46 square miles—an area larger than Manhattan—came under military control. In the end, 1,000 buildings were damaged, burned, looted, or completely destroyed; almost 4,000 people were arrested; more than 1,000 were injured seriously enough to require medical treatment; and 34 were dead, all but three black.[37]

As horrifying as Watts was, it was merely the beginning. Soon came up-risings in Chicago, New York, Newark, Detroit, and in many other cities, large and small, in every section of the country. In 1967 alone, more than 250 serious disturbances took place. For one long hot summer after another, Americans watched what appeared to be the coming apart of their own country. On the front page of their morning newspapers and on their television screens in the evening appeared dramatic and frightening pictures of devastation and ruin: cities on fire, mobs of blacks looting stores and hurling rocks at police, tanks rumbling down the avenues of American cities. Along with the riots came a new rhetoric that frightened many whites and splintered black leadership: there was less talk of nonviolence and more of self-defense; less yearning for integration and more for solidarity and black nationalism; "We shall overcome" was replaced by Black Power and "burn, baby, burn."

If the civil rights movement and the flagrantly racist reaction it incited com-pelled many white Americans to express their support for racial equality as a matter of principle, the riots and the new belligerent rhetoric pushed them in quite a different direction. As we saw earlier, civil rights was widely regarded as the nation's most important problem in 1964 and 1965, but began to fade soon thereafter and disappeared entirely by the mid-1970s. Whites seemed to believe that the national government had successfully swept away all the barriers and obstacles that had stood in the way of black participation in American society. Segregation was being dismantled. Discrimination was illegal. Voting rights were being enforced. In the view of many white Americans, the problem of race was solved.

Or rather *that* problem of race was solved. Public discussion of the "race problem" in America no longer referred to ensuring equal rights and opportu-nities for blacks—that, apparently, had already been accomplished. Instead, discussion centered on the threat that inner-city blacks posed to social order and public safety. This point is made emphatically in figure 5.2. As Americans lost interest in civil rights, they became preoccupied with violence and disorder in the cities.[38]

This change reflects a transformation in the characterization of race relations dominating news reports and public discourse. Before Watts, the typical picture looked something like this: neatly dressed blacks, petitioning peacefully for their basic rights, crouched on the ground, being pummeled with nightsticks and set upon by police dogs. After Watts, Americans were instead witness to pictures of mobs of young city blacks, hurling bricks at police cars, torching their own neighborhoods, and looting stores of all that they could carry. Such pictures invited the conclusion from whites that after all that had been done for blacks, after all that had been given to them, it was not enough. Blacks wanted more, they demanded more—and they took it.

The riots opened up a huge racial rift. Fear and revulsion against the violence were widespread among both white and black Americans, but whites were much more likely to condemn those who participated in the riots and more eager for the police and National Guard to retaliate against them.[39] Where blacks saw the riots as expressions of legitimate grievances, whites were inclined to explain them as eruptions of black hatred and senseless criminality incited by outside agitators. To many white Americans, then, the civil disorders of the 1960s amounted to an appalling collective mugging.[40]

Understood in this way, the riots created a crisis for liberalism. President Johnson attempted to distinguish between the movement for civil rights—the "orderly struggle for civil rights that has ennobled the last decade"—and the violence and destruction that were sweeping through American cities. This was a difficult distinction to sell, and the political advantage moved decisively to the conservatives:

> Liberals faced the burden of explaining why the riots occurred after so many of the things which they had promised would solve the problems had already been done. They faced accusations that they were unwilling to uphold public order and were proposing to reward rather than punish communities that had spawned mass violence. Politically, liberals suddenly found themselves on the defensive, no longer occupying the high moral ground. Intellectually, they were far from certain about what was required or what would work.[41]

After the riots, conservative arguments took on new appeal, now in tune with white apprehensions. There was less talk about equality and more about law and order. Onto the national stage strutted George Wallace, followed in short order by the "new" Richard Nixon and by Ronald Reagan. Each, in his own way, gave public expression to simmering racial resentments. By interpreting inner-city violence and poverty as glaring manifestations of the failure of blacks to live up to American values, and by placing these problems at the center of their campaigns, Wallace, Nixon, and Reagan, among others, helped to create and legitimize a new form of prejudice. They did not promote biological racism: they were not white supremacists; they did not allege genetic impairments; they did not promise a return to segregation; they did not imply that blacks were second-class citizens or that they should be treated differently than anyone else. Their message was subtle, rather than blatant: it was that blacks should behave themselves. They should take quiet advantage of the ample opportunities now provided them. Government had been too generous, had given blacks too much, and blacks, for their part, had accepted these gifts all too readily. Discrimination was illegal, opportunities were plentiful. Blacks should work their way up without handouts or special favors in a society that was now color-blind.

At the core of this new resentment was not whether blacks possessed the inborn ability to succeed, but rather whether they would try. Now that all major obstacles to their improvement had supposedly been removed, would blacks apply themselves, as others had before them? One might say that black Americans would now be judged as Martin Luther King had wished, that is, by the "content of their character." The riots specifically and inner-city life generally were interpreted by many whites as repudiations of individualism, sacred American commitments to hard work, discipline, and self-sacrifice.

And more was to come. The riots that had handed the political advantage to conservatives were followed by a series of contentious public issues entangled in race, which, to many whites, exposed both the misguided benevolence of major American institutions and the moral deficiency of blacks unwilling to make it honestly on their own. These included allegations of fraud and abuse in the welfare system, explosions of crime, the dissolution of the traditional family, the plague of drugs, and dependence on government handouts. Most recently, public debate on matters of race has focused on affirmative action. Opponents of affirmative action see government requiring employers to give jobs and promotions to underqualified blacks, schools filling up with ill-prepared and undeserving black students, judges redrawing district lines to guarantee black candidates safe election, and colleges caving in to black students with codes that restrict speech and multicultural curricula that ridicule traditional learning.

Each of these episodes has provided a public stage for the creation and expression of racial animosity. A new form of prejudice has come to prominence, one that is preoccupied with matters of moral character, informed by the virtues associated with the traditions of individualism. At its center are the contentions that blacks do not try hard enough to overcome the difficulties they face and that they take what they have not earned. Today, we say, prejudice is expressed in the language of American individualism.

THE MEANING AND MEASUREMENT OF RACIAL RESENTMENT

With these developments in mind, we attempted to measure racial resentment with a battery of six questions included in the 1986 NES.[42] Each question was presented as an assertion; whites were asked to indicate whether they agreed or disagreed with each, and how strongly they did so:

> *Irish, Italian, Jewish and many other minorities overcame prejudice and worked their way up. Blacks should do the same without any special favors.*

> *Generations of slavery and discrimination have created conditions that make it difficult for blacks to work their way out of the lower class.*

> *It's really a matter of some people not trying hard enough; if blacks would only try harder they could be just as well off as whites.*

> *Over the past few years, blacks have gotten less than they deserve.*

> *Most blacks who receive money from welfare programs could get along without it if they tried.*

> *Government officials usually pay less attention to a request or complaint from a black person than from a white person.*

Compared with most efforts to measure racial animosity, these questions should appear rather subtle. They do not require whites to declare in straightforward fashion that blacks are dim-witted or lazy or promiscuous. Their approach is more roundabout. The questions distinguish between those whites who are generally sympathetic toward blacks and those who are generally unsympathetic. It could be said that our questions do for race what Adorno's *Authoritarian Personality* did for anti-Semitism. The famous "F-scale" that Adorno and his research team employed to measure authoritarianism was composed of questions that resemble ours, in that they were carefully formulated, as Roger Brown put it, "to express a subtle hostility without seeming to offend the democratic values that most subjects would feel bound to support. Each question has a kind of fair-minded and reasonable veneer. It is sometimes rather difficult to find the sting."[43]

As table 5.1 reveals, many white Americans are quite prepared to express such a "subtle hostility" toward blacks. Substantial majorities agreed that if

Table 5.1 Racial Resentment among White Americans

1. Most blacks who receive money from welfare programs could get along without it if they tried.	
Agree strongly	25.4%
Agree somewhat	35.3
Neither agree nor disagree	14.2
Disagree somewhat	18.7
Disagree strongly	6.5
2. Over the past few years, blacks have gotten less than they deserve.	
Agree strongly	3.3
Agree somewhat	15.4
Neither agree nor disagree	22.8
Disagree somewhat	38.0
Disagree strongly	20.5
3. Government officials usually pay less attention to a request or complaint from a black person than from a white person.	
Agree strongly	3.9
Agree somewhat	17.8
Neither agree nor disagree	28.3
Disagree somewhat	30.5
Disagree strongly	19.4
4. Irish, Italian, Jewish and many other minorities overcame prejudice and worked their way up. Blacks should do the same without any special favors.	
Agree strongly	32.9
Agree somewhat	33.7
Neither agree nor disagree	12.4
Disagree somewhat	16.2
Disagree strongly	4.7

[In past studies, we have asked people why they think white people seem to get more of the good things in life in America—such as better jobs and more money—than black people do. These are some of the reasons given by both blacks and whites.]

5. It's really a matter of some people not trying hard enough; if blacks would only try harder they could be just as well off as whites.	
Agree strongly	22.4
Agree somewhat	36.9
Neither agree nor disagree	13.3
Disagree somewhat	19.1
Disagree strongly	8.2
6. Generations of slavery and discrimination have created conditions that make it difficult for blacks to work their way out of the lower class.	
Agree strongly	17.0
Agree somewhat	41.1
Neither agree nor disagree	9.8
Disagree somewhat	19.2
Disagree strongly	12.9

Source: 1986 National Election Study.

blacks would only try harder they could be just as well off as whites; that most blacks who receive money from welfare programs could get along without it if they tried; and that blacks should overcome prejudice on their own without any special favors. Likewise, many rejected the assertion that blacks have gotten less than they deserve in recent years; that blacks receive less attention from government officials than whites do; or that generations of slavery and discrimination have created conditions that make it difficult for blacks to work their way into the middle class.[44]

Racial Resentment = Racial Prejudice?

Are white Americans who express such views prejudiced? The answer depends on what is meant by prejudice. This is an important and delicate point, worth a bit of our time.

Prejudice, according to Gordon Allport, is "an antipathy based on a faulty and inflexible generalization. It may be felt or expressed. It may be directed toward a group as a whole, or toward an individual because he is a member of that group."[45] The questions we use to measure racial resentment certainly fulfill some of Allport's requirements. For one thing, our questions focus on blacks as a group. The questions are categorical and abstract; they take as their frame of reference blacks as a whole.

The questions also have a strong evaluative component; they were designed to reveal "antipathy." They do so, notice, without making reference to genetic inferiority, so common to white supremacist ideology and to southern campaigns of a generation ago. In recognition of the decline of biological racism, the questions focus not on the inborn abilities of blacks, but on how hard blacks are willing to try. The questions are preoccupied with character: effort, enterprise, and determination. As portrayed in these questions, the "problem of race" is not the threat that blacks might pose to whites' personal safety or to their material well-being, but to their sense of civic virtue. To whites who agree with the premise of these questions, blacks constitute a moral threat, one that challenges "how we are to order our lives and our life as a community."[46]

So far our questions fit the classic definition of prejudice reasonably well. But what about Allport's insistence that prejudiced beliefs are erroneous, that prejudice is rooted in a "faulty" generalization?

It would not be hard to make a case that the assertion "if blacks would only try harder they could be just as well off as whites" is wrong, just as it is wrong to deny that generations of slavery and discrimination have created conditions that make it difficult for blacks to work their way out of the lower class. In both cases, what we are calling the racially resentful position *is* faulty. But on our other questions, it is more difficult to determine which answer is correct. For example, the first question presented in table 5.1 implies that the prejudice faced by blacks is no different from the prejudice faced by the Irish, the Italian, or the Jews—which is false. But the core of the question goes to whether blacks deserve special help, and it is hard to imagine authoritative evidence on whether whites who claim blacks should work their way up without any special favors are, or are not, mistaken. If we insist that prejudice is thinking ill of others without sufficient warrant, then we cannot say here with perfect confidence that we have a measure of prejudice.[47]

Prejudice, finally, is defined also by its inflexibility. Implicit here is a distinction between ordinary errors of misjudgment and the more serious and sinister case of prejudice. As Allport put it, "If a person is capable of rectifying his erroneous judgments in the light of new evidence, he is not prejudiced. Prejudgments become prejudice only when they are not reversible when exposed to new information."[48] We simply do not have any evidence that goes directly to this point. People hold on to their racial resentments with unusual tenacity, as we will see later, but this does not satisfy Allport's stronger claim.

In short, "racial resentment," as we use the term here, should not be confused with racial prejudice, as Allport defines it. We cannot be certain that the racially unsympathetic sentiments spelled out in table 5.1 are expressions of presumption and ignorance, and we do not know for sure whether whites might reverse their position should they be presented with evidence on the other side. This is tricky business, and we are not done with it yet: in the book's final chapter, we will come round again to the question of prejudice.

In other respects, our measure of racial resentment lives up to the empirical requirements normally expected of prejudice, as we will see over the next several pages. That is, racial resentment is coherent and stable, just as racial prejudice is expected to be; its expression is curtailed in the presence of black Americans, a sign that whites recognize that blacks would take offense; it powerfully predicts derogatory racial stereotypes, which are often thought to be the core of prejudice, and it is associated with, but distinct from, biological forms of racism, which it has largely replaced.

Racial Resentment Is Coherent

It is conceivable for people to answer the questions set out in table 5.1 in ways that have little to do with race. For example, those who say that if blacks only tried harder they could be as well off as whites might be expressing faith in individual initiative in general. Or those who agree with the notion that blacks should work their way up without special help might be signaling commitment to the ideal of equal treatment. It is conceivable, but this would mean that the sentiments expressed in table 5.1 would not really belong together.

Table 5.2 Pearson Correlations between Answers to the Racial Resentment Questions

	1	2	3	4	5	6
1	—					
2	.39	—				
3	.19	.40	—			
4	.50	.43	.19	—		
5	.51	.37	.16	.56	—	
6	.31	.40	.24	.37	.38	—

Source: 1986 National Election Study.
Note: Questions are given in full in table 5.1.

They would be a hodge-podge of complaints, each reflecting a different belief or value. Against this, we say that the various resentments expressed in table 5.1 constitute a coherent system of ideas, one centering on black Americans. Resentment over blacks getting ahead unfairly is the one theme that runs through *all* six questions. If we are right, then whites who agree that if blacks would only try harder, they would be as well off as whites should also be inclined to deny that slavery and discrimination have created conditions that impede black progress, to agree that blacks should work their way up without any special favors, and so on through all the questions.

Table 5.2 reveals that white Americans show just this kind of consistency. The table presents evidence on the degree of association between answers to each pair of questions, as indexed by the Pearson correlation coefficient.[49] Judged against normal standards, the correlations displayed there are quite strong, ranging from .16 to .56, and averaging .36. Thus the ostensibly diverse sentiments expressed by the racial resentment questions are not in fact a miscellaneous collection; they do indeed reflect an empirically coherent outlook. White Americans answer these questions as if they had one thing primarily in mind.[50]

Racial Resentment Is Stable

Prejudice is an acquired taste. Children enter the world free of any such animosity, but their innocence is temporary, for they are born into a world in which socially significant distinctions are already in place. By the time American children enter elementary school, they know that racial groups exist, and that persons belong to such groups on the basis of observable characteristics: skin color, facial features, the texture of their hair. They know which racial group they belong to, and they know which racial groups are good and which are bad. White children have strong positive associations with the term "white," referring both to color and to race, and strong negative associations with "black"; and they almost never express a wish to be a member of a racial

SUBTLE PREJUDICE FOR MODERN TIMES

group other than their own.[51] As children's cognitive abilities mature, they come to understand racial categories as permanent and immutable and their perception of differences between racial groups is accentuated.[52] By the early adult years, racial ideas are difficult to reverse; at this stage, race has become a standard and automatic way of categorizing and evaluating the social world. As Allport once put it, "A prejudice, unlike a simple misconception, is actively resistant to all evidence that would unseat it."[53]

If we have measured racial resentment well, then white Americans should answer the NES questions in essentially the same way when offered a second chance. We can see whether this is so by taking advantage of the 1990–92 NES panel design. Roughly one-half of those interviewed in the 1992 NES study were first questioned in 1990, and on both occasions they were asked the same four racial resentment questions, a subset of the original six.

One standard way to give mathematical representation to individual stability is through the Pearson correlation coefficient. In this context, a Pearson correlation of 1.0 would mean perfect stability: an ordering of white Americans by their scores on the racial resentment scale administered in 1990 would correspond exactly to the ordering revealed by their 1992 scores. A correlation of 0.0, in contrast, would mean perfect instability: racial resentment scores in 1990 bear no relation to scores two years later.

For the racial resentment scale, the Pearson correlation between the 1990 and 1992 observations is .68. This estimate of continuity is well above the zero chaos point, but falls visibly short of perfect stability. So how stable is racial resentment? How big is .68?

One answer is provided by comparing the Pearson correlation of .68 with continuity estimates of other political sentiments. From this perspective, racial resentment looks quite stable: substantially more stable than views on equality (Pearson $r = .49$), ideological identification ($r = .49$), or positions on various matters of public policy (Pearson r's hover around .4). Whites' racial resentments even approach the stability of their identification with a political party ($r = .79$), widely regarded as providing the stability benchmark for political attitudes.[54]

Thus a Pearson correlation of .68, viewed comparatively, is quite impressive, and it is the more impressive when we recognize that it almost certainly underestimates the real stability of racial resentment. Our observations of change over time reflect a mixture of real instability (white Americans' changing their minds about black Americans) and artificial instability (produced by inevitable errors in our measures). With this in mind, it would be useful to produce an estimate of the stability of racial resentment once the intrusions of unreliability are removed.

We do this in two ways. Both procedures require that we have multiple measures of racial resentment on more than one occasion, as we do. The first follows the standard recommendation from test theory in psychometrics.[55] With estimates of the reliability of the racial resentment scale in each year, we can correct the correlation of .68 for the unreliability due to random measurement error (correction for attenuation, as it is called). When we do so, the correlation rises to .89. This means that if we had in our possession perfectly reliable measures of racial resentment (in place of the fallible measures employed in the 1990–92 NES panel study), we would have found a correlation of .89 (rather than .68). And a correlation of .89 over a two-year period, though not quite perfect, is certainly consistent with the claim that racial resentment, like prejudice, is difficult to reverse.[56]

A second way to partition unreliability from stability makes use of confirmatory factor analysis. Here we treat racial resentment as a latent variable in order to estimate the correlation between resentment in 1990 and 1992, with unreliability once again removed. The results, shown in table 5.3, indicate that the model fits the data reasonably well. Each of the four questions loads substantially on the racial resentment factor, and the pattern of the loadings is highly similar across the two years. This model estimates the stability correlation between resentment in 1990 and resentment in 1992 to be .78. Once the random and systematic components of unreliability are removed, therefore, racial resentment is once again revealed to be stable—not perfectly stable, not fixed, but predominantly stable.[57]

Table 5.3 Stability of Racial Resentment, 1990–1992 (confirmatory factor analysis)

	Factor Loadings	
	$Resentment_{90}$	$Resentment_{92}$
Blacks gotten less than deserved$_{90}$	.57	
Blacks should work their way up$_{90}$	.82	
Blacks need only try harder$_{90}$	.79	
Slavery and discrimination$_{90}$	.53	
Blacks gotten less than deserved$_{92}$		.65
Blacks should work their way up$_{92}$		.76
Blacks need only try harder$_{92}$		.80
Slavery and discrimination$_{92}$		.57

Correlation between $Resentment_{90}$ and $Resentment_{92}$ = .78
Chi-square with 15 degrees of freedom = 90.41
Goodness of fit = .960
Adjusted goodness of fit = .905
Root mean square residual = .053

Source: 1990–92 National Election Panel Study.

Racial Resentment Is Conditioned by Race of Interviewer

In Chapter 2 we argued that in a society like our own, characterized by racial segregation and tension, an extended conversation between a black person and a white person is unlikely to be experienced as innocuous by either party. And indeed we found that whites interviewed by blacks expressed less conservative views on matters of race policy than did whites interviewed by whites.

The same should hold true for the expression of racial resentment—and it does. When questioned by black interviewers, whites appeared less resentful than they did when they were questioned by white interviewers. The effect is not large, but it holds for five of the six questions taken individually, for the scale as a whole, and with the effects due to social background characteristics statistically held constant. Race-of-interviewer effects also show up, this time more sizably, in both the 1988 and 1992 National Election Studies. That whites present themselves differently to a black interviewer than to a white interviewer is consistent with the claim that we are really measuring *racial* resentment.[58]

Racial Resentment Predicts Derogatory Stereotypes

Social animosity is often expressed through stereotypes, pejorative beliefs that in-group members hold toward members of outgroups. As a further test of the validity of our measure of racial resentment, we examined the extent to which scores on the racial resentment scale predict endorsement of traditional racial stereotypes. This analysis is possible because the 1992 NES included both our measures of racial resentment and a set of stereotype questions originally developed at the National Opinion Research Center for the General Social Survey.[59]

In some ways the GSS stereotype questions are similar to the questions we have been analyzing. Like their NES counterparts, the GSS questions are categorical and abstract, in that they take as their frame of reference blacks as a group. But the GSS questions mix old, or biological, and new, or individualistic, forms of animosity. One item questions blacks' intelligence, consistent with a central claim of biological racism; another questions blacks' effort and motivation, consistent with a central claim of racial resentment. And finally, the GSS questions take quite a different form from what we have used to measure racial resentment. Here citizens are presented with a series of paired antonyms (hardworking versus lazy, say) and asked to judge whether members of some designated group (blacks, for example) are mostly hardworking, mostly lazy, or somewhere in between. In the 1992 NES, three pairs of antonyms were included: hardworking versus lazy, unintelligent versus intelligent, and violent versus peaceful.

By comparing the judgments whites offer about blacks to those they make about their own racial group, it is possible to derive a measure of racial stereotyping. And according to the 1992 NES results, most white Americans do in fact subscribe to racial stereotypes. That is, they believe that blacks are less hardworking than whites, that blacks are more violent than whites, and that blacks are less intelligent than whites. Some whites see no difference between the races, but most of the variation among white Americans is in *how* inferior black Americans are, whether the racial superiority that whites enjoy in essential capacities and fundamental qualities is overwhelming or slight.

Can racial resentment predict, as to our way of thinking it must, the extent to which white Americans subscribe to such stereotypes? To find out, we coded the three stereotype measures 0–1, with 1.0 representing complete endorsement of the stereotype, 0.0 its complete reversal, and 0.5 the color-blind view that blacks and whites differ not at all. We then simply regressed each of the stereotype measures against our measure of racial resentment (also coded 0–1).

The results, shown in table 5.4, indicate that racial resentment and racial stereotyping are indeed closely related. White Americans who express racial sympathy on the racial resentment scale (a perfect score of 0) show up almost precisely at the color-blind 0.5 neutral point on all three stereotype measures: they say whites and blacks are indistinguishable. At the same time, white Americans at the other end of the racial resentment scale (with a perfect score of 1) are predicted to score around .65 on the stereotype measures: they say whites are much smarter, much harder working, and much less violent. The impact of racial resentment on racial stereotypes is strong in all three cases, but it is least strong, by some 50%, for beliefs about intelligence, the one item of the

Table 5.4 Predicting Racial Stereotypes from Racial Resentment

	Blacks Are Comparatively		
	Lazy	Unintelligent	Violent
Racial resentment	.18	.12	.19
	(.01)	(.01)	(.01)
Constant	.48	.50	.50
	(.01)	(.01)	(.01)
R-squared	.11	.05	.11
Standard error	.12	.11	.12
Number of cases	1,797	1,780	1,782

Source: 1992 National Election Study.
Note: Table entry is *B*, the unstandardized ordinary least squares regression coefficient, with standard errors in parentheses underneath.

three closely associated with biological forms of racism. This suggests the distinctiveness of contemporary racial resentment from its biological predecessor, an issue we take up more directly next.

Racial Resentment Is Distinct from Biological Racism

We have argued that contemporary expressions of prejudice no longer center on claims of racial inferiority rooted in biology. Today, we say, prejudice is preoccupied less with inborn ability and more with effort and initiative. But does racial resentment really constitute a new form? Or is it in fact indistinguishable from nineteenth-century biological racism?

Remember that the 1986 NES included a question that was intended to elicit in straightforward fashion the unvarnished racism of the American past, the claim that blacks are genetically inferior. Respondents were asked whether they agreed or disagreed with the assertion that blacks were less well off in America because they "come from a less able race." As noted earlier, by 1986, most whites, but far from all, rejected biological inferiority as an explanation for racial differences.[60]

It would be surprising and, from a theoretical point of view, disconcerting if the position white Americans took toward the claim of black genetic inferiority turned out to be completely unrelated to racial resentment as we have defined and measured it here. Old-fashioned bigotry and contemporary racial resentment share an attitude of hostility toward black Americans, and this should be reflected in a positive relationship between them. On the other hand, we would be equally disconcerted if the relationship turned out to be strong. Whites who believe blacks to be their biological inferiors might resent the special help that blacks supposedly receive, but they also might think that blacks require such help precisely because of their genetic handicap. Similarly, whites who express indignation over blacks failing to live up to the standards of self-sacrifice and self-reliance may genuinely reject the claim of biological inferiority. Old-fashioned bigotry and contemporary racial resentment are related, but distinct, concepts—or so we say.

The relevant evidence runs this way. Answers to the genetic inferiority question are related to answers to the six resentment questions, but ever so slightly: the Pearson correlation between the scale of racial resentment and opinions on blacks' inborn inferiority is just .12. Biological inferiority no longer appears to be the centerpiece of American racial thinking.[61]

RACIAL RESENTMENT AND PUBLIC POLICY

All this evidence suggests that we have in hand a reliable and valid measure of racial resentment, one well suited to modern-day American race relations.

But our interest lies less in racial resentment for its own sake, and more in how it is played out in public life. Here it is our purpose to determine the effect of racial resentment on the views white Americans take on a wide variety of social policies.

To estimate this effect, we must first place racial resentment in a larger theoretical framework. The evidence we have just presented is reassuring on the quality of our measures, but does nothing to relieve us of the obligation to take into account alternative interpretations of public opinion on matters of race. It would be foolish to assume that whites' views on, say, affirmative action are *only* expressions of racial resentment. To generate estimates of the political effect of racial resentment that anyone should take seriously, we must at the same time take into account the effects due to other plausible considerations. These include, most notably, whatever threats to material interests that appear to be at stake, general opposition to government intervention in private affairs, commitment to the abstract American ideal of individualism, and principled reservations about the application of equality to society.

Mindful of this obligation, we will estimate the impact of racial resentment in several rounds of analysis. Each round represents a distinct, but plausible, specification. We rely first of all on data provided by the 1986 NES, but move beyond it when we can. We begin with simple specifications, adding complexity as we proceed.

Racial Resentment and Race Policy

Our immediate purpose is to estimate the impact of racial resentment where it is likely to be most pronounced: on policies that deal explicitly and unambiguously with race. On matters of school desegregation and affirmative action, black Americans are the intended primary beneficiaries, and all our questions name them as such. If racial resentment is to come into play in public opinion at all, it should show up most plainly here.

In this first analysis, we also take into account, in addition to racial resentment, the effects due to material threats to self-interest, opposition to the intrusions of government in private affairs, a wide array of social background characteristics (age, region, gender, Hispanic ethnicity, family income, education, occupational status), as well as race of interviewer.[62]

Column 1 of table 5.5 presents the results. The rows of the table correspond to each of the six race policies included in the 1986 NES. The estimated effect of racial resentment is provided in each case by ordinary least squares regression. Keeping in mind that the policy questions, like the racial resentment scale, are coded on the 0–1 interval, the coefficients on display in column 1 of table 5.5 indicate a very substantial effect of racial resentment on white opinion.

Table 5.5 Impact of Racial Resentment on White Americans' Opinions on Race Policy

Policy	1986			1988	1992	
	(1)	(2)	(3)	(4)	(5)	(6)
Fair employment	.57	.57	.51	.63	.63	.51
School desegregation	.30	.28	.18	—	.40	.17
Federal spending	.45	.44	.36	.41	.59	.73
Government effort	.44	.44	.37	.53	.51	.59
Preferential hiring	.40	.40	.38	.42	.47	.41
College quotas	.60	.61	.59	.63	.71	.60

Source: 1986, 1988, 1992 National Election Studies.
Note: Table entry is B, the unstandardized regression coefficient representing the effect of racial resentment (coded 0–1) on whites' views on race policy (also coded 0–1). All coefficients are statistically significant. The standard errors range from .05 to .10. Estimates provided by ordinary least squares regression, except in column 6, which are provided by two-stage least squares.

Consider, as a typical example, the question of whether the federal government should provide special assistance to black Americans. According to table 5.5, the regression estimate of the effect of racial resentment on this question of policy is .44. This means that two white Americans, identical in social background and political outlook, who differ only in that one is racially sympathetic (scoring 0 on the racial resentment scale) while the other is racially resentful (a score of 1.0), will differ from each other on the question of federal assistance by a value of .44. When we consider that the effects due to other considerations are taken into account, and that the policy scale itself ranges from 0, meaning that the government has a special obligation to blacks, to 1, meaning that blacks should get ahead on their own without the help of government, a difference of .44 is large.

Indeed, column 1 of table 5.5 presents nothing but sizable coefficients. The effect of racial resentment is greatest on the question of quotas in college admissions and smallest—though still appreciable—on the question of school desegregation. These results imply that white Americans' objections to policies intended to diminish racial inequalities are expressions, in large part, of racial resentment.

Racial Resentment and General Individualism

What happens to our results, and to the conclusion they imply, when we take abstract individualism into account? To find out, we simply added a measure of individualism into our first round regression analysis. For the purpose of this analysis, the six individualism questions included in the 1986 NES are ideal: the questions are abstract, they make no specific reference to blacks or whites, and they concentrate for the most part on the virtue of self-reliance and the power of individual initiative (e.g., "Most people who don't get ahead

should not blame the system; they have only themselves to blame"). Individualism, measured in this way, will play a prominent role in the next chapter, as
part of our more general argument that public opinion is shaped by American principles. Our purpose here is limited to establishing whether the effect of racial resentment diminishes when we also take into account general
individualism.[63]

Adding individualism changes nothing. For each of the six race policies, the
estimated impact of racial resentment is completely unaltered. This can be seen
by comparing the string of coefficients in column 1 of table 5.5 with the corresponding string of coefficients in column 2. The two are indistinguishable. The
effect of racial resentment is completely unaffected by the presence of individualism. In the meantime, the estimated effect of individualism itself in these six
cases is essentially zero.[64] We will have more to say about individualism in
Chapter 6, but this is what we can say now: white opposition to racial change
appears to be motivated not by commitment to individualism in general, but by
resentment directed against blacks in particular.[65]

Racial Resentment and Race Policy in Different Settings

That our estimate of the impact of racial resentment is unaffected by individualism is both important and convenient, for it allows us to replicate our
analysis in NES studies that do not include measures of individualism. Thus we
can see whether the effects of resentment so dramatically on display in 1986
also show up under a variety of circumstances, free of the worry that our estimate is biased because of the omission of individualism.

In particular we can repeat our analysis twice, making use of the 1988 and
1992 NES presidential election studies. The 1988 NES carried all but one of the
six race policy questions that have been the center of our attention so far; the
1992 NES carried them all. Both studies also included virtually the same array
of social background characteristics that we made use of in our analysis of the
1986 NES, and both included a measure of limited government. Most important, both studies carried four of the original six questions that made up the
1986 NES racial resentment scale—the first four questions, as they appear on
page 106. The resulting resentment scale is briefer and slightly less reliable in
each case than the 1986 version, but in some ways it may be better. The two
questions that were set aside in the 1988 and 1992 studies are those least justi-
fiable as measures of prejudice (on the interpretation that prejudical beliefs are
erroneous). Moreover, uniquely among the original set of six, the two explicitly
invoke government, referring to "welfare" in one case and "government officials" in the other. This means that the 1986 NES racial resentment scale incor-

SUBTLE PREJUDICE FOR MODERN TIMES

porates elements that are uncomfortably close to what we are trying to explain, namely, public policy on race. In short, the 1988 and 1992 NES studies may provide us with more than precisely calibrated replications; they may actually provide the better test of the power of racial resentment.

The results from 1988 and 1992 are presented in columns 4 and 5 of table 5.5, and they are striking. The powerful effects of racial resentment first detected in 1986 are even more powerful in 1988 and in 1992. These findings, based on a sharpened measure of racial resentment, strengthen our original conclusion. White opposition to policies that would provide opportunity and assistance to blacks is primarily an expression of racial resentment.[66]

Resentment and Equality

So far we have found powerful effects of racial resentment on white opinion toward various aspects of racial policy. But this evidence is not fully convincing, because we have not yet taken into account the real possibility that white opinion on racial matters is derived at least in part from beliefs about equality. In the next chapter, we develop the argument that American public opinion has a foundation in principles, and in claims about equality in particular. As we will see there, much scholarship on the American political tradition takes as a central point what Tocqueville referred to as the American "passion for equality." The implication of this line of analysis is to suggest that opinion on matters of race might well turn on the extent to which Americans subscribe to doctrines of equality. And this point takes on immediate relevance here when we recognize that racial resentments and beliefs about equality are likely to be correlated. It should not surprise us to discover that racially sympathetic whites are inclined to embrace egalitarian principles, while racially resentful whites tend to express reservations about equality. And this means we need to take views on equality into account here, as we try to ascertain the political effect of racial resentment.

One way to do this is simple and straightforward. To our first round of analysis, we just add a measure of principled reservations about the application of equality to American society. This measure is based on an averaged response to six equally weighted questions that primarily concern the desirability of equality of opportunity, pitched at an abstract level (e.g., "Our society should do whatever is necessary to make sure that everyone has an equal opportunity to succeed").[67]

Bringing in equality in this way diminishes the effect of racial resentment. These results, which are taken from the 1986 NES, are presented in column 3 of table 5.5. They show that in the presence of equality, the estimated direct effect of racial resentment is somewhat reduced. The reduction is appreciable in just one case, however, on school integration, where the direct effect of resentment diminishes by about 40%. In all other cases, the impact of racial resentment declines either modestly or not at all. Thus under stringent statistical controls, racial resentment remains a powerful force in white opinion.

Indeed, the impact of racial resentment is probably stronger than it appears in these last results. As we said, this first way of bringing equality into the analysis is straightforward but also, if we are not careful, misleading. That the direct effect of racial resentment declines in the presence of equality does not necessarily mean that the we should readjust downward our assessment of its political potency. This is so because beliefs about equality may be in large part a *product* of racial animosity. Views about equality of opportunity in general are, perhaps, reflections of sentiments toward the social groups that have been at the center of particular and conspicuous struggles over equality. Put more strongly than we actually believe, when white Americans are asked to turn their minds to equality in the abstract, they are really turning their minds to equalities in the concrete, and especially to racial disputes over equality in particular. By not taking this *indirect* effect of racial resentment into account, our first results on equality may lead us to underestimate its real (or total) effect.

It is of course possible to turn this argument around, to claim that resentment toward blacks is a product of general egalitarian sentiments. Should this be true, then the strong direct effects of racial resentment displayed in column 3 of table 5.5 provide a good reading of its real power.

The general difficulty here of settling by assumption the relationship between equality and racial resentment suggests an additional analysis. In this specification, we estimate the impact of racial resentment and equality on white opinion toward racial policy. As we do so, racial resentment is assumed to be a cause of equality, and, simultaneously, equality is assumed to be a cause of racial resentment. The practical obstacles that stand in the way of estimating these effects can be surmounted by taking advantage of the 1990–92 NES panel design, which includes measures of resentment and equality on both interviews, along with the standard set of race policy questions in 1992.[68]

The results are shown in the last column of table 5.5. They tell a by now familiar story, that of the political power of racial resentment. They suggest that previously we may have exaggerated a bit the power of racial resentment on matters of school desegregation and fair employment (where views on equality turn out to be very important), and at the same time, underestimated the power of resentment on issues of federal responsibility. But everywhere, our results say, racial resentment is important.

Resentment and Opinion beyond the Racial Domain

Finally we wondered about the impact of racial resentment on issues that lie outside the domain of race. To inform this analysis, we made use of the categories introduced in Chapter 2 and the rich set of policy questions included in the 1992 NES. We distinguished among explicit racial issues, where, as we have just seen, the impact of racial resentment is substantial; implicit racial issues, which make no mention of blacks and whites but that may be widely understood to have a racial implication (e.g., federal support for Food Stamps); broad-based social programs (e.g., government spending on Social Security); moral issues raised by the religious right (e.g., parental consent for abortion); new issues arising out of surges in immigration (e.g., restricting the flow of immigrants into the country); and, finally, matters of foreign policy (e.g., U.S. relations with what used to be the Soviet Union). Heading into this analysis, we expected that the impact of racial resentment would be most pronounced in policy disputes where the racial dimension is explicit and out in the open, substantially smaller but still visible on implicit race policy, and essentially disappear thereafter, as issues of public contention become farther and farther removed from American race relations.

The results are displayed in table 5.6, organized by category, from explicit racial policy at the top to foreign policy at the bottom. Each entry in the table is the unstandardized version of the ordinary least squares regression coefficient, giving the effect of racial resentment on white opinion on each of the various policies. In all cases, the estimated effect of racial resentment is over and above the effects due to limited government, social background, race of interviewer, and (most important) equal opportunity. If anything, then, the effects presented in table 5.6 may underestimate the actual impact of racial resentment.[69]

Results generally conform to expectations: the effects of racial resentment are huge at the top and small at the bottom, as the issue domain proceeds from race to foreign relations. But the table contains some surprises as well. One is the strong effect of racial resentment on issues where race is present only by assumption. Racially resentful whites are a good bit less enthusiastic about increasing federal support for the Food Stamps program, for example, and they are a good bit more enthusiastic about capital punishment for convicted murderers. And so it goes for welfare, urban unrest, and sanctions against South Africa: even when policies are described in ways that make no mention of race, racial resentment plays a prominent role. These results suggest how far race has infiltrated discussions of American policy.

Far, but not all the way. Much as we had expected, the effect of racial re-

Table 5.6 Effect of Racial Resentment on White Public Opinion

Integrated Schools	Fair Employment	Government Assistance	Preferential Hiring	College Quotas
.37	.67	.47	.43	.68
(.06)	(.06)	(.03)	(.04)	(.04)

Food Stamps	Welfare	Remedies for Urban Unrest	Federal Spending	Sanctions against South Africa[86]	Capital Punishment
.27	.22	.23	.49	.46	.33
(.04)	(.04)	(.04)	(.04)	(.10)	(.04)

Homeless	Medicare	Family Leave	Social Security	Education	Childcare	Poor
.05	−.08	.18	−.16	−.05	.12	.10
(.03)	(.03)	(.05)	(.04)	(.03)	(.04)	(.04)

Gay Rights

Protect against job discrim.	Gays in military	Gays adopt children	School choice
.21	.15	.24	.12
(.06)	(.06)	(.05)	(.08)

Sexual Harassment

Serious problem	Requires legislation
.11	.14
(.05)	(.05)

Abortion

Women's right	Parental consent	Government subsidy	Spousal notification
−.05	.26	.15	.19
(.04)	(.04)	(.05)	(.06)

Prayer in School	Restricting Immigration	Withholding Benefits from Immigrants	English Official Language
.07	.21	.22	.26
(.03)	(.03)	(.06)	(.06)

Compete with Soviet Union	Keep out of Central America	Defense Spending
.29	.14	.10
(.06)	(.05)	(.03)

Source: 1986 and 1992 National Election Studies.

Note: Table entry is *B*, the unstandardized form of the ordinary least squares coefficient, with standard error in parentheses underneath. Each regression equation included measures of limited government, equal opportunity, social background, and race of interviewer.

sentment diminishes sharply on broad social programs, the next category in table 5.6. Racially resentful whites are no more likely to oppose Medicare, or to cut federal aid to the homeless, or to disapprove of federal support for public education, or to press for reductions in Social Security. All in all, racial resentment seems quite irrelevant to white Americans' views on social programs that distribute benefits and opportunities widely. Two exceptions stand out in table 5.6, however, and they may be related in that both entail intrusions upon traditional family arrangements. On child care and family leave, racially resentful whites are a bit less inclined to support policies that would make it easier for women to raise a family and to continue working outside the home. But these are modest effects, and as a general matter, racial resentments have little influence over white Americans' opinions on social spending.

A second major surprise comes with the issues of morality and rights. We expected that racial resentment would have negligible effects here, and in some respects this turned out to be true. Resentments of a racial sort had little or no effect on the views white Americans took on school prayer, on choice in public education, or on whether or not women have a right to abortion. But as table 5.6 shows, racial resentment had a substantial impact on other aspects of opinion within this domain. Racially resentful whites are less impressed with sexual harassment than are racially sympathetic whites: less likely to assign sexual harassment high priority and less likely to say that more needs to be done to control it. Racially resentful whites are no more likely to deny women the right to abortion as a matter of principle, but they are more likely to support various practical limitations on abortion: they favor parental consent; they oppose government subsidies; and they support spousal notification. And last, whites who express resentment toward black Americans are reluctant to extend rights and protections to gay and lesbian Americans: they are more opposed to allowing gays in the military, they are less persuaded that homosexuals require protection against discrimination on the job, and they are more opposed to the adoption of children by gay couples. The effects of racial resentment here are not overwhelming, but neither are they dismissable. They indicate an impressive breadth to the political power of racial resentment, one that we had not anticipated.

This story line continues in the next row of table 5.6, where we see quite strong association between racial resentment and white opinion on matters of immigration. Whites who resent blacks are also more inclined to favor restrictions on the flow of immigrants into the country, more likely to say that those who do come into the country should not be eligible for government benefits, and more likely to favor the establishment of English as an official language. Nativist reactions to immigration are nothing new in American political life; it is perhaps no surprise to see another.[70] What *is* surprising, however, is that the connection is so visible in our results, even though current immigration comes predominantly from Central and South America and the Pacific rim, while our measure of "nativism" is directed exclusively at black Americans.

Last of all, and a final surprise, the impact of racial resentment is also detectable in the domain of foreign relations. As the bottom row of table 5.6 reveals, racially resentful whites seem to be generally more apprehensive over foreign threats: more inclined to favor increases in defense spending, more likely to advocate a tough posture toward the Soviet Union, and more likely to support U.S. involvement in Central America. The effects are not gigantic, but they are far from zero. They suggest, once again, that resentment toward blacks is part of a broader system of beliefs and feelings about social difference in general.[71]

CONCLUSIONS

The origins of race prejudice in America are tangled and distant. They recede far into our shared past, rooted most plainly in the experience of slavery. Closer to our own time, the public form and private meaning of prejudice have undergone two important alterations, one reflected in the decline of the doctrine of biological racism, the other provoked by the sweeping changes and turbulent events that made up the racial crisis of the 1960s. As a consequence of these developments, animosity toward blacks is expressed today less in the language of inherent, permanent, biological difference, and more in the language of American individualism, which depicts blacks as unwilling to try and too willing to take what they have not earned.

Defined this way, racial resentment plays an important and expansive role in white public opinion. On equal opportunity in employment, school desegregation, federal assistance, affirmative action at work, and quotas in college admissions, racially resentful whites line up on one side of the issue, and racially sympathetic whites line up on the other. Racial resentment is not the *only* thing that matters for race policy, but *by a fair margin racial resentment is the most important*. This result comes shining through, across various specifications, under different political circumstances, and with close attention to alternative considerations.[72]

Such results would be enough to establish the political significance of racial resentment in contemporary American society, but we found more. We found that racially resentful whites also tend to push for a strong national defense and a tough stance toward the Soviet Union (back when there was a Soviet Union), to favor limits on foreign imports to save American jobs, and to oppose sanctions against South Africa. On the home front, racially resentful whites oppose legislation that would protect gays from employment discrimination and are comparatively unenthusiastic about federal efforts to cope with the AIDS epidemic. They favor the death penalty. They tend to oppose increases in federal money for Food Stamps. They would like to see government services denied to immigrants.

We should hasten to say that not everyone who resents blacks fears homosexuals, and not everyone who supports a strong defense believes that blacks have gotten ahead unfairly. We have uncovered tendencies and inclinations, that is all. Still, the tendencies and inclinations are surprisingly strong, and most especially, they reach surprisingly far. We began with resentment toward blacks in particular, but here we are at the end with something rather different—with, evidently, apprehensions and fears set off by a variety of social differences.

In this way, our findings recall those reported by Adorno and his colleagues nearly fifty years ago in *The Authoritarian Personality*. Adorno's team found that the fear and contempt that some Americans felt for Jews were often accompanied by comparable sentiments directed at other "alien elements": criminals, Japanese-Americans, conscientious objectors, immigrants, blacks, foreign ideas, and more. Our results suggest a similar ethnocentric pattern to American opinion today. The resemblances between our conception of racial resentment and the point of view put forward in *The Authoritarian Personality* are sufficiently striking, and the differences sufficiently important, to warrant further discussion. We will return to the relationships between racial resentment, prejudice, and ethnocentrism in our final chapter.

For now we want to emphasize the contrast between our results, which reveal racial resentment to be the most potent force in white public opinion on race today, and most contemporary scholarship on white racial attitudes, which tends to be impressed by the transformation in race relations that has taken place in the United States in the latter half of the twentieth century and optimistic about the future. In much of this work, America is portrayed as moving inexorably toward a racially integrated and egalitarian society. There are authoritative references to "revolutionary changes in ancient beliefs about Negroes,"[73] and to the "steady, massive growth in racial tolerance."[74] There is the confident inference that "white Americans have shown in many ways that they do not want a racist government and that they will not follow racist leaders."[75] The most recent report from the General Social Survey's monitoring of white racial attitudes begins with the characteristically sunny announcement that "despite widespread and vocal concerns about a resurgence of racism and the decline of support for civil rights during the 1980s, public support for racial equality continued to grow throughout the decade and, in 1990, support on many measures was at or near all time highs."[76]

Not to worry is the main message here. Prejudice is a problem, but a small and shrinking one; more impressive is the massive improvement in white attitudes. Reynolds Farley, in the conclusion to his superior review of the evidence on differences between blacks and whites in economic and social standing, expresses this point of view superbly:

> Whites have confronted the American dilemma described by Gunnar Myrdal and have accepted the principles that all should be allowed to vote and that blacks and whites should have equal opportunities for jobs and education. To be sure, racism is not dead. A small number of whites are still active in the Ku Klux Klan, crosses are still burned on the lawns of some blacks who dare to move into white neighborhoods, and proposals to build low-income housing or to integrate public schools still meet heated opposition. But no more than a small minority of whites would prefer to overturn the civil rights laws of the 1960s and go back to a legally segregated society.[77]

This is not so much wrong as it is incomplete. Real progress *has* taken place. As a rule, white Americans now reject the idea that blacks originate from an inferior race, and they accept equal opportunity and racial integration as matters of principle. These are genuine accomplishments—but there is more to be said, and more to worry over.

For one thing, we see no reason why biological racism might not return. In a scathing commentary on *A Common Destiny,* the National Academy of Sciences report on the condition of black Americans and the state of race relations today, the Harvard psychologist R. J. Herrnstein complained of the report's unwillingness to confront the possibility that racial differences in socioeconomic achievement or intellectual performance might be due to "differing average endowments of people in the two races."[78] Herrnstein argued that restrictions on public discourse and scientific investigation on matters of racial difference are both pervasive and powerful. In Herrnstein's view, to mention genetic explanations is "taboo in polite company"; "open discussion of the [genetic] model is our obscenity, much as public discussion of sexuality was the Victorian obscenity."[79]

Herrnstein has a point, even if he carries it too far. Liberal environmentalism did take over the social sciences, and no doubt did discourage the consideration of biological explanations for racial differences. But liberal environmentalism now seems to be in retreat. Biological and evolutionary models have made a considerable splash in recent years throughout the social sciences. Carl Degler argues that this revival of biological thought is politically innocent—and much of it appears to be.[80] Certainly it differs conspicuously from the flagrant racism of late nineteenth-century Social Darwinism. But Degler's thick and learned volume devotes only a dismissive footnote to the work of Arthur Jensen, the well-known Berkeley educational psychologist who has argued that racial differences in performance on intelligence tests should be understood in genetic terms.

And Degler's book was published too soon to take account of the ostentatious arrival of *The Bell Curve*, in which Herrnstein and Charles Murray imply, again and again, that racial differences in achievement and social standing are biologically based; and that in the face of this genetic imperative, social reform and government intervention are powerless.[81] *Newsweek* called *The Bell Curve* "frightening stuff," which it is, and worried that it "plays to public anxieties over crime, illegitimacy, welfare dependence, and racial friction," which it does. At the *National Review*, meanwhile, contributors to a symposium welcomed it as "magisterial," noting that it "confirms ordinary citizens' reasonable intuition that trying to engineer racial equality in the distribution of occupations and social positions runs against not racist prejudice but nature, which shows no such egalitarian distribution of talents." It is simply too early to tell whether or not Jensen and then Herrnstein and Murray represent the leading edge of what will turn into an outpouring of research, once again altering the mix of ideas about race circulating through American society. We may not have seen the last of biological racism.

Even if we have seen the last of biological racism, we surely have not seen the last of racial resentment. It may be comforting to equate prejudice with the doctrine of white supremacy and to imagine racists parading around in white sheets. Defined this way, prejudice is now confined primarily to the backwaters of white society and very well may be on the way out altogether. But the decline of blatant racial bigotry should not be equated with the disappearance of racial resentment. There is still plenty of that around, expressed in assumptions about black character. Informed by the individualistic virtues of hard work and self-reliance, racial resentment remains a very popular and exceedingly potent force in white opinion. More than 130 years after emancipation, on the eve of a new century, views on politics and society are still powerfully shaped by the black image in the white mind.

Matters of Principle

One strong current in the history of Western political thought, closely associated with Aristotle, insists that politics and morality never be divorced. Aristotle argued in the *Ethics* that moral judgments must be integrated into political life. In the *Politics,* he suggested that a necessary criterion for judging the worthiness of a governmental regime or constitution was whether it allowed a good man to be a good citizen. Our purpose here is to investigate the proposition that public opinion on matters of race is based in part on principles, much as Aristotle would have wished.

Our analysis takes for granted that people are neither detached nor indifferent to their world; that they "do not stop with a sheerly factual view of their experience. Explicitly or implicitly, they are continually regarding things as good or bad, pleasant or unpleasant, beautiful or ugly, appropriate or inappropriate, true or false, virtues or vices."[1] Americans, like people everywhere, engage in these kinds of normative assessments in politics as in other realms of human experience. Indeed, Americans may do this more than others; principles may play a more prominent role in American political life than elsewhere. For America, it is said, originated in a conscious political act, in the proclamation of certain basic political principles. And Americans, it is argued, are unified by a commitment to a "creed"—a set of governing principles that guides their views on politics and society. We are skeptical of such sweeping claims, but we shall see. Here we consider the possibility that public opinion on matters of race is influenced by core American principles, by the ideas of *equality, economic individualism,* and *limited government,* in particular.[2]

We take up these three and not others because each has received detailed attention in studies of the American political tradition. Each has played a prominent role in national debates on issues of race. Each is neither so general as to be vacuous nor so specific as to be of little use in guiding the variety of views that make up an outlook on politics.[3] And finally, each of the three provokes genuine disagreement. Not all Americans are swept away by the call of equality; not everyone takes hard work and individual initiative to be virtues; not all Americans think of the national government as encroaching on their rights. Differences on these general matters of principle may therefore translate into corresponding differences on specific matters of policy. That, at least, is the hypothesis that we bring to our analysis here.[4]

It may seem odd that we consider this a working hypothesis rather than a settled conclusion. Starting with Alexis de Tocqueville, many perceptive observers, liberal and conservative, white and black alike, have confidently placed these three themes at the center of the American political experience.[5] And yet we have just begun to accumulate systematic evidence on what ordinary Americans think about such principles—whether they think about them at all—and the extent to which they might take such principles into account as they reach their political views.

We believe that principles are important to opinion, but we want to begin our analysis cautiously, grounded in realistic expectations. Too often, it seems to us, principles are imbued with a kind of wondrous and awesome power. Sometimes it seems as if American principles did work on their own, that people had nothing to do with ideas, or at least that once ideas appeared on the scene, people could do little to stop them. By some accounts, the American Creed virtually defines the nation. More so than a common religion, ethnic heritage, or linguistic background, a commitment to principles is supposedly what unifies the American people. And if principles can define and build a nation, then why shouldn't they also provide the means for the country to overcome its most vexing problem, that of slavery and its lingering aftermath of racial conflict?

This is the position taken by Gunnar Myrdal, in his justly celebrated and massive study of American race relations, now fifty years old. Myrdal was shocked at the place of blacks in American society and impressed with how deeply entrenched were patterns of racial segregation and discrimination. Nevertheless, Myrdal emerged from his investigation optimistic about America's future, and his optimism derived from the power he invested in the American Creed: "Americans of all national origins, classes, regions, creeds, and colors, have something in common: a social *ethos*, a political creed. It is hard to avoid the judgment that this 'American Creed' is the cement in the structure of this great and disparate nation."[6]

For Myrdal, the creed was the ideological inheritance that drove American political development. As discrimination and prejudice were supported by "mere" tradition and interest, surely they would retreat in the face of the inexorably advancing creed, where "the American thinks, talks, and acts under the influence of high national and Christian precepts."[7] Myrdal's faith in the power of American principles to set things right is striking, given the object of his study, and also, we think, naive, but it is by no means unusual.[8]

A common companion to the claim that principles exercise an extraordinary power is the contention that they transcend their times. If not quite eternal, principles are often portrayed as if they were essentially unchanging. Thus Myrdal's reference to the American Creed, an ideological inheritance traced back in a straight line to Enlightenment ideals. Thus Lipset's influential argu-

ment that the entire length of American political history can be read as a perpetual struggle between two essentially fixed ideas, equality and achievement.[9]
Thus Tocqueville's observation that "two things are surprising in the United
States: the mutability of the greater part of human actions, and the singular
stability of certain principles. Men are in constant motion; the mind of man
appears almost unmoved."[10]

We don't think so. America is no longer a dependent colony but free and
independent, the world's only superpower. Where once the country was largely
rural and sparsely populated, it is now predominantly urban, industrial, and
heavily populated. At special moments and again now, the nation has faced the
challenge of absorbing huge numbers of "alien elements." Is it reasonable to
assume that in the face of all these dramatic transformations, the founding principles have somehow been perfectly preserved?

We believe to the contrary, that the core principles of equality, economic
individualism, and limited government are not fixed but evolving. Principles
are used in political argument, they help to shape political reality, and are themselves altered as certain constructions become obsolete and new political conditions arise. Like Rodgers, we believe that the history of political principles in
America is not a story of "a slowly unfolding tradition" but rather an account
of "contention, argument, and power." Like Rodgers, we are interested in how
principles are "put to use, and in this way fashioned and re-fashioned: not what
the American political tradition *means*, but how various aspects of the Creed
have been *used:* how they were employed and for what ends, how they rose in
power, withered, and collapsed, how they were invented, stolen for other ends,
remade, abandoned."[11]

Finally, we presume that opinions typically reflect conflict and compromise
among *multiple* principles. We do not wish to repeat the search for the Holy
Grail of ideology, the largely fruitless pursuit for the one sweeping ideological
idea that would unlock the mysteries of American public opinion that has so
preoccupied research over the last thirty years. Rather, we assume here multiple principles at play simultaneously. Opinions on race policy are likely to
reflect a person's thinking about the importance and desirability of equality, the
claim of individualism, the propriety of government intervention, and perhaps
more. People ordinarily take into account more than a single principle when
confronting public policy.

Not only is this the way things likely are, it's the way things should be, according to Robert Lane:

> Just as the person who is bound entirely by his ideology, so that
> experience does not have the power to change its elements, is an
> ideologue and unfree, so the person who governs all his policy rec-
> ommendations by a single value is close to "obsession" or borders

on "fixation" and is similarly unfree. The healthy person has multiple values, and he finds them often in conflict; his health is revealed in his toleration of the conflict and the means he chooses to reconcile the conflict, not in the way he makes all policy recommendations serve a single value, however economical that might be for him.[12]

Our framework takes Lane's point a few steps further. We also think that Americans take into account several principles, not just one. But we also insist that Americans are juggling other considerations as well: they are pursuing their own diverse interests, they are concerned about the interests of their group, and they are using policy questions as an opportunity to express their various social sympathies and resentments. All of these elements shape opinions on race policy. Principles play a role, but probably not the overriding one often attributed to them. Our analysis must be sensitive to the malleability and complexity of values and to the particular ways they may be constructed and activated in political debate. Mindful of these qualifications and warnings, our purpose now is to introduce the trio of distinctively American principles—equality, economic individualism, and limited government—that we suspect contribute to the views white and black Americans take on matters of public policy.

EQUALITY

Much writing on the American political tradition, and on American exceptionalism in particular, takes as a central fact what Alexis de Tocqueville referred to as the American "passion for equality." In the opening pages of *Democracy in America*, Tocqueville wrote that

> nothing struck me more forcibly than the general equality of condition among the people. I readily discovered the prodigious influences that this primary fact exercises on the whole course of society; it gives a peculiar direction to public opinion and a peculiar tenor to the laws; it imparts new maxims to the governing authorities and peculiar habits to the governed.
>
> The more I advanced in the study of American society, the more I perceived that this equality of condition is the fundamental fact from which all others seem to be derived and the central point at which all my observations constantly terminated.[13]

As usual, Tocqueville was on to something. Certainly by European standards, American politics and society were remarkably egalitarian, free of monarchy and aristocracy alike. The American revolutionaries renounced the authority of the British king and invested political power instead in republican institutions. American democratic customs in social affairs both delighted and shocked European sensibilities. Public education and universal suffrage came relatively early here. More generally, upheavals of reform that have punctuated American history—from the Revolution to Reconstruction to the campaign for women's suffrage to the civil rights movement—are often taken as evidence for Americans' special and recurring demand for more and more equality.[14]

Yet the American commitment to equality has never been complete. Alongside the passion for equality, Tocqueville detected evidence of a longing for aristocracy in America. While America may have seemed egalitarian from European perspectives, inequalities of practice and belief flourished here. Men were thought naturally suited to rule over women, at home and in the realm of politics; Protestants were regarded as theologically and morally superior to Catholics, Jews, and others; Americans of northern European ancestry were thought naturally better than those Americans who were here first.

Most conspicuous is the anomaly of race. Slavery, segregation, and racial discrimination stand as especially flagrant violations of the fabled American commitment to equality. According to Rogers Smith, celebrations of American egalitarianism must either treat the American racial experience as an aberration or ignore it altogether.[15]

Ambivalence and complexity also characterize the attitudes toward equality expressed by contemporary citizens. Americans differ over the importance and desirability of equality as a political ideal and as a practical reality, and these differences translate into sharp differences on matters of public policy.[16] In some ways this is mysterious, since, as Rae and his colleagues point out, equality

> is the simplest and most abstract of notions, yet the practices of the world are irremediably concrete and complex. How, imaginably, could the former govern the latter? Equality and other formal terms float freely across the layers of time, the points of the compass, the bounds of topical reference. Can we imagine that the simple, formal idea of equality contains enough information, enough specificity, enough texture, to be capable of direct and consistent application to a concrete, complex world?[17]

Of course not: equality is not and cannot be a single coherent program. The formal principle of equality fissions into many equalities of practice.[18]

Other analysts also recognize the complexity of equality in application, distinguishing among political, legal, social, and economic equalities; or differentiating among equality at work, in politics, and at home; or as Michael Walzer does in his defense of pluralism, arguing that the application of equality hinges decisively on the nature of the social good being allocated.[19]

The Measurement of Equality

An appeal to equality, because it seems so familiar, manages to say a lot and obscure a lot at the same time. Douglas Rae and his associates acknowledge this difficulty by suggesting that because equality means so many things, it may be more sensible to speak of *equalities*. Similarly, the six equality questions included as part of the 1986 and 1992 National Election Studies, presented below, probably refer to many things, and surely to more than one:

> *Our society should do whatever is necessary to make sure that everyone has an equal opportunity to succeed.*

> *We have gone too far in pushing equal rights in this country.*

> *One of the big problems in this country is that we don't give everyone an equal chance.*

> *This country would be better off if we worry less about how equal people are.*

> *It is not really that big of a problem if some people have more of a chance in life than others.*

> *If people were treated more equally in this country we would have many fewer problems.*

All six questions address the idea of equality. Each is abstract; each refers to a broad principle; none refers to any specific policy. But they address different aspects of equality. To our eyes, the questions differ most prominently in the kind of equality they seem to advocate.[20] Should equality be restricted to opportunities? Should it include rights? Should it extend further to cover results? Our questions concern different kinds of equality: the first, third, and fifth questions seem to us to refer primarily to equal opportunities, the fourth to equal rights, and the remaining pair to equal results.[21]

The findings presented in table 6.1 suggest that among these types, equality of opportunity is the most popular, among black and white Americans alike. Resoundingly, and indeed almost unanimously, Americans endorse the idea that "our society should do whatever is necessary to make sure everyone has an equal opportunity to succeed." Large proportions also agree with the other two propositions on equality of opportunity, though, especially among whites, with more qualification. Whites seem to be saying: try to insure equal opportunity, but should the effort fail, it is no disaster.

On the face of it, references to "equal rights" might seem comparatively innocuous. When equality is understood as formal or procedural, as in the Fourteenth and Fifteenth amendment guarantees of equal protection of the laws and the right to vote, equality seems relatively uncontroversial. But according to the opinions offered by both black and white Americans in response to our survey questions, guaranteeing equal rights appears to be more controversial than insuring equality of opportunity. In this, Americans may be harking back to the heated controversies surrounding the civil rights legislation of the nineteen sixties.

Table 6.1 Support for Equality among White and Black Americans

	Whites		Blacks	
	1986	1992	1986	1992
Our society should do whatever is necessary to make sure everyone has an equal opportunity to succeed.				
Agree strongly	62.7%	61.4%	84.5%	74.9%
Agree somewhat	25.6	28.9	10.5	20.6
Neither agree nor disagree	4.9	4.5	2.8	1.7
Disagree somewhat	4.7	3.7	1.5	1.4
Disagree strongly	2.1	1.5	0.6	1.4
We have gone too far in pushing equal rights in this country.				
Agree strongly	19.3	15.8	7.7	5.9
Agree somewhat	31.9	32.8	13.0	12.6
Neither agree nor disagree	17.0	16.0	11.1	11.9
Disagree somewhat	17.0	20.3	19.2	26.9
Disagree strongly	14.8	15.3	48.9	42.7
One of the big problems in this country is that we don't give everyone an equal chance.				
Agree strongly	19.4	27.1	58.8	62.7
Agree somewhat	28.3	32.8	22.6	25.8
Neither agree nor disagree	13.9	11.7	8.0	3.5
Disagree somewhat	26.7	20.3	4.6	5.2
Disagree strongly	11.7	8.0	5.9	2.8
This country would be better off if we worried less about how equal people are.				
Agree strongly	19.5	17.6	15.8	13.3
Agree somewhat	28.5	32.3	13.9	18.9
Neither agree nor disagree	18.4	12.4	8.4	9.1
Disagree somewhat	19.2	22.6	22.0	22.5
Disagree strongly	14.3	15.1	39.0	36.1
It is not really that big a problem if some people have more of a chance in life than others.				
Agree strongly	6.8	7.7	10.5	8.7
Agree somewhat	25.7	25.3	15.5	12.5
Neither agree nor disagree	21.2	16.1	12.1	11.5
Disagree somewhat	26.4	30.3	18.6	28.9
Disagree strongly	19.9	20.6	43.3	38.3
If people were treated more equally in this country we would have many fewer problems.				
Agree strongly	25.2	36.9	70.3	63.1
Agree somewhat	30.8	36.4	15.5	25.4
Neither agree nor disagree	18.5	11.4	5.9	6.6
Disagree somewhat	18.0	11.6	5.6	3.8
Disagree strongly	7.5	3.7	2.8	1.0

Source: 1986 and 1992 National Election Studies.

Equality of results (or treatment) goes beyond equality of opportunity and equal rights by scrutinizing distributive mechanisms that confer greater or lesser benefits upon individuals. Asking whether Americans are treated equally implicates questions of whether opportunities are really equal, and whether all have the same access to the rights guaranteed in the Constitution. Table 6.1 suggests that equality becomes a contested ideal in American political life really only here, where it is construed as equality of results. Black and white Americans seem genuinely divided among themselves when they are asked to say whether the country would be better off if we worried less about how equal people are.

Regardless of the kind of equality in question, black Americans are much more enthusiastic than white Americans are. The most striking feature of the results displayed in table 6.1 is the huge difference by race. Consider, for example, that while just 14.8% of whites strongly reject the claim that "we have gone too far in pushing equal rights in this country," 48.9% of blacks do (1986 NES data). Or that 36.9% of white Americans agree strongly that "if people were treated more equally in this country we would have far fewer problems," as against 63.1% of black Americans (from the 1992 NES). Comparable differences show up on each of the six questions, in 1986 and 1992, and in roughly equal measure. In all cases, support for equality as an aspiration and an ideal comes much more from blacks than from whites. "Equality," J. R. Pole wrote, "is normally the language of the underdog."[22]

This racial divide raises the question of whether we should regard ideas about equality as a general principle, as intended, or as equality for particular groups. When Americans say that they are unhappy that not everyone is given an equal chance, do they really have an abstract "everyone" in mind, or just some particular ones? When Americans say that the nation would be better off if people were treated more equally, are they thinking of people in general, or particular kinds of people? Later in this chapter, as a way of probing these questions, we will see whether ideas about equality influence opinion on race policy alone, or whether equality's influence is felt on redistributive policies in general.

ECONOMIC INDIVIDUALISM

Like equality, individualism occupies a place of privilege in standard accounts of American political culture. To James Bryce, individualism was among the American people's "choicest" and most "exclusive" possessions. More than a half a century later, the distinguished American historian Richard Hofstadter came to essentially the same conclusion. In America, Hofstadter argued, the "economic virtues of capitalist culture" were transformed and celebrated as the "necessary qualities" of mankind. More recently still, Robert Bellah and his associates launched their extended complaint against individualism with the sweeping assertion that "individualism lies at the very core of American culture." Individualism, according to Bellah, is our "first language." [23]

Despite these confident declarations, we are just now beginning to accumulate evidence on the importance of individualism in shaping Americans' views on matters of politics. The preliminary evidence we have in hand, moreover, is not always straightforward to interpret. The idea of individualism is notoriously complicated, embracing, as Weber once put it, "the utmost heterogeneity of meanings." [24] Because different conceptions give rise to different measures, it is not always obvious that those of us who claim to be undertaking empirical investigations of individualism are actually studying the same thing. Like equality and limited government, individualism is not one thing, but many. Here we will try to be clear about which individualism we have in mind.

Individualism is a nineteenth-century word, invented in the aftermath of the French Revolution. To conservative writers in Europe and Britain, individualism was a dangerous idea that meant the disintegration of social solidarity and the collapse of communal purpose. To them, the revolution was bloody proof of the social consequences of ideas that exalt the individual. Individualism was a menace; it threatened the stability of government and the harmony of traditional social relations. Overtaken by individualism, citizens become "rapacious wolves" and society disintegrates into "an unsocial, uncivil, unconnected chaos of elementary principles." [25]

In America, however, individualism was treated not as a threat but as a virtue. It came to stand for the beneficence of capitalism and the goodness of liberal democracy.[26] How such a perspective could develop was of course a central preoccupation of Weber's *Protestant Ethic and the Spirit of Capitalism*. Weber traces the origins of individualism to Puritan doctrines stressing the need for individuals to arrive at their own accounting with God. In such doctrine, as Weber made it out, work was transformed from a burden into a calling. Work became a vital form of moral activity, just as idleness became a sign of a fall from grace. Under Puritan doctrine, men were required to work in a profoundly new way: unceasingly, conscientiously, and diligently. Every moment had to be spent soberly and well.

In Weber's account, Puritans and Quakers carried this view to the new world as articles of faith, where it was reshaped in subtle ways, harnessed to the American experience. The idea of a calling faded from common speech and with it the idea that in work one labored in the first instance for the glory of God. Instead, work served the national purpose. An intense, nervous fear of idleness filled the sermons and essays of nineteenth-century American moralists. Only work could provide protection against sexuality, despair, violence, and radicalism.

This American inclination to define the moral life as a "mustering of the will against the temptations within and the trials without" was commonly joined to the American dream of success. The nineteenth century witnessed a massive production of popular literature on behalf of the argument that hard work, effort, and determination were the keys to wealth and position. We were a nation of self-made men, or so we were told: "No boy, howsoever lowly—the barefoot country boy, the humble newsboy, the child of the tenement—need despair. . . . They have but to master the knack of economy, thrift, honesty, and perseverance, and success is theirs." Such was the advice provided the nation by John D. Rockefeller, and it was echoed in countless sermons, homilies, and popular tracts.

The sanctity of work, and especially the moral stain attached to idleness, survived the dramatic transformations industrialization brought to nineteenth-century American society.[27] As the work ethic became an increasingly abstract ideal, further and further divorced from the reality of work itself, Americans clung to their faith in work as the moral center of life ever more tenaciously. The morally charged language of work and idleness became the "distinctive propaganda of industrial America," put to use by publicists of all political persuasions. Socialists denounced capitalists for their idleness, pointing to "their delicate hands, their yachts and horses, and their ample, brocaded bellies." Conservatives saw in every radical proposal "some device that would enable the idle and incompetent to live at the expense of the frugal and the industrious." European immigrants were regarded as "bummers" and "dead heads," failures who had no place in America. Labor union strikes were portrayed by their opponents as "organized idleness." Thus all political perspectives helped to fashion idleness into "one of the most popular weapons in the arsenal of rhetorical invectives."[28]

The worldly asceticism that Weber identified in Puritan thought is of course now rather difficult to detect in the American consumer culture. Still, most Americans continue to subscribe to the intrinsic values of exertion and hard work. Idleness is still a moral defect; hard work, in and of itself, a moral virtue; dependence on others a disreputable condition, one that ought to be avoided.[29]

Moreover, such sentiments appear to figure prominently in many Americans' opposition to various manifestations of the modern welfare state. For example, when Americans are asked what runs through their minds as they answer questions on social welfare policy, they refer often to individualistic themes: people should make it on their own; they should be responsible for themselves; welfare induces dependency; the poor deserve their poverty; some people are just naturally lazy; work induces pride and self-esteem; welfare is unfair to those who work. Such references carry a moral charge and, not surprisingly, are expressed more often by the opponents of such policies than by supporters. What is surprising is how prominent such sentiments are even among those who favor more generous welfare programs, a sign of the difficulty that redistributive policies face in the United States.[30] Other investigations reveal that those Americans who subscribe to the view that hard work pays off are less inclined than others to support an expansion of government services or to see a role for government in providing a decent standard of living.[31] Popular remedies for poverty also bear the stamp of individualistic thinking: the prevalent view is that economic hardships can and should be surmounted primarily through individual enterprise.[32]

The Measurement of Economic Individualism

Taken all together, the evidence suggests that individualistic principles are an important part of American thinking on social welfare policy. The ambivalence and hesitation that have long characterized the American version of the modern welfare state is perhaps reflected in the American public's enthusiasm for individualism. But notice that the survey evidence we have reviewed does not speak directly to public opinion on policies in the realm of race. Does individualism in fact provide a principled foundation for white opposition to egalitarian policies on racial matters? We simply don't know.[33] The current state of the evidence also provides us no guidance on the role of individualism in black public opinion. It is these two gaps in our understanding that our analysis seeks to fill, making use of the following questions taken from the 1986 NES:

Most people who don't get ahead should not blame the system; they have only themselves to blame.

Hard work offers little guarantee of success.

If people work hard they almost always get what they want.

Most people who do not get ahead in life probably work as hard as people who do.

Any person who is willing to work hard has a good chance at succeeding.

Even if people try hard they often cannot reach their goals.

The core idea running through these questions is the extent to which, in American society, effort is repaid. The underlying concept is what we will call economic individualism, more specifically, beliefs about the degree to which individual striving finds its just reward. The questions therefore provide only selective coverage of the broader and more complex idea of individualism. In partial compensation, the questions are coherent, they center on an important theme, and taken all around, they suggest the priority given to the abstract individual in classical formulations of individualism. Their major drawback, as we see it, is that they are formulated for the most part as matters of rather neutral and unemotional belief. The questions are not, with the exception of the first on the list, morally charged. They do not probe reactions to work and idleness treated as ethical categories; they do not inquire as to whether hard work *should* be rewarded. We would have preferred more questions in the spirit of the first, which raises the issue of blame and does so in moralistic language. We must live with the questions dealt us, but we should keep our sense of limitations alive as we proceed with the analysis.[34]

Responses to the various economic individualism questions are summarized in table 6.2, separately for white and black Americans. The results suggest that on balance, Americans generally support the idea of economic individualism. Most Americans, white and black, agree that people who fail to get ahead have only themselves to blame; that, in America, anyone who is willing to try hard has a good chance of finding a place in the sun. Not everyone subscribes to the sentimental view expressed by John D. Rockefeller—that children born to poverty need only "master the knack of economy, thrift, honesty, and perseverance, and success is theirs"—but there is nevertheless running through these questions a persistent faith in the virtue and practicality of hard work.

Striking by contrast to the case of equality, we see virtually no race differences on individualism. Americans generally believe in economic individualism, and this is as true for blacks as it is for whites. On some questions, whites express slightly more faith in hard work; on others, slightly less. But on a scale of economic individualism, based on a combination of answers to all six questions, we detect scarcely any race difference at all.[35] This result is hardly decisive by itself, but it does challenge the popular view that black Americans suffer from a culture of dependency, that the American virtues of self-reliance and individual effort apply to whites alone. We find little support for that here. Whether economic individualism influences opinions on policy is another matter, of course, one that we will get to shortly.

LIMITED GOVERNMENT

Ever since Jefferson's famous announcement at the dawn of the American republic—"That government is best which governs least"—suspicion of government power has been a staple of American political thought. Indeed, Samuel Huntington places Jefferson's claim at the precise center of the American political tradition. In no other society, Huntington asserts, is suspicion of government power such a widespread and deeply ingrained habit. While acknowledging that American ideology encompasses an amalgam of contradictory ideas, Huntington nevertheless insists that such ideas "do have a common thread and import for the relations between society and government: all the varying elements in the American Creed unite in imposing limits on power

Table 6.2 Support for Economic Individualism among White and Black Americans

	Whites	Blacks
Most people who don't get ahead shouldn't blame the system; they have only themselves to blame.		
Agree strongly	25.1%	25.0%
Agree somewhat	47.4	37.5
Neither agree nor disagree	12.2	11.7
Disagree somewhat	11.7	12.7
Disagree strongly	3.7	4.6
Hard work offers little guarantee of success.		
Agree strongly	10.8	14.4
Agree somewhat	26.1	33.8
Neither agree nor disagree	10.1	10.0
Disagree somewhat	32.8	26.3
Disagree strongly	20.3	15.6
If people work hard they almost always get what they want.		
Agree strongly	16.1	22.0
Agree somewhat	39.4	32.7
Neither agree nor disagree	11.9	8.8
Disagree somewhat	26.0	23.9
Disagree strongly	6.6	12.6
Most people who do not get ahead in life probably work as hard as people who do.		
Agree strongly	10.7	26.3
Agree somewhat	28.7	26.9
Neither agree nor disagree	14.3	14.4
Disagree somewhat	32.6	31.1
Disagree strongly	13.7	10.0
Any person who is willing to work hard has a good chance of succeeding.		
Agree strongly	42.5	56.6
Agree somewhat	43.6	28.3
Neither agree nor disagree	5.4	6.9
Disagree somewhat	7.1	5.7
Disagree strongly	1.3	2.5
Even if people try hard they often cannot reach their goals.		
Agree strongly	19.4	28.8
Agree somewhat	56.3	44.4
Neither agree nor disagree	10.2	10.0
Disagree somewhat	10.9	13.1
Disagree strongly	3.2	3.8

Source: 1986 National Election Study.

and on the institutions of government." Huntington goes on to say, even more flatly, that "the distinctive aspect of the American Creed it its antigovernment character. Opposition to power, and suspicion of government as the most dangerous embodiment of power, are the central themes of American political thought."[36]

Huntington overstates the case, but suspicion of government power does occupy an important place in contemporary American opinion, and it does have a distinguished history in classical liberal thought. The view that the purpose of government is to protect individuals' rights and allow them maximum scope to pursue their own interests owes much to Locke. Lockean liberalism stresses a view of government as restricted in scope and constrained in practice. Government was an institution best conceived of as an instrument for the defense of the "life, liberty, and estate" of its citizens, its authority conditional on the consent of the governed. Politics was a distinct, separate, and limited sphere, one set apart from economy, culture, and home.[37]

For a time, this idea of limited government was joined and strengthened by the doctrine of laissez-faire, the somewhat more specific idea that government interference in the market economy should be held to a bare minimum. Laissez-faire had its origins in the economic theories of Adam Smith and David Ricardo as they were promoted in mid-nineteenth-century England but was consistent with the views championed by such distinguished and prominent Americans as Jefferson and Emerson. Laissez-faire had an obvious affinity for American individualism. Both held that individuals should bear sole responsibility for their own economic affairs and should neither seek nor receive assistance from government.

According to Arieli, such ideas reigned virtually unchallenged through the nineteenth century, and then took an extreme turn toward the end of century with the triumph of Social Darwinism.[38] As interpreted by Herbert Spencer and William Graham Sumner, Darwin's *On the Origin of Species*, published in 1859, seemed to offer a scientific rationale for a ruthlessly competitive society. Competition was glorious, selecting for success those with the greatest store of economic virtue: as Sumner put it, those possessed of "courage, enterprise, good training, intelligence, and perseverance."[39] Survival of the fittest carries society forward, favors all its best members, and gives no reason to worry over those left behind. Thus Spencer argued against virtually all forms of state interference in economy, culture, and family, and against the Poor Laws in particular, since "the whole effort of nature is to get rid of them [the poor], to clear the world of them, and make room for better."[40]

Darwin's ideas were also seized upon by American racists bent on promoting the idea of the permanent inferiority of the black race. Toward the turn of the century, from accomplished natural scientists, physicians, statisticians, and demographers poured forth confident and authoritative predictions of black extinction through natural causes. Following emancipation and the protection that slavery had afforded them, blacks, now on their own, sank into disease, sexual vice, crime, and indolence. Absent the discipline provided by slavery, young Negroes were "reverting through hereditary forces to savagery."[41] Applied to "the Negro problem," social Darwinism was at once an attack upon the policies of Reconstruction, an explanation for freed blacks' "reversion to savagery" that was so obvious to scientific observers, and a justification for even more repressive policies still to come.

As we learned in Chapter 5, such biological forms of racism have for the most part disappeared from popular commentary (and from white Americans' attitudes). But according to Huntington, the distinct and more general opposition to government power ran unabated through the twentieth century. To Huntington, "Government was still conceived of as the servant of society; the idea of the state as a legitimizing authoritative entity remained foreign to American thinking."[42]

This is too simple. It ignores the decline in popularity of laissez-faire ideas. By the late 19th century, as wealth and power became more concentrated in corporate hands, disagreements began to spill into the public realm. Progressive reformers, intellectuals, and spokesmen for the working class began to call for government to intervene in the economy and to remedy the social ills an unfettered market seemed to produce. It ignores as well the blow struck against free market doctrines by John Maynard Keynes, whose *General Theory of Employment, Interest, and Money*, published in 1936, transformed economic theory and economic policy for generations to come. And most conspicuously, it ignores the fact that the responsibilities and powers of the central government grew enormously through the twentieth century. Washington now provides pensions and subsidies and services at a level unimaginable in an earlier era. Americans have come to expect, if not depend on, an interventionist state.

Does this mean that suspicion of central government authority has disappeared from the American scene? Absolutely not. It is clearly present in the rise to power of the Republican right, in the views of free marketeers such as Milton Friedman who argue that the effects of government policies are nullified by the workings of the market, in the popular idea that the government in Washington regularly, if not inevitably, makes a mess of things, and in the continual appeal of what Hirschman calls the "perversity argument": that progressive reforms, however well intentioned, always backfire.[43]

According to survey evidence of various sorts, Americans' views on limited government are mixed. They are conservative in the abstract, in that they don't like the idea of big government, but they are liberal programmatically, supporting a wide array of particular policies and regulations that require government intervention.[44] The evidence also suggests that abstract opposition to a powerful national government tends to go along with a tendency to oppose government policies designed to benefit blacks in particular.[45] This evidence is restricted for the most part to the views held by white Americans, the analysis is not always as rigorous as we would like, and the effects are often small. Still, the results suggest the plausibility that public opinion on race has a principled foundation in ideas about the proper scope of government power.

The Measurement of Limited Government

Measurement is always an imperfect business, but the questions available to assess the theme of limited government seem to us rather more imperfect than most. We make use of two kinds of questions. The first, available in a pair of items that appear in both the 1986 and 1992 National Election Studies, assumes that the principle of limited government can be revealed by consistent opposition to government policies. One of the pair refers to government's obligation to provide services in general; the other refers to the federal government's responsibility to guarantee the economic welfare of its citizens:

> Some people think the government should provide fewer services, even in areas such as health and education, in order to reduce spending. Other people feel it is important for the government to provide many more services even if it means an increase in spending. Where would you place yourself on this scale?

> Some people feel the government in Washington should see to it that every person has a job and a good standard of living. Others think the government should just let each person get ahead on their own. Where would you place yourself on this scale?

The obvious worry here is that these questions may pick up both an attitude about government in general and more specific opinions elicited by particular policies and groups. A minimal test for treating these questions as a measure of the more general sentiment about government is that responses to them be correlated—and they are. Citizens who favor the expansion of government services also tend to think it is the government's responsibility to provide citizens a good standard of living.[46]

As table 6.3 shows, Americans do not appear to be all that suspicious about government, at least as revealed by their answers to these questions. They are quite divided over whether government services should be cut back, and divided as well over the government's responsibility for citizens' economic welfare. What we have here appears to be a case at least as much of programmatic liberalism as it is of abstract conservatism.

In exploring the theme of limited government, we will also make use of

Table 6.3 Support for Limited Government among White and Black Americans

	Whites		Blacks	
	1986	1992	1986	1992
Some people think the government should provide fewer services, even in areas such as health and education, in order to reduce spending. Others feel it is important for the government to provide many more services even if it means an increase in spending.				
Government should provide many fewer services; reduce spending a lot	4.5%	5.3%	5.3%	1.9%
*	7.2	8.8	1.2	2.2
*	14.2	13.7	4.0	6.6
* Intermediate positions	36.4	44.7	24.8	42.1
*	18.0	15.1	15.5	16.7
*	10.9	6.6	12.9	12.6
Government should provide many more services; increase spending a lot	8.8	5.8	30.1	17.9
Some people feel the government in Washington should see to it that every person has a job and a good standard of living. Others think the government should just let each person get ahead on their own.				
Government see to a job and a good standard of living	6.6	6.3	30.7	20.4
*	4.7	7.2	13.5	10.1
*	8.8	9.7	6.1	13.5
* Intermediate positions	28.0	31.6	27.6	34.9
*	17.8	18.7	8.0	11.0
*	15.7	13.5	6.1	4.1
Government let each person get ahead on own	18.3	12.9	8.0	6.0
One, the less government the better; or two, there are more things that government should be doing.				
Less government	—	37.4	—	10.8
Both, depends	—	4.1	—	2.8
Do more	—	58.5	—	86.5
One, we need a strong government to handle today's complex economic problems; or two, the free market can handle these problems without government being involved.				
Strong government	—	65.9	—	81.6
Both, depends	—	6.9	—	8.0
Free market	—	27.2	—	10.4
One, the main reason that government has gotten bigger over the years is because it has gotten involved in things that people should do for themselves; or two, government has gotten bigger because the problems we face have been getting bigger.				
People should do for themselves	—	40.0	—	17.0
Both, depends	—	7.5	—	5.9
Bigger problems	—	52.5	—	77.1

Source: 1986 and 1992 National Election Studies.

instrumentation included for the first time in the 1992 NES. These questions are formulated more abstractly, at a level above policies, and so resemble more closely our assessment of the principles of equality and individualism:

One, the less government the better; or two, there are more things that government should be doing?

One, we need a strong government to handle today's complex economic problems; or two, the free market can handle these problems without government being involved.

One, the main reason that government has gotten bigger over the years is because it has gotten involved in things that people should do for themselves; or two, government has gotten bigger because the problems we face have been getting bigger.[47]

The central issue raised by these questions is whether a strong central government is desirable. Many Americans think that it is. That is, many disagree with Jefferson, that the less government the better; many reject the claim that economic problems would dissolve if the market were left alone to work its magic; and many resist the notion that government has taken over responsibilities better left to the initiative of private citizens. And they do so reasonably consistently, as if they were in possession of a settled view about government as a matter of principle.[48] On these questions at least, Americans seem quite free of the deep suspicions of government power that Huntington places at the center of our political tradition.

In referring to Americans, we do not mean to gloss over the racial differences apparent in table 6.3, differences that are every bit as large as those that emerged on equality. Limited government is much more popular among white Americans than among black Americans. This shows up on all questions, whether formulated as matters of principle or as matters of policy, in both 1986 and 1992. For example, in 1986, while just 8.8% of whites supported the idea that government should provide many more services, 30.1% of blacks did. Or consider that in 1992, 37.4% of white Americans subscribed to Jefferson's view that the less government the better, as against just 10.8% of black Americans. In every case, the idea that government should be constrained and limited is prized much more by whites than by blacks.[49]

This result raises again the question of the extent to which our measures are tapping a general and abstract principle. As in the case of equality, we will want to examine the scope of limited government. Do Americans' views on limited government have across-the-board effects on opinion, which would support the conclusion that we have measured limited government as a general, abstract principle? Or do we find that views on limited government have narrow and specific effects, which would support the conclusion that our measure of limited government is less a general, abstract principle and more a specific orientation, contingent perhaps most of all upon for whom government is acting?

IMPACT OF PRINCIPLES ON PUBLIC OPINION

Equality, economic individualism, and limited government seem to represent distinctive and separate ideas. But it could be that the three are highly related—so highly related that we should consider them to be indistinguishable parts of the same ideological package. Perhaps what we have been writing about in this chapter, and trying to measure, is not so much a set of distinct principles as one general point of view, perhaps even the fabled American Creed itself.

One simple way to find out is to compute correlations between the three principles. We report these results in table 6.4, separately for blacks and whites. As indicated there, the structure of empirical relationships among the several political principles is similar for whites and blacks, and it follows the form we would expect. For whites and blacks alike, faith in economic individualism goes together with support for limited government, and both these ideas are opposed by belief in equality. Perhaps most important, the correlations shown in table 6.4 support the conclusion of loose linkages between the three principles. Equality, economic individualism, and limited government are related to one another, but the relationships are quite modest; they fall well short of what would be required for claims about such sweeping abstractions as the American Creed. The modesty of the correlations also increases the likelihood that the three principles will have separate and independent effects on matters of opinion, our next and most important topic.[50]

Table 6.4 Relationships between Political Principles among White and Black Americans (Pearson r)

	Whites			
	1986		1992	
	Economic individualism	Limited government	Economic individualism	Limited government
Equality	−.14	−.39	—	−.32
Economic individualism	—	.25	—	—
	Blacks			
	1986		1992	
	Economic individualism	Limited government	Economic individualism	Limited government
Equality	−.24	−.31	—	−.12
Economic individualism	—	.19	—	—

Source: 1986 and 1992 National Election Studies.

Table 6.5 Effect of Whites' Belief in Equality, Economic Individualism, and Limited Government on Their Opinions on Racial Policy

	Federal Responsibility		Equal Opportunity		Affirmative Action	
	Special effort	Federal spending	Integrated schools	Fair employment	Hiring	College admissions
Equality	.23	.25	.47	.31	.08	.04
	(.05)	(.06)	(.12)	(.12)	(.06)	(.07)
Economic	−.05	−.01	.09	.01	.00	−.01
individualism	(.05)	(.06)	(.12)	(.12)	(.06)	(.08)
Limited	.23	.25	.35	.34	.17	.26
government	(.04)	(.05)	(.10)	(.10)	(.05)	(.06)
R-squared	.30	.25	.25	.24	.20	.22
Standard error	.22	.27	.43	.44	.27	.33
Number of cases	804	836	545	567	814	832

Source: 1986 National Election Study.
Note: Table entry is B, the unstandardized ordinary least squares regression coefficient, with standard errors in parentheses underneath. All variables coded 0–1. Each equation also included measures of racial resentment and social background.

Impact of Principles on White Opinion

We begin with whites' racial views, as assessed by the familiar policy questions included in the 1986 NES. In addition to the three political principles, our analysis takes into account the effects due to racial resentment and social background. As usual, we estimate these effects with regression, and we code each variable on the 0–1 scale in such a way that positive coefficients are predicted in all cases.[51] The results are shown in table 6.5.

Indicated there first of all is a reasonably strong effect due to equality. Whites who subscribe to egalitarian ideals tend to favor policies intended to narrow inequalities between the races. The effect of equality is especially noteworthy on school integration and fair employment, issues that exemplify the struggle to bring equal opportunity to life. Equality's imprint is also visible on federal obligations to blacks. On affirmative action, however, equality disappears entirely.[52]

A roughly similar pattern holds for limited government, though it takes a less drastic form. Here we see modest to strong effects, in the expected direction. Whites who oppose the interventions of government in general tend to oppose interventions on behalf of blacks in particular. The effects are most apparent where the issues are posed as whether or not the federal government should act—specifically to ensure school integration and to guarantee equal opportunity in employment. The effects of limited government are somewhat diminished on affirmative action, but in some ways it is interesting that the effects show up here at all, since neither affirmative action question mentions government.

The empirical record for economic individualism reported in table 6.5 is altogether different. In the case of economic individualism, we turn up no positive evidence whatsoever. The coefficient on the economic individualism term never approaches statistical significance. It is smallest (and takes the wrong sign) precisely where we would expect it be largest: on whether the federal government is obliged to provide special assistance to blacks or, rather, blacks should make it on their own. Formulated this way, the policy would seem to play directly into economic individualism. Nevertheless, we see no evidence that whites' opinions on this policy are influenced by their views on individualism. Taken overall, the average effect over the six policies is a practically perfect .00.[53]

We can undertake a partial replication of all these results by moving on to the 1992 NES. The replication is partial because the 1992 NES did not include measures of economic individualism, in part for empirical reasons of the sort we have just reviewed. In some ways this is regrettable, since we would have welcomed another opportunity to test the idea that faith in individualism contributes to conservative positions on matters of race. But if our 1986 results are correct in documenting the irrelevance of economic individualism to white opinion on race—and these results are replicated in the fine grain in our analysis of the 1985 NES—then the omission of individualism in the 1992 study is not troubling.[54] In particular, the exclusion of economic individualism in 1992 should not distort our estimates of the effects due to equality and limited government. And analyzing the 1992 NES has two clear advantages: first, the 1992 study includes a measure of limited government formulated as an abstract principle; and second, the 1992 NES carries a rich set of policy questions outside the realm of race, which we will take advantage of a little later on. With the exception of the necessary disappearance of economic individualism, we estimate the effects of principles on public opinion in 1992 just as we did in 1986. We begin with the measure of limited government expressed as consistent opposition to federal interventionist policies, as we were required to do in 1986.

The results, presented in table 6.6, suggest that principles play a substantial role in white opinion on racial issues in 1992. Notice first that the coefficients indexing the importance of equality are roughly the same size in 1992 as in 1986, and they assume the identical pattern. In 1992, the impact of equality is greatest on the issues of school integration and fair employment, as in 1986; intermediate on issues involving federal responsibility for blacks' welfare, just as before; and fades away rather completely on matters of affirmative action, as in 1986.[55] Taken all around, the results from our analysis of the 1992 NES strongly reinforce those based in the 1986 study. In combination, they support the conclusion that egalitarian ideals figure prominently in white opinion on racial poli-

Table 6.6 Effect of Whites' Belief in Equality and Limited Government on Their Opinions on Racial Policy

	Federal Responsibility		Equal Opportunity		Affirmative Action	
	Special effort	Federal spending	Integrated schools	Fair em- ployment	Hiring	College admissions
Equality	.10	.23	.57	.54	.02	.11
	(.04)	(.05)	(.08)	(.08)	(.05)	(.05)
Limited	.36	.22	.22	.23	.02	.10
government	(.03)	(.05)	(.07)	(.07)	(.04)	(.04)
R-squared	.34	.26	.20	.25	.20	.26
Standard error	.23	.29	.44	.44	.27	.31
Number of cases	1,236	1,683	1,175	1,193	1,204	1,722

Source: 1992 National Election Study.
Note: Table entry is *B*, the unstandardized ordinary least squares regression coefficient, with standard errors in parentheses underneath. All variables coded 0–1. Each equation also included measures of racial resentment and social background.

cies, especially those policies that aim to guarantee equality of opportunity to Americans regardless of color.[56]

Where limited government is concerned, the results do not repeat themselves quite so neatly. As in 1986, we find modest and mostly consistent effects of limited government on white opinion on racial matters. Compared with 1986, however, the differences are somewhat less impressive on integrated schools and fair employment, and a good bit less impressive for affirmative action policies. These changes produce a different overall picture in 1992, one that is more in keeping with our original expectations. As we began this analysis, we thought that whether private employers choose to pursue some version of affirmative action in their hiring practices would not engage views on government; likewise, whether colleges and universities reserve openings for black students is not the same question as what the policies of the government should be. The disappearance of limited government from the affirmative action equations in 1992 is consistent with these expectations. According to the 1992 results, white opinion on racial policies reflects broader views on the role of government insofar as the policies have their origin clearly and conspicuously in the authority of the federal government.

So much for limited government expressed as consistent opposition to particular government interventions. In the 1992 NES, we can also assess the importance of limited government expressed in terms of abstract opposition. The two forms of limited government are reasonably well correlated, so it would be surprising if we did not find roughly the same results across the two.[57] In fact, when we repeated the analysis summarized in table 6.6, substituting the one measure of limited government for the other, similar results are just what we find. Indeed, on integrated schools, fair employment, preferential hiring, and college quotas, the estimated effects of limited government are virtually identical. Whether we assess this sentiment through consistent opposition to federal policies or through abstract opposition to big government, the impact of limited government is modest on equal opportunity policies and invisible on affirmative action. The one difference comes on issues of federal responsibility, especially on the question of whether the federal government should make special efforts on behalf of blacks, where the estimated effect of limited government is greater when opposition to federal power is measured as a reaction to concrete policies. Even with this one discrepancy, however, the various results support the same broad conclusion: white opposition to racial policy draws in part on the American suspicion of government as an instrument for social change.[58]

Impact of Principles on Black Opinion

Next we take up the importance of political principles for black opinion on matters of race, following essentially the same procedures set out above in our analysis of white opinion. We begin, as before, with the familiar race policy questions first included in the 1986 NES. Our first round of regression analysis estimates the independent effects of equality, economic individualism, and limited government while controlling on the effects due to self-interest, group interest, and a variety of social background characteristics. The 1986 results are presented in table 6.7.[59]

Shining up out of table 6.7 is the clear importance of equality. Despite the small sample size (and therefore imprecision in our estimates), the regression coefficient on equality surpasses statistical significance in three cases, and in substantive terms, the effect is noteworthy in four. If anything, the effects due

Table 6.7 Effect of Blacks' Belief in Equality, Economic Individualism, and Limited Government on Their Opinions on Racial Policy

	Federal Responsibility		Equal Opportunity		Affirmative Action	
	Special effort	Federal spending	Integrated schools	Fair employment	Hiring	College admissions
Equality	.47	.17	.45	.43	.29	.03
	(.17)	(.15)	(.19)	(.17)	(.23)	(.21)
Economic	.29	−.03	−.15	.01	−.17	−.01
individualism	(.14)	(.13)	(.16)	(.14)	(.20)	(.18)
Limited	.14	.17	.22	.13	.14	.14
government	(.11)	(.10)	(.12)	(.11)	(.15)	(.14)
R-squared	.20	.14	.16	.09	.08	.05
Standard error	.28	.25	.31	.28	.40	.36
Number of cases	138	138	138	138	138	138

Source: 1986 National Election Study.
Note: Table entry is B, the unstandardized ordinary least squares regression coefficient, with standard errors in parentheses underneath. All variables coded 0–1. Each equation also included measures of interests and social background.

to equality are more impressive for blacks than they are for whites (compare the top rows of tables 6.5 and 6.7). In a pattern that resembles the results for whites, blacks' beliefs about equality were most important for their opinions on school integration and fair employment, and faded away completely in just one place, on racial quotas in college admissions.

In the third row of table 6.7, we see that blacks who oppose the interventions of government in general tend to oppose interventions on behalf of their racial group in particular. These are modest effects—indeed, we can be confident that the effect is real in just one case, on the question of whether or not the federal government should intervene to ensure integration of the public schools—but they are consistent. According to these results, opposition to government intervention plays a small but regular role in black opinion on matters of race.

Finally are the results for economic individualism, which look nearly as dreary for blacks as they did for whites. A clear effect shows up in just one case. We had anticipated that ideas about economic individualism would have their biggest impact on whether the federal government was obliged to make special efforts for blacks, or whether blacks should get ahead on their own. And, as table 6.7 reveals, this turned out to be true. Elsewhere, however, the effect of economic individualism was essentially zero. Black opinion on policy in the domain of race, like white opinion, appears to have little to do with faith in hard work.[60]

Replication of these results is especially important, since our 1986 sample of blacks is small. The 1985 NES pilot study cannot help us: it provides too few black Americans to sustain even the simplest analysis. Thus we turn immediately to the 1992 NES, with its large and representative sample. In the spirit of replication, we follow as closely as we can our 1986 analysis.

The 1992 results, shown in table 6.8, tell a familiar story. As before, equality comes booming through. Black Americans' opinions on issues of race are powerfully shaped by their views on matters of equality. In 1992 the effects of equality are noteworthy even in the case of affirmative action in college admissions, the one place where the equality thesis faltered in our 1986 analysis.[61]

Meanwhile, limited government also influences black opinion on racial policy in 1992. Indeed, running against the tendency we noticed in our analysis of white opinion, the impact of limited government is more apparent in 1992 than in 1986. The effect of limited government is quite strong on affirmative action, as it was not in 1986, and it is very strong—perhaps suspiciously strong—on the particular question of whether the federal government is obliged to make special efforts for black Americans.[62] We would have liked to check these results with the abstract version of limited government available in the 1992 NES, as we did in our analysis of white opinion. In contrast to the case for whites, how-

Table 6.8 Effect of Blacks' Belief in Equality and Limited Government on Their Opinions on Racial Policy

	Federal Responsibility		Equal Opportunity		Affirmative Action	
	Special effort	Federal spending	Integrated schools	Fair employment	Hiring	College admissions
Equality	.23	.22	.26	.50	.09	.45
	(.10)	(.09)	(.13)	(.10)	(.15)	(.13)
Limited	−.67	.21	.20	.16	.30	.36
government	(.09)	(.08)	(.12)	(.09)	(.14)	(.12)
R-squared	.20	.05	.03	.09	.11	.13
Standard error	.28	.25	.36	.30	.41	.36
Number of cases	285	285	286	284	280	282

Source: 1992 National Election Study.
Note: Table entry is B, the unstandardized ordinary least squares regression coefficient, with standard errors in parentheses underneath. All variables coded 0–1. Each equation also included measures of social background.

ever, black views on limited government elicited by the three abstract questions added to the 1992 NES were poorly correlated with each other and were virtually uncorrelated with the measure of limited government based on reactions to specific policies.[63] Given this state of affairs, it is perhaps not surprising that when we repeated the analysis summarized in table 6.8, substituting the one measure of limited government for the other, the estimated effect of limited government collapses to zero. We take these particular results to reflect less on the real role of limited government in black opinion, and more on our inability to measure such beliefs well.

At a more general level, we interpret the 1992 results as confirming our results from the 1986 NES. On issues of race, black opinion, like its white counterpart, is partly, but importantly, a reflection of principle. Equality most of all, limited government to some extent, and in special circumstances, economic individualism, all are implicated and entangled in public opinion in affairs of race.

Equal Opportunity and Public Opinion outside the Racial Realm

Of the three values we have examined, our results leave us most impressed with the importance of equality. Differences of opinion on topical matters of race can often be traced to differences over equality. But these same results do little to settle what it is, exactly, that equality means. We are especially interested in trying to determine the extent to which equality represents an abstract principle, as against sympathy for a particular group. This question comes up for blacks and whites alike. In both instances we want to know whether the strong connections we see in the domain of race reflect a general commitment to equality in principle, or a belief in equality for black Americans in particular.

Our question simply is: equality for whom? That we find strong effects of equality on opinion regarding policy within the racial domain does not help us; we need to extend our analysis beyond race. Are views on equality just as important for redistributive and rights policies generally as they are for policies intended to narrow racial inequalities specifically?

Our answer takes advantage of the rich variety of policy questions included in the 1992 NES. The results for whites are presented in table 6.9; comparable results for blacks are presented in table 6.10.[64] In both instances, the findings are organized around seven clusters of issues. Starting at the top of each table and proceeding downward, these are: first, the familiar race policy items, included for purposes of comparison (the coefficients in the first row of tables 6.9 and 6.10 are simply lifted from tables 6.6 and 6.8); next, covert racial issues (e.g., remedies for "urban unrest"); then social spending that would go primarily to the poor (e.g., federal spending on the homeless); next, programs targeted at the elderly (e.g., federal support for Medicare); next, social programs with broad mandates and huge constituencies (e.g., government support for public education); next, issues involving minority rights (e.g., protecting gays and lesbians from discrimination at work); and finally, issues that have arisen around immigration (e.g., loosen restrictions on entry). Taken all together, the issues on display in tables 6.9 and 6.10 roam over a large territory, but each arguably raises questions of equality. And diversity over issues is precisely what we want here, since our object is to assess how far ideas about equality reach.

The answer for white Americans is that equality reaches a long way. The effects of equality are not confined to policy questions in the realm of race, whether explicit or covert. As table 6.9 makes plain, the importance of equality is also perfectly clear on a variety of policies that would redistribute resources—to the poor, to the elderly, and to the working and middle classes, generally. Even more impressive, perhaps, are the effects of equality on abortion, on sexual harassment, and especially on the need for laws to guarantee gays and lesbians freedom from discrimination in the work place. On such questions, ideas on equality have much to say.

Thus various groups, not blacks alone, are part of white Americans' wish for a more egalitarian society. The list includes women, the elderly, the poor and working class, gays and lesbians, and perhaps children. The list is long, but it omits immigrants. Egalitarians do not support easing immigration restrictions, nor are they more opposed to the establishment of English as an official language. Equality seems to mean, then, equality for *us*, not for *them*.

The results for black Americans, shown in table 6.10, resemble in most important respects the results we have just reviewed for white Americans. For blacks as for whites, ideas about equality have broad range and wide application. And in one interesting case—that of school choice—the role of equality

Table 6.9 Effect of Whites' Belief in Equality on Their Opinion on Policy beyond the Realm of Race

Policy	B (SE)
Special Effort	.10 (.04)
Federal Spending	.23 (.05)
Integrated Schools	.57 (.08)
Fair Employment	.54 (.08)
Preferential Hiring	.02 (.05)
College Admissions	.11 (.05)
Welfare	.15 (.05)
Remedies for Urban Unrest	.19 (.05)
Sanctions against South Africa	.43 (.12)
Food Stamps	.08 (.05)
Poor	.27 (.05)
Medicare	.20 (.04)
Social Security	.16 (.05)
Homeless	.28 (.04)
Child Care	.24 (.04)
Health Insurance	.22 (.05)
Education	.22 (.04)
Sexual Harassment	.26 (.06)
Gay Rights	.50 (.07)
School Choice	.15 (.10)
Abortion	.26 (.05)
Restricting Immigration	.07 (.03)
English Official Language	.11 (.08)

Source: 1986 and 1992 NES.

Note: Table entry is B, the unstandardized form of the ordinary least squares regression coefficient, with standard errors in parentheses underneath. All variables coded 0–1. All results come from the 1992 NES, except for policy on South Africa, which comes from the 1986 NES. Each regression equation included measures of racial resentment and social background.

Table 6.10 Effect of Blacks' Belief in Equality on Their Opinion on Policy beyond the Realm of Race

Policy	B (SE)
Special Effort	.36 (.11)
Food Stamps	.20 (.11)
Homeless	.13 (.08)
Education	.34 (.08)
Abortion	.30 (.13)
Federal Spending	.26 (.09)
Welfare	.17 (.13)
Poor	.24 (.09)
Sexual Harassment	.16 (.13)
Restricting Immigration	−.13 (.09)
Integrated Schools	.28 (.14)
Remedies for Urban Unrest	.41 (.11)
Child Care	.28 (.10)
Fair Employment	.52 (.11)
Medicare	.14 (.08)
Gay Rights	.40 (.14)
Preferential Hiring	.15 (.15)
Sanctions against South Africa	.52 (.17)
Social Security	.14 (.09)
Health Insurance	.40 (.11)
School Choice	.59 (.19)
English Official Language	−.47 (.11)
College Admissions	.55 (.14)

Source: 1986 and 1992 NES.

Note: Table entry is *B*, the unstandardized form of the ordinary least squares regression coefficient, with standard errors in parentheses underneath. All variables coded 0–1. All results come from the 1992 NES, except for policy on South Africa, which comes from the 1986 NES. Each regression equation included measures of racial resentment and social background.

was dramatically more pronounced for blacks. From the black perspective, school choice looks like a program to deny equal opportunity. School choice proposals have been criticized on the grounds that they would have the effect of subverting integration of the public schools. We seem to be detecting more than a whiff of that criticism here, in black opposition to school choice. The racial difference could hardly be sharper: it implies that whites and blacks understand the issue of school choice in fundamentally different ways.

A second racial difference worth noting concerns immigration. In the case of white Americans, equality proved to be generally irrelevant to opinion on various facets of immigration policy. Thus, in the last row of table 6.9 the coefficients fade to zero. But for black Americans, the coefficients do not go to zero; they change sign. It is not that equality is irrelevant to immigration; it is that the direction of the relationship contradicts our expectations. Egalitarians were *more* likely, not less, to favor tougher restrictions on immigration; and were *more* enthusiastic, not less, about establishing English as an official language. Among blacks, increased immigration seems to threaten equal opportunity.

These racial differences are interesting, but they should not distract us from the larger lesson. For black and white Americans alike, equality appears to be an idea of broad range, encompassing a wide variety of groups and issues. Equality appears to be, in short, not an utterly abstract and empty pronouncement, and not merely a plank in a platform, but something in between: a principle.

Limited Government and Public Opinion outside the Racial Realm

We can ask precisely the same question of limited government that we have just asked of equal opportunity. The motivating facts in the two cases are roughly the same: first, we have produced rather impressive results on the power of limited government to shape opinion on race policy; and second, we have discovered that the doctrine of limited government is much less popular among black Americans than among white Americans. Now, finally, we want to know the extent to which limited government represents a general principle as against a position regarding government intervention on behalf of black Americans in particular. As in the case of equality, our answer comes from an analysis of the rich array of policy questions available in the 1992 NES. In fact, the results of this analysis, on display in tables 6.11 (for whites) and 6.12 (for blacks), are derived from the identical equations that gave rise to tables 6.9 and 6.10 for equality. The analysis is identical, but the tables are arranged a bit differently for limited government, since the policies that we deemed relevant to the theme of limited government overlap with, but are not identical to, those useful for testing the empirical scope of equality.

Table 6.11 Effect of Whites' Belief in Limited Government on Their Opinion on Policy beyond the Realm of Race

Special Effort	Federal Spending	Integrated Schools	Fair Employment
.36	.22	.22	.23
(.04)	(.05)	(.07)	(.07)

Food Stamps	Welfare	Remedies for Urban Unrest
.39	.48	.26
(.05)	(.04)	(.05)

Homeless	Poor	Medicare	Social Security	Education	Child Care
.41	.47	.28	.28	.31	.42
(.03)	(.04)	(.04)	(.04)	(.03)	(.04)

Sexual Harassment	Gay Rights
.16	.27
(.05)	(.06)

Source: 1992 NES.
Note: Table entry is *B*, the unstandardized form of the ordinary least squares regression coefficient, with standard errors in parentheses underneath. All variables coded 0–1. Each regression equation included measures of racial resentment and social background.

The results for white Americans suggest that, like equal opportunity, limited government should be understood to be a principle, one with considerable scope. Limited government clearly applies to opinions on explicitly racial policy that originate in the actions of the federal government (top row), and to domestic versions of covert racial issues as well: Food Stamps, welfare benefits, and remedies for urban unrest (second row of the table). But the real test for limited government comes in the next two rows, and it is a test that it passes with flying colors. According to these results, limited government figures prominently in white opinion on a variety of social programs. On aid to the homeless, assistance to the poor, on Medicare and social security, on federal support for child care and education, whites who indicate skepticism, if not hostility, toward government intervention are strongly inclined to oppose the policy in each instance. Indeed, the effects of limited government are more impressive here than they are on matters of race. And finally, in the bottom row of table 6.11, we see that white Americans who believe in limited government as a general matter are also less inclined to support government legislation against sexual harassment or to protect gays and lesbians from discrimination at work. We say "believe in limited government as a general matter" because that seems to be just what we have discovered. Among white Americans, limited government applies not to just one group, or one kind of policy, but broadly and generally.

The same cannot be said for black Americans. These results are presented in table 6.12. Among black Americans, there is a precipitous falloff in the impact

Table 6.12 Effect of Blacks' Belief in Limited Government on Their Opinion on Policy beyond the Realm of Race

Special Effort	Federal Spending	Integrated Schools	Fair Employment
.67	.21	.20	.16
(.09)	(.08)	(.12)	(.09)

Food Stamps	Welfare	Remedies for Urban Unrest
.41	.26	.32
(.10)	(.11)	(.09)

Homeless	Poor	Medicare	Social Security	Education	Child Care
.09	.12	.06	.11	.07	.05
(.07)	(.05)	(.07)	(.08)	(.07)	(.09)

Sexual Harassment	Gay Rights
.07	−.03
(.10)	(.13)

Source: 1992 NES.
Note: Table entry is B, the unstandardized form of the ordinary least squares regression coefficient, with standard errors in parentheses underneath. All variables coded 0–1. Each regression equation included measures of social background.

of limited government outside the realm of race. On overt and covert racial issues, limited government plays a strong role in black opinion. But once outside the domain of race, its role virtually evaporates. For example, whether the government should provide more assistance to the poor, or whether legislation is required to protect women against sexual harassment, is almost completely unconnected to blacks' views on government in general. In the case of black Americans, then, we should not say "government in general," since here limited government appears to be less an abstract principle and more a position on the federal government's responsibility to black citizens in particular.[65]

CONCLUSIONS AND IMPLICATIONS

In scores of commentaries over more than a century, principles have been given a prominent place in the analysis of American politics, and none more than the three we have just examined: equality, economic individualism, and limited government. Bold claims are not the same as systematic evidence, of course, and it is systematic evidence (of a particular kind) that we have done our best to supply here.

In some respects, what we found supports the widespread and apparently growing enthusiasm for principles as a way to understand American public opinion. Principles do matter; they are, by our evidence at least, an important part of the story of public opinion. This is particularly true for equality, but it also applies, if less forcefully, for limited government. Our results stand up well to replication, and they hold for black Americans as for whites.

Principles matter, then, but the imprint they leave on opinion is not uniformly strong. Indeed, in the case of economic individualism, the imprint is faint almost to the vanishing point. But even more generally, the effects that we manage to turn up here have a contingency and specificity about them that are out of keeping with the common portrayal of principles as unstoppable forces that level all opposition. Equality may be, as Douglas Rae and his colleagues maintain, "the most distinctive and compelling element of our national ideology," but not all Americans find equality compelling.[66] And it may even be that, as Huntington would have it, "Opposition to power, and suspicion of government as the most dangerous embodiment of power, are the central themes of American political thought," but not all Americans seem to regard government as dangerous, and even when they do, they do not necessarily take such sentiments into account as they form opinions on policy.[67] In their modesty and specificity, our results do not measure up all that well to the grand declarations often made on behalf of American political principles.

Modesty and specificity do not trouble us, of course. We would have been surprised had things turned out the other way. We don't mean to imply that we were clear-eyed about exactly what form such contingency and specificity would take. There were more than a few surprises, and two seem worth noting here.

The first concerns equality. Of the three principles we examined, equality loomed the largest in public opinion on matters of race. What we find most impressive is not so much that equality made a large difference as that the magnitude of equality's effect depended so acutely on exactly which issues were under consideration. In Chapter 2 we suggested that the six race policy questions examined in greatest detail here reflect three distinct, but closely related, facets of current debate. But what we took to be rather fine distinctions among the three related domains the American public obviously takes very seriously: we see this in the highly variable role played by equality across the domains. Equality is extremely important when it comes to school desegregation and fair employment, the two issues that best represent the struggle for equal rights and opportunities carried forward by the civil rights movement. It is perhaps not surprising that the principle of equality would enter most forcefully into public opinion on precisely these questions. But the extent to which this is true, for whites and blacks alike, in 1992 and in 1986, is surprising.

At the same time, equality simply disappears from public opinion on issues of affirmative action. This disappearance is instructive: it tells us something both about affirmative action and about equality; it suggests that opponents and supporters of affirmative action can enlist equality as justification for their views. Opponents can reject affirmative action in the name of equality by arguing that affirmative action violates equal treatment; supporters can embrace affirmative action in the name of equality by arguing that affirmative action brings the formal idea of equal opportunity to life. Equality is complicated and elastic; it can be stretched to more than one use, "furnishing rival interests," as Pole once wrote, "with equally satisfying terms of moral reference."[68]

Yet another surprise was the quite spectacular failure of economic individualism. Faith that hard work brings success has very little to do with opinions on matters of race. This holds generally for whites as for blacks, and in the 1985 NES data as in the major study of opinion on issues of race undertaken by NES in 1986. These results challenge the contention that contemporary debate over affirmative action and welfare reform is first and foremost a discussion about the virtues of hard work and individual responsibility.[69]

Finally, that principles matter at all in public opinion implies a particular conception of politics, one that puts justification and discussion at the center of political life. Stoker puts this point well:

> Politics is not simply an arena where citizen preferences are articulated and aggregated but one where public goals and policies are debated and political goals must be publicly justified. When citizens assess public policies, events, and leaders or consider their own political choices, they are not merely trying to figure out what or who they like or what it is they want. They are also trying to figure out what or who is *good* and what is *right*.[70]

This figuring out of what is right is complicated business. When Stoker asserts that politics takes place in public arenas where goals and policies are debated and justified, she reminds us that citizens in a demoncracy are not on their own; that indeed they might be on the receiving end of a fair amount of help as they try to draw connections between principles and policies. Such assistance is in fact being constantly supplied by political elites, who are always searching for advantageous ways to structure public debate. By framing issues in particular ways, elites hope to induce citizens to make particular connections, to see how certain policies embody (or violate) certain of their principles. With this in mind, it is to political elites and the issue frames they are continually promoting that we turn next.

PART III

FRAMES AND CAMPAIGNS

CHAPTER SEVEN

Framing the Issue: Elite Discourse
and Popular Understanding

In 1990, liberals in Congress introduced legislation intended to strengthen federal protection against racial discrimination in employment. They referred to their bill as the Civil Rights Bill of 1990 and argued that it was necessary to counteract a series of recent Supreme Court decisions that had made it more difficult to prove discrimination. Edward Kennedy in the Senate and Augustus Hawkins in the House portrayed the bill as a straightforward extension of the Civil Rights Act of 1964, required in 1990 because of the persistence of racial discrimination. In their view, America's commitment to equal opportunity was incomplete. Detractors of the bill, most notably George Bush, then president of the United States, disagreed, arguing that the pending legislation was in fact a perversion of American principles. Bush maintained that the bill would coerce employers to establish hiring quotas; that the bill was not about civil rights at all, but about "quotas, quotas, quotas." William Bennett, then national chairman of the Republican National Committee, backed the president up, calling quotas "contemptible," and arguing that the bill would reward blacks for mediocre achievement and institutionalize expectations of racial inferiority. For Bennett as for the president, blacks should compete without favor in an American society that was now free of racial discrimination.[1]

In one respect, at least, the debate over the 1990 Civil Rights Bill—or was it the 1990 Quota Bill?—was utterly commonplace: just another example of the words and symbols that swirl around any public issue. Advocates always try to define issues their way, hoping that others, including the general public, will find their formulations persuasive. The press reports the debate and, as it does so, necessarily if unconsciously privileges some definitions at the expense of others.

Here we want to suggest that such debate among elites—what we will call momentarily a war of *frames*—is a central component of public opinion. For public opinion depends not only on the circumstances and sentiments of individual citizens—their interests, feelings toward social groups, and their political principles—but also on the ongoing debate among elites. This debate becomes available to citizens in a multitude of ways: through the reporting of daily events in television news programs, newspapers, and radio; through editorials, syndicated columns, political talk shows, cartoons, newsletters, and the like; and most directly through press conferences, debates, advertisements, speeches, and so forth. Through all these channels, individual citizens are bombarded with suggestions about how issues should be understood. The issues taken up by government are always complex; they are always subject to alternative interpretations. What exactly is affirmative action? Is it reverse discrimination? Is it compensation for the injustices of the past? Is it a giveaway that blacks do not deserve? Which of these interpretations prevails in popular discourse may substantially affect how citizens understand affirmative action and, in the end, what their opinions on affirmative action turn out to be.

How citizens understand an issue, which features of it are central and which are peripheral, is reflected in how the issue is framed. Allowing for some variation in definition, the concept of frame is currently at the center of a variety of high profile theoretical projects scattered across the social sciences. Our analysis borrows (this is a polite term for it) most from William Gamson.[2] Gamson presumes, as we do, that politics are in part a competition of ideas. Every issue is contested; advocates of one persuasion or another attempt to define the issue their way. At the heart of each issue definition is a frame: "a central organizing idea or story line that provides meaning to an unfolding strip of events, weaving a connection among them. The frame suggests what the controversy is about, the essence of the issue."[3] Thus the Arab-Israeli conflict might be framed as a matter of U.S. strategic interests, or as the struggle of a tiny, embattled nation surrounded by hostile forces, or as a fight between two liberation movements. The debate over abortion policy might be couched in terms of a woman's right to choose or as the fetus's right to life. AIDS might be portrayed as a lethal disease that poses a dire public health threat or as divine retribution for sinful habits. As these examples are meant to suggest, alternative frames are never even-handed: they define what the essential problem is and how to think about it; often they suggest what, if anything, should be done to fix it.

In our analysis, frames lead a double life. As we have suggested so far, frames are interpretive structures embedded in political discourse. In this use, frames are rhetorical weapons created and sharpened by political elites to advance their interests and ideologies. Perhaps more often, they are implicit and unconscious, journalistic habits rather than explicit attempts to persuade. Either way, frames are a central part of political debate.

At the same time, frames also live inside the mind; they are cognitive structures that help individual citizens make sense of the issues that animate political life. They provide order and meaning; they make the world beyond direct experience seem natural. Without a frame in mind, citizens are likely to be bewildered by political debate; it will appear to them as "one great, blooming, buzzing confusion."[4]

Citizens occasionally generate frames on their own, but for the most part we believe frames are assembled and promoted by others. They are the creation of a handful of intellectuals and activists, then brought to public attention by issue entrepreneurs and journalists. No doubt elites create and promote frames with public reaction very much in mind. And citizens certainly may reject frames they dislike and rework those they adopt. But by and large, citizens consume frames rather then produce them.[5]

We intend to show here that frames, conceived of in this fashion, are consequential: that public opinion on race—and, by implication, public opinion generally—depends in a systematic and intelligible way on how the issues are framed. We investigate this proposition through a sequence of experiments. In each, we ask respondents for their views on the same policy, but framed in alternative ways. We compose these alternative frames carefully; our project requires that they mimic the rival frames that prevail in contemporary elite discourse. Because our goal is to understand the relationship between elite discourse and public opinion, we must formulate our policy questions in a way that captures the essence of the ongoing debate among rival elites. By examining the kinds of alterations in opinion that are set in motion by variations in question wording that reenact the ongoing debate among elites, we can learn about how changes in public opinion are induced by changes in the setting beyond the survey, in everyday public discussion.[6]

Or so we say. We develop and test this line of argument in four experiments. The first is taken from the 1989 NES and explores whether public opinion on government programs for black Americans deteriorates in the absence of popular debate, when elites and institutions fail to provide citizens with frames that might aid their understanding. The second experiment, drawn from the 1985 NES, investigates whether the foundations of public opinion on affirmative action can be altered by supplying citizens with alternative frames. And the third and fourth experiments, one based in the 1988 NES, the other taken from the 1990 General Social Survey, examine whether public support for egalitarian policies is enhanced under issue frames that direct attention to inequalities of class rather than race. Before we get to the studies themselves, we should first say a few words about experimentation in general.

REENACTING ELITE DISCOURSE THROUGH EXPERIMENTS IN QUESTION WORDING

In the summer preceding the otherwise forgettable 1924 presidential contest between Calvin Coolidge and John W. Davis, Harold Gosnell decided to conduct an experiment.[7] He assigned neighborhoods lying within twelve typical districts in the city of Chicago to one of two conditions. Residents living in neighborhoods designated as experimental were sent postcards that pointed out voter registration deadlines and locations, and went on to suggest that citizens of Chicago who failed to exercise their sacred right to vote were little different from the "slackers" who refused to defend their country in time of war. Residents of otherwise comparable neighborhoods assigned to the control condition, meanwhile, were left alone. Come election day, about 8% more of the experimental group than the control group made it to the polls. The result confirmed Gosnell's hunch that turnout could be increased through information and exhortation. But decades later, we remember his research less for the finding than for the method. Way ahead of his time, Gosnell tested his hypothesis through experimental means, by actively intervening in the political process.[8]

It is this feature of intervention, and the control that such intervention brings, that distinguishes experimental research from other systematic empirical methods. In the fully realized experiment, the investigator arranges settings in order to exclude various nuisance factors, creates treatments so as to isolate precisely the relevant causal factor (or factors) of interest, and schedules observations in such a way as to reduce the likelihood that the measured effects are contaminated by other causes. Perhaps most important, in true experiments, it is the investigator who determines which subjects receive which treatments. The investigator decides this not by intuition or convenience but by deliberately turning assignment over to chance. By assigning subjects to treatments randomly, the experimenter can be assured that any observed differences between conditions is due to differences in the treatments themselves. Absent random assignment, there is no way to guarantee equivalence of groups before the treatments are applied. In a single stroke, then, random assignment sweeps aside a host of possible alternative interpretations. It is, as Cook and Campbell put it, "the great *ceteris paribus* of causal inference."[9]

Like all empirical methods, experimentation has its liabilities as well as its strengths. When it comes to internal validity—providing unequivocal evidence on causal relationships—experiments really have no serious competition. But on matters of external validity—providing assurance about the generalizability of results—experiments are generally less persuasive. Concern about the external validity of experimental results finds various expression, but the standard complaint, and the most powerful, questions the typicality of experimental subjects. Many experiments are conducted with samples of convenience: most notably, for social scientists situated in universities, the local student body. This leads to understandable skepticism over whether experimental results can be generalized to broader populations. After all, as Carl Hovland warned some years ago, the typical college sophomore may be a rather peculiar creature.[10]

This line of argument poses a serious challenge to some experiments, but it does no damage to ours. For our experiments are carried out within national surveys that go to unusual lengths to ensure that their samples resemble as closely as possible the national population of voting age citizens. For a study of elite frames and public opinion, this is of course precisely the population of real interest.[11]

Enough, in general, about experimentation. The proof, as always, is in the pudding—here, in the four particular experiments that we have cooked up to probe the impact of frames on public opinion on matters of race. Our experiments take as their point of departure the notion that those of us who design surveys find ourselves in roughly the same position as elites who create and promote the terms of political discourse. Both of us must decide how public issues are to be thought about and discussed. By examining the kinds of alterations in opinion that are induced by systematic alterations in the way that questions are framed within the survey, we hope to learn how public opinion is shaped by the conversation that takes place between leaders and citizens in democratic societies.

EXPERIMENT I: FRAMED VERSUS STRIPPED OPINION

Informing our first experiment are long-standing disputes about the capacity of ordinary people to participate in their own governance. Democracy—rule by the people—can be justified only on the assumption that average citizens are, in general, qualified to govern themselves. At the core of arguments for democracy is what Dahl calls the presumption of personal autonomy: "In the absence of a compelling showing to the contrary, everyone should be assumed to be the best judge of his or her own good or interests."[12] The same point is reflected in John Dewey's insistence that asking people what they want, not telling them what they need or what is good for them, is "an essential part of the democratic idea."[13]

Many perceptive analysts of politics have questioned whether citizens really are up to the demands of democracy. H. L. Mencken, for one, wrote that "democracy is the theory that the common people know what they want, and deserve to get it good and hard."[14] Mencken's cynicism took a particularly sour form, but on the general point he was hardly alone. Walter Lippmann, Joseph Schumpeter, and most recently Philip Converse have all expressed strong reservations about the political capacity of ordinary citizens in modern mass society. Converse made his case with evidence, in a series of brilliant papers based upon the analysis of national surveys carried out in the 1950s, concluding that most Americans glance at public life innocent of ideological concepts and unguided by any broad outlook on government policy.

It may be that Americans are innocent of sweeping ideological ideas, but they are hardly innocent of personal and political considerations that bear on matters of public debate. As we have seen over the last three chapters, the American political mind is not so much empty as it is teeming with potentially relevant considerations: the interests at stake, feelings of resentment or sympathy toward social groups, general views on equality and the intrusive (or commendable) interventions of government, and no doubt more. This same point is made nicely in Jennifer Hochschild's in-depth discussions with ordinary Americans about justice in politics, the workplace, and at home. On the one hand, the people Hochschild interviewed display the same symptoms that Converse detected: inconsistency, hesitation, ambivalence, confusion and more. On the other hand, their fundamental problem was not that they had no ideas about taxes or unemployment or income distribution, but that they had too many. They suffered not so much from a shortage of relevant considerations, as from an impoverished ability to integrate them. What they lacked, perhaps, were frames.[15]

Insofar as elite debate provides useful frames, citizens will be more likely to develop informed opinions. With helpful frames in mind, citizens should be better able to overcome their ambivalence and arrive at an overall position. Experiment I tests this claim by comparing public opinion on government assistance to blacks elicited in one of two ways: either by a question that referred explicitly to the rival frames that dominate elite discourse, the "framed" treatment, or by a question that did not, the "stripped" treatment. Here the framed treatment mimics the political condition in which citizens witness a debate between opposing elites, each pushing an alternative definition of the issue. Meanwhile, the stripped treatment is intended to simulate the political condition where there is no elite debate, where citizens are on their own in formulating what the issue is about. We expected that opinion on government assistance to black Americans elicited under framed conditions would differ systematically from opinion elicited under stripped conditions, that it would display the benefits of democratic debate.

More specifically, we expected, first, that such opinion would be more widespread: when asked the framed version of the question, more citizens would express an opinion. Second, that such opinion would be more stable: when asked the framed version of the question, more people would take the same position from one occasion to the next. Third, that such opinion would be more consequential: when citizens are asked the framed version of the question, their views on government assistance would better predict their evaluations of prominent public officials who themselves are identified with a particular position on government assistance. And fourth, that such opinion would be better anchored: when citizens are asked the framed version of the question, their views on government assistance would be predicted better by the interests, group resentments, and political principles that the frame highlighted. In short, framed opinions should more closely resemble the real opinions that democracy would seem to demand of citizens. Finally, while our expectations refer to citizens and public opinion, much of our analysis is limited, regrettably, to white citizens and white public opinion. Experiment I was embedded within the modest-sized 1989 NES pilot study, which included interviews with just fifty-eight black Americans—too few to support any but the simplest of comparisons.

Respondents to the 1989 NES were randomly assigned to one of two experimental groups. Citizens assigned to the first (n = 300) were asked about the desirability of government assistance to blacks in a way that reminded them of the dominant justifications for and against the policy. Drawing primarily on the work of Gamson and Modigliani, we took the dominant supportive frame to be that blacks lack opportunities; the dominant oppositional frame we understood to be undeserved advantage. Hence the question suggests that government assistance might be supported out of a belief that blacks are still denied equal opportunity, and that government help might be opposed out of the sense that blacks should get ahead on their own, without any special advantages, as other groups had presumably done before them.[16]

Citizens assigned to the second experimental condition (n = 314) were asked the same question and were offered the same response alternatives, but this time the question was stripped of any justification either for or against government help. In this condition, the issue comes to citizens unframed; they are much more on their own in trying to determine what the issue is really about. Here are the two versions of the question, with the differences between them highlighted in italics:

FRAMED

Some people feel that the government in Washington should make a special effort to improve the social and economic position of blacks, *because blacks still don't have the same opportunities to get ahead as everyone else.* Others feel that the government should not make any special effort to help blacks; *that blacks should help themselves, just as other groups have done.* Do you have an opinion on this issue, or haven't you thought much about it?

STRIPPED

Some people feel that the government in Washington should make a special effort to improve the social and economic position of blacks, while others feel that the government should not make any special effort to help blacks. Do you have an opinion on this issue, or haven't you thought much about it?

Before our four hypotheses about framed versus stripped opinions can be tested, it is necessary first to establish that respondents randomly assigned to the two conditions are actually comparable. It would of course complicate things if one group were more liberal, or more educated, than the other. With this worry in mind, we undertook a series of comparisons, examining the two groups on a full roster of standard demographic and political variables. The results are reassuring on the point that the two groups really are comparable, that the only feature that sets them apart is the experimentally induced one: some citizens were asked to think about government assistance to black Americans under relatively enriched circumstances, while others were asked to think about the same policy under relatively impoverished conditions.[17]

The Expression of Opinion

That citizens are reluctant to provide answers to some of the questions they encounter in the course of a political survey is due, at least in part, to the way questions are posed. In particular, citizens might not know quite how to think about an issue when it comes at them free of context. But when the issue is presented within a familiar frame, they might more readily give an answer. With a friendly frame in mind, citizens should be better equipped to integrate various competing considerations, to overcome ambivalence, and to arrive at an overall position.

To test this hypothesis, we simply distinguished between those NES respondents who declared that they had no opinion on the issue of government assistance to blacks and those who declared that they did, irrespective of what their opinion might be. We did so separately within the framed and stripped conditions to see whether opinions were more likely to appear when the issue was framed. The results conform to expectations. Whites were significantly more likely to express an opinion on government assistance to blacks when the issue was framed than when it was stripped: 69.4% took a position when the issue was framed compared to 58.0% when it was not.[18]

More opinions aren't necessarily a good thing, of course. Are the additional views expressed under the framed condition real opinions? Or are they flimsy fabrications, created by the momentary presence of persuasive-sounding frames? We cannot settle this question decisively with the evidence in hand, but we are inclined toward the former characterization, that the opinions are real and should be taken seriously. When we repeated the analysis just reported, after first partitioning respondents by level of political information, we found that the presence of frames produced more opinions even among the comparatively well informed. Another way to put this result is that frames facilitated the expression of opinions among citizens in general, not just among "know-nothings." Frames, it would seem, help citizens find their political voice.

The Stability of Opinion

It was the observation of flagrant instability in public opinion that led Converse to the troubling conclusion that on many pressing matters of public debate, citizens possessed not real attitudes but nonattitudes. Here we suggest that unstable opinions may be a reflection in part of fluctuations in the way the issue is framed or, more likely, the absence of a guiding frame altogether. If citizens are left to their own devices, their views on government assistance to blacks might be shaped on one occasion by concerns over interests, on another by considerations that special assistance violates equality, and on still a third primarily by feelings of group resentment. Such cycles might be broken by framing the issue consistently, as we did in the 1989 NES, where the same citizens were questioned first in July and then again in September. On both occasions they were asked about government assistance to blacks, and on both occasions in the identical way. In July and in September, citizens randomly assigned to the framed condition were invited to think about government assistance as a matter of squelched opportunities versus equality of treatment. If these frames were in fact successful in inducing people to think about the issue in the same way, then opinion should be more stable across the two interviews in the framed than in the stripped condition.

Alas, it seems not to be. Our calculation of the Pearson correlation coefficient, r, between the July and September responses to the government assistance question, separately under framed and stripped conditions, provides another case of a plausible hypothesis running into inconvenient facts. By this test, the presence of frames does nothing to enhance the stability of opinion. Indeed, the Pearson correlation is slightly higher in the stripped condition (.74 versus .70), though the two are statistically indistinguishable. Much the same conclusion is obtained if we simply calculate the percentage of respondents who expressed exactly the same view on both occasions. In this case, framed responses show more consistency than stripped responses, in line with our expectation, but the difference is small (62.0% versus 58.7%) and in statistical terms impossible to distinguish from no difference at all. With different issues, or with different formulations, frames may increase opinion stability, but we see little evidence of that here.

The Consequences of Opinion

Next we examined the impact of whites' opinions on the federal government's obligation to blacks on their evaluations of a quartet of prominent public

Table 7.1 Effect of Whites' Opinions on Government Assistance to Blacks on Their Evaluation of Prominent Political Leaders, by Issue Frame

	Stripped	Framed
Bush	.087	.138
	(.055)	(.055)
Dukakis	−.079	−.126
	(.059)	(.063)
Jackson	−.162	−.314
	(.065)	(.066)
Reagan	.135	.141
	(.060)	(.060)

Source: 1989 National Election Study.
Note: Table entry is the unstandardized regression coefficient, with standard errors in parentheses. Each of the estimated effects shown in the table controls on the effects due to age, region, education, gender, level of political information, ideological identification, and party identification, all measured in the 1988 National Election Study. All variables are coded on the 0–1 interval.

figures: George Bush, Michael Dukakis, Jesse Jackson, and Ronald Reagan, the four principals from the just-concluded 1988 presidential campaign. To the extent our frames faithfully reflected the nature of elite debate, framed opinions should predict sentiments toward Bush and company better than stripped opinions.

And they do. Table 7.1 presents the relevant results. The column on the left corresponds to the impact due to opinions on government help to blacks in the stripped condition, and the column on the right corresponds to the impact of such opinions in the framed condition. Impact is given by the unstandardized ordinary least squares regression coefficient. The coefficient estimates the effect of whites' opinions on government assistance to blacks on their evaluations of each of the four political leaders, controlling on the effects due to social background and political outlook.[19]

Notice that the coefficients are positive for Republican leaders and negative for the Democrats, as they should be. Whites who say that blacks should get ahead on their own tend to admire Bush and Reagan and dislike Dukakis and Jackson, while the sympathies of whites who believe that the federal government has a special obligation to black Americans run in the opposite direction. Among the four leaders, opinions on the issue figure most prominently in evaluations of Jesse Jackson, himself black and closely identified with the plight of the black poor.

These are sensible patterns, but the real news in table 7.1 has to do with the greater power of the issue of government assistance when it is framed. Among white Americans, opinions on assistance to blacks took on greater significance when elicited by a framed question. This was true in each of the four tests, though the increase was trivial in evaluations of Reagan and modest for both Bush and Dukakis. It was most pronounced in evaluations of Jackson: there the impact due to opinions on government assistance to blacks nearly doubled (from −.162 in the stripped condition to −.314 in the framed). These results suggest again that frames may help citizens discover their views. In the presence of familiar frames, citizens are better able to assemble an opinion that is connected to how they feel about the commanding political personalities of the day.

The Antecedents of Opinion

Our fourth and final analysis of Experiment I examines the extent to which opinions on government assistance are rooted more firmly in their antecedents under framed conditions, where citizens are invited to consider those antecedents, than under stripped conditions, where citizens are left on their own. Our general expectation is that the pattern of antecedent relationships discovered in the framed condition would resemble the pattern of relationships in the stripped condition but in amplified form. Modest relationships should become strong. Strong relationships should become stronger still.

Recall that in the framed condition, support for government help was justified on the grounds that American society failed to provide equal opportunities to blacks. Meanwhile, opposition to government help was justified on the grounds that blacks must take individual responsibility for their own lives, as other groups had done. Encouraged to think about government assistance in this way, whites should attach more weight to their views on equal opportunity and to their assessment of the moral qualifications of black Americans than they otherwise would.

Framing the question in the way that we did might also diminish the importance of other possible considerations. While equality and racial sentiments were being brought to center stage, other ways of seeing the question—especially relatively race-neutral ways—were being shunted aside. In particular, opposition to government intervention as a matter of principle might get less play under framed than under stripped conditions, and so might sympathy for the poor.

Table 7.2 presents the results.[20] As expected, racial resentment and equal opportunity had a bigger impact on opinion in the framed condition. The differences are large and statistically significant.[21] At the same time, framing the issue in this fashion—converting government assistance into a referendum on the character of blacks and the importance of equality as an ideal—also appeared to diminish the relevance of limited government and sentiments toward

Table 7.2 Antecedents of Whites' Opinions
on Government Assistance to Blacks, by Issue Frame

	Stripped	Framed
Racial resentment	.49	.69
	(.11)	(.12)
Equal opportunity	.09	.38
	(.13)	(.13)
Limited government	.09	.01
	(.11)	(.11)
Attitude toward poor	.14	−.08
	(.13)	(.12)
R-squared		.34
Number of cases		324
Standard error		.26

Source: 1989 National Election Study.
Note: Table entry is the unstandardized regression coefficient,
with standard errors in parentheses. The equation also included
measures of party identification and question frame (see text for
details). All variables are coded on 0–1 interval.

the poor. As table 7.2 indicates, the effect of limited government, noticeable in the stripped condition, becomes invisible in the framed condition; meanwhile, sentiments toward the poor are quite prominent in the stripped condition, but fade away in the framed condition.[22] These results suggest that when frames draw attention to some considerations, they deflect attention away from others.

EXPERIMENT II: ALTERNATIVE FRAMES AND AFFIRMATIVE ACTION

We undertook Experiment I to see whether providing citizens with helpful frames might encourage them to overcome their ambivalence. Our results suggest that for the most part, frames do play this role. When whites are asked the framed version of the question on government assistance to blacks, their opinions reflect more vividly the group resentments and political principles that the frames highlight. In Experiment II, we investigate whether by sponsoring and successfully promoting alternative opinion frames, advocates can shape how issues are understood. Our claim is that which ingredients Americans pay attention to and which they ignore has partly to do with the ongoing political debate. As particular frames rise to prominence, some opinion ingredients are highlighted and made more accessible while others are shunted to the side. In the process, elite frames transform the meaning of opinion.

We test this claim by examining public opinion on affirmative action. Conveniently for our purposes, Gamson and Modigliani analyzed the evolution of elite debate on this complex and controversial issue.[23] To identify elite frames, they examined the opinions of Supreme Court justices in pivotal cases, *amicus curiae* briefs, speeches and statements delivered by prominent public officials, and the views expressed in various political journals. Gamson and Modigliani then went on to chart each frame's public "career" by tracing its changing prominence from 1969 to 1984 in national news magazines, network news programs, editorial cartoons, and syndicated opinion columns.

According to Gamson and Modigliani's analysis, supporters of affirmative action have typically defended their position throughout this period by referring to the need for *remedial* action. Under this frame, race-conscious programs are required to offset the continuing pernicious effects of America's long history of racial discrimination. On the other side of the issue, opponents argued that affirmative action constitutes *unfair advantage*. This frame questions whether rewards should be allocated on the basis of race and expresses the particular concern that blacks are being handed advantages that they do not deserve. Unfair advantage has gradually given way among elite opponents of affirmative action to *reverse discrimination*. Like unfair advantage, reverse discrimination questions whether rewards should be allocated on the basis of race, this time by raising the particular concern of whether the interests of whites must be sacrificed in order to advance the interests of blacks.

With Gamson and Modigliani's results in hand, we developed alternative frames for a pair of specific issues, both tied to affirmative action. The first refers to affirmative action in hiring decisions, the other to affirmative action in college admissions. For both issues, support for affirmative action was framed in terms of remedial action; for both, opposition to affirmative action was framed either in terms of reverse discrimination or in terms of unfair advantage. The questions were then included in the 1985 NES. The 380 people interviewed in December 1985 and reinterviewed three weeks later—over the telephone in each instance—constituted a subsample of respondents to the 1984 NES, a probability sample of Americans of voting age. Because the 1985 sample is on the small side, our analysis will be confined to whites alone.[24]

To compare the alternative versions of the affirmative action questions, respondents to the 1985 study were randomly assigned to one of two groups. People assigned to the first (n = 192) were asked a pair of questions on affirmative action that offered as justification for opposing affirmative action the assertion that such policies discriminated against whites. We refer to this version as the "reverse discrimination" frame. People assigned to the second group (n = 188) were asked the same pair of questions, but this time the questions contained as justification for opposing affirmative action the assertion that such policies gave blacks advantages they had not earned. This formulation of the question we call the "undeserved advantage" frame:[25]

REVERSE DISCRIMINATION FRAME

Some people say that because of past discrimination against blacks, preference in hiring and promotion should be given to blacks. Others say preferential hiring and promotion of blacks is wrong because it *discriminates against whites.* What about your opinion—are you for or against preferential hiring and promotion of blacks?

Some people say that because of past discrimination, it is sometimes necessary for colleges and universities to reserve openings for black students. Others oppose quotas because they say quotas *discriminate against whites.* What about your opinion—are you for or against quotas to admit black students?

UNFAIR ADVANTAGE FRAME

Some people say that because of past discrimination against blacks, preference in hiring and promotion should be given to blacks. Others say preferential hiring and promotion of blacks is wrong because it *gives blacks advantages they haven't earned.* What about your opinion—are you for or against preferential hiring and promotion of blacks?

Some people say that because of past discrimination, it is sometimes necessary for colleges and universities to reserve openings for black students. Others oppose quotas because they say quotas *give blacks advantages they haven't earned.* What about your opinion—are you for or against quotas to admit black students?

These questions suggest that affirmative action might be supported on the grounds that such policies are necessary to overcome past discrimination, in line with Gamson and Modigliani's claim that remedial action constitutes the dominant frame among supporters of affirmative action. The questions differ in that one version suggests that affirmative action might be opposed because such policies constitute discrimination against whites (reverse discrimination), while the other version suggests that affirmative action might be opposed because such policies give to blacks advantages they have not earned (unfair advantage).

Apart from these frame differences, which were introduced deliberately and experimentally, the two samples were otherwise virtually interchangeable. On demographic, social, and political characteristics, they were impossible to distinguish. Should we detect differences in opinion on affirmative action across the samples, they can safely be attributed to the effects of alternative frames.[26]

Table 7.3 Antecedents of Whites' Opinions of Affirmative Action, by Alternative Issue Frame

	Reverse Discrimination Frame	Unfair Advantage Frame
Self-interest	.14	.02
	(.07)	(.09)
Racial resentment	.17	.29
	(.11)	(.12)
Equal opportunity	.21	−.33
	(.13)	(.15)
Economic individualism	−.23	.09
	(.13)	(.12)
Limited government	.21	.01
	(.13)	(.11)
R-squared	.21	
Number of cases	256	
Standard error	.25	

Source: 1985 National Election Study.
Note: Table entry is unstandardized least squares regression coefficient, with standard errors in parentheses. All variables are coded on 0–1 interval.

Alternative Ingredients for Opinions for Affirmative Action

Different survey questions, like the different opinion frames promoted by political elites, should alter the ingredients that go into public opinion on affirmative action. The results of our analysis are reported in table 7.3; the left-hand column of coefficients gives our best estimate of the importance of the various opinion ingredients under the reverse discrimination frame; the right-hand column does the same for the unfair advantage frame. We expect to see differences across the two frames—different question frames should induce citizens to consider different antecedents—and we do.[27]

Notice first that under the reverse discrimination frame, self-interest makes a difference. When invited to think about affirmative action as discrimination against whites, Americans who were convinced that affirmative action might harm the education of their own children were more likely to oppose the policy. But this effect disappeared when opposition to affirmative action was framed as unfair advantage. This result at once points to the power of alternative frames and suggests again the weakness of self-interest as a general motive underlying public opinion. Consistent with the findings reported in Chapter 4, we find here that the perception of personal racial threat at work has nothing to do with opinion on affirmative action policies. Its failure is so complete it does not even appear in table 7.3. The personal threat posed by affirmative action in school admissions does make a (modest) difference to opinion, but only when the policy is framed in such a way as to underscore its zero-sum quality. If affirmative action is understood to be discrimination against whites, then self-interest—of a particular sort—becomes relevant to opinion. These results suggest that interests can be activated but that more often they are not.

If self-interest is less consequential under the unfair advantage frame, racial resentment is more. Framing opposition to affirmative action in terms of advantages to blacks that they do not deserve evokes white Americans' racial feelings powerfully. This result can be put the other way round: the impact of racial resentment diminishes when affirmative action is framed as reverse discrimination. This suggests that even on controversial issues that are transparently about race, racial resentment need not play a dominant role in public opinion. By structuring issues one way, elites can bring simmering racial resentments to full boil; but by framing issues in other ways, elites can lower the racial temperature and turn public opinion into a more complex stew, one that includes a variety of ingredients in addition to racial resentment.

Finally, table 7.3 indicates that principles weigh more heavily in affirmative action opinions when the issue is framed as reverse discrimination than when framed as unfair advantage. Under reverse discrimination, views on affirmative action are supported by classic American values—in particular, by belief in equal opportunity, economic individualism, and limited government. Neither of the last two principles is engaged in the debate over affirmative action when that debate is framed in terms of unfair advantage. Equality of opportunity does, but—and this is perhaps our most arresting result—*equality supports affirmative action in one case and moves against it in the other.* Under the unfair advantage frame, those whites who endorse the principle of equal opportunity most are also most likely to support affirmative action. But under the reverse discrimination frame, those whites who endorse the principle of equal opportunity most are least likely to support affirmative action. When invited to think about affirmative action as discrimination against whites, egalitarians stand against the policy.

Alternative Frames and Racial Thinking

According to our results so far, white opinion on affirmative action policy can be more or less dominated by racial resentment depending on the way the policy is framed. This result is sufficiently important to warrant further investigation. Here we see whether we can detect additional evidence that the reverse discrimination frame diminishes racial thinking. On the assumption that racial resentment is a central ingredient in white opinion on race, and that the reverse discrimination frame pushes such resentment somewhat to the side, we should find that whites' views on race become less coherent, less tightly coupled, in the presence of the reverse discrimination frame.

The 1985 NES Pilot included questions in two other domains of race policy in addition to affirmative action. The first concerns the federal government's general responsibility to blacks; the second addresses the federal government's responsibilities to promote equal opportunity. Thus we can see whether relationships between opinions in these two domains and opinions on affirmative action were conditioned by how affirmative action was framed.

To test this in a pointed way, we turned to confirmatory factor analysis. Because we want to see whether the structure of white opinion on racial policy varies by opinion frame, we analyzed the two samples separately: those who were encouraged to think about affirmative action as undeserved advantage and those who were invited to think about affirmative action as reverse discrimination. In both samples, our model presumes that whites possess distinct, but correlated, views about three aspects of policy on race: the general responsibility of the federal government to provide assistance to blacks (measured by three questions); the specific obligations of the federal government to ensure that blacks can attend integrated schools, purchase homes without prejudice, and be free from discrimination on the job (three questions); and the appropriateness of affirmative action policies in employment and college admissions decisions (the familiar pair of questions).[28]

As the results presented in table 7.4 show, the three-factor model fits the data quite well, and does so without regard to the way the affirmative action questions were framed.[29] Indeed, with one exception, there is little in these results to distinguish between the two samples: the structure of the model is identical, and the factor loadings are virtually the same. The single exception is important, however. Under the reverse discrimination frame, opinion on affirmative action correlates much less strongly with opinion on federal assistance and on equal opportunity than it does under the unfair advantage frame. The relevant correlations, displayed at the bottom of table 7.4, are .52 and .32 versus .70 and .57.[30]

Thus when opposition to affirmative action is justified on the grounds that such policies hand to blacks advantages they have not earned, opinion on affirmative action is closely tied to the opinions whites express on other policies that concern blacks. Affirmative action then fits snugly within a coherent package of policy ideas on race. When, on the other hand, opposition to affirmative action is justified on the grounds that such policies discriminate against whites, opinion on affirmative action is less closely coupled to the white public's assessment of appropriate government policy in providing help and guaranteeing

Table 7.4 Structure of White Opinion on Race Policy, by Issue Frame (maximum likelihood factor analysis)

| | Reverse Discrimination Frame | | | | | | Unfair Advantage Frame | | | | | |
| | Federal Assistance | | Equal Opportunity | | Affirmative Action | | Federal Assistance | | Equal Opportunity | | Affirmative Action | |
Race Policy	Coef	se	Coef	se	Coef	se	Coef	se	Coef	se	Coef	se
Government guarantee opportunity	.181	(.028)					.170	(.028)				
Federal spending	.201	(.025)					.219	(.026)				
Government help	.174	(.024)					.183	(.023)				
Government/school discrimination			.219	(.028)					.205	(.024)		
Government/housing discrimination			.233	(.026)					.237	(.025)		
Government/job opportunity			.256	(.024)					.251	(.023)		
Preferential hiring					.189	(.033)					.204	(.027)
Preferential admissions					.253	(.041)					.260	(.032)
Chi-square with 17 degrees of freedom					28.08 (p = .044)						27.30 (p = 0.54)	
Adjusted goodness of fit					.914						.903	

Factor Correlations

	Federal Assistance	Equal Opportunity	Affirmative Action		Federal Assistance	Equal Opportunity	Affirmative Action
Federal assistance	1.00				1.00		
Equal opportunity	.72	1.00			.68	1.00	
Affirmative action	.52	.32	1.00		.70	.57	1.00

Source: 1985 National Election Study.

Note: Estimates based on variance-covariance matrix.

Table 7.5 Associations between Whites' Opinions on Affirmative Action and Their Views on Other Matters of Race, by Issue Frame

	Reverse Discrimination Frame	Unfair Advantage Frame
Implicit race policy		
Spending on cities	.07	.27
Spending on jobs	.04	.11
Spending on welfare	.06	.26
Emotional reactions to preferential treatment		
Angry	−.21	−.30
Disgusted	−.09	−.41
Infuriated	−.11	−.28

Source: 1985 National Election Study.
Note: Table entry is Pearson correlation coefficient.

opportunities to black Americans. Affirmative action then drifts away; it becomes less and less part of that package of policy ideas.

Just the same kind of result is apparent in the top panel of table 7.5. There we present simple (Pearson) correlations between opinions on affirmative action and views on three implicit racial policies carried in the 1985 NES: whether federal spending on *cities, jobs,* and *welfare* should be increased, decreased, or remain about the same. As table 7.5 makes clear, correlations between opinions on affirmative action and opinions on implicit race policy are consistently stronger when affirmative action is framed in terms of undeserved advantage than when framed in terms of reverse discrimination.[31] Indeed, when people are encouraged to consider that affirmative action should be opposed because such a policy constitutes reverse discrimination, the correlations virtually vanish. But when they are invited to consider that affirmative action policies should be opposed because they hand to blacks advantages they have not earned, then those who oppose affirmative action tend to be the same people who oppose federal money for cities and welfare.

As a final analysis on this point, we examined whether the pattern of emotional reactions evoked by affirmative action depends upon the way affirmative action is framed. In the 1985 NES, respondents were asked whether they had ever experienced a variety of emotional reactions to the "preferential treatment of blacks" and specifically whether they had ever felt angry, disgusted, or infuriated. The bottom half of table 7.5 presents the correlations between opinion on affirmative action and each emotional response, separately by frame. These correlations suggest that affirmative action framed as unfair advantage evokes indignation in a way that affirmative action framed as reverse discrimination does not.[32]

We take all this evidence—the regression analysis of the antecedents of opinion on affirmative action summarized in table 7.3, the factor analysis results on the coherence of views on racial policy reported in table 7.4, and the correlational analysis results on the relationship between opinions on affirmative action and views on implicit racial policy and emotional reactions summarized in table 7.5—as further indication that the power of racial resentment is contingent on elite discourse. Whatever its liabilities, the reverse discrimination frame appears to have the virtue of reducing the part played by racial resentment in white opinion on issues of race.

Experiment III: Race-Conscious Frames and Government Assistance

How might popular support for government assistance to blacks be strengthened? One answer is through policies that cut across racial lines. Perhaps the best known advocate of this position is William J. Wilson. First in *The Declining Significance of Race*, then more forcefully in *The Truly Disadvantaged*, Wilson argues that proposals intended to eliminate race discrimination or provide preferential treatment are off the mark. According to Wilson,

> In the coming years the best political strategy for those committed to racial justice is to place more emphasis on race-neutral programs that would not only address the plight of the disadvantaged among minorities but would apply to all groups in America. After all, Americans across racial and class lines continue to be concerned about increased unemployment, decreased job security, deteriorating real wages, poorer public education, escalating medical and hospital costs, the lack of good child care, and more crime and drug trafficking in their neighborhoods. Because these problems are more highly concentrated in the inner cities as a result of cumulative effects of decades of racial subjugation, programs that aggressively address them will disproportionately benefit the underclass.[33]

Wilson's argument is based partly on political calculations. Coalitions to support affirmative action for blacks or more generous welfare benefits that would go disproportionately to blacks are often too weak or fragile to carry the day. Wilson, like Heclo, Skocpol, and others, is well aware of the political obstacles that stand in the way of government programs for black Americans.[34]

Our third experiment begins to address the likely success of a race-neutral political strategy. The experiment involves the familiar question on government assistance to blacks that has figured prominently in much of our previous analysis. The question was asked in two slightly different forms in the 1988 NES and put to alternative, but otherwise comparable, half samples.[35] One refers to federal efforts to improve the social and economic position of blacks; the other refers to federal efforts to improve the social and economic position of blacks and other minorities. More precisely:

RACE-CONSCIOUS FRAME

Some people feel that the government in Washington should make every effort to improve the social and economic position of blacks. Suppose these people are at one end of the scale at point number 1. Others feel that the government should not make any special effort to help blacks because they should help themselves. Suppose these people are at the other end, at point 7. And, of course, some other people have opinions somewhere in between at points 2, 3, 4, 5, or 6. Where would you place yourself on this scale, or haven't you thought much about this?

RACE-NEUTRAL FRAME

Some people feel that the government in Washington should make every effort to improve the social and economic position of blacks *and other mi: nority groups.* Suppose these people are at one end of the scale at point number 1. Others feel that the government should not make any special effort to help *minorities* because they should help themselves. Suppose these people are at the other end, at point 7. And, of course, some other people have opinions somewhere in between at points 2, 3, 4, 5, or 6. Where would you place yourself on this scale, or haven't you thought much about this?[36]

All in all, the difference between the two question frames seems quite subtle. In both cases it is the government in Washington that should or should not provide assistance; in both cases the liberal option is to make special efforts; and in both cases the conservative reply is to insist on self-reliance. The only difference goes to the apparent beneficiaries of government help—what Rae and his colleagues would call the "subjects" of equality.[37] In the first version of the question, the subjects of government policy are explicitly designated to be black Americans and black Americans alone. In the second, the subject class is expanded to include other minorities. Is this one difference in how the issue is framed sufficient to produce differences in opinion?

Public Support for Government Assistance

Indeed it is. In line with Wilson's political calculation, whites are significantly more likely to support government assistance to blacks and other minorities than they are to blacks alone (see table 7.6). In the 1988 NES survey, 24.8% favor assistance in the first instance, while just 17.7% do so in the sec-

Table 7.6 White and Black Support for Government Assistance to Blacks, by Issue Frame

		Whites		Blacks	
		Blacks Only Frame	Blacks and Minorities Frame	Blacks Only Frame	Blacks and Minorities Frame
Government should make special effort	1	4.1%	6.6%	29.6%	41.0%
	2	4.1	5.2	8.7	6.0
	3	9.5	13.0	6.1	11.1
	4	24.8	23.9	24.3	21.4
	5	16.4	18.0	10.4	6.0
	6	15.7	14.9	12.2	8.5
Blacks should help themselves	7	25.2	18.4	8.7	6.0
Chi-square		17.81, p < .01		7.38, p = .29	

Source: 1988 National Election Study.

ond.[38] This difference, though predicted, is curious in one respect, in that government programs for blacks and other minorities would presumably cost whites more than would programs for blacks by themselves. Despite the greater implied expense, the white public is nevertheless more enthusiastic about government assistance broadly distributed—perhaps another strike against the political importance of self-interest. More curious, perhaps, is that black Americans are *also* more likely to support government assistance to blacks and other minorities than they are to blacks alone. The difference among blacks—58.1% support under the first frame versus 44.4% under the second—is even larger than among whites.[39] Consistent with several lines of political argument, race-neutral programs do appear to be more popular among the American public, black and white.[40]

Race-Conscious Frames and Race of Interviewer

Strictly speaking, "race neutral" does not really describe our more popular frame: to refer to blacks and other minorities is hardly race neutral. This frame is race neutral only by comparison with its alternative, which presents the policy as providing assistance to blacks alone. Compared with a frame that targets blacks as the sole beneficiary of government assistance, it is more race neutral, or so we say.

Back in Chapter 2, we discovered that liberal views on matters of race were expressed more often in the presence of black interviewers, and less often in the presence of white interviewers, and that this held for both black and white citizens. Here we see that same pattern repeated for government assistance, *but only when blacks were singled out as the sole beneficiary.* When framed in a race-neutral way, the issue of government assistance elicits opinions that are unaffected by race of interviewer, for black and white citizens alike. When the issue is framed in a race-conscious way, however, the familiar result returns: now both blacks and whites express more support for government assistance when questioned by a black interviewer than when questioned by a white—roughly fifteen to sixteen percentage points more support. These results suggest that framing the policy of government assistance as providing support for blacks and other minorities goes some distance toward race neutrality.[41]

Race-Conscious Appeals and the Complexity of White Opinion

Why do whites support government assistance more when the issue is formulated in race-neutral ways? One possibility is that putting the question in this way shifts how the issue is understood, thereby altering the mix of ingredients that go into opinion. Specifically, race-neutral formulations may diminish the role otherwise played by racial resentment. If formulating the issue in a more race-neutral way (and the evidence we have just presented on race of interviewer suggests that we have at least partially succeeded in doing so) defines the issue less as a referendum on black Americans, then white Americans may look more favorably upon government initiatives. At the same time, putting the issue as a question of support for minorities in general may also enhance the importance of equality. If assistance is intended to be applied universally to persons who need help, regardless of race, then whites' commitment to the idea of equal opportunity—which, as we saw in Chapter 6, is both considerable and powerful—may be brought more centrally into play. In short, the race-neutral frame may both suppress racial resentment and activate equal opportunity, thereby enhancing the popularity of government help.

Formulating the issue in a race-neutral fashion may also bring other considerations into greater prominence. Broadening the issue to include other minorities has the most direct and immediate relevance to minorities themselves. From the perspective either of self- or group interest, Hispanic Americans should be more apt to support a policy if they are likely to benefit. For Hispanic Americans, support for government assistance to blacks is one thing; support for government assistance to blacks and other minorities should be quite another.

Minorities might come more visibly into play under the race-neutral formulation in at least one other way. As we have seen repeatedly, whites' views on public policy on race hinge importantly on their feelings toward blacks, all the more so when the issue is formulated in such a way as to make clear that blacks are the intended beneficiaries of the proposed policy. It follows that when the issue is formulated in terms of assistance not just to blacks but also to

Table 7.7 Antecedents of Whites' Opinions on Government
Assistance to Blacks, by Issue Frame

	Blacks Only Frame	Blacks and Minorities Frame
Racial resentment	.51	.44
	(.05)	(.05)
Equal opportunity	−.01	−.15
	(.06)	(.06)
Hispanic descent	−.16	−.13
	(.04)	(.04)
Attitude toward Hispanics	−.02	−.18
	(.05)	(.05)
Limited government	.29	.33
	(.05)	(.05)
R-squared		.36
Number of cases		1146
Standard error		.23

Source: 1988 National Election Study.
Note: Table entry is the unstandardized regression coefficient with standard errors in parentheses. All variables are coded on 0–1 interval.

blacks and other minorities, whites' views on the policy may turn importantly on their feelings, one way or the other, toward these other minorities. In particular, we expect that when the issue is framed in this broader way, whites' sentiments toward Hispanic Americans will become part of the mix of ingredients that make up public opinion.

To test these several claims, we turned to an analysis of the antecedents of opinion on government assistance, and whether the power of such antecedents depends upon how the issue is framed. Our analysis considers the independent effects associated with racial resentment, equal opportunity, Hispanic origins, attitude toward Hispanics, and limited government. We include limited government not because we expect its effect to vary by frame—we do not—but because we know from previous analysis (reported in Chapter 6) that limited government is related to racial resentment and equal opportunity and is itself an important determinant of opinions on issues of race.[42]

The results are shown in table 7.7. In the left-hand column of the table appear our estimates of the effects on opinion due to the various ingredients under the race-conscious frame. The column of coefficients to the right provides the identical estimates, this time under the race-neutral frame. As expected, when the race-conscious frame is replaced by the race-neutral formulation, the effect of racial resentment declines and the impact of equal opportunity increases.[43] Meanwhile, the impact due to limited government remains about the same—it increases a bit, but not enough for us to be sure that the increase is real.[44] These results suggest that race-neutral frames can alter the ingredients of opinion, and in a way that enhances the popularity of government support for blacks.

The results also indicate that Hispanics tend to favor government assistance without regard for how the issue is formulated. Hispanics are actually more supportive of government help when that assistance is targeted at blacks alone than when it is distributed among blacks and other minorities, but the difference is tiny. Better we should think of it as no difference at all.[45] This result amounts to another disconfirmation of a politics based in self-interest. From an interest point of view, Hispanics should favor policies insofar as they or their group would directly benefit, but we see no evidence of it here.

This failure may reflect the diversity that flourishes within the Hispanic category. Mexican Americans, Puerto Ricans, Cuban Americans and other Americans of Hispanic heritage are distinguished from one another by their history, cultural practices, economic success, and, not least, by their politics. No doubt some of those we have classified as Hispanic do not consider themselves to be minorities. And in any case, the question frame in the race-neutral condition does not mention Hispanics or Mexican Americans or Cubans or any other group by name. So the frame difference, from the perspective of Hispanic Americans, may be quite subtle.

Against this last interpretation, however, is the fact that whites' attitudes toward Hispanics play precisely the role we expected. Under the race-conscious formulation, feelings toward Hispanics, good or bad, have nothing to do with support for government help. But when the issue is put in terms of assistance to blacks and other minorities, then feelings toward Hispanics suddenly become relevant. Evidently, the frame manipulation was not *that* subtle.

Finally, it is worth stepping back a moment from the details of these various results to consider them taken all together. Compare the two columns of coefficients presented in table 7.7, each associated with a different frame. Notice that they add up to quite a different story about public opinion. Under the race-conscious frame, whites' views on government assistance are dominated by their feelings toward blacks. Other considerations pale by comparison: whether they also support or oppose government intervention matters less; whether they favor equal opportunity matters not at all; their sentiments toward Hispanics are utterly irrelevant. Under the race-neutral frame, the meaning of public opinion is quite different. Now opinion on government assistance appears to be shaped by a mix of considerations, not just feelings of racial resentment or sympathy alone. Views on whether or not the government is obliged to make a special effort to help minorities still depend in part on racial feelings. But they also depend on beliefs about limited government, views on equal opportunity, and on sentiments toward other Hispanic Americans. Under a race-neutral frame, white opinion is much less a referendum on the character of black Americans.

EXPERIMENT IV: CLASS, RACE, AND ASSISTANCE TO THE POOR

In some respects, the results from Experiment III are surprising in that they are produced by what appears to be a subtle difference in issue frames: one refers to blacks alone, while the other refers to blacks and other minorities. Our fourth and final experiment sharpens this contrast. Experiment IV provides a clearer empirical representation of the claim that popular support for egalitarian policies will increase if such policies are color-blind; if, that is, they deliver benefits and programs to the poor and the disadvantaged, regardless of race.

We test this claim not once but three times by analyzing an experiment that was part of the 1990 General Social Survey.[46] The 1990 installment of the GSS carried three policy questions that present what might be called individualistic remedies for racial inequality. Each calls for government intervention, consistent with New Deal liberalism, but each also attempts to create circumstances that enable people to provide for themselves, consistent with American individualism. The first proposes the establishment of enterprise zones, the second recommends spending more money on early education, and the third calls for funding college scholarships for students who maintain good grades. Respondents to the 1990 GSS were asked about enterprise zones, early education en-rich-ment, and college scholarships for *blacks* (the race frame), or they were asked about the identical policies but this time with the *poor* in mind (the *class* frame):

RACE FRAME	CLASS FRAME
Giving business and industry special tax breaks for locating in *largely black* areas.	Giving business and industry special tax breaks for locating in *largely poor* and *high unemployment* areas.
Spending more money on the schools in *black* neighborhoods, especially for preschool and early education programs.	Spending more money on the schools in *poor* neighborhoods, especially for preschool and early education programs.
Providing special college scholarships for *black* children who maintain good grades.	Providing special college scholarships for children *from economically disadvantaged backgrounds* who maintain good grades.

Table 7.8 White and Black Support for Egalitarian Policies, by Issue Frame (race versus class)

	Whites						Blacks					
	Enterprise Zones		School Funds		College Scholarships		Enterprise Zones		School Funds		College Scholarships	
	Race	Class	Race	Class	Race	Class	Race	Class	Race	Class	Race	Class
Strongly favor	7.7%	18.4%	17.4%	29.4%	16.6%	36.7%	27.8%	25.7%	50.6%	45.8%	56.1%	47.2%
Favor	35.5	52.2	50.8	56.8	53.1	54.7	41.8	45.7	43.4	45.8	39.0	44.4
Mixed	25.0	16.2	15.3	7.9	14.1	5.7	21.5	14.3	3.6	4.2	4.9	5.6
Oppose	24.6	9.9	12.3	4.5	11.5	1.6	5.1	10.0	2.4	2.8	0.0	2.8
Strongly oppose	7.2	3.3	4.3	1.4	4.8	1.3	3.8	4.3	0.0	1.4	0.0	0.0

Source: 1990 General Social Survey.

In each of the three pairs, the proposals are identical but for the intended beneficiaries. In the first instance of each pair, the benefits and programs are to go to
blacks; in the second instance, they are intended for the poor.

Support for Individualistic Remedies for Social Inequality

Our first question is what difference this distinction makes for public support. The answer is clear: it makes a large difference. These results are presented
in table 7.8, for white and black Americans taken separately.

Notice first that under the race frame, all three policies attract considerable
support among white Americans. Clear majorities approve of both education
initiatives, and, on balance, white opinion also favors tax breaks for businesses
willing to locate in black communities. Whites are certainly more likely to back
these initiatives than they are the race policies we have been analyzing, especially those dealing with federal responsibilities or affirmative action. But the
most important lesson of table 7.8 is that white support for the three policies
increases dramatically under the class frame. When enterprise zones, school
funding, and college scholarships are directed toward the poor, white approval
skyrockets. Framed in class terms, white support for enterprise zones increases
some twenty-seven percentage points; school funding gains eighteen points;
and white approval of college scholarships jumps nearly twenty-two percentage points.

In the meantime, among black Americans, differences associated with the
two frames are much harder to see. The relevant percentages are also on display
in table 7.8. As revealed there, when policies are specifically and explicitly designed with blacks in mind, black Americans are somewhat more likely to register their strong support. This difference shows up on each of the three policies,
but it is noteworthy only in the case of college scholarships. Moreover, once
we move beyond the category of strong approval, differences in black opinion
induced by the different frames fade away entirely.

Taken together, these two sets of results have an arithmetically inevitable
implication for the racial divide in opinion. When poverty policies are targeted
at the poor and the disadvantaged, regardless of race, the racial divide in opinion contracts rather spectacularly. White opinion becomes decisively more liberal; black opinion becomes slightly less liberal. Under these circumstances,
blacks are still more likely than whites to favor the egalitarian option, but the
differences are much diminished and quite modest, nothing like what we see
when policies are formulated in terms of race.

Table 7.9 Impact of Racial Stereotyping on Whites'
Opinions toward Egalitarian Policies, by Issue Frame

Enterprise Zones	
Race frame	Class frame
.18	.16
(.14)	(.14)

School Funds	
Race frame	Class frame
.29	−.01
(.13)	(.11)

College Scholarships	
Race frame	Class frame
.13	.03
(.13)	(.11)

Source: 1990 General Social Survey.
Note: Table entry is the unstandardized regression coefficient,
with standard errors in parentheses. Each equation also included
measures of individualism, limited government, equality, and social background.

Racial Resentment and the Class Frame

One reason why white support for redistributive policies increases so
sharply under the class frame might be that providing benefits to the poor,
without respect to race, removes or at least downplays the importance of racial
resentment. Perhaps the class frame operates to defuse the racial connotations
that would otherwise be associated with antipoverty policies.

We test this proposition by making use, one last time, of the racial stereotyping measure available in the 1990 GSS. Remember that most white Americans
do in fact subscribe, in some degree, to traditional racial stereotypes. Most
whites believe that their racial group is more industrious, smarter, more loyal,
less violent, and more self-reliant than blacks. Does racial resentment, defined
in terms of these stereotypes, figure less prominently in white opinion when
policies are framed in terms of class?

The answer, spelled out in table 7.9, is yes.[47] For each of the three policies,
table 7.9 provides two estimates. The one on the left is the regression coefficient
indexing the importance of racial stereotyping under the race frame; its companion to the right is the corresponding coefficient under the class frame. As
the table indicates, when individualistic remedies are formulated with the poor
in mind, the effect of racial resentment diminishes. Indeed, it disappears entirely in the cases of early education enrichment and college scholarships, and

we cannot be certain that it isn't also zero for white opinion on enterprise zones. On these several policies, then, when assistance is directed to poor Americans rather than to black Americans, white support jumps and the importance of racial resentment plummets.

CONCLUSIONS AND IMPLICATIONS

Members of Congress, presidents, corporate public affairs officers, activists, policy analysts, reporters and editors, and all the rest who devote themselves to the public sphere are perpetually engaged in a war of words and symbols, and with good reason. As we discovered repeatedly over the course of our four experiments, words and symbols make a difference: the underpinnings of opinion, and thus the very meaning of opinion, can be shifted by inducing citizens to think about issues in particular ways.

In Experiment I we asked whether elite frames contribute to an informed public opinion. Do framed opinions, compared with their stripped counterparts, resemble more the opinions that advocates of democracy hope for? The answer is (a qualified) yes. We found that enriching the question with a frame induces more opinions, more consequential opinions, and opinions more firmly rooted in the antecedents stressed by the frame. The effects are not overwhelming, but they are quite consistent, and they are produced by a modest experimental intervention. Several well-chosen phrases are all that distinguishes the framed from the stripped condition, and yet this difference visibly enhances the structure of public opinion.[48]

In Experiment II, we discovered that the mix of ingredients that goes into whites' opinions on affirmative action can be systematically altered by the way that the issue is framed. One especially noteworthy result here is that when encouraged to think of affirmative action as reverse discrimination, the white public's response is comparatively free of racial resentment. This finding, which we have been able to replicate in two independent tests, is consistent with Gamson and Modigliani's argument that the reverse discrimination frame was created in order to mobilize opposition to affirmative action in a manner that could be defended against the charge of racism.[49]

As the power of racial resentment wanes under the reverse discrimination frame, opinion on affirmative action tends to be dominated instead by interests and principles. Among these, the effect of self-interest is especially noteworthy—not because the effect is large (it is not), but because it goes against much previous research. Here we see that the personal threat posed by affirmative action in school admissions makes a difference to opinion: whites who feel personally threatened oppose the policy more. But we also see that the effect appears only when the policy is framed to emphasize its zero-sum quality, when whites are encouraged to understand affirmative action as reverse discrimination. This result suggests that self-interest can take on political significance, but perhaps only when the issue is framed in such a way as to underscore the personal benefits and costs at stake.

No doubt the most striking shift across the two frames in Experiment II involves the power associated with ideas about equality. Under the unfair advantage frame, citizens who endorsed the principle of equal opportunity tended to support affirmative action; under the reverse discrimination frame, citizens who supported equal opportunity tended to oppose affirmative action. Thus equality facilitates affirmative action in one case and stands in its way in the other. This result tends to support Gamson's contention that affirmative action's ideological battleground centers on the idea of equal opportunity and that partisans on both sides can lay claim to it.[50] To its supporters, affirmative action is required to bring true equality of opportunity to life. As Justice Blackmun wrote in his opinion on the Bakke case in 1978, "In order to get beyond racism, we must first take into account race. And in order to treat some people equally, we must treat them differently." Opponents of affirmative action also invoke equality of opportunity, this time to argue against taking race into account. Race-conscious policy—"thinking in blood," as Eastland and Bennett put it— inevitably leads to preferential treatment for some groups and necessarily violates the principle of equal opportunity for individuals.[51] More generally, our result on equality suggests the malleability of principles that we tried to emphasize in Chapter 6. In the end, just as Rae and his colleagues suspected, "The idea against which equality must struggle most heroically is equality itself."[52]

In Experiment III, we turned directly to the question of how frames might alter overall support for policy. The chief distinction tested here was between government assistance targeted at black Americans in particular as against assistance directed to blacks and minorities in general. As expected, whites were significantly more likely to support government assistance to blacks and other minorities than they were to blacks alone. To our surprise, black Americans showed exactly the same tendency. Race-neutral programs are more appealing to the American public, both white and black. These shifts in opinion are not huge—they amount to about ten percentage points—but they are statistically reliable, they reappear in virtually identical form in independent tests, and they are induced by what would seem to be slight alterations in how the question is framed.

In Experiment IV, finally, where we sharpen the contrast between policies whose benefits go exclusively to blacks and those whose benefits go to the disadvantaged, the results are stronger. Enterprise zones, special schooling, and college scholarships are dramatically more popular among white Americans when they are designated for the poor than when they are aimed at blacks. Moreover, when framed in terms of class rather than race, such policies were less likely to stir up racial resentments.[53]

The large shifts in opinion that we detect in Experiment IV may not be typical, but neither do they seem to be remarkable. Consider these two additional examples, one concerning desegregation of neighborhoods, the other affirmative action. Over the years, NES and the National Opinion Research Center (NORC) have asked comparable samples of Americans for their views on residential integration using similar but not identical questions. While the NORC version makes mention only of a strong reason to oppose racial integration of neighborhoods (white people have a right to keep blacks out of their neighborhoods), the NES version of the question refers to reasons on both sides of the issue. In the NES question, the right of whites to determine the racial composition of their neighborhoods is balanced by the rights of blacks to live wherever they can afford. In our vocabulary, the issue of residential integration is framed differently by the two questions. The NORC version mimics the case in political debate where a single frame dominates, where the opposition is silent; the NES version represents the classic case where two opposing frames collide. By encouraging whites to consider reasons to support as well as oppose neighborhood integration, the NES version of the question should evoke more support for the policy. And it does: white support for neighborhood integration is some twenty-five percentage points stronger under the NES frame.[54]

This result suggests the vital importance of an effective opposition. Frames may be especially powerful when they do not compete with rival interpretations. When there is only one line, many citizens seem to swallow it.

The second illustration comes from Stoker's recent experiment on public opinion toward affirmative action.[55] Stoker finds that support for government's requiring large companies to give a certain number of jobs to blacks increases when the question is framed to include the information that such companies have been found to discriminate against blacks. Under this frame, support increases among white and black Americans alike, by roughly fifteen percentage points.

This result is important not just because it demonstrates that alternative frames can tip the balance of public opinion. The greater significance of the result comes from the fact that Stoker's experimental manipulation was designed to mirror the thinking evident in recent Supreme Court decisions on affirmative action. In recent years, the court has ruled that affirmative action should be applied only as a narrowly tailored remedy for discriminatory practice. In effect, the court has decided that, as Stoker puts it, "because this institution has been discriminating against blacks, it is this institution whose procedures must change, and those subject to this discrimination that deserve restitution."[56] Thus Stoker's result suggests that affirmative action programs that follow the court's rulings are more likely to be favorably received by the American public, white and black.

Finally, that a policy can be framed in different ways, to highlight or downplay certain of its features, and that different frames can influence what public opinion turns out to be, obviously complicates the business of gauging public sentiment accurately. If policies are typically framed in different ways in the political context outside the survey, we should certainly expect that the policy descriptions we use inside the survey will influence opinion as well. Our experiments show that they do, thereby demonstrating why the design of issue questions is one of the most vexing problems faced by survey researchers.

Our remedy for this problem may seem peculiar, but it follows directly from our results on framing. Our remedy is this: issue questions must incorporate the frames that prevail in the contemporary political debate. Because such debate is almost always partisan and contentious, our recommendation moves against the conventional view that would have us compose innocuous questions. In the conventional view, questions should be sanitized, stripped of arguments, symbols, and reasons, anything that might sway citizens to one side or the other. Our taste, instead, runs to questions that are surrounded by arguments, symbols, and reasons. Like the political debate they are intended to mimic, issue questions should be provocative and contentious, dirty rather than clean.

In somewhat different ways, each of our experiments illustrates the point that surveys not only measure public opinion but also shape, provoke, and occasionally create it. This is a problem and a headache, but as we have tried to show here, it is an opportunity as well. By examining the kinds of alterations in opinion that are induced by variations in question wording that mimic the rival frames that prevail in popular discourse, we can learn about how changes in public opinion are induced by changes in the ongoing, everyday process of political debate. We will take up the implications of our experimental results for democratic debate in the final chapter, as part of a broader discussion of the power of ideas in politics and the importance of deliberation to democratic process. That discussion is best postponed until we have considered how issues of race are framed in the special democratic moment that is the American presidential campaign, which is the business of Chapters 8 and 9.

CHAPTER EIGHT

The Electoral Temptations of Race

One hundred and fifty years ago, at the peak of the abolitionist agitation, Wendell Phillips was inspired to proclaim that "a man with a ballot in his hand is the master of the situation. He defines all his other rights. What is not already given him, he takes. . . . The Ballot is opportunity, education, fair play, right to office, and elbow room."[1] In these remarks Phillips was feverish, carried away, but in a characteristically American direction. The right to vote has been at the center of racial conflict in the United States, just as elections have loomed large in American theories of democracy.

Indeed, in America, elections are widely regarded as *the* democratic moment, providing the ennobling occasion for citizens to pass judgment on their government. They are the "critical technique," as Robert Dahl once put it, for making sure that leaders will take into account the aspirations and interests of the voters. If elections are "the linchpin of the [democratic] machine," then voting must be, in William Riker's words, "the central act of democracy."[2] When Americans condemn other nations for being insufficiently democratic, they usually have in mind the absence of fair and competitive elections.

Elections as a general matter and elections in the American style in particular are not without their problems, of course. For one thing, they are notoriously blunt instruments of influence: insofar as elections shape policy, they do so partially and retrospectively, sometimes well after the damage has been done.[3] Moreover, voters are to some degree captives of the choices and the campaigns they are presented, which rarely meet the standards set by those who place deliberation and discussion at the center of democratic politics.[4] Despite such shortcomings, citizens seldom choose to give elections up; they would rather have them than not. The American electoral system in particular is singled out by Converse, Eulau, and Miller as "one of the great institutional wonders of the political world." Why? Because

> periodically and regularly, tens of millions of citizens go to the polls on a single day to cast secret ballots and, through the simple act of voting, to give direction to what is properly called popular government. Changes in the composition of representative offices and changes in public policies occurring as a result of voting may

not be many, rapid, or great, but they do impart some important short-term and many critical long-term consequences for the circulation of government elites, the representation of diverse interests, and the evolution of public policies.[5]

Here Converse and his colleagues are celebrating the instrumental role of elections: elections as the "critical technique" for ensuring that public preferences influence government action.[6]

The significance of voting and elections goes beyond power, however, particularly in matters of race. For black Americans, securing the right to vote has been a long, arduous, and often dangerous process. White Americans resisted extending the vote to blacks ferociously and blacks demanded the vote unflaggingly not just because the vote gives to blacks the power to choose policies and candidates. In addition, the right to vote was understood, on both sides of the color line, to convey symbolic authority, a special kind of democratic recognition.

To whites, the right to vote was a public and prominent sign of superiority, one not easily relinquished. According to Myrdal:

> Already in the *ante-bellum* elections, political campaigning and voting had acquired a ceremonial significance as marking off a distinct sphere of power and responsibility for the free citizen. From Reconstruction on, voting remained to the white Southerner more than a mere action: it was, and still is, a symbol of superiority. Partly because it is a public activity and does not lend itself to privacy or segregation, it becomes so hard for the white Southerner to admit the Negro to full participation in it.[7]

To black Americans, the symbolic weight attached to being denied the vote was no less. As Frederick Douglass put it:

> Men are so constituted that they derive their conviction of their own possibilities largely from the estimate formed of them by others. If nothing is expected of a people, that people will find it difficult to contradict that expectation. By depriving us of suffrage, you affirm our incapacity to form intelligent judgments respecting public measures.[8]

Such observations and testimonials lend support to Judith Shklar's contention that the right to vote is a primary feature of democratic citizenship in America. Denied the vote, individuals feel "scorned" and "dishonored"; with it, they are invested with democratic responsibility and dignity. In Shklar's analysis, participation in elections is "an affirmation of belonging."[9]

For several reasons, then, campaigns and elections are an important site for continuing our examination of the racial divide. The investigation of campaigns and elections is especially appropriate since it allows us to carry forward two central themes in our findings so far: the power of racial resentment among white Americans and the ability of political elites to frame popular debate on race. The deep reservoir of resentment and the artful ways elites have learned to draw upon it are central ingredients in what we will call the *electoral temptations of race*.

American national elections, we believe, are infected by racial troubles; they are mired in a racial predicament more than a generation in the making. The predicament is over campaign strategy, about how to frame winning appeals to the American public given the persistence of racial resentment. For the Democratic party, the predicament is how to maintain the loyalty and enthusiasm of blacks without alienating conservative whites. The Democratic temptation is silence and evasion. For the Republican party, the predicament is how to enlist the support of white conservatives without appearing racist. The Republican temptation is racial codewords.

The purpose of this chapter is to provide an account of the origins and evolution of this predicament. As we hope to show, the electoral temptations of race are the result of historical changes in society and politics set in motion by the rise of the civil rights movement in the 1950s. It is a story with four moving parts: the rearrangement of the political parties over matters of race dramatically expressed in the Goldwater-Johnson campaign of 1964; the expansion of the black Democratic vote, occasioned in part by the historic Voting Rights Act of 1965; the demise of the Solid (Democratic) South, a response to the Democratic party's move to the left on race; and the change in social norms governing political speech on racial questions, represented by the virtual disappearance of blatant racist appeals, on the one hand, and their replacement by racial code, on the other. Together, these various developments tell us much about the transformation of the American presidential election system over the last quarter-century, and about American democracy as well.

TURNING POINT: PARTY SWITCH IN 1964

The story of 1964 begins, in a way, with the election of 1948. Remembered best for Truman's miraculous comeback, the real political lesson of 1948 was exposure of the deep rift in the Democratic party over race. Early in that election year, in an abrupt departure from the ambivalence and inaction that had characterized the Roosevelt administration, President Truman began to move boldly on civil rights. In 1946 he had appointed a presidential Committee on Civil Rights to review the condition of black Americans. Packed with liberals, the committee issued a sweeping denunciation of racial discrimination and segregation. "The pervasive gap between our aims and what we actually do," the committee concluded, "is a kind of moral dry rot which eats away at the emotional and rational bases of democratic beliefs."[10]

Truman embraced the report, calling it "an American charter of human freedom." South of the Mason-Dixon line, however, it was received rather less cordially. In his inaugural address of January 20, 1948, Governor Fielding Wright of Mississippi issued an angry pledge of defiance, one that others promptly echoed. Wright attacked the committee's proposals and called for a break with the Democratic party if its leaders continued to support legislation "aimed to wreck the South and our institutions."[11]

Undeterred by the governor's warning, President Truman sent to Congress early in 1948 a series of legislative proposals on civil rights. The president's plan would establish fair employment practices, prohibit segregation in interstate transportation, make lynching a federal crime, and protect the voting rights of blacks. If Truman's initiatives fell short of the presidential committee's recommendations, they nevertheless represented a sharp break with the past. Certainly the Southern Governors' Conference thought so. In session as Truman was sending these proposals to Congress, the conference promptly announced that the "president must cease attacks on white supremacy or face full-fledged revolt in the South."[12] But Truman kept pushing: later in the same year he issued executive orders forbidding discrimination in federal employment and banning segregation in the armed services.

President Truman took these initiatives partly at the urging of his special counsel and principal political strategist at the time, a young lawyer by the name of Clark Clifford. Clifford argued that the increasing numbers of blacks in northern cities might well tip the vote their way in the upcoming November election, and that, "as always, the South can be considered safely Democratic."[13]

Clifford was wrong. When the Democratic National Convention adopted an aggressive civil rights plank in the summer of 1948—the first time in its history that the party had taken a strong position in support of racial equality—the Mississippi delegation and portions of the Alabama delegation walked out. Several days later, in Birmingham, Alabama, Governor Strom Thurmond of South Carolina was nominated to lead the Dixiecrat revolt against the Democratic party, with Governor Wright of Mississippi at his side. According to Simkins and Roland's account, the assembled company in Birmingham—some 6,000 white southerners—"waved the Confederate flag, snake-danced under the portrait of Robert E. Lee, and condemned as 'infamous and iniquitous' the suggestion of equal rights for Negroes."[14] In accepting the nomination, Thurmond declared, "There are not enough laws on the books of the nation, nor can there be enough laws, to break down segregation in the South."[15]

Thurmond and Wright set out not so much to win the presidency as to deny it to Truman. Their purpose was to punish the Democratic party for betraying the interests of the (white) South, to make perfectly clear that the South could *not* be "considered safely Democratic." With this object in mind, Thurmond and Wright campaigned actively along a southern arc from Texas to Maryland, making Truman's civil rights program their primary target. Thurmond referred to Truman's proposals as "a cheap political trick" and "the wedge which can force open the doorway to tyranny." His speeches generally avoided flagrant racist declarations. In fact, he often said that he was neither prejudiced against nor even opposed to blacks. But the centerpiece of his campaign was opposition to Truman's initiatives on civil rights and defense of segregation. "In the best interests of law and order, for the integrity of the races," Thurmond declared, "whites and Negroes should be kept separate in schools, theaters, and swimming pools." Racial intermingling might be all right for the people of Massachusetts, but "we will have none of it here."[16]

Come fall, Thurmond took 56% of the vote in the Deep South. He carried four states, winning every county in Mississippi and all but one in Alabama.[17] As third party efforts go, the Dixiecrats did splendidly in 1948—though not quite well enough to deny Truman the election.[18]

There can be little question that the defection of southern whites from the Democratic party in 1948 was precipitated primarily by Truman's newfound and well-publicized interest in civil rights. Thurmond did best in the black belt, the "hard core of the political South," where blacks lived in greatest numbers and where appeals to racism were a familiar part of the political landscape.[19] Moreover, the defection came precisely in 1948, just after Truman began to push his civil rights initiatives. As James Sundquist put this point,

> The aggressive civil rights stance of the national Democratic party was the one big *new* event, from the southern viewpoint, of the 1944–52 period. Its traumatic effect can hardly be overestimated. The South, after all, had managed, without leaving the national Democratic party, to accept the Wagner Act, minimum wages, public housing, public power, federal welfare programs, the Farm Security Administration, deficits and debt and devaluation of the dollar, Roosevelt's "purge," and his attack on the Supreme Court. But in the single year of 1948 the issue of civil rights drove out of the national Democratic party almost nine-tenths of its supporters in Mississippi, almost three-fourths in South Carolina, and more

than half in Louisiana, and all of its support (by providing the pretext for keeping it off the ballot) in Alabama.[20]

With the advantages of hindsight, we can now see the Dixiecrat Revolt as a rehearsal for the trouble that race would pose to the Democratic party later on, a persistent split that Thurmond's successors would be able to exploit even more successfully.

None of this was apparent at the time, however. After Truman's scare, the national Democratic party quickly canceled its experiment with civil rights. Truman's support in Washington came primarily from northern Republicans, and it was not enough: Congress failed to enact any of Truman's proposed legislation. In 1952 the party selected Adlai Stevenson as its presidential nominee and Alabama Senator John Sparkman as his running mate. Stevenson was acceptable to the southern wing of the party; his priorities for the country did not include civil rights for black Americans. As an issue of national politics and governmental policy, race once again disappeared from center stage.[21]

The Democratic party's retreat from racial liberalism left voters without an obvious choice on matters of race. If anything, through the 1950s and early 1960s, the Republican party was the more progressive. Insofar as support existed within Congress for civil rights, it came predominantly from liberal Republicans. It was the Republican platform that endorsed racial equality, civil rights, and the 1954 Supreme Court decision on school desegregation. It was with the support of a Republican administration that the Civil Rights Bills of 1957 and 1960 became law, the first legislation designed to protect the rights of black Americans since Reconstruction. And however reluctantly, it was a Republican president who dispatched federal troops to enforce desegregation of the public schools in Little Rock in 1957. Civil rights was central to neither party's agenda, but for those voters determined to throw their support to the party that was more sympathetic to the interests of blacks, Republican was the party of choice.[22]

This changed dramatically in 1964, when Senator Goldwater came storming out of the conservative wing of his party to seize the Republican presidential nomination. Arguing against the encroachments of the federal government in private affairs in general and against the civil rights legislation sponsored by the Johnson administration in particular, Goldwater went where Republican presidential candidates had feared to campaign: Goldwater went South. As he did so he moved the Republican party, the party of emancipation and Abraham Lincoln, decisively to the right on matters of race.

Goldwater meant to achieve the presidency by giving voice to the moral uneasiness and discontent he sensed stirring in the country. He presented himself "as a straightforward and principled man, one who felt deeply that public service was too important to be left to the politicians."[23] In comparison, Lyndon Johnson was, in the Republican view, "a politician of dubious ethics, questionable associations, and brutal egoism."[24] Goldwater himself put the point this way, in characteristically blunt language:

> To Lyndon Johnson, running a country means . . . buying and bludgeoning votes. It means getting a TV monopoly . . . and building a private fortune. It means surrounding himself with companions like Bobby Baker, Billie Sol Estes, Matt McCloskey and other interesting men. . . . It means craving and grasping for power—more and more and more, without end.[25]

Goldwater's purpose was not only to draw personal contrasts with his opponent but also to sharpen the policy differences that divided them. In international relations, Goldwater was an implacable anticommunist. Examining the Kennedy-Johnson record on foreign affairs, he discovered evidence of "drift, deceptions, and defeat."[26] And on matters of domestic policy, Goldwater called for major redirections: "a revival of individual responsibility, a reduction of federal 'welfare' programs, and a decentralization of government power."[27]

The most important feature of the Goldwater campaign from our point of view was its so-called southern strategy. In the spring of 1963, the National Draft Goldwater Committee had circulated a scheme that was intended to propel its candidate to the White House. Breaking with Republican tradition, it conceded most of the Northeast and Midwest to Johnson and gave up on blacks entirely. The key to victory rested instead with holding on to the western states that Nixon had won in 1960 and launching an intensive campaign to win the votes of southern whites.

In some important ways, Goldwater followed this script closely. In the South and elsewhere, Goldwater articulated a forceful defense of states' rights, reminding his audiences that he had stood against the Civil Rights Act of 1964. He also denounced "forced integration" and spoke against transporting children out of their neighborhoods for the sake of achieving racial balance in the schools. He attacked the Supreme Court. He condemned the "wave after wave of crime in our streets and in our homes," the "riot and disorder in our cities." And he expressed contempt for political leaders who had sought "political advantages by turning their eyes from riots and violence."[28]

Certainly all this could be expected to play well among southern whites disenchanted with what they took to be the liberal excesses of the Kennedy-Johnson administration, and certainly there was little in it that would appeal to blacks. But it does a disservice to the ambitions of the Goldwater strategists to call the scheme a southern strategy alone. Stanley Kelley calls it, more fittingly, a "southern-backlash strategy," and indeed it was. Governor George Wallace's striking success in the Democratic primaries in Wisconsin and Indiana in the spring of 1964 suggested to the Goldwater campaign the political profit that might be realized south and north. After Goldwater's nomination was assured, Wallace abandoned his candidacy for the presidency, leaving the Arizona senator the chief beneficiary of the racial resentments that seemed to be simmering throughout the nation. (Wallace eventually endorsed Goldwater.) When race riots erupted in Harlem, Bedford-Stuyvesant, and Rochester in late July, and in Jersey City, Elizabeth, Paterson, and North Philadelphia in August, prospects for a genuine backlash vote in the north brightened. Goldwater repeated his objections to busing and condemned the riots and violence. In the end, although he spent more of this time in the South than Nixon did before him, and there is some reason to think that the Goldwater campaign was better organized and more amply supported in the South than elsewhere, Goldwater in fact brought his campaign to every section of the country.[29]

If read literally, the Goldwater campaign was not racist. Goldwater's vote against the Civil Rights Bill should probably be understood as a principled expression of his general conservatism, a complaint lodged against what he took to be inappropriate encroachments of the federal government. Likewise, Goldwater's opposition to busing for the purposes of racial integration need not be taken as a sign of antagonism toward the rights and interests of black Americans. Indeed, Goldwater claimed to oppose racial discrimination. During the campaign, he said—if infrequently and without enthusiasm—he would enforce the Civil Rights Act of 1964 should he be elected president. His references to riots and violence were no fabrication: riots and violence were occurring. And forsaking the votes of blacks was perhaps just shrewd political strategy.[30]

As pure or careful as the original intentions might have been, however, the Goldwater campaign obviously appealed to racism. In the South especially, the rhetoric of states' rights was, in part, familiar code for keeping blacks in their place.[31] Richard Rovere, political correspondent for *The New Yorker*, accompanied Goldwater on his campaign in the South and was struck by the fact that the senator drew crowds that were large, enthusiastic, and virtually all-white. To Rovere it appeared that "by coming south, Barry Goldwater had made it possible for great numbers of unapologetic white supremacists to hold great carnivals of white supremacy."[32] Strom Thurmond, now the Senator from South Carolina, was so delighted by the Goldwater campaign that he ostentatiously switched parties, endorsed Senator Goldwater, and proceeded to campaign for him enthusiastically.

Goldwater closed his campaign for the presidency in Columbia, South Carolina, delivering a televised speech carried over the entire South. Surrounded at the podium by famous heroes of southern resistance (including Thurmond), Goldwater chose the moment to repeat his attack on the Civil Rights Act of 1964. Of this episode, Earl and Merle Black write, "Goldwater was pitching his anti-civil rights message so low to the ground that even the least astute of his audience would get the point." [33]

As the Republican party was moving to the right on race in 1964, the national Democratic party, pushed hard by the civil rights movement, was moving to the left. During the preceding presidential campaign, Kennedy and Nixon had debated the accomplishments and failures of the Eisenhower years, the nature of the Soviet threat, and the place of religion in American political life. But they said barely a word about the struggle for civil rights under way in the American South.[34] Kennedy's razor-thin victory in 1960 provided no mandate in any case. The new president found himself dependent on the powerful and racially reactionary southern wing of his party, much as Franklin Roosevelt had before him. As a result, ambivalence and moderation marked the Kennedy administration's early efforts on civil rights.[35]

Meanwhile, boycotts, demonstrations, and sit-ins continued. CORE began to sponsor freedom rides through the Deep South to contest segregation in interstate travel, provoking violent reactions from whites, often aided and abetted by local law officials. In the fall of 1962, the State of Mississippi was required under federal court order to enroll James Meredith, a resident of the state and a black, at the University of Mississippi at Oxford. Meredith's appearance incited not just a riot, but, in C. Vann Woodward's perhaps melodramatic terms, "an insurrectionary assault on officers and soldiers of the United States government and the most serious challenge to the Union since the Civil War."[36] The following spring the civil rights movement selected Birmingham, Alabama, as a site for concerted protest. Birmingham was known among civil rights leaders as the "Johannesburg of the South" and home to Police Commissioner Eugene Connor, a notorious racist. Civil rights protesters who sat in at segregated lunch counters or hotels were hauled away and jailed; those who marched were flattened by high pressure water hoses, mauled by police dogs, and pummeled by Connor's forces. In September, when the public schools of Birmingham were under federal court order to desegregate, Governor Wallace placed national guardsmen at the doors to ensure that no black child would enter. In response, President Kennedy federalized the guardsmen, commanded them to return to their barracks, and insisted that desegregation proceed. The following Sunday, an explosion ripped through the Sixteenth Street Baptist Church, killing four black teenage girls, and setting off a riot. All these developments were given extensive coverage in the national (and indeed the world) press, eventually forcing Kennedy's hand. Within the week, Kennedy sent an ambitious civil rights bill to Congress. There it languished, done in by southern Democrats.

Following Kennedy's assassination, President Johnson declared to a joint session of Congress that "no memorial oration or eulogy could more eloquently honor President Kennedy's memory than the earliest passage of the civil rights bill." It required the longest legislative debate in the history of the U.S. Congress, but finally, over the fierce objection of southern Democrats, the Civil Rights Bill became law. Discrimination against black Americans in important arenas of public and private life was now officially illegal.

At the same time that President Johnson was maneuvering the Civil Rights Bill through Congress, he recognized that Goldwater threatened his support among racially conservative whites in 1964, especially in the South. Accordingly, Johnson spent more time in the South in 1964 than Kennedy had in 1960, and when he was there, he did his best to reassure whites that he was not abandoning them. Here is what the Johnson campaign looked like to Stanley Kelley, writing at the time:

> The President repeatedly identified himself with his fellow southerners: "I know the burdens the South has borne. I know the ordeals that have tried the South all these years." He appealed to feelings that it would be good to have the fight on civil rights over and done with: "Our first work must be to bind out wounds and heal our history—and make this nation whole." He made "the Klan and the Birch Society and those others who preach hate" the villains of the civil rights drama.[37]

Johnson also spoke forcefully for the preservation of law and order, no doubt with Goldwater's references to riots and violence in mind. Three days after rioting broke out in Harlem, in late July, Johnson dispatched 200 FBI agents to New York City to investigate the causes of the violence. He used the occasion to declare, pointedly, that "American citizens have a right to protection of life and limb—whether driving along a highway in Georgia, a road in Mississippi or a street in New York City."[38] The president also did his best, according to Theodore White's account, to pressure civil rights groups to direct their energies into voter registration rather than, as the president put it, "hell-raising."[39]

In the end, Johnson was lucky as well as astute. As the campaign entered its final stage, not only did demonstrations and rioting subside but other major events helped push civil rights off center stage. The central thrust of the Democratic campaign had little to do with civil rights in any case; it had to do instead with attempting to portray Goldwater as politically extreme and personally untested. Johnson characterized his own policies as "prudent" and "progressive" when set against the radical proposals of his opponent, while other prominent Democrats made the argument that Goldwater was dangerous.[40]

On election day, Goldwater's presidential aspirations were buried under an avalanche of votes for Lyndon Johnson, who had come a long way from the hill country of east Texas. But in some ways the Republicans' new racial strategy proved to be remarkably cunning. Goldwater took 87% of the vote in Mississippi, nearly 70% in Alabama, 59% in South Carolina, 57% in Louisiana, and 54% in Georgia, all states that had eluded the Republicans since Reconstruction. In the Deep South as a whole, Goldwater ran some forty percentage points better than he had reason to expect, given the distribution of party strength in the region, more than doubling the vote whites had bestowed on Richard Nixon just four years before.[41] The problem from the Republican point of view, of course, is that while Goldwater did astonishingly well in the South, scarcely anywhere else did he do well enough. Outside the Deep South, the Goldwater campaign was in fact a disaster: he captured only his home state of Arizona and was buried in a landslide of historic proportions.[42]

The Goldwater defeat provoked volumes of speculation on realignment, widespread apprehension that the Republican party was on the verge of extinction, and smug analysis from liberal commentators that the conservative movement in America was dead—all of which would look quite foolish in just a few years' time. A more important and enduring legacy of the 1964 campaign was a transformation in the public's perceptions of the political parties. Thanks in large part to Goldwater and Johnson, Americans came to see the Democratic and Republican parties in a completely different way. Before 1964, voters were quite evenly divided over whether the Republican or Democratic party was the more liberal on matters of race; most professed to see no difference between them. But in 1964, a clear majority claimed to see a difference, and most of those were convinced that the Democratic party was the more liberal. This transformation, presented in graphical form in figure 8.1, testifies to the ability of racial disagreements to penetrate a public normally quite inattentive and indifferent to the world of politics.[43]

Figure 8.1 also makes clear that 1964 was no momentary aberration. The events that have unfolded since 1964 have consolidated the changes in party position and public perception first noticed in the Goldwater-Johnson contest. For one thing, Johnson's landslide had consequences for the Congress: a raft of liberal Democrats were brought in on Johnson's coattails, mainly replacing liberal Republicans. Starting in 1965, then, core support for racial liberalism, in the Senate and House alike, was to come from the Democratic party.[44] And for his part, the president continued to push civil rights hard. Johnson worked tirelessly for passage of the Voting Rights Bill of 1965 and the Fair Housing Bill of

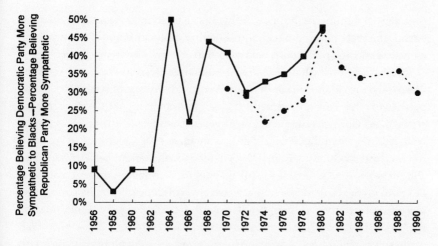

FIGURE 8.1 American public's perception of parties' positions on race, 1956–1990. *Source:* 1956–1980 series (solid line), Carmines and Stimson 1989, p. 165; 1970–1990 series (dotted line), 1970–1990 National Election Studies.

1968; he established the Department of Housing and Urban Development with Robert Weaver its head, the first black cabinet member in U.S. history; he appointed Thurgood Marshall to the Supreme Court, the ninety-sixth justice and the first black; he insisted on a proliferation of programs—VISTA, Head Start, Model Cities, the Office of Economic Opportunity, and more—designed to eradicate poverty and establish the Great Society. In all these conspicuous ways, Johnson succeeded in pushing and hauling the national Democratic party to the left on matters of race.

As Johnson was completing his work, efforts were under way within his own party to overhaul the institutions that govern the selection of a presidential nominee. Following the spectacularly unsatisfying experience of 1968, which featured Johnson's surprise withdrawal, Robert Kennedy's murder, the "police riot" at the Democratic National Convention, and loss of the White House in November, the reform elements within the Democratic party succeeded in changing the rules. These changes—which Byron Shafer called "the most extensive in 140 years" and "the most extensive *planned* changes in the entire history of American parties"—ensured that nominees would be selected less by party leaders and more by the party rank and file, in a dispersed sequence of primaries and open caucuses.[45] The new system allowed a greater voice for black Democrats, whose numbers were increasing rapidly, as we will see momentarily. The proportion of black delegates to the Democratic National Convention doubled between 1964 and 1968, and doubled again in 1972.[46] One consequence of party reform, then, has been to improve the chances that the Democratic presidential nominee will follow in Lyndon Johnson's footsteps. For the most part, Democrats have nominated presidential candidates out of the programmatic liberal wing of the party, committed to civil rights and racial equality.

Meanwhile, on the Republican side of the street, the riots that swept through American cities in the middle and late 1960s, and the apparent failure of liberal policies that the violence seemed to signal, were reviving the Goldwater racial strategy. As violence erupted in Los Angeles, Chicago, New York, Newark, Detroit, and in many other cities, large and small, in every section of the country, the Goldwater position no longer looked misguided. Rather than writing off the 1964 experience as a terrible miscalculation, the Republican party remained to the right on race. Liberal Republicans began to disappear from the corridors of power, replaced by such figures as Governor Ronald Reagan of California and the "new" Richard Nixon, who followed a southern strategy of his own in 1968.

In short, differences between the parties on race set in motion by the events of 1964 have, if anything, hardened over the succeeding years. Nothing is permanent in politics. Bill Clinton gives off signs—in his presidential campaign in 1992, and in his interest in welfare reform and crime control—of trying to move his party closer to the Republicans. But as a general matter, it would appear that the experiment undertaken by the two parties in 1964 has become a settled habit. On matters of race, American voters are now being offered a clear choice.

EXPANSION OF THE BLACK DEMOCRATIC VOTE

The dramatic switch in the position of the parties expressed so vividly in the 1964 election induced predictable alterations in the partisanship of American voters, black and white. While the Democratic party began to lose its historic grip on the political loyalties of white southerners (more on this later), black Americans moved almost unanimously to the Democratic party.

Viewed in historical perspective, the 1964 campaign was the culmination of a process set in motion by the economic dislocations of the 1930s. Before the Depression, from Reconstruction onward, blacks had cast their political lot with the Republican party—where and when they were permitted to vote. The Republican party had history on its side; it was the party of abolition, emancipation, and Abraham Lincoln.[47] But the collapse of the American economy in 1929 signaled the beginning of the end of black Republicanism and the formation of a new Democratic majority.

No group was more devastated by the Great Depression than black Americans. Economic privation, malnutrition, disease, family disintegration: all these fell especially hard upon blacks, particularly in the rural South.[48] But for a time at least, black loyalty to the Republican cause persisted. In 1932, despite economic devastation, despite President Hoover's insistence that the federal government had no obligation to assist those struck down, despite the Republican administration's indifference, if not outright hostility, to the interests of blacks—despite all this—black Americans stood by the Republican candidate. Roosevelt, after all, was a Democrat, and during the campaign he gave blacks no reason to suspend their historically grounded suspicions. More generally, the 1932 campaign, like those since 1876, was not about race: it was preoccupied with more pressing matters:

> Throughout the campaign Roosevelt and Hoover clashed over the causes of the Depression and the best means of coping with it— how to deal with the problem of relief; how to stimulate and stabilize economic activity; and how to keep federal expenditures in check. They differed over farm policy and the relationship of the federal government to public utilities. They debated the repeal of Prohibition. They worried over the gold standard, the protective tariff, and a balanced budget. But they did not concern themselves about blacks. Both national campaign committees mounted "colored divisions," which cranked out publicity for black newspapers and sent prominent blacks on the campaign trail. But these efforts were limited and late, and they were peripheral to the central business of the campaign. Neither candidate addressed a predominantly black audience. Neither took the initiative to issue statements that appealed specifically to black voters.[49]

Presented with such a choice, blacks evidently chose what they took to be the lesser of two evils. While the nation was giving Roosevelt a landslide victory, black Americans voted overwhelmingly for Hoover. As late as 1932, voting Democratic was still viewed within many black communities as "the equivalent of a traitorous act"; "Anybody who wasn't a Republican was somehow or another a kind of questionable character."[50]

But 1936 was another story. While Roosevelt's share of the popular vote diminished between 1932 and 1936 in the country as a whole, his support among black voters shot up. Roosevelt won almost three-quarters of the black vote in 1936, more than double his support from just four years before.[51]

How did this happen? In *Farewell to the Party of Lincoln*, Nancy Weiss points to the "vital role of New Deal relief and economic recovery programs." The great migration of black Americans out of the rural South and into the cities made this political transformation possible, but the change was triggered, according to Weiss, by Roosevelt's relief programs: "Blacks in northern cities in the 1930's voted Democratic because the New Deal brought them some relief from the Depression. . . . It was Franklin Roosevelt's ability to provide jobs, not his embrace of civil rights, that made him a hero to black Americans."[52]

Weiss is quite right to insist that the outpouring of black support for Roosevelt in 1936 cannot be explained by Roosevelt's policy initiatives on civil rights over the previous four years, for there were none. The president refused to support antilynching legislation and, for the most part, refused even to deplore the act of lynching, which was undergoing a resurgence in the South. Likewise, the president did nothing to amend the National Labor Relations Act of 1935 to prohibit or discourage pervasive racial discrimination by labor unions. Roosevelt stood by silently as southern Democrats excluded agricultural and domestic workers from coverage by the Social Security Act. And on the systematic disfranchisement of blacks in the South, Roosevelt had nothing to say.

To move his economic recovery program through Congress, Roosevelt desperately needed the support of his party, which was dominated by southerners. Roosevelt believed, undoubtedly with good reason, that pushing civil rights would jeopardize his economic program. Black voters amounted to only about 3% of the national electorate; most were impoverished and politically disorganized. Even if Roosevelt were personally disposed to push civil rights, the political incentives all ran in the opposite direction. Always there was more pressing business: the economy, the court, the third term, war on a global stage.[53]

This analysis may partially excuse Roosevelt's sorry legislative record on civil rights and economic opportunity for blacks, but it does nothing to explain why blacks threw their support so wholeheartedly to a president who did nothing to advance their political interests. What Roosevelt did provide, according to Weiss, was some relief from economic calamity. Insofar as the New Deal programs enhanced the capacity of the federal government to help those who were suffering, such help was extended to blacks as well as whites. Weiss offers as her best case in point the Works Progress Administration, or WPA, created in May of 1935. The WPA eventually employed thousands of blacks—construction workers, architects and engineers, musicians and writers—and brought schools, community centers, swimming pools, and athletic fields to black neighborhoods. Weiss acknowledges that race discrimination infected the administration of WPA, as it did other New Deal programs, but not fatally: that "blacks were not excluded from the economic benefits of the New Deal was a sufficient departure from past practice to make Roosevelt look like a benefactor of the race."[54]

The emphasis upon economic recovery was one centerpiece of the Democratic appeal to black voters in the 1936 campaign, but there was another message as well, present both in the campaign and in the first four years of the Roosevelt presidency. The message was one of inclusion: that the president sympathized with the predicament of black Americans, and his administration was at least partially open to black demands and aspirations. One expression of this outlook was the establishment of the Black Cabinet, an informal network of blacks within the federal government well known to the black community. Another was Eleanor Roosevelt's highly publicized interest in the plight of black Americans. Mrs. Roosevelt both provided a sympathetic ear to black organizations and became an advocate for their causes with the president. During the 1936 campaign itself, the Democratic National Convention seated black delegates for the first time; representatives of the black press were permitted to sit with other journalists; a black clergyman delivered the invocation; and a black member of Congress gave one of the speeches renominating FDR. Meanwhile, the "colored division" of the campaign, which in years past had been window dressing, apparently meant business in 1936.[55] Members of the Black Cabinet went out on the stump; members of the clergy campaigned from their pulpits; the black press switched over to Roosevelt; the head of the NAACP publicly endorsed the president, breaking his lifelong affiliation with the Republican party; and in the last few weeks of the 1936 campaign, at the dedication of a chemistry building at Howard University erected by the Public Works Administration, FDR delivered his first address to an entirely black audience, taking the opportunity to declare that "among American citizens there should be no forgotten men and no forgotten races."[56]

Some have read this entire episode as symbolic politics at its most cynical.[57] There is some merit to this view, but as Weiss maintains, black Americans did share in the economic benefits distributed by the New Deal, if not in full measure. And the message of inclusion conveyed by various symbolic gestures should not be dismissed. It was not a trivial matter that Roosevelt, from the highest office in the land, began to say to blacks that they were citizens, too. If now the economic benefits seem paltry and the symbolism pathetic, way out of proportion to the transformation of the black vote in 1936, it should serve as a reminder of how desperate things were then, of how thoroughly blacks were excluded from American politics and society.

One good reason for taking the Roosevelt administration's racial symbolism seriously is that Roosevelt's opponents did. By 1936, southern conservatives had begun to worry that the growth of federal powers would undermine the doctrine of states' rights, thereby endangering their ability to "manage" the race problem. Governor Talmadge of Georgia was one leader of this anti–New Deal movement. In an effort to build support for his cause, Talmadge appealed to whites' racial pride and fears. And at the center of Talmadge's effort, according to Harvard Sitkoff, was Eleanor Roosevelt:

> Eleanor Roosevelt was made the symbol of everything wrong with the "damnyankee," race-meddling New Deal. The followers of Tal-

madge attacked her for hosting a garden party for inmates of the
National Industrial Training School for Girls, labeling it just enter-
tainment for "a bunch of 'nigger whores.' " They distributed thousands of pictures throughout the South of 'Nigger Lover Eleanor'
dancing with a black youth. Another widely-reproduced picture
showed Mrs. Roosevelt with some ROTC cadets at Howard University. Its caption read: "A picture of Mrs. Roosevelt going to some
nigger meeting, with two escorts, niggers, on each arm." They also
circulated rumors that blacks "come to the White House banquets
and sleep in the White House beds," and popularized the ditty:

> You kiss the negroes,
> I'll kiss the Jews,
> We'll stay in the White House
> As long as we choose.

Virtually all their speeches against the New Deal included at least
one accusation against Eleanor Roosevelt of having Negro blood or
a black lover.[58]

If Eleanor Roosevelt's attitudes seem mild and her actions innocuous when
judged from the perspective of the present, they most certainly were not in her
own time. What she said and did gave hope to black Americans and infuriated
many whites. However "merely symbolic" and detached from tangible benefits they may have been, these visible signs of access and influence were taken
seriously by blacks and racist whites alike.

Whatever the precise reasons, nearly three-quarters of black Americans
gave their votes to Franklin Roosevelt in the 1936 presidential election. More
important for the long term, they gave their loyalty to the Democratic party.
This point is established in figure 8.2, which reveals two roughly stable periods
of Democratic support among black Americans, one running up to and the
other leading out of 1964. On the left-hand side of the figure appears one high
plateau, signifying substantial black support for the Democratic presidential
ticket from 1936 to 1960. On the right-hand side appears an even higher plateau,
signifying overwhelming black support for the Democratic presidential ticket
from 1964 to the present. The two plateaus are connected by a steep cliff, centered on 1964. Put another way, the Goldwater-Johnson contest and the events
that followed converted a decisive Democratic majority among black Americans into a supermajority. Blacks came late to the Democratic coalition—after
the Irish, the Italians, and the Jews—but they have stayed the longest, and are
now the most loyal members of what remains of the New Deal majority party.

That black voters abandoned the party of Lincoln so completely is impressive, but it is just part of the story of the increase of the black Democratic vote.

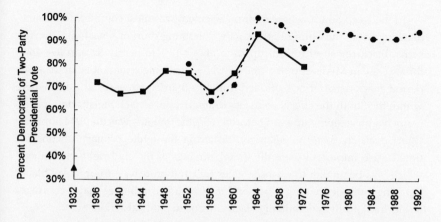

FIGURE 8.2 Black Americans' presidential vote, 1932–1992. *Source:* 1936–1972 series (solid line), Ladd and Hadley 1978, p. 158; 1952–1992 series (dotted line), 1952–1992 National Election Studies; 1932 (triangle), estimated from voting statistics assembled by Weiss 1983.

More important was the expansion of the black electorate. After long delay, the right to take part in elections regardless of race was about to become real.

The modern campaign to secure the vote produced savage resistance in the Deep South and, on three separate occasions, in 1957, 1960, and 1964, federal legislation with no teeth. Prompted in part by the violence in Selma, Alabama, Congress finally passed a serious voting rights bill. President Johnson signed the bill into law on August 6, 1965, thereby bringing to completion a year of remarkable legislative achievements for civil rights.

At the time of its passage, the Voting Rights Bill was widely regarded as a drastic measure, one required by the grotesque distortions of democratic practice that then prevailed over much of the South. Its main provisions pertained to "covered" jurisdictions, found for the most part in the Deep South, states and counties that made use of literacy tests and that had a voter turnout below 50% in the 1964 presidential election. In such jurisdictions, literacy tests, which gave enormous discretion to local registrars in order to exclude blacks from the polls, were immediately suspended. In this way, the Voting Rights Act supplemented the Twenty-fourth Amendment to the Constitution, ratified the previous year, which prohibited the poll tax, still another device for discouraging black participation.[59] The act also stipulated that covered jurisdictions could institute no new voting qualification or procedure without prior approval, or "preclearance." At the discretion of the Justice Department, federal registrars and election observers could be dispatched to covered jurisdictions to guarantee blacks their right to vote—and they were.

In the Deep South, where disfranchisement was most complete, the immediate impact of the Voting Rights Act was nothing short of sensational. In Alabama, black registration shot up from about 19% to nearly 52% in less than three years. In Mississippi the figures were even more remarkable: in the same period, black registration exploded from less than 7% to nearly 60%. Elsewhere within the South the effects were less dramatic, since black registration had already begun creeping upward before 1965. One impetus was the 1944 Supreme Court decision, *Smith v. Allwright*, declaring the white primary unconstitutional. Also important were the initial stirrings of the civil rights movement, which was beginning to sponsor voter registration drives, to organize blacks into single-minded voting blocs, and to persuade candidates that there might be electoral profit in mobilizing black citizens to political action.[60]

Over and above these effects, however, the Voting Rights Act (and the Twenty-fourth Amendment) visibly increased black participation in elections. The suspension of literacy tests and the prohibition of poll taxes produced large gains in registration.[61] Registration rose further in those jurisdictions faced with the prospect that the U.S. Attorney General might dispatch federal officers to oversee the registration of voters and observe the conduct of elections. In fact, few examiners and observers descended from Washington, but the threat that they might—or in the colorful language of the attorney general of Mississippi at the time, that federal officers might "swarm in here like grasshoppers on a spring morning and register one group of people on a wholesale basis"—evidently persuaded many local election officials that it was better to open the registration process to blacks than risk federal interference.[62] At the same time, the distinct possibility of federal intervention "gave hope and legal protection to the efforts of CORE, SNCC, the N.A.A.C.P., and the Voter Education Project."[63] In these various ways, then, the Voting Rights Act went a long way in the direction of securing "for black Americans what the Fourteenth and Fifteenth Amendments, passed during the first Reconstruction, had not—the right to vote, the very bedrock of democracy."[64]

• The consequences of all this considerable activity are summarized in figure 8.3, which presents the growth in black registration in the South from 1940 to the present. In 1940, despite a voting-age population of nearly five million, only about 150,000 blacks were registered to vote, little more than 3% of those eligible. Today in the American South, almost 6 million blacks are officially registered, a *forty-fold* increase. One can scarcely imagine a more consequential transformation of the southern electoral landscape.

With many more blacks voting, and voting overwhelmingly Democratic, black Americans had become a sizable and important constituency for the Democratic party. Indeed, the black vote was now indispensable to Democratic

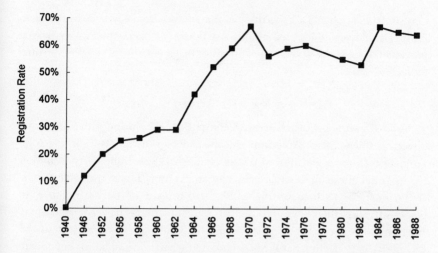

FIGURE 8.3 Black registration in southern states, 1940–1988. *Source:* Jaynes and Williams 1989, p. 233.

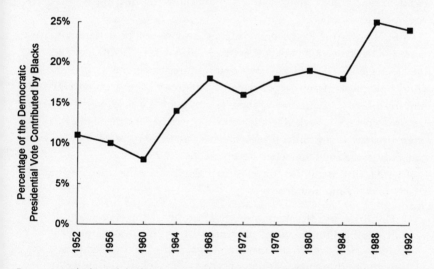

FIGURE 8.4 Blacks and the Democratic coalition, 1952–1992. *Source:* Stanley and Niemi 1995.

success. In figure 8.4 we display the percentage of the Democratic party presidential vote contributed by black Americans from 1952 to 1992. Before 1964, blacks supplied something less than 10% of the Democratic total. In 1988, however, after Goldwater and Johnson's positions on race had become a settled habit, and after the Voting Rights Act and the civil rights movement had pried open the electoral system, blacks provided more than 20% of the Democratic vote. In 1988, Michael Dukakis drew as many votes from blacks as he did from Catholics or from union households. As figure 8.4 makes plain, Democratic presidential candidates need the support of black Americans; they have come to depend on it.

DEMISE OF THE SOLID SOUTH

As a consequence of changes in the parties and in the procedures that govern elections, black Americans became active participants in the electoral struggle for power and moved decisively to the Democratic party. All other things equal, these quite remarkable alterations should have strengthened the Democratic party's hold on the South, where disproportionate numbers of blacks still make their home. Quite clearly, all other things have not been equal. Far from it. The dramatic switch in the position of the parties expressed so vividly in the 1964 election induced changes in the partisan affiliations not only of black voters but of white voters as well. As a consequence, the Democratic party began to lose its hold on the South. A "momentous reversal of party fortunes" was about to take place.[65]

From Reconstruction through the New Deal, no section of the country was more solidly Democratic than the South. In 1924, when Calvin Coolidge somehow managed to secure 1,100 votes in the entire state of South Carolina, Governor Cole Blease, Democrat, demagogue, and race baiter par excellence, was moved to say: "I do not know where he got them. I was astonished to know they were cast and shocked to know that they were counted."[66] An apocryphal story, perhaps, but one that reveals much about the sorry state of the Republican party in the South following Reconstruction.

There is little doubt that the one-party South was built upon a foundation of racism and white supremacy:

> Of all the ties that bound the South to the Democratic party in the first half of the twentieth century, by far the most compelling and sacrosanct was the shared understanding that the Democratic party was the party of white supremacy. This belief was the essence of the traditional southern political culture. In return for unswerving loyalty to the Democratic party in national elections, southern Democratic leaders expected ample freedom to control race relations within the region.[67]

Such expectations were directly and visibly challenged by President Truman's experiment with racial liberalism, which led immediately and dramatically to the Dixiecrat revolt. Thurmond's success in 1948 suggested that the days of the Solid South might finally be numbered. But when the national Democratic party retreated on civil rights, southern whites returned home, voting Democratic in 1952 and 1956.

Writing in 1963 on the possibility of a political realignment in the South, Philip Converse pointed out that analysts and strategists alike "have awaited a collapse of the Democratic grip on the region with notable impatience. For some time the collapse has seemed 'just around the corner.' Although the signs of impending change persist, the South has yet to see anything like the major partisan realignment which appeared so imminent fifteen years ago."[68] Instead of realignment, Converse detected secular processes at work—migration, urbanization, and industrialization—that were gradually bringing the South into the mainstream of American political life. Converse concluded that political change in the South was "proceeding at a snail's pace. It smacks more of a slow erosion of regional differences than of any dramatic partisan realignment, even in its early stages."[69] Extrapolating from the slight and gradual movement detected in the survey materials available to him at the time, Converse offered a facetiously precise prediction: that the South would become indistinguishable from the rest of the country in its partisan loyalties in June 1983.[70]

As we know now, the eve of the Goldwater campaign was exactly the wrong moment to be making forecasts about the political future of the South based on linear extensions from the past. A revolution in partisan loyalties was about to take place. Converse's mistake was that he failed to anticipate that the major parties were on the verge of offering voters a clear choice on race. Realignment not only requires the kind of urgency and immediacy supplied by the crisis in race relations brewing in the South; it also requires that there be no ambiguity in voters' minds about which party is championing whose interests. Before 1964, many southern voters, black and white, were vitally concerned about civil rights, but they saw neither party speaking for them. In 1964, all that changed. The 1964 presidential campaign made it possible for voters to act on their racial views. In 1964, the question of civil rights, so central a preoccupation of southern society, was unleashed onto the electoral arena by the clear and opposing positions staked out by President Johnson and Senator Goldwater.

As we have seen, the Johnson-Goldwater contest precipitated a massive shift in political allegiances among black Americans, moving them almost unanimously to the Democratic party. The point we wish to add here is that as blacks moved *into* the Democratic party, southern whites moved *out*. These opposite and partially offsetting movements in party attachment are summarized and displayed in figure 8.5. The movements shown there are remarkable in two respects: in their magnitude, and in their speed. As late as 1960, native-born southern whites were much more Democratic in their partisan affiliations than were blacks—according to figure 8.5, they were twenty-eight percentage points

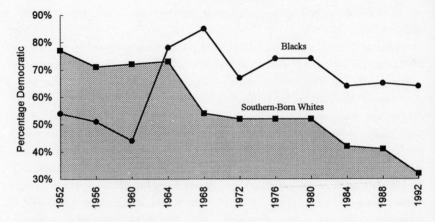

FIGURE 8.5 Democratic identification among blacks and southern-born whites, 1952–1992. *Source:* Stanley and Niemi 1995.

more Democratic. By 1968, just eight years later, this large difference had completely reversed: now blacks were much more Democratic in their partisan affiliations than were southern whites—by thirty-one percentage points.[71]

This is a breathtaking change, centered once again on 1964, one that cannot be understood by referring to urbanization, industrialization, or migration. Such processes have helped to nudge the South closer to the nation as a whole over the last seventy years, but they cannot account for sharp swings in partisanship accomplished in less than a decade.[72] Likewise, although recession and war can produce shifts in party strength, it is hard to see why these forces would move whites in the South but not whites elsewhere, or why they would push whites in one direction and blacks in the other.[73] Something else was going on.

All in all, the movements depicted in figure 8.5 certainly resemble what V. O. Key, Jr. meant by a "realignment," one induced by changes in the parties over the question of race. Key introduced the concept of realignment to draw attention to those special junctures in American political history when the coalitions supporting the parties break and re-form. For Key the hallmark of such turning points was the "critical election," characterized by a "sharp and durable electoral realignment between parties."[74] By a near consensus, critical elections and the national realignments that accompany them have occurred three times since the origins of the modern party system, at intervals of about a generation: first in the 1850s, second near the turn of the century, and third and most recently during the 1930s, in the depths of the Great Depression.

If as Burnham and others argue, there is a generational rhythm to realignments, then the fourth case of realignment is long overdue.[75] The tardiness of the next realignment—and the accompanying inability of realignment theory to account for what has happened lately in American politics on a national scale—has produced a crisis of confidence in the theory.[76] But whatever its problems and ambiguities in explaining national trends, realignment theory fits the particular case under examination here almost to perfection.

Consider these facts, which follow the classic realignment script closely. First of all, it is not hard to argue that the challenge to race relations posed by the civil rights movement and the savage response it often provoked produced the necessary precipitating crisis in the South—and perhaps for blacks nation-wide. Protests, sit-ins, marches, and other forms of demonstrations increased through the early 1960s. Such activities, and the flagrantly racist reactions they often provoked, reached their absolute peak in 1965, when they were still taking place predominantly inside the South.[77] The second ingredient required to set off a realignment, according to the classic theory, is that the parties must offer voters a choice. Goldwater and Johnson did so in 1964, as Kennedy and Nixon had not four years earlier, and as their successors would in presidential elections to come.

Third, not only did voters take notice of this historic transformation in party positions on race, but southern voters in particular marched to the polls in record numbers. Turnout in the South was greater in 1964 and 1968 than in any other election in the twentieth century.[78] High turnout is characteristic of critical elections in the classic mold. Finally, remember that the shift in party allegiance was more rapid among blacks than among southern whites. Blacks moved expeditiously into the Democratic party, with much of this change accomplished by 1964. Movement in the opposite direction among southern whites was more gradual, apparent first in 1966 and continuing on through 1970 or so.

This difference of pace may reflect differences in strength of partisanship among blacks and whites, especially in the South. Most black Americans lived in the South at this time, and many lived in desperate circumstances: economically depressed, educationally impoverished, excluded from mainstream society, shut out of politics for generations.[79] That blacks moved so promptly and so completely to the Democratic party in 1964 suggests successful mobilization rather than conversion. By comparison, southern whites were faced with relinquishing historic commitments, something that requires more time. A mix of mobilization and conversion is consistent with the standard realignment story.

In short, we interpret the rearrangement of party loyalties described in figure 8.5 as an exemplary case of realignment, one set in motion by the historic reversal of party positions in 1964 in the context of a racial crisis that was every bit as gripping in its own way as was the economic dislocation of the 1930s. The Goldwater and Johnson campaign of 1964 gave electoral expression to the simmering racial changes under way in the South. As a consequence, blacks moved into the Democratic party, and white southerners moved out.[80]

These shifts in partisanship had predictable consequences for the emergence of a Republican party and the eventual return to political competition in the South. That white southerners were leaving the Democratic party in great numbers did not translate immediately into a politically potent Republican party, however. White southerners left the Democratic party, but it took some time for them to arrive fully at the Republican.[81] Moreover, the institutional barriers to the emergence of a competitive Republican party in the South were high. The party was badly organized, commanded few resources, and was led, if that is the right word, by a demoralized leadership.[82] The emergence of a Republican challenge to the Democratic South required a reinvigorated organization and new leadership. According to Sundquist, the Goldwater campaign provided both. Although clobbered in the country, Goldwater revived Republican organizations in the South.[83]

Indications of the return of political competition below the Mason-Dixon line are provided in figure 8.6. The figure displays, in two separate lines, the percentage of House seats and the comparable percentage of U.S. Senate seats won by the Republicans. In each instance, Republican success is plotted from the 1940s, across the critical turning point of 1964, on into the early 1990s.

Figure 8.6 displays the overwhelming dominance enjoyed by the Democratic party early in the series. As late as 1958, southern Republicans mounted official challenges in only 33 of the region's 106 House elections! Republican

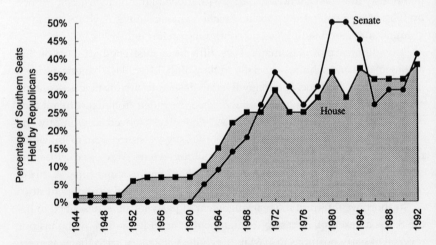

FIGURE 8.6 Emergence of Republican political strength in the South, 1944–1992. *Source:* Black and Black 1992, p. 356; 1992, *Who's Who in Congress 1993, 103d Congress* (Washington, D.C.: Congressional Quarterly Press, 1993).

success was essentially invisible until the early 1960s but then took off sharply. This timing meshes perfectly with the rearrangement of the national parties on race in 1964. At the presidential level, apart from the Carter and Clinton interludes, the Solid South is now, and has been since 1964, solidly Republican.

After examining numbers of the sort we present in figure 8.6, Black and Black concluded that the "breadth of the Democratic collapse is staggering," as indeed it is.[84] From the Republican point of view, the prospects for a new majority, and for regaining and holding the presidency, now lay in the South. In 1992, the eleven states of the Old Confederacy offered up more than one-quarter of the nation's electoral votes: sweeping the South provides more than one-half of the electoral votes required to capture the presidency. Goldwater's "southern strategy," so widely ridiculed in the immediate aftermath of 1964, has become a standard part of the Republican presidential campaign.

THE EMERGENCE OF RACIAL CODE

While the parties were changing places, blacks were registering and voting Democratic in record numbers, and southern whites were moving toward the Republican party, something else was happening that would help to define the character of our current predicament. Racism, which for generations had been an entirely respectable point of view, was losing respectability. The old norms of white supremacy and racial segregation were giving way. White voters were serenaded less and less by candidates who expressed unqualified support for segregation and who appealed in straightforward fashion to race prejudice.

This represents a clear departure from the not-so-distant past. In his successful campaign for governor in 1959, Ross Barnett told Mississippi voters, "I don't believe God meant for the races to be integrated. God placed the black man in Africa and separated the white man from him with a body of water. . . . Integration has ruined every community in which it has been practiced. I would rather lose my life than to see Mississippi schools integrated."[85] Barnett's remarks were quite representative for his time (and place), but his time was passing. The passionate defense of segregation and the deliberate appeal to racism that characterized Barnett's campaign were about to disappear. As a general rule, we don't hear this kind of talk any longer—not from public officials, or from candidates, or from those in public life more generally.

The best evidence on this point comes from Earl Black's careful examination of the campaigns of every serious candidate for governor in each of the eleven Old Confederacy states across nearly a quarter-century, from 1950 through 1973. Black finds that, prior to the *Brown* school desegregation case, racial segregation was seldom the centerpiece of gubernatorial campaigns. The racial caste system was simply taken for granted; the inferior status of the Negro was a settled question. Campaigns were dominated by segregationists, to be sure, but rival candidates saw little profit in reminding their white audiences of where they stood on this most historic and sacred of commitments. As Black put it, "There might be differences of style, tone, and emphasis, but white politicians in the years before *Brown v. Board of Education* were united by 'a common resolve indomitably maintained—that it shall be and remain a white man's country.' "[86]

Then in 1954 came the Supreme Court's decision that racial segregation in public schools was unconstitutional. The court's unanimous declaration that "in the field of public education the doctrine of 'separate but equal' has no place" altered the political landscape in the South, bringing segregation and its defense to the center of public discourse. In just a few years' time, militant segregationists like Ross Barnett of Mississippi and George Wallace of Alabama came to dominate Southern gubernatorial elections. Such candidates expressed unqualified opposition to race mixing, appealed directly and crudely to racism, and ridiculed their opponents as racial moderates. The successful gubernatorial campaign of J. Lindsay Almond of Virginia in 1957 provides an excellent case in point:

> A champion of massive resistance to school desegregation, Almond dismissed the *Brown* decision as the "sociological predilections and wild hallucinations of nine men contrary to the language of the Constitution." His moderate segregationist opponent might favor a pupil placement plan even though it "opens the door for mass integration" and "embraces, accepts, promotes, and legalizes race-mixing," but Almond promised to "defend our way of life" and to "fight relentlessly to prevent amalgamation of races in Virginia."[87]

Such talk began to diminish through the 1960s, and by the 1970s, according to Black's analysis, it had practically disappeared. Federal efforts to desegregate public accommodations and public schools in the South persisted and eventually prevailed. In the meantime, a newly mobilized and sizable black electorate stood ready to support racial moderates. In the face of these sweeping changes, militant segregationism was no longer a winning position. It was replaced not by full-fledged racial liberalism, but by what might be called "benign neglect." Candidates of this persuasion essentially avoided questions of race: they neither defended nor attacked segregation and they said as little as possible about the racial caste system. Campaigns that avoided race, which were no more than a curiosity in the 1950s, typified Southern gubernatorial contests by the early 1970s.

This change in public speech about race finds a parallel in white Americans' views on integration and equal opportunity, which have also undergone a transformation over the past forty years. White Americans once gave their support to the principles of segregation and discrimination; now they support racial integration and equality of opportunity, at least in principle. This transformation is consistent with Black's conclusion that political appeals based in white supremacy or fears of racial amalgamation are no longer broadly acceptable. Public speech on race is now calibrated, cautious. Officials are careful what they say.

The disappearance of racial segregation and white supremacy from public discourse does not mean that appeals to racism have disappeared. It means something less: that racial antagonism is expressed in more subtle and socially acceptable ways. Earl Black makes exactly this point, as he cautions us not to be swept away by changes in southern campaign rhetoric on racial segregation. Black predicted that "many white candidates . . . will find ways to appeal to anti-black prejudices without describing themselves as segregationists" and that "truculent demands for the preservation of racial segregation" will give way "to more euphemistic language."[88] The new rules governing public discussion of race require not the abandonment of racism, but rather that appeals to prejudice be undertaken carefully, through indirection and subterfuge. Political debate on matters of race now often takes place in code. Racial codewords make appeals to prejudice electorally profitable even when, as in contemporary American society, prejudice is officially off limits.

More precisely, we define racial code, following Himelstein, as:

> a word or phrase which communicates a well-understood but implicit meaning to part of a public audience while preserving for the speaker deniability of that meaning by reference to its denotative explicit meaning. . . . Code words are intended as rhetorical winks, and if they are too easily detected they lose their deniability and thus their effectiveness.[89]

Himelstein's interest in codewords was motivated by his observations of racial politics in Mississippi in the late 1970s, where increases in black voter strength and changes in the etiquette of race relations seemed to have "sanitized the language of political rhetoric."[90] Conservative white politicians needed the support of racially resentful white voters, but they also needed to avoid being tagged as racists. The solution to their problem was provided by codewords. Repeated references to "racial discord," or "federal intrusion," or "outside agitation" served to remind white Mississippians that whatever novel issue they seemed to be facing was really the familiar one of race. They were encouraged to place themselves in the middle of an old fight, and to think (and vote) accordingly.

Himelstein was writing about Mississippi, but his analysis has implications for the nation as a whole. As early as the middle 1960s, codewords were becoming prominent in public discourse about race. Witness, for example, the campaign to overturn fair housing in California in 1964, couched in the language of liberty and property rights. In the summer of 1963, the California legislature, at the insistence of Democratic Governor Pat Brown, had passed the Rumford Bill, which prohibited racial discrimination in the housing and rental markets. Having fought and lost with the legislature, California real estate and property management interests took their case to the people. On the November ballot appeared Proposition 14, which promised both to repeal the Rumford Act and to prevent the state or any locality within from adopting fair housing legislation of any sort.

According to Wolfinger and Greenstein's analysis, public debate on Proposition 14 was structured around competing claims of principle: between equal opportunity, on the one side, and liberty and property rights, on the other:

> Opponents of Proposition 14 based their case on the desirability of providing equal housing opportunity for minority groups, especially Negroes. The "no" vote was solicited, in the phrase of the bumper stickers, as "a vote against prejudice and discrimination." Needless to say, the proposition's proponents did not argue in favor of "prejudice," "discrimination," and "inequality," at least not in their public messages. The "yes on 14" forces stressed the principles of "property rights" and "non-compulsion."

Thus Proposition 14 was at once an embodiment of cherished American principles and, for those tuned to hear it, an expression of racial animosity aimed at keeping blacks out of white neighborhoods. In the end, after the kind of intense and lavishly financed campaign that we have come to expect of California initiatives, Proposition 14 carried easily, by a two to one margin.[91]

Consider, as another example, Goldwater's vigorous defense of states' rights in the 1964 presidential campaign. To Richard Rovere, who accompanied the senator on his tour of the South, the groundswell of southern support for Goldwater appeared "to be a racist movement and very little else." Not that Goldwater presented himself as a defender of segregation or a proponent of white supremacy. According to Rovere, Goldwater

> did not, to be sure, make any direct racist appeals. He covered the South and never, in any public gatherings, mentioned "race" or

"Negroes" or "whites" or "segregation" or "civil rights." But the fact that the words did not cross his lips does not mean that he ignored the realities they describe. He talked about them all the time in an underground, or Aesopian language—a kind of code that few in his audiences had any trouble deciphering. In the code, "bullies and marauders" means "Negroes." "Criminal defendants" means "Negroes." "States' rights" means "opposition to civil rights." "Women" means "white women."[92]

Or contemplate the 1968 presidential campaign of Richard Nixon, who pursued a southern strategy in every corner of the country. Nixon's transformation between 1960 and 1968 is striking, a revelation of the shift in party positions on race embodied within a single person. In 1960, Nixon actively sought the votes of blacks and ran on the standard progressive Republican platform. In 1968, Nixon wrote blacks off and instead pursued the votes of racially disaffected whites. He did so quietly and indirectly. Nixon neither endorsed segregation nor gave voice to white supremacist sentiments. Indeed, Nixon's formal positions on matters of civil rights and desegregation, as routinely expressed in the campaign, did not differ that much from the positions expressed by his Democratic opponent, Hubert Humphrey, who for twenty years had fought tirelessly for civil rights.[93] Still, the subtext was there to read, not very far beneath the surface.

In 1968, Nixon chose as his running mate Spiro T. Agnew, an obscure governor from the border state of Maryland known best for his punitive response to racial unrest, a striking contrast to Henry Cabot Lodge, a representative of the liberal New England wing of the Republican party, who ran beside Nixon in 1960. Nixon campaigned hard in the South in 1968, embraced southern cultural symbols, and identified himself with heroes of southern resistance, most notably Senator Thurmond of South Carolina. As the 1968 Republican National Convention opened, Nixon met with southern delegations to assure them that he understood and sympathized with their "racial predicament."

And the new Nixon—post-1964 Republican, post-Goldwater—is revealed finally in the battering he gave to the Johnson-Humphrey administration on the issue of law and order.[94] Early in 1968 Nixon condemned the official Kerner Commission report on civil disorders for blaming "everybody for the riots except the perpetrators of violence" and promised "retaliation against the perpetrators" that would be "swift and sure."[95] He began his acceptance speech at the Republican National Convention this way: "As we look at America, we see cities enveloped in smoke and flame. We hear sirens in the night. . . ." Later in the same address, Nixon adroitly connected fears provoked by the urban riots with resentments over assistance to blacks: "For the past five years we have been deluged by government programs for the unemployed; programs for the cities; programs for the poor. And we have reaped from these programs an ugly harvest of frustration, violence, and failure across the land. . . . I say it is time to quit pouring billions of dollars into programs that have failed." During the campaign itself, Nixon's television advertisements played upon Americans' fear of crime. While voiceovers pointed to sharp increases in violent crime and blamed the Democrats, the television viewer witnessed scenes of riots and buildings in flames, montages of urban decay, a lonely policeman on the beat, a mugging, crowds taunting the police, faces of anxious and perplexed Americans, and a woman walking alone on a deserted city street as darkness fell.

In 1960, before Goldwater and Johnson, before the Voting Rights Act, and before the riots, Nixon took nearly one-third of the black vote. In 1968, in the aftermath of Watts and Detroit, he won less than one black vote in ten.[96]

Consider, as a final and telling example, George Wallace, who had built a substantial political career, first in Alabama, and then in the country as a whole, by giving an angry voice to Americans frightened of racial change. In 1962 Wallace made defense of segregation the centerpiece of his successful gubernatorial campaign. Defiance rang through his inaugural address, delivered on a cold, bleak day in Montgomery:

> This nation was never meant to be a unit of one, but a unit of the many . . . and so it was meant in our racial lives. Each race, within its own framework, has the freedom to teach, to instruct, to develop, to ask for and receive deserved help from others of separate racial station . . . but if we amalgamate into the one unit as advocated by the Communist philosopher, then the enrichment of our lives, the freedom for our development is gone forever. We become, therefore, a mongrel unit of one under a single all-powerful government. And we stand for everything, and for nothing. . . . Today I have stood where Jefferson Davis stood, and took an oath to my people. It is very appropriate then that from this Cradle of the Confederacy, this very heart of the great Anglo-Saxon Southland, that today we sound the drum for freedom. . . . In the name of the greatest people that have ever trod this earth, I draw the line in the dust and toss the gauntlet before the feet of tyranny. And I say, Segregation now! Segregation tomorrow! Segregation forever![97]

Wallace's national aspirations were fueled by the pending civil rights legislation in Washington and the demonstrations and riots that seemed to be happening everywhere. In early 1964, he entered a series of Democratic presidential primaries, running in each case against home-state candidates standing in for President Johnson. Wallace's success astonished the country: he took 34% of the vote in Wisconsin, nearly 30% in Indiana, and 43% in Maryland. There was nothing subtle in Wallace's appeal: he declared himself to be against racial inter-mingling, arguing that, as he once put it to a *Newsweek* reporter, "countries with niggers in 'em have stayed the same for a thousand years."[98]

By the time of his campaign for the presidency in 1968, however, even Wallace had mastered the new etiquette. He no longer endorsed segregation; he did not declare that blacks were inferior; he no longer referred to race mixing or to the mongrelization of the white race in his speeches. Indeed, Wallace steered scrupulously away from explicitly racist language of any kind.[99]

But while Wallace did not mention blacks by name, he referred to them con-stantly. They were the clear, if unnamed, beneficiaries of what Wallace regarded as the federal government's relentless and arrogant intrusion upon the rights of ordinary citizens to send their children to the schools they wished and to sell their homes to whomever they pleased. They were the murderers and rapists constantly lurking in city alleyways and parks, coddled by the liberal courts. They were the outlaws and thugs who felt free to burn and loot "our" cities. To a long-time associate of Wallace's from Alabama, these allusions were not diffi-cult to decipher: "He can use all the other issues—law and order, running your own schools, protecting property rights—and never mention race. But people will know he's telling them 'A nigger's trying to get your job, trying to move into your neighborhood.' What Wallace is doing is talking to them in a kind of shorthand, a kind of code."[100]

Millions of whites got the message. In 1968, Wallace mounted the most suc-cessful third party presidential campaign since Theodore Roosevelt in 1912. He won close to two-thirds of the white vote in the Deep South, carried five states, and received forty-six electoral votes. In 1972, having returned to the Demo-cratic fold, Wallace was the clear front runner for the Democratic presidential nomination, winning primaries south and north, when a hail of bullets ended his presidential ambitions.

Perhaps the most notorious purveyor of racial codewords today is David Duke. Duke is an elected member of the Louisiana state house and in 1991 a serious, but not quite successful, candidate for the U.S. Senate. He is also for-merly national grand wizard of the Ku Klux Klan. There is little reason to doubt that Duke owes his political appeal to racism. But out on the campaign trail, speaking to poor whites in small, dusty towns, what does Duke say? Does he hold forth on the innate superiority of the white race? No. Does he promise a return to segregation? He does not. Instead, Duke expresses indignation over reverse discrimination and welfare abuse, and boasts of his legislative triumphs over the allegedly powerful black caucus back in Baton Rouge. This is code, of course, but if we cannot detect overt racism in Duke's campaign—if a former grand wizard of the KKK, the most destructive racist organization in the history of the United States, has managed to master the new lessons of American racial politics—then we can be sure that something important and widespread has changed in public discourse on race.[101]

THE ELECTORAL TEMPTATIONS OF RACE

Transported to the national stage, the Duke phenomenon speaks to the electoral temptations of race. The balance in national elections now rests in the hands of what are often referred to as "Reagan Democrats" (though we could just as well call them Wallace Democrats or Nixon Democrats). They are white and culturally conservative. They generally think of themselves as Democrats, and they may even vote that way in state and local elections, but they often cross over to support Republicans for president. Though sympathetic to the idea of racial integration in principle and racial equality as an ideal, they are generally hostile to policies designed to bring integration and equality about. Both the Democrats and Republicans need their support—and therein lie the electoral temptations of race.

From the Democratic perspective, the electoral problem is to maintain the loyalty and enthusiasm of blacks without alienating conservative whites. Where Democratic candidates and black voters are concerned, the temptation is benign neglect. The problem from the Republican point of view is to enlist the support of white conservatives without appearing racist. Where Republican candidates and white voters are concerned, the temptation is racial codewords.

So we say, and so we hope to show. Chapter 9 will take us from theory to practice. From the general formulation of the electoral temptations of race set out here we proceed next to take up in detail the 1988 American presidential campaign, treating it as a flagrant and dispiriting case in point.

CHAPTER NINE

Benign Neglect and Racial Codewords in the 1988 Presidential Campaign

The 1988 contest for the presidency between George Bush and Michael Dukakis has few defenders. It has been characterized as the meanest and least edifying in modern memory, the most dismal of presidential campaigns, a national embarrassment. Critics say that no real discussion of the nation and its future took place, that serious debate disappeared in a blizzard of sound bites, negative advertisements, and misinformation.[1]

Maybe so. Certainly we have no interest in championing the 1988 campaign. As an exercise in civic education, at extravagant public expense, it left much to be desired. But our response differs from the standard complaint. Our point rather is that the 1988 campaign exemplified the electoral problem that race now poses to both parties. That problem, as we attempted to show in the preceding chapter, has two faces: for the Democratic party, to maintain the loyalty and enthusiasm of blacks without alienating racially resentful whites; and for the Republican party, to enlist the support of racially resentful whites without appearing racist. The purpose of this chapter is to illuminate the electoral temptations of race in practice, taking the 1988 presidential campaign as a theoretically splendid, if democratically disheartening, case in point. First we recapitulate the campaign as voters saw it, and then, in the core of the chapter, analyze white and black voters' reactions, paying special attention to racial resentment among whites and racial group solidarity among blacks.

CODEWORDS AND NEGLECT IN 1988

Governor Dukakis of Massachusetts entered the nomination season well organized, well financed, and politically well positioned in the center of his party.[2] He was the chief beneficiary of Senators Hart's and Biden's early self-destruction, of New York Governor Mario Cuomo's refusal to run, and of a nomination system that placed disproportionate importance on Dukakis's neighboring state of New Hampshire. After winning the New Hampshire primary handily, and doing well in states outside the Old South on Super Tuesday, Dukakis was widely regarded to be the Democratic front runner. At this juncture, only the Reverend Jesse Jackson stood between Dukakis and the nomination.

But Jackson posed a considerable obstacle. Four years before, Jackson had entered the nomination contest late, without the unanimous endorsement of black leaders, many of whom had already committed to Walter Mondale. He went on to win just two primaries and 18% of the total vote cast. In 1988, by contrast, Jackson won seven primaries and 29% of the primary vote, more than doubling his support among whites. He won more votes than any other candidate on Super Tuesday. Indeed, at the close of voting on Super Tuesday, Jackson had pulled even with Dukakis in the popular vote, and trailed him only slightly in the count of delegates. A week later, Jackson defeated Dukakis decisively in the Illinois primary, and then as March drew to a close, won an overwhelming victory in the Michigan caucus.

Jackson's successes were greeted with pride and exhilaration by many black Americans. The black press complimented Jackson on the stands he took on economic questions and on drug abuse (and complained that other Democratic candidates were stealing his views). Black newspapers and magazines began to argue that because of his strong showing, Jackson had earned a prominent place in the party; that his attacks on the social and economic policies of the Reagan-Bush administration and his forthright position on the drug menace should become part of the Democratic platform; and that serious consideration as a vice-presidential candidate was due Jackson should his run for the nomination fall short. A central and persistent theme in this coverage was that Jackson had earned the respect of the Democratic party and of the nation as a whole.

Not everyone agreed. Jackson's stunning victory in Michigan sent shivers of apprehension through the Democratic leadership, who quickly began to call, discreetly, for closer scrutiny of Jackson. They also began to argue that the nomination of Dukakis was inevitable, and that Democrats should unite behind his candidacy. In response, the black press began to complain about a Democratic party conspiracy to frustrate Jackson's bid for the presidency, including allegations that the convention was rigged against him. Things came to a head in the New York primary, a contest riddled with racial and religious acrimony and dominated by New York City Mayor Koch's biting attacks upon Jackson. Conservative and Jewish Democrats, who preferred Gore to Dukakis, but both of them by a wide margin to Jackson, were evidently persuaded that a vote for Gore might lead to the "unthinkable"—a Jackson victory—and so voted instead for their second choice.[3] Partly as a result, Dukakis defeated Jackson soundly in New York and then more decisively in subsequent contests. Jackson pressed on, hopeful of extracting concessions, but the nomination belonged to Dukakis.

Meanwhile, the struggle for the presidential nomination among Republicans was notable perhaps most of all for the extinction of liberalism. All six of the Republican candidates presented themselves as conservative, as indeed they were. With the exception occasionally provided by New York Congressman Jack Kemp, not one seemed interested in appealing to black voters. Each claimed to be Ronald Reagan's true heir; each argued that he would be the proper guardian of the president's conservative legacy. Given Reagan's reputation among black Americans, this competition for the Republican nomination was obviously not calculated to appeal to them; the Republican candidates had other constituencies in mind.

With the nomination struggle framed in this fashion, George Bush had a natural advantage. It was Bush, after all, who had served two full terms as the president's loyal assistant. After a startling and embarrassing loss in the Iowa caucus, where Bush finished third behind Senator Robert Dole and evangelist Pat Robertson, the Bush campaign recovered in New Hampshire. Bush abandoned his vice-presidential limousine, put on a down jacket, and mingled with the voters. He attacked Dole for his willingness to impose taxes and made excellent use of Governor Sununu's extensive political organization. Perhaps most important, Bush emphasized his ties to the president, an overwhelmingly popular figure among New Hampshire Republicans. In the end Bush defeated Dole by a comfortable margin. Three weeks later, on Super Tuesday, Bush won all fifteen contests, most by lopsided margins. For all practical purposes, the Republican nomination process was complete.

By sewing up the nomination early, the Bush campaign was able to turn its full attention to Michael Dukakis and the contest to come. One Bush objective was to reinforce the voter's inclination to treat the 1988 election as a referendum on the previous eight years. Bush presented himself as a loyal and experienced partner to President Reagan, determined to complete the mission they had begun together in 1980. Reagan, meanwhile, campaigned hard for his vice-president, imploring voters to stay the course. In his final campaign appearance, in San Diego on election eve, the president put it this way: "If my name isn't on your ballot tomorrow, something more important is: a principle, a legacy. . . . So if I could ask you one last time, tomorrow, when the mountain greets the dawn, will you go out there and win one for the Gipper?"[4] It is an obvious point, perhaps, but worth underscoring nevertheless, that President Reagan's pitch was not destined to win over the hearts and minds and, finally, the votes of black Americans. The "Reagan legacy" played to whites but not to blacks; the majority of black Americans considered the Reagan years a political nightmare.[5]

Throughout the campaign, Bush emphasized the accomplishments of the Reagan presidency. He pointed to economic growth, the creation of jobs, and control over inflation. He looked beyond the borders of the United States and saw a world at peace, democracy sweeping the Pacific rim, and fundamental reform under way in the Soviet Union. He reminded voters of the worst moments of the Carter presidency and argued that America was the chosen land and must remain the dominant force for good in the world.

While taking credit for the achievements of the previous eight years and allying himself with the president, Bush also sought to amplify the risks of a Dukakis presidency. Given peace and prosperity, the Bush campaign attempted to convince the public that Dukakis was dangerous: that he would wreck the economy, weaken the nation's defense, and threaten its virtue. With this last objective in mind, the Bush campaign sought to portray Dukakis as out of step with American values. The liberal Democrat from Massachusetts, as he was often called, was far too generous with government programs, unwilling or unable to recognize the world as a dangerous place, and most of all, too liberal on social questions. Characterizing his own views as "just common sense" and drawing a sharp contrast with his opponent's views, Bush placed social issues squarely at the forefront of his campaign. Bush argued that teachers be required to lead their students in the pledge of allegiance at the start of the school day; that convicted murderers and "drug kingpins" be permanently incarcerated or executed; that children be allowed to pray in school; that Americans be allowed to purchase firearms without restriction; and that abortion be outlawed. In this way, Bush portrayed himself as the forceful champion of conservative values.

As we would expect from our analysis of the electoral predicament of race, Bush made virtually no direct appeals to blacks. In fact, it would be fair to say that the Bush campaign wrote off the votes of blacks, following the now well-traveled path established by Barry Goldwater in 1964. Bush rarely spoke before black audiences, he failed to show at the annual meeting of the Urban League, and he declined an invitation to appear at a ceremony honoring the memory of Martin Luther King, Jr. Bush said virtually nothing about racial discrimination, or racial inequality, or the underclass, or the Third World, and his campaign spent virtually no money on "outreach activities" aimed at black voters.[6]

Ignoring black voters is one thing; appealing to white voters on the basis of racial resentment is another. Did the Bush campaign succumb to this temptation? We believe it did. The Bush campaign did so first of all by exploiting the prominence and success of the Jackson campaign. Bush strategists were privately delighted by Jackson's early victories, by the visible role he played at the Democratic National Convention, and by the sheer number of blacks on the convention floor (blacks constituted 21% of convention delegates). In the event that white voters might have missed the point, Republicans kept reminding them of Jackson's stature within the Democratic party. Several speakers at the Republican National Convention—Reagan, Ford, and Bush himself—insinuated that Jackson was the third member of the Democratic ticket. In his acceptance speech, Bush referred to the "three blind mice" in a clever rebuttal to Democratic claims that the Reagan-Bush years had produced an uneven prosperity, a "Swiss cheese economy." The third mouse, of course, was Jackson.

Jackson was also prominently featured in letters and fliers distributed by state Republican party organizations, all of which pushed the idea that a vote for Dukakis was a vote for Jackson. California voters, to take one example, received a letter that juxtaposed, on the first page, a photograph of Bush standing next to Reagan with a photograph of Jackson towering over Dukakis. The letter claimed that "if [Dukakis] is elected to the White House, Jesse Jackson is sure to be swept into power on his coattails." On the letter's next page was displayed a photograph of Republican California Governor George Deukmejian on one side, and on the other, a photograph of Willie Brown, the speaker of the California Assembly, and, perhaps more to the point, a black American.

Certainly it was fair to raise the question of how much influence Jackson might exert in a Dukakis administration. But it is odd and revealing that the question was raised about Jackson alone, especially given the troubled and prickly relationship that had grown up between Jackson and the Democratic nominee. And it is odd and revealing that the question was raised visually: Jackson was not merely mentioned but presented photographically, lest any white voter forget the color of his skin.

None of this was missed by the black press. Republican efforts to tether Jackson to Dukakis were given extensive coverage in black newspapers. The coverage was not only extensive but negative as well: the black press had no trouble calling these various maneuvers racist.

Jackson was important to the Republican campaign for white votes, but not nearly as important as Willie Horton turned out to be. The most effective Republican overture to racially intolerant whites in 1988 did not on the surface deal with race at all; it dealt instead with crime. Horton, a black man convicted of murder and sentenced to life imprisonment, was granted a weekend leave by the Massachusetts prison furlough program while Dukakis was governor. Horton fled the state and terrorized a white couple in Maryland, beating the man and raping the woman before being recaptured and returned to prison. In the local uproar that followed, Dukakis defended the furlough program and appeared indifferent to Horton's victims.

The Horton story was uncovered by a research team assembled by the Bush campaign whose purpose was to scour Dukakis's past in the hope of turning up exploitable liabilities. The team actually found two: the Horton story, and Dukakis's declaration as unconstitutional an effort to require Massachusetts school children to recite the pledge of allegiance. In late May 1988, the Bush

campaign brought together small groups of Democratic voters who had supported Reagan in 1984 but were inclined to vote for Dukakis in 1988. Both episodes were recounted to them, with explosive consequences. Senior members
of the Bush campaign—Teeter, Ailes, and Atwater—recognized immediately
that they had stumbled on to issues of enormous power. Later, Atwater would
recall thinking at the time that he knew that the pledge of allegiance and the
furlough stories could "blow up" Dukakis.

Shortly thereafter, Vice President Bush began making regular references in
his campaign speeches to the furlough (and to the pledge). In early June, Willie
Horton became a fixture in Bush's speeches and in three weeks, the large lead
that Dukakis had been enjoying was sliced in half. The apparent success of this
pitch guaranteed that Americans would be hearing much more about prison
furloughs, and seeing much more of Horton, later. As a member of the Bush
campaign staff boasted to Elizabeth Drew, "Every woman in this country will
know what Willie Horton looks like before this election is over."[7]

Beginning the day after the vice-presidential debate, in early October, the
furlough issue and Horton moved to the center of the Bush campaign. Again
and again, Bush recounted the gruesome and horrific details of Horton's crimes,
often against a dramatic visual backdrop provided by rows of police officers in
full dress. Bush insisted that Dukakis cared more about the rights of criminals
than he did the victims of crimes, and he lambasted Dukakis for opposing the
death penalty. Bush referred to his opponent contemptuously as a "liberal theo-
rist" who had forgotten that law enforcement's first priority must be "to protect
the safety of our neighborhoods and law abiding citizens."[8]

At about this time, Clifford Barnes, the man who had been beaten up
by Horton, was becoming a public figure. With financial assistance provided by
the Committee for the Presidency, a political action committee based in Los
Angeles that claimed to be independent of the Bush campaign, Barnes went on
tour, to speak about his experiences and to criticize Dukakis. Barnes visited
cities in the pivotal states of Texas, California, New York, and Illinois, holding
press conferences wherever he went. He showed up on the television talk-show
circuit, making appearances on the Oprah Winfrey, Geraldo Rivera, and Mor-
ton Downey, Jr., programs. Barnes also appeared in a television commercial and
was featured in what Republican strategists called "saturation" radio advertisements for Bush in the late stages of the campaign in Texas and California.

Republican party organizations also played an important and, at the time,
underpublicized role in the Horton initiative. In New York, the Republican
party distributed thousands of Bush fliers that prominently featured Horton's
face. The citizens of Illinois were deluged with handbills that referred to Horton
and then proceeded to claim that "all the murderers and rapists and drug push-

ers and child molesters in Massachusetts vote for Michael Dukakis." As this was happening, the Republican National Committee was busy reprinting and distributing copies of a commissioned article, "Getting Away with Murder," which had appeared in the July *Reader's Digest.* The article began, "In Massachusetts, convicted murderers roam the streets on weekend passes" and went on from there, recounting in grisly detail Horton's crimes and describing Governor Dukakis's unwillingness to terminate the furlough program. In Maryland, where Horton's crime spree came to a brutal end, a campaign leaflet circulated by the Republican state party displayed photographs of Horton and Dukakis, followed by the warning that "you, your children, your parents, and your friends can have the opportunity to receive a visit from someone like Willie Horton if Mike Dukakis becomes President." Republican party organizations in other states mailed out fliers contrasting a menacing photograph of Horton with that of a small white child.

Horton himself starred in a commercial sponsored by Americans for Bush, an arm of the National Security political action committee. Entitled "Weekend Passes," the commercial ran nationwide on CNN, A&E, CBN, and Lifetime cable networks. In thirty seconds, this is what viewers saw and heard:

> Side-by-side photographs of Bush and Dukakis appear on the screen. An unseen announcer says, "Bush and Dukakis on crime."
>
> Switch to a picture of Bush. "Bush supports the death penalty for first-degree murderers."
>
> Switch to a photograph of Dukakis. "Dukakis not only opposes the death penalty, he allowed first-degree murderers to have weekend passes from prison."
>
> Switch to a menacing mugshot of Willie Horton. "One was Willie Horton, who murdered a boy in a robbery, stabbing him 19 times."
>
> Switch to another photograph of Horton, in a wild afro and raggedy beard, dressed in army fatigues, and towering over a white police officer, who is evidently placing him under arrest. "Despite a life sentence, Horton received 10 weekend passes from prison. Horton fled, kidnapped a young couple, stabbing the man and repeatedly raping his girl friend." The words "kidnapping," "stabbing," and "raping" flash on the screen.
>
> Finally is a photograph of Dukakis. "Weekend prison passes. Dukakis on crime."

"Weekend Passes" was designed by Larry McCarthy, previously a senior vice-president of Ailes Communication (Roger Ailes was Bush's director of campaign communications). When critics charged that the advertisement was inflammatory and racist, staff members of the Bush campaign responded that like other political action committees, and like state party organizations, Americans for Bush was an autonomous venture, not subject to their influence. Perhaps—but perhaps what we have here is an organizational equivalent to a racial codeword: the nasty business is claimed to be carried out by a wholly independent entity; the campaign is protected; all the while, appeals to racism continue.[9]

The Bush campaign designed and put out its own television commercial on the furlough issue, "Revolving Door," the most memorable television advertisement of 1988.[10] In it, a line of prisoners trudges steadily into a prison and then immediately out again through a revolving door in the prison wall. The commercial does not mention Horton. Nor does it suggest, if it is examined with a microscope, that criminals are black. According to Lee Atwater, Bush's chief campaign adviser, the commercial actually was reshot, because in its original version, the line of prisoners included too many black faces:

> When we first shot the furlough spot of the revolving door that we used on television, we used regular prisoners. Roger [Ailes] and I looked at it. It was a totally natural thing in the prison. Frankly, we worried there were too many blacks in the prison scene, so we made sure that on the retake there were but one or two.[11]

No doubt there were "but one or two" black faces in the grim parade that appeared on national television, but the shot is so distant, and the color so washed out, that it is difficult to tell.

While the Republicans attempted to lure racially conservative whites through coded appeals, the Democrats "solved" the electoral predicament of race through evasion and neglect. Dukakis aimed his campaign at the "pinched middle class," trying to give expression to the apprehensions many Americans seemed to feel about their own and their country's economic futures. Dukakis argued that too many Americans were working hard just to break even; too many could no longer afford to purchase even a modest home for their families; too many could no longer send their children to college. The governor did his best to tie these apprehensions to the trade and budget deficits of the Reagan-Bush administration. Dukakis did not abandon this pitch until the desperate last weeks of the campaign. Suddenly, and finally, Dukakis took off his dark suits, rolled up his sleeves, and became a populist, telling crowds that he was on "their side" and that Bush and the Republicans were the champions of greed and privilege. In the end, he even embraced the liberal label—though according to Elizabeth Drew's account, without meaning to.[12]

As Dukakis sought the votes of the middle class, issues of race simply disappeared from the Democratic presidential campaign. Like his Republican opponent, Dukakis said little about racial discrimination, or affirmative action, or the underclass, or the plight of American cities. Dukakis had gained no experience in Massachusetts in the delicate business of assembling biracial coalitions, and he secured the Democratic nomination with virtually no black support.[13] The relationship between Dukakis and Jackson grew strained and tense. Dukakis did not consult with Jackson on the selection of his vice-presidential running mate, nor, in a much publicized flap, did he inform Jackson of his choice personally. This snub was given much attention in the black press, sometimes accompanied by calls to black Americans to sit the 1988 election out. Moreover, Dukakis's selection of Lloyd Bentsen, a southern conservative, as his running mate sent at best an ambiguous signal to black Americans. At the Democratic National Convention, elaborate precautions were taken to ensure that photographs of Dukakis, Bentsen, and Jackson—or worse yet, Dukakis and Jackson alone together—would not show up in the next morning's newspapers. Such measures were widely interpreted in the black press as insulting not just to Jackson but also to black Americans everywhere.

For the most part, Dukakis stayed out of the central cities, and appeared ill at ease when he appeared before black audiences. Dukakis did make his way to Philadelphia—Philadelphia, Mississippi, that is. On a sweltering August afternoon, Dukakis appeared at a county fair, twenty-four years to the day that the corpses of James Chaney, Andrew Goodman, and Michael Schwerner, three murdered civil rights workers, were hauled from beneath a nearby earthen dam. Speaking to a virtually all-white crowd, Dukakis chose not to mention the anniversary—and was immediately taken to task by Jackson.

Finally there was Dukakis's reaction to the Bush campaign's use of the Horton incident. Dukakis first ignored it. When Donna Brazile, deputy national field director for the Dukakis campaign and its highest-ranking black official, complained to the press that the Bush campaign was employing racist tactics, she was fired. The Dukakis campaign press secretary immediately disavowed Brazile's charge; Paul Brountas, campaign chairman, went on record to say that the Bush campaign was not racist; and Dukakis personally apologized to Bush. Eventually, Dukakis did express outrage over some of the Horton material, but not, evidently, because it was racist. Rather, as Dukakis said again and again, it constituted a cynical use of a human tragedy, something he would never do.[14]

Dukakis's evasions left it up to Lloyd Bentsen and Jesse Jackson to charge the Bush campaign with racism. In the final weeks of the campaign, Jackson reappeared, campaigning hard for Dukakis, urging blacks to vote, and openly calling the Republican presidential campaign racist—a charge the Republicans naturally rejected. Bush himself, his voice rising in moral indignation, insisted in an election eve speech that *"I'm* the one who said let's leave the tired baggage of bigotry behind us . . . there's not a racist bone in my body." Vice-presidential candidate Quayle turned the charge around, chastising the Democrats for "fanning the flames of racism in the country." With few exceptions, the mainstream media also treated the accusation of racism as a fraudulent and desperate move by a campaign in deep trouble. An editorial running in the *Washington Post*, for example, referred to the charge of racism as "phony," while the *Wall Street Journal* accused the Democrats of "waving the bloody shirt of race." The black press reacted quite differently, though the controversy over the place of Horton in the Republican campaign did not loom very large there. For the most part, the black press had already written off the Republican campaign as incorrigibly hostile to the interests of black Americans. In the black press and in the black community, the Horton controversy simply was not news.

Perhaps most interesting of all was the reaction of Michael Dukakis himself. When asked about Bentsen's charge that the Bush campaign was pursuing a racist strategy, Dukakis replied that Bentsen would never have volunteered such a charge himself; to be fair to Bentsen, said Dukakis, you must understand that he was pressed by reporters for an opinion. Dukakis himself said nothing about the charge itself.[15] In a lengthy interview on the "McNeil/Lehrer News Hour" on Monday, October 31, with just a week remaining until election day, Dukakis was asked pointblank whether the prominent place of Horton in the Republican campaign constituted a racist appeal. Dukakis replied by acknowledging that his vice-presidential running mate had expressed the view that there were racist elements in the Bush campaign and that he [Dukakis] agreed with Bentsen.

Notice that in his answer, Dukakis both softened the charge and hid behind his running mate. Dukakis never said, with conviction and in his own voice, that the Bush campaign was trafficking in racism. Indeed, Dukakis said nothing about racism and virtually nothing about race, one way or the other, during the entire campaign. Nor did Dukakis grant Jackson the respect that many black Americans believed he had earned during the primary season. Little wonder that in the final two weeks of the contest, when the Dukakis campaign turned finally to the black community in an effort to turn out the vote, the black press reacted with skepticism and coolness.

Consider this image, which appeared on "ABC News" during the last week of the campaign, after the Bentsen and Jackson claims of racism had received considerable attention, and which seemed to condense the Democratic solution to the predicament of race in 1988 into a single moment. The reporter Sam Donaldson shouted a question to Dukakis about *his* view on racism in the campaign. Dukakis looked toward Donaldson, shook his head, and trudged wearily up the gate into the waiting airplane. Exactly right: Dukakis turned his back; silence and neglect in 1988. A more apt visual metaphor for the Democratic campaign could scarcely be imagined.

ANALYZING VOTERS IN 1988

It is one thing to describe the campaign, quite another to demonstrate that the 1988 campaign, as we have styled it here, actually made a difference to voters. Because the typical American is consumed for the most part by the demands and vicissitudes of private life, it is hazardous to assume that the Bush and Dukakis campaigns left an impression. Still, we believe that campaigns generally matter and that the 1988 campaign in particular made a difference. In our vocabulary, campaigns are grand and expensive exercises in "priming." By drawing attention to some considerations while suppressing others, campaigns attempt to prime prospective voters to think about the election in ways that work to the advantage of their candidate and damage their opponent.[16]

Priming theory is rooted in some elementary aspects of cognitive psychology. Following Herbert Simon, we believe that "human thinking powers are very modest when compared with the complexities of the environment in which human beings live. Faced with complexity and uncertainty, lacking the wits to optimize, they must be content to satisfice—to find 'good enough' solutions to their problems and 'good enough' courses of action."[17] One consequence, or symptom, of satisficing in the political realm is that few voters even attempt to take into account everything that they know about the rival candidates. Instead, they draw upon a sample of what they know—and a sample of convenience at that. Some considerations prove decisive; others are ignored. The relative importance of each depends upon its mental accessibility.[18] Thus voters' decisions depend less on an exhaustive examination of their views and sentiments and more on which aspects of their views and sentiments happen to come to mind. "Happen" isn't quite right, since what comes to voters' mind may be determined, in no small part, by the various activities of the rival campaigns. With vast resources and formidable expertise, campaigns do their best to prime voters to think about the choices they face in advantageous ways.[19]

Suppose that our characterization of the 1988 presidential campaign corresponds reasonably closely to what voters actually saw and heard. From the point of view supplied by priming, what consequences then follow? White voters no doubt brought to the 1988 campaign a variety of considerations potentially relevant to their eventual choice. But instead of undertaking an "exhaustive examination of their views and sentiments," they took into account only some considerations, setting others aside. This selective review was influenced by the Republican campaign, which invited white voters to pay particular attention to their feelings toward blacks. From the perspective of priming, the role of the Republican campaign in 1988 was to activate racial resentments, to move racial resentment to a more central place in the white vote than it would have otherwise occupied.

What should we expect of black voters given the campaign of neglect from the Democrats and racial codewords from the Republicans? On the one hand, the Republican campaign gave black Americans little reason to embrace Bush and many reasons to reject him: we should see evidence of this in black voters' reactions to the Bush candidacy. At the same time, the strategy of neglect followed by Dukakis should leave many black voters ambivalent about the Democratic candidate. More generally, a campaign which the black press reads as either incorrigibly hostile, in the case of the Republicans, or as disrespectful of the Jackson candidacy, in the case of the Democrats, might serve as a reminder to black Americans of their double identity as both black and American, what Du Bois called "two-ness." The implication here is that, thanks in part to the 1988 campaign, many black voters would have prominently in mind identification with their racial group.

To test these expectations, we draw primarily upon the 1988 NES. Overall, 52.4% of the 1988 NES respondents cast their ballot for Bush—a figure that is indistinguishable from the official tally.[20] But this narrow margin in the national popular vote conceals a huge racial divide: Bush won a comfortable victory among whites, taking 57% of their votes, while being routed among blacks, winning just 9% of their support.[21] This difference is of course thoroughly reminiscent of the wide political divide between black and white that we first witnessed back in Chapter 2. It suggests, as does our description of the 1988 campaign itself, that we take up the task of explaining the white and black vote separately, and so we do.

WHITE VOTERS IN 1988: THE POLITICS OF RACIAL RESENTMENT

Evidence that the 1988 campaign made a difference to voters can be read first of all in the widespread impression among white voters that Bush would be tougher on crime than his Democratic opponent. This emerges clearly in responses to the open-ended questions in the 1988 NES, which permit voters to say whatever they please about the two major party candidates. It turns out that references to crime in these free commentaries were remarkably common among white voters, and were directed much more often at Dukakis than at Bush (by a margin of nearly four to one). Most important, while virtually all the references to crime and Bush were positive (95%), virtually all the references to crime and Dukakis were negative (98%). Put differently, nearly one-quarter of white voters who had something bad to say about Dukakis specifically mentioned his opposition to the death penalty or his apparent unwillingness to crack down on criminals.[22] This is an extraordinary figure, all the more so because serious crime was actually declining at the time of the 1988 campaign.[23] That so many white voters were preoccupied with crime in the 1988 presidential campaign testifies to the effectiveness of the Bush campaign.

So, too, do results from a pair of questions present in the postelection survey that inquired directly into citizens' perceptions of Bush and Dukakis on the issue of crime. Among white voters, Bush was much more likely to be seen as a vigorous opponent of crime. In the immediate aftermath of the campaign, two-thirds of white voters (66%) said that the phrase "tough on crime and criminals" fit Bush either "extremely well" or "quite well," compared with just 30% who said so for Dukakis. This difference is huge and, although it is hard to make exact comparisons, greater by far than the differences that show up in assessments of Bush and Dukakis on other political dimensions.[24] Furthermore, Bush's advantage on the issue of crime at the end of the campaign represented a dramatic reversal in political fortunes. According to evidence from national campaign polls carried out by CBS/*New York Times*, as late as the first week of July, voters regarded Dukakis, not Bush, as the stronger candidate on the question of crime. By late October, this Democratic advantage not only had disappeared; it had turned into a serious, perhaps fatal liability.[25] All the speeches and commercials and fliers and letters evidently paid off. Bush and the Republicans won the debate.

But what was that debate about, exactly? Was it about crime alone, or crime and race together? We have argued that the Republican party attempted to use crime to signal its racial sympathies to white voters. But did this initiative succeed? Were white voters primed by the campaign to vote in accordance with the resentments they felt for black Americans?

To find out, we took advantage of the fact that four of the six racial resentment questions that first appeared in 1986 NES were part of the 1988 election survey.[26] As we learned in great detail in Chapter 5, racial resentment, measured by such questions, is strongly implicated in the views white Americans take on political questions that are in some conspicuous fashion entangled in race, such as the desirability of affirmative action. And now we see that racial resentment is also powerfully associated with the vote in 1988. Racially resentful whites were more likely to vote for Bush; racially sympathetic whites were more likely to vote for Dukakis. This association is spelled out in figure 9.1. As indicated there, support for Bush builds steadily from left to right, as resentment increases.[27] Bush does miserably among the most racially sympathetic

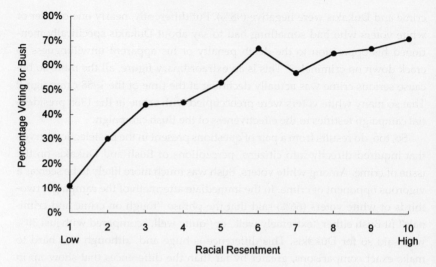

FIGURE 9.1 Support for Bush in 1988 among white voters by level of racial resentment. *Source:* 1988 National Election Study.

whites, receiving just 11% of their support, and splendidly among the most racially resentful, taking 71% of their votes.[28]

Figure 9.1 is an essential starting point, but that resentment and the vote are associated is not the same as demonstrating that resentment was a cause of the vote in 1988. To get closer to the causal question, we need to ascertain whether, all other things equal, racially resentful whites were more likely to vote for Bush. In doing so, we confront exactly the same problem we encountered in our analysis of public opinion. As then, no single sovereign theory of the voter will do: voting is a complex act, subject to a variety of considerations. To estimate the impact of racial resentment on the white vote in 1988 requires us to take into account alternative theories about the motivations of voters and the nature of presidential campaigns (just as we will later, when we attempt to estimate the impact of racial group solidarity on the black vote).

More precisely, we claim that Americans contemplating the choice between Bush and Dukakis in the fall of 1988 were pushed and pulled by their loyalty to party; their views on the direction that government policy should take, both at home and abroad; their assessments of national economic conditions; and, far from least, by their evaluations of the incumbent and retiring president, Ronald Reagan, who cast a long shadow across the 1988 campaign, as Dwight David Eisenhower and Lyndon Johnson had in comparable situations before him.[29]

To this already rich stew, we need add one final ingredient: white voters' attitude toward Jesse Jackson. Jackson was far and away the most prominent black figure on the national stage in 1988, a position that his string of victories and strong showings during the primary season only enhanced. Although he failed to win the nomination and mostly faded away after the Democratic National Convention, Jackson could still have played an important role in the 1988 vote. Insofar as white voters disapproved of Jackson—because of his inexperience, or his liberal policies, or his intemperate remarks directed at American Jews, or because of the color of his skin—they should be more inclined to vote for Bush.[30]

With all these effects taken into account—those due to partisanship, views on policy, assessments of national economic conditions, and evaluations of Reagan and Jackson—should we expect racial resentment to have a direct effect on the vote in 1988? Probably not. If racial resentment influenced the vote in 1988, it most likely would have had to do so indirectly, by affecting those considerations that influenced the 1988 vote in a direct way. In fact, when we added our measure of racial resentment into the vote analysis that takes into account all these considerations, we found the direct effect of racial resentment to be indistinguishable from zero. Not racial resentment, but assessments of the parties, policies, national conditions, and the commanding political personalities of the moment constituted the immediate determinants of the 1988 vote (and perhaps of any vote).

Concluding, as we have just done, that racial resentment had no direct effect on the 1988 presidential vote is not the same as concluding that it had no effect at all.[31] For racial resentment might have influenced those considerations that influenced the white vote directly. This indirect route seems especially likely given the coded and subterranean nature of the racist appeals that infiltrated the 1988 campaign. Disapproval of Jesse Jackson, opposition to social welfare policies, support for Reagan, even approval of an aggressive foreign policy, could all have been shaped, in part, by racial resentment.

To take these several indirect possibilities into account—to determine the total effect of racial resentment on the vote in 1988—we estimated the reduced-form version of the vote. Included in the equation as predictor variables, in addition to racial resentment, were party identification, assessments of national economic conditions, race of interviewer, and an elaborate set of electorally relevant social background characteristics: education, occupation, family income, union household, gender, employment status, region, religion, Hispanic origins, and size of current location. Dropping out of the equation are evaluations of Reagan and Jackson, and views on social welfare and foreign policy, those considerations that the effects of racial resentment might work

Table 9.1 Estimated Total Effect of Racial Resentment on Support for Bush in 1988, White Voters Only (reduced-form equation)

Variable	Probit Estimate	Standard Error
Racial resentment	1.07	.29
National economic conditions	2.81	.40
Republican identification	1.09	.15
Democratic identification	−.96	.14
Union household	−.46	.15
Jewish	−.83	.40
Protestant fundamentalist	.42	.19
Westerner	−.15	.15
Southerner	.16	.16
Hispanic	−.38	.26
Unemployed	−.85	.44
Disabled	.22	.49
Family income (> $75,000)	.40	.26
Family income (refused)	.49	.24
Rural	.22	.22
Town	−.21	.15
City	−.11	.17
High school degree	.09	.19
Some college	.30	.20
College degree	.42	.22
Advanced degree	.09	.28
Unskilled worker	.16	.28
Service worker	.26	.20
Gender	.09	.12
Race of interviewer	.26	.41
Constant	.53	.52
Number of cases	821	
−2 times the log likelihood ratio	501.74	
Degrees of freedom	25	

Source: 1988 National Election Study.

through. The results of this analysis are summarized in table 9.1. They indicate a significant and sizable total effect of racial resentment on the 1988 vote (probit coefficient = 1.07, standard error = .29, t = 3.69, p < .01).

Just how sizable an effect this is can be seen in table 9.2, where we have converted the probit coefficients into probabilities. Table 9.2 presents predicted votes for Bush, expressed as percentages, by levels of racial resentment and political partisanship. By partisanship, we distinguish among Democrats, Independents, and Republicans; with respect to racial resentment, we distinguish among racially sympathetic whites (a score of 0 on the scale), racially resentful whites (a score of 1), as well as several intermediate positions (.25, .50, .75). For the purpose of these calculations, variables present in the equation other than racial resentment and party identification assume their actual sample values.

According to the estimates displayed in table 9.2, racial resentment had a substantial effect on the vote in 1988. For white voters as a whole, support for Bush rises steadily and quite sharply with increases in resentment (bottom row of the table). Racially resentful whites (given by a score of .75 on the scale) were some twelve percentage points more likely to vote for Bush than were their racially sympathetic, but otherwise comparable, neighbors (as given by a score of .25).

Table 9.2 also shows that the effect of racial resentment was conditioned by partisanship: it was most pronounced among Independents, noticeable among Democrats, and least visible among Republicans, who were approaching unanimity in their support of the Bush candidacy. These results suggest that the Bush campaign solved the electoral predicament of race adroitly. By playing upon racial resentments in an indirect way—through racial codewords—the Bush campaign cut deeply into Dukakis's support among Independents and Democrats, meanwhile losing little support among racially tolerant Republicans.

Racial Resentment and American Conservatism

Our analysis of the 1988 election presumes that voting is, among other things, a way for citizens to express their values. From this perspective, voting is a symbolic act, the campaign a national ritual.[32] George Bush expressed this point well in his nomination acceptance speech when he ridiculed Dukakis's claim that the election was about competence, not ideology: "Competence is the creed of the technocrat who makes sure the gears mesh but doesn't for a second understand the magic of the machine. The truth is, this election is about the beliefs we share, the values we honor, the principles we hold dear." Bush presented himself as someone who cared deeply about America, who understood

Table 9.2 Effect of Racial Resentment on Support for Bush in 1988, among White Democrats, Independents, and Republicans

	Racial Resentment				
	0	.25	.5	.75	1.0
Party Identification					
Democrats	08	12	17	23	30
Independents	35	44	53	62	69
Republicans	80	86	90	94	96
TOTAL	43	49	55	61	66

Source: 1988 National Election Study.
Note: The number in each cell is based on the probit estimate from the reduced-form equation. The probits have been converted to probabilities and are expressed here as percentages.

the menace posed by enemies abroad and the threats to safety and virtue at home. This is a politics of symbols and values, not of debates over policy and performance, and it is a politics that Bush and his advisers seemed to understand vastly better than did the other side.

The primary exhibit for Republican superiority in this respect we take of course to be race. But the 1988 campaign was not only about race and crime, and the white vote was certainly not a matter of racial resentment alone. When Bush recited the pledge of allegiance, when he wrapped his campaign in the flag, when he suggested that Dukakis was outside the American mainstream, he appealed to patriotism. When Bush spoke for the rights of the unborn, when he presented himself as a loving grandfather, when he assailed purveyors of pornography, he appealed to moral conservatism. When Bush insisted that his opponent was a liberal, when he linked Dukakis with the American Civil Liberties Union and with, as he put it, the expensive and failed policies of the 1960s, he attempted to mobilize hostility to liberalism. In short, various strands of American conservatism were prominently on display in the 1988 campaign—and so could have been prominent in voters' minds as well. Indeed, it is possible that the effect we have just attributed to racial resentment really belongs instead to patriotism, moral conservatism, or illiberalism.

It is possible, but it appears not to be so. The 1988 NES included questions that allowed us to construct reliable measures of various aspects of contemporary American conservative values, including the three that the Bush campaign tried to mobilize. When we modified the vote equation described earlier to include measures of patriotism, moral conservatism, and illiberalism, the estimated impact of prejudice was scarcely affected.[33] Thus when President Bush declared the 1988 election to be about "the beliefs we share, the values we honor, the principles we hold dear," he was referring at least in part, whether he knew it or not, to resentments rooted in race.

Racial Resentment and Willie Horton

Racial resentment made a difference in 1988, but we have so far provided no evidence that there was anything special in this—that the notable impact of racial resentment in 1988 had anything to do with the nature of the Republican campaign. Conveniently for this question, the Horton initiative moved to the center of the Bush campaign on October 5, the day after the vice-presidential debate, and remained there until the election.[34] This is convenient because October 5 cuts our preelection sample virtually in half: 473 white voters were interviewed before October 5 (51.8%); 440 were questioned after, as the Horton initiative was earnestly under way (or 48.2%). Taking advantage of this serendipitous fact, we reestimated the vote equation, adding one new variable to capture the possibility that the impact of racial resentment might increase among white voters inundated with the Horton story. We call this variable {E * Racial Resentment}, where E is exposure to the Horton initiative. We set E at 0 for white voters interviewed before October 5, and assign a value between 0 and 1 for those interviewed after October 5, corresponding in linear fashion to the exact date of interview (i.e., those interviewed close to election day were assigned scores on E close to 1; those interviewed close to October 5 were assigned scores close to 0; and so on in between). If the coefficient on this multiplicative term—{E * Racial Resentment}—turned out to be zero, it would suggest that the power of racial resentment was independent of the prominence of the Horton initiative in the Bush campaign.[35]

The coefficient is *not* zero. We estimate the probit coefficient on {E * Racial Resentment} to be 1.22, standard error = .35 (t = 3.45, p < .01), while the probit coefficient on Racial Resentment is .94, standard error = .32, (t = 2.98, p < .01). These coefficients mean that, on average, the impact of racial resentment more than doubled for white voters interviewed on the eve of the election as compared with those interviewed before October 5.[36] Thus, by activating racial resentments, the Horton story seemed to play precisely the role written by Republican strategists.

BLACK VOTERS IN 1988:
THE POLITICS OF RACIAL GROUP SOLIDARITY

From the vantage point provided by history, the lopsided support blacks gave Dukakis in 1988 is neither new nor remarkable. As we learned in the preceding chapter, Dukakis's margin among blacks in 1988 reflects long-standing differences between the parties originating in the Great Depression and consolidated by the racial crisis of the 1960s. With this history in mind, we will explore several aspects of black political response in 1988: black voters' wholesale rejection of Vice-President Bush; their ambivalence toward Governor Dukakis; their nuanced reading of the racial sympathies of the political figures that dominated the political landscape in 1988; prospects for Republican inroads among middle-class blacks; and last, the power of racial group solidarity to tie blacks to the Democratic party.

Rejection of Bush

Beginning with Barry Goldwater's southern-backlash strategy, Republican presidential candidates have done miserably among black Americans, a tradition that the 1988 election merely extended. It is nevertheless worth pausing for a moment to consider the 1988 case in particular, to contemplate the thoroughness with which blacks rejected Vice-President Bush. Consider, first of all, that when asked whether there was anything in particular about Bush that might make them want to vote for him, 83% of black voters said no. As a general matter, blacks were unimpressed with the vice-president's intelligence, knowledge, and honesty, and they were especially unmoved by his compassion. Nearly two-thirds of black voters reported that Bush had made them feel angry; three-quarters that Bush had made them feel afraid. Little wonder that most blacks could think of no reason to vote for Bush; little wonder that he received less than one out of ten black votes cast in 1988.

Ambivalence toward Dukakis

Although black voters preferred Dukakis to Bush by an overwhelming margin, this turned more on rejection of the Republican than on enthusiasm for the Democrat. Black voters regarded Dukakis as more capable and trustworthy than Bush, it's true, and as much closer to their own views on policy (documented ahead). In the eyes of most black voters, Dukakis was clearly better than the Republican alternative—but he was no Jackson.

While blacks preferred Dukakis to Bush, they revered Jackson. Ninety-one percent of black voters reported that Jackson made them feel hopeful; 96% said that Jackson made them feel proud. More than two-thirds of black voters—69% to be exact—gave Jackson extremely favorable ratings. When asked which of the Democratic presidential candidates would have made the best president, 62% of black voters chose Jackson; only 31% selected Dukakis, then the official Democratic nominee.

Interpretations of the Candidates' Racial Sympathies

Black voters generally saw Dukakis and Bush as offering quite different solutions to national problems. Across a range of policy questions, Dukakis was viewed as somewhat liberal and Bush as very conservative. These differences showed up on the general tradeoff between government services and government spending, on money for defense, on the federal government's responsibility to provide jobs and a good standard of living, on government health insurance, on cooperation with the Soviet Union, and, with particular relevance for the question of racial sympathy we wish to examine here, on whether the federal government should make special efforts to provide assistance to black Americans. On this matter, nearly three out of four black voters saw Bush as hostile, with one out of three placing him at the extreme conservative end of the scale, labeled "government should not make any special effort to help blacks because they should help themselves." Dukakis came across quite differently, though not because he was regarded as an enthusiastic supporter of federal efforts to help blacks. Rather, most black voters placed him squarely in the middle. Meanwhile, black voters themselves gravitated disproportionately to the liberal end of the debate. Slightly more than one-third of blacks selected the most liberal option available, the position that the federal government should make special efforts to help black Americans; by comparison, fewer than 5% of white Americans did so. In short, Bush comes through these materials as the enemy of black interests; Dukakis as a perhaps not altogether reliable friend.

Unremarkably, on matters of public policy generally, black voters took President Reagan to be conservative—and more conservative than Bush. On cuts in government services, defense spending, government guarantee of jobs, general philosophy, an equal role for women: on all these public questions, black voters regarded Reagan as more conservative than his vice-president. Instructively, this difference failed to show up on federal assistance to blacks.[37] On this question, Bush and Reagan were indistinguishable. This suggests that the campaign we described earlier was also seen that way by many black Americans; that the Bush campaign's trafficking in racism did not escape their notice.

Also unremarkably, black voters understood Jackson to be more liberal than Dukakis across a wide range of policy questions. The most pronounced difference emerged on the question of the government's obligations to black Americans. Roughly 59% of black voters saw Jackson as advocating special federal help for blacks, while just 32% saw Dukakis that way. This large difference in perception *doubles* the average difference between Dukakis and Jackson on other matters of policy. These results suggest again that many blacks may have harbored doubts about Dukakis's commitment to their interests.

Finally, both these findings—Dukakis's unusual centrism and Bush's unusual conservatism—disappear when the policy question regarding federal assistance to blacks is slightly reframed, as it was for one-half the 1988 NES sample. The question we have been analyzing here refers to blacks alone. But in the other half of the 1988 sample, the question refers to assistance the government might provide to blacks *and other minorities*. Under this frame, the standard difference between Bush and Reagan reemerges: now Reagan is seen by black voters as the more conservative, in this domain as in others. Similarly, the unusually large difference in black voters' perceptions of Jackson and Dukakis shrinks to average size when the issue is not special help for blacks, but special help for blacks and other minorities. In short, on the particular question of black interests and aspirations, Bush was interpreted as unusually conservative, and Dukakis as unusually equivocal. All these results suggest a special sensitivity on the part of black voters in reading the racial subtext of the 1988 campaign.

Middle-Class Black Republicanism?

Despite what we have said so far, some blacks did indeed vote for Bush in 1988. Here we determine whether they did so for reasons of class. Did middle-class black voters take the 1988 presidential contest as an opportunity to express the interests of their class, siding ultimately with George Bush and the Republican party?

In the last forty years, a visible, if precariously based, black middle class has emerged.[38] This development implies the possibility that blacks might at last prepared to enact the role scripted for them by pluralist accounts of American society.[39] Their politics would finally reflect not merely or even mostly their position in the racial hierarchy, but increasingly their position in the class hierarchy. As more and more blacks made their way to the middle class, they would begin to entertain political views commensurate with their new social and economic position. They would appreciate the virtue in conservative policies; they would regard the Republican party as their natural home; and they would be predisposed to give their support to George Bush in 1988.

Contrary to the pluralist prediction, the black middle class does not seem to be abandoning the Democratic party. The relevant results are displayed in table 9.3, for several measures of class taken separately: income, education, and occupational status. As we have already noted, only a handful of black NES respondents cast a Republican ballot in 1988, making the analysis of vote itself hazardous. Hence our analysis mixes nonvoters and voters together and examines not choice but preference, measured as the difference between the thermometer score ratings given to Bush and to Dukakis.

Table 9.3 Black Support for Bush in 1988 as a Function of Class (% expressing preference for Bush)

Family Income	
<$12K	10.1
$12-30K	6.2
$30K+	4.5
Education	
<High school	13.0
High school	6.8
Some college	0.0
Occupational Status	
Service	9.5
Unskilled	17.4
Skilled	12.9
Sales	4.0
Professional/managerial	0.0

Source: 1988 National Election Study.

The various cross-tabulations, shown in table 9.3, lend little support to the class thesis. The relationships between class and support for Bush are uniformly weak, and, if anything, they run in the opposite direction from that predicted. Black support for Bush was strongest among the poor, not the well off; among those who failed to graduate high school, not those with college degrees; and among unskilled and service workers, not professionals and managers. No indication here of a black middle-class exodus from the Democratic party.[40]

Racial Group Solidarity and the 1988 Vote

Finally we turn from class to race, to consider the possibility that black voters took the 1988 presidential contest as an opportunity to express the interests and aspirations not of their class but of their racial group. In one form or another, the notion of attachment to racial group is at the center of scholarly efforts to understand such diverse episodes as the emergence of the civil rights movement, the eruption of racial violence in American cities, participation in the presidential campaigns of Jesse Jackson, and support for liberal policies.[41] We take the key concept here to be racial group identification, defined as a combination of membership and attachment, rooted in shared interests and common values. The basic proposition we wish to examine is that support for Bush will come most from those blacks least identified with their racial group.

The measure of racial group identification available to us is regrettably crude. In one series of questions in the 1988 NES, respondents were shown a long list of groups that included blacks and then were asked to identify those that they felt particularly close to—"people who are most like you in their ideas and interests and feelings about things." In a second and separate question, respondents were asked to evaluate, on the 101-point thermometer scale, a series of social and political groups, which once again included blacks. Because responses to the two questions were correlated, we constructed a scale of *racial group identification*, which weighs each response equally.[42]

To estimate the electoral impact of racial group identification, we once again combined nonvoters and voters. As before, the dependent variable in this analysis is preference, measured as the difference between the thermometer score ratings given to Bush and to Dukakis, recoded to the 0–1 interval.[43] The regression results, shown in table 9.4, indicate that Bush's support among blacks in 1988 did come disproportionately from those least identified with their race. The effect of racial group identification is not huge, but the effect is visible, and our estimate here is consistent with the results from other vote models, using alternative measures and different data.[44] Most black Americans identified with their racial group; those who did not were inclined to sympathize with Bush and the Republicans in 1988.

Table 9.4 Effect of Racial Group Identification on Black Support for Bush in 1988

Variable	Regression Estimate	Standard Error
Racial group identification	−.10	.06
Personal economic condition	.28	.07
Assessments of national economy	.03	.08
Gender	.05	.03
Age (elderly)	−.07	.04
Mainstream Protestant	.09	.06
Charismatic Protestant	.11	.05
Income (poor)	.02	.04
Young × Poor	−.06	.06
Young × Affluent	.07	.09
Professional	−.11	.05
Manager	−.08	.11
Sales	−.04	.04
Farmer	−.18	.12
Student	−.15	.08
Disabled	.15	.07
Race of interviewer	−.06	.04
R-squared	.25	
Number of cases	170	
Standard error	.19	

Source: 1988 National Election Study.

CONCLUSIONS

Race creates divisions more notable than any other in American life—economic divisions, social divisions, and, as we have seen here repeatedly, political divisions as well. And yet these racial differences are often invisible, denied, or suppressed. During the 1988 campaign, Bush and Quayle distanced themselves from accusations of bigotry and racism, promoting the notion that their campaign had nothing to do with race. In the meantime, the Democratic campaign avoided black audiences and ignored black interests. Race was likewise invisible to a surprising number of ordinarily sophisticated observers: academic accounts of the Bush campaign often made no reference to race whatever, and many reporters seemed puzzled over why so much of the 1988 campaign was being devoted to the issue of law enforcement.[45]

It may have been difficult to see at the time, but race was in fact central to the 1988 contest: in the coded appeals to whites' racial resentments offered by the Republicans, in the studied avoidance of appeals to the core constituency of blacks by the Democrats, and, finally and ultimately, in the decisions of white and black voters on election day. In these ways, the 1988 campaign offered a near-perfect illustration of the electoral temptations of race.

These temptations are a product in part of the persistent power of racial resentment among American voters, combined with a willingness to exploit such resentment among American politicians. As we have seen here, racial resentment had a sizable impact on the vote of white Americans in 1988. The effect was greatest among Democrats and Independents, precisely those voters the Bush campaign had to attract to capture the White House; independent of strands of American conservatism that were also on display in the Bush campaign; and most pronounced among those whites most inundated by the Horton initiative.[46]

For the Democrat party, race offers the temptation of benign neglect, also on display in 1988. One consequence was that while black Americans rejected Bush wholeheartedly, they were unenthusiastic about Dukakis. Moreover, presented with a campaign that featured racism on the Republican side and evasion on the Democratic, many black Americans sat the election out. Black turnout fell sharply in 1988; the gap between black and white turnout is about as large now as it was two decades ago.[47] This withdrawal of black Americans from participation in elections undermines the prospects for meeting the standards of even an adversarial democratic politics, where conflicts of interest are assumed to be accommodated in processes like voting.

When Bentsen and Jackson complained late in the campaign that the Republicans were appealing to racism, the press brushed the accusation away, treating it as if it were an act of partisan desperation, no different in kind from other claims. This was a mistake. The charge of racism is different. At issue are not merely the "real facts" behind Bush's support for Social Security or Dukakis's record on environmental protection. Systematic appeals to racial prejudice go beyond disputes over errors of fact; they degrade the democratic process. If democracy is, in part, government by discussion, and if a prominent part of such discussion takes place during presidential campaigns, then the accusation of racism deserves special examination. In 1988, the press failed to provide it. Pursuing an "objective" and "neutral" description of the campaign, journalists played into the hands of elite strategists who were willing to indulge in coded racist appeals or in racial silence. Members of the press thus became, in Michael Schudson's phrase, "mere stenographers for the official transcript of social reality."[48]

Was the Republican Initiative Racist?

The question here is not whether the Republican campaign had racist consequences—the evidence we have provided on that point seems, at least to us, persuasive—but rather whether Republican strategists intended this effect. To

C. Vann Woodward, writing shortly after the 1988 results were in, the answer was perfectly obvious:

> More fundamental are the skill and expertise, the cynicism and unscrupulous methods, by which the electorate was successfully gulled and deceived. All the tested methods of McCarthyite character assassination and phobia spreading were employed, but the main reliance was upon race. Not only familiar code words—crime, rape, public housing, urban conditions—but blatantly outright racism such as use made of Willie Horton. The people who did this were not rednecks or Western toughs from the boondocks. George Herbert Walker Bush, Yale 1948, and James Addison Baker III, Princeton 1952, come from a higher level of social, economic, and educational elite than any other front running leaders since Franklin Roosevelt. They knew exactly what they were doing.[49]

The Republican principals, not surprisingly, presented a different view. Atwater, Ailes, and Teeter steadfastly defended the campaign they designed in 1988, arguing in particular that the Horton fliers, radio spots, television advertisements, and the central place Horton assumed in Bush's speeches had nothing to do with race.

Accepting this claim requires us to swallow the idea that the Bush campaign was not responsible for what was going on in its name elsewhere. It requires us to believe that Teeter, Ailes, and Atwater, among the most successful campaign operatives in the business, were blind to the consequences of their own advice. Most of all, accepting the Republican defense requires a serious case of political amnesia. It requires us to forget Lee Atwater's personal history and meteoric rise to power. Atwater grew up in South Carolina. He served as a college intern in the Washington office of Senator Strom Thurmond, one of the fiercest opponents of desegregation, who led the Dixiecrat Southern revolt from the Democratic party in 1948. By 1978, Atwater had become political director of Thurmond's successful reelection campaign and a minor legend in southern political circles. Apart from Thurmond, Atwater's most important mentor was Harry Dent, a South Carolinian widely given credit for devising Richard Nixon's southern strategy in 1968. Looking back on the Republican's effort in the South in 1968, Atwater called it "a model campaign," saying, "I've used it as a blueprint for everything I've done in the South since then."

That Atwater was unable to overcome his past is apparent from his own words, what he was willing to say in public about the 1988 campaign. To a

Republican Unity meeting in June, Atwater promised that "by the time this election is over, Willie Horton will be a household name" (a promise he delivered on). Later during the campaign he asserted that "the Horton case is one of those gut issues that are value issues, particularly in the South, and if we hammer at these over and over, we are going to win." And in a speech intended to boost party morale in late July, Atwater said, "There is a story about Willie Horton, who, for all I know, may end up being Dukakis's running mate. . . . The guy [Dukakis] was on TV about a month ago, and he said, you'll never see me standing in the driveway of my house talking to these [vice-presidential] candidates. And guess what? Monday I saw in his driveway of his home Jesse Jackson. So anyway, maybe he [Dukakis] will put this Willie Horton on the ticket after all is said and done."

A Dukakis-Horton ticket is a "joke," of course, and a revealing one. It reflects a confusion between Jackson, a prominent minister, successful politician, and protégé of Martin Luther King, Jr., and Horton, a convicted murderer and rapist. Atwater's confusion is perhaps understandable, since from his strategic point of view, Jackson and Horton might as well be the same person. And there is the irony that Horton owes his notoriety less to Dukakis than to Atwater and his associates: it was the Bush campaign that was attempting to place Horton on the Democratic ticket.

In a public forum hosted by Harvard's Kennedy School of Government less than a month after the presidential election, Atwater (and Ailes) vigorously defended the Republican campaign. Atwater denied that racial prejudice continues as a force in American politics. With this point established, the Democratic accusation then becomes insulting to the American people—by which Atwater meant, evidently, American people of pale complexion. Ailes made a similar point, arguing that the American people are now color-blind. Atwater and Ailes also defended their use of the furlough issue, arguing that it had nothing whatever to do with race. The real issue, according to Atwater, was a policy that permitted convicted murderers with no chance of parole to be furloughed. Atwater said that he was "sickened" by the Horton story, and by the furlough program. This is how Atwater recounted Horton's original crime:

> When I first heard about this issue, I didn't know who Willie Horton was. I didn't know what race he was. I was told a story about a guy—I didn't know the name—who had gone to a gas station. There was a 17-year old kid there who was trying to work his way through college. The guy [Horton] stabbed this kid 24 times, cut his sexual organ off, stuck it in his mouth, cut his arms and legs off, and stuck the guy in a trash can.[50]

The boy who died in the robbery attempt was not mutilated. Atwater's assertion that Horton had cut off the boy's penis and stuffed it in the boy's mouth is wrong. This is, to say the least, an interesting mistake. Stories of cross-race mutilations are a prime exhibit of what folklorists call *modern legends:* "highly captivating and plausible, but mainly fictional, oral narratives that are widely told as true stories."[51] Mutilations of just the sort Atwater imagined are notonly the stuff of legend, of course. They actually took place as a dehumanizing accompaniment to the lynching of black men by white mobs in the decades following the Civil War. Atwater's confusion has a deep racial resonance—as did the campaign he orchestrated.

Was the Democratic Evasion Racist?

Looking back at the campaign she helped to manage, Susan Estrich expressed regret at failing to speak directly on questions of race. On the Bush campaign initiatives on Horton in particular, Estrich wrote:

> The Democratic Party has been assaulted on the crime issue, and we have behaved as a timid and frightened victim, afraid that we have done something wrong. We have not been soft on crime, and we ought not act as if we have. But we have been soft on racism and political demagoguery.
>
> "We can't afford to alienate white voters," I was told by many in my party and my campaign, whites may be put off if we "whine" about racism. I am not proud of our silence, broken finally by Lloyd Bentsen.
>
> When we see racism, we need to say so. It begins to lose its power only when we make it explicit.
>
> When Democrats are attacked as soft on crime—by a campaign using a black rapist as a symbol—our substantive response on the "crime issue" is largely beside the point. The point is race, not crime. That we do not say so—or that we say so only late in the game, and only for a day, and only with kid gloves—only enhances the power of a race-based appeal.[52]

Estrich is embarrassed, and she should be, but her critique does not go far enough. Silence in the face of an opponent's racist campaign does confer legitimacy on the political uses of racism and does thereby participate in the degradation of political discourse. That's bad enough, but there's more. By evading discussions of racial questions and avoiding black audiences, the Democratic campaign in 1988 withheld democratic recognition from black Americans. If elections are ritualistic affirmations of belonging, then by the evidence of 1988, some Americans belong to their political society more fully than do others.

Postscript on 1992

Some may read our conclusions and commentary as cynical. They will say that we are blind to the unmistakable signs of racial progress, that we are "in love with pessimism."[53] In the few years since the 1988 campaign passed into history, they might point out, David Dinkins was elected mayor of New York City; Douglas Wilder moved into the governor's mansion of Virginia; and the number of blacks serving in the House of Representatives nearly doubled.

We quite agree that there has been genuine progress—even if Dinkins lost his bid for reelection; even if Wilder has been retired unceremoniously from public life; and even if recent gains in black representation in Congress are in serious jeopardy because of court challenges to the Voting Rights Act. Granting all this, it is still the case that black Americans hold public office today in numbers that would have seemed inconceivable just a quarter century ago. In a political system where public office confers both power and recognition, this is an essential fact, one well worth celebrating.

If the 1988 presidential campaign reminds us of how far we have yet to go, of how easily we can fall victim to the electoral temptations of race, the lessons of 1992 are more complex. The 1992 experience suggests that there is nothing inevitable about the prominent place taken by racism in 1988. Temptations can be resisted; they can be overcome or set aside. Although the 1992 campaign had problems of its own, it was comparatively free of the racism that stained the 1988 contest.

In part, this was the result of events that took place before the campaign itself. In November 1991, after an initial veto, and while using the occasion to advertise his staunch opposition to racial quotas, President Bush nevertheless signed into law the 1991 Civil Rights Bill. When Thurgood Marshall retired from the Supreme Court, Bush chose another black American, Clarence Thomas, to replace him, and then stood behind the furious challenge that was mounted against his confirmation. Lee Atwater, the chairman of the Republican National Committee, a close adviser to the president, and a principal architect of the 1988 strategy, died of cancer, and so was not available to manage the president's reelection bid. And during the campaign itself, the religious right was better organized and more visible than in 1988. One consequence was the conspicuous display of moral conservatism and family values at the Republican National Convention. For all these reasons, the Bush campaign was tempted less by racial codewords in 1992 than in 1988.

On the Democratic side, meanwhile, Jesse Jackson was to play a much smaller part in the 1992 campaign than he had four years before. Governor Clinton of Arkansas, the eventual nominee, entered the campaign less vulner-

able to the kinds of veiled racial attacks that had been directed at his predecessor, Governor Dukakis of Massachusetts. Clinton was southern, moderate,
experienced at building biracial coalitions, and had made work requirements a
prominent part of his welfare program in Arkansas.

And then there was the massive intrusion on the 1992 proceedings by Ross
Perot. In spite of the formidable hurdles that the American electoral system
places before third-party candidates, Perot managed to win nearly one in five
votes in 1992, the second best showing by a third-party candidate since the
Civil War. His quixotic and lavishly financed campaign centered on the federal
deficit and the ways things work, or don't, in Washington. Perot's campaign
amounted to a huge distraction from the politics of race.

In short, for a variety of reasons, the electoral temptations of race were apparently less tempting in 1992 than in 1988. If this is so—if nothing like the
elaborate Horton initiative of 1988 can be found in the serenade voters were
sung in 1992—then racial resentment should have played a less prominent role
in the white vote in 1992. And it did. The 1992 NES carried questions that allowed us to undertake exact, side-by-side comparisons with 1988. When we did
so we found that the impact of racial resentment among white voters declined
between 1988 and 1992. We found also that while the impact of racial resentment increased in 1988 as the election came to a close and as the Horton story
moved to the center of the Bush campaign, it diminished in importance as the
campaign neared its end in 1992. As a result, at the climax of the campaign,
racial resentment was a powerful ingredient in the white vote in 1988 but barely
present in 1992.[54]

The 1992 campaign reminds us that racial resentment is not an automatic
part of American political discourse or public opinion. Its prominence is contingent, not fixed. How deeply resentment infiltrates our politics depends importantly on decisions made by elites. If the 1988 campaign is a disheartening
reminder of how potent the electoral temptations of race remain, 1992 shows
that campaigns need not be run that way; that there is nothing inevitable about
white voters casting their ballots preoccupied with matters of race.[55]

PART IV

IMPLICATIONS AND CONCLUSIONS

CHAPTER TEN

Racial Politics and Democratic Ideals

W. E. B. Du Bois began *The Souls of Black Folk* with an immodest claim and a bold prophecy: "Herein lie buried many things which if read with patience may show the strange meaning of being black here in the dawning of the Twentieth Century. This meaning is not without interest to you, Gentle Reader; for the problem of the Twentieth Century is the problem of the color-line."[1] Du Bois wrote at the turn of the new century, with a fine sense of history, and he was right, twice over. His collection of essays remains an authoritative source on the black experience in America, and his prophecy accurately foretold the struggle for freedom that would mark the twentieth century. Du Bois was a perceptive analyst of American race relations, but we wonder now whether he cast his famous prediction far enough into the future. Du Bois, perhaps, was too optimistic.

In this final chapter, we review our findings on racial politics in America and place them in a broader context. We will say something both about the politics of race in contemporary American society (the way things are) and about how the character of our racial politics might be made more democratic (the way things might be).

INTERESTS AND OPINIONS

When we began, the general claim on behalf of self-interest seemed persuasive. Of course people support policies that promote their own material interests and oppose policies that threaten them. Opinions on public policy are a direct and immediate reflection of "primitive self-interest" and little else, is how *The American Voter* put it.[2]

The presumption is strong, but the evidence is weak. In our analysis, whites who felt personally threatened by affirmative action policies, either at the workplace or in schools, were generally no more opposed to such policies than were whites whose personal lives were free from racial threat. Likewise, the perception of personal gain from affirmative action policies did not generally inspire more support for such policies among black Americans (if anything, the relationship ran the other way). Whites whose families were experiencing economic trouble were not any more likely to oppose federal programs and employment policies designed to help blacks; black Americans who had recently run into economic difficulty or who expressed apprehensions about their economic future were not especially favorable toward government assistance. And on it went: we uncovered little empirical justification here for building a theory of public opinion upon the foundations of self-interest.

These results may seem surprising, but they are in fact consistent with the generally anemic effects of self-interest on public opinion reported in scores of investigations over the last decade or so. On such diverse matters as government health insurance, aid to education, racial busing for the purpose of school desegregation, employment policy, gun control, and more, self-interest turns out to be quite unimportant.[3] Together, these studies suggest that self-interest packs much less political punch than commonly assumed. Public opinion resembles religion more than it does commerce.[4]

If we have added anything to this conclusion, it comes from having pursued the implications of self-interest for black Americans as least as vigorously—indeed, more vigorously—as we have for white Americans. Up to now, research on self-interest and public opinion on race has been preoccupied with whites' racial fears. Thus the general collapse of self-interest in our various analyses, for white and black Americans alike, *is* news. Like whites, blacks do not appear to be single-minded seekers of advantage, even on matters that seem to engage their interests directly. As a result, the huge racial divide in opinion cannot be accounted for by what Hume once called the "universal passion" for personal advantage.

Contingent Self-Interest

We do not mean to imply that self-interest never makes a difference for public opinion. Such a conclusion would be contradicted by our own results, to say nothing of the broader empirical literature. While self-interest is generally unconnected to public opinion, it can take on political significance under special conditions: when the material benefits or harms of a proposed policy are substantial; when benefits and harms are well publicized, so that citizens do not have to figure this out on their own; and when benefits and harms are virtually certain to take effect, should the policy pass.[5]

This general formulation of the conditions under which self-interest influences opinion seems to fit our few cases of self-interest making a noticeable difference in public opinion on matters of race. For example, in our results, self-interest figured into white opinion only when whites were encouraged to think about affirmative action in terms of the harm that might befall them. Only then did self-interest emerge as a significant (if modest) predictor of opinion. Then those whites who believed that affirmative action was likely to set back the education of their own children were more likely to oppose the policy.[6]

This result was induced by framing a survey question in a certain way, but we carried out this experiment and others like it in order to simulate the effects provoked by actual campaigns. With this in mind, it is interesting to note that while studies of public opinion set in the context of real campaigns for tax relief—contentious and expensive campaigns like that of Proposition 13 in California in 1978—show noticeable effects of self-interest, otherwise comparable studies that inquire about taxes in the abstract or about hypothetical changes in the tax code do not.[7] These results point again to the importance of elite frames. Unless campaigns do for citizens what they seem disinclined to do for themselves—that is, first ascertain and then keep prominently in mind the personal price tags of proposed policies—self-interest is likely to remain politically insignificant.[8]

Group-Interest and Public Opinion

In our preoccupation with self-interest, we should not forget that our results do support the importance of interests in public opinion—interests that are collective rather than personal. Many white Americans believe that affirmative policies threaten their collective interests, that powerful institutions cater to black Americans, and that it is now white Americans who operate at a disadvantage. This sense of group threat and disadvantage, moreover, is systematically related to opinion. White Americans who believe that black Americans threaten their collective interests are less supportive of policies designed to reduce racial inequalities. We take this result to mean that interests matter to whites' opinions on racial affairs, that group interests matter.

We also find group interest at work in black public opinion, though the results here are more complex. Black Americans believe that affirmative action generally works to their racial group's advantage, but they also express considerable skepticism that this happens very often: many blacks believe instead that American institutions discriminate against their racial group, some thirty years after the Civil Rights Act made it illegal to do so. Both these aspects of group interest registered an effect on black opinion. Black Americans were consistently more likely to support government policies on race if they believed that affirmative action programs enhance opportunities for blacks (not for themselves, but for blacks as a whole); and, independently, if they believed that racial discrimination obstructs the progress of blacks (not their own progress, but the progress of blacks as a whole).

Our results on group interest are consistent with the general finding that citizens are quite capable of distinguishing between their own experiences and interests, on the one hand, and the experiences and interests of their group, on the other, and that between the two, the latter appears to be the more important politically. Much of this work builds on the concept of relative deprivation, introduced by Samuel Stouffer and his associates in their landmark study, *The American Soldier*. In an effort to understand why soldiers who experienced the best conditions expressed the lowest morale, Stouffer argued that feelings of deprivation were relative, based less in objective condition and more in social comparison. Later, Runciman introduced the distinction between egotistical and fraternal deprivation: the first refers to a sense of personal relative disadvantage; the second refers to a sense of group relative disadvantage.[9] This turns out to be not just a neat analytic distinction, but one with real political bite. Thus, to take one example, participation by black college students in the civil rights movement is predicted better by their anger over society's treatment of black Americans in general than by any discontent they felt about their own predicament. In this instance as in others, it appears that the political power of deprivation is located in the sense of collective disadvantage.[10]

Our results are also consistent with the major positive finding to emerge from the quest for the ideological underpinnings of American public opinion. The positive finding is this: when Americans are asked to evaluate political parties and presidential candidates, they very often refer to social groups.[11] Campbell and associates call this inclination "ideology by proxy," since there

> is little comprehension of "long-range plans for social betterment," or of basic philosophies rooted in postures toward change or abstract conceptions of social and economic structure of causation. The party or candidate is simply endorsed as being "for" a group with which the subject is identified or as being above the selfish demands of groups within the population. Exactly *how* the candidate or party might see fit to implement or void group interests is a moot point, left unrelated to broader ideological concerns.[12]

However unsophisticated the reasoning, citizens nevertheless find political significance in collective benefits and deprivations, and such interests appear to shape their assessments of candidates and parties powerfully.[13]

So interests have a part to play in public opinion, interests that are collective rather than personal, group centered rather than self-centered. In matters of public opinion, citizens seem to be asking themselves less "What's in it for me?" and more "What's in it for my group?" In this way, our findings sustain a line of analysis reaching back to Marx and Sumner and carried forward by contemporary group conflict theorists.[14]

Fears of the Imagination

Empirical research has taken the origins of interests mostly for granted; its primary business has been to ascertain the effects of interests, not their antecedents. From the perspective of psychological research on risk and uncertainty, however, an equally interesting question is how people go about deciding whether they are threatened or safe. And on this question, our results suggest a large divorce between perception and reality. Connections between sense of threat, on the one hand, and actual conditions, on the other, were weak to nonexistent in our analysis. We found instead that the racial threats whites saw were almost entirely a consequence of the racial sentiments they felt. Whites experience racial threat because they are inclined to look at their social world that way; they feel threatened when others, in comparable circumstances, feel safe.

That racial fear is in an important way a fear of the imagination is also suggested by other investigations of American race relations. For example, the urban riots of the 1960s appeared to set off fears and apprehensions among whites that were disproportionate to the events taking place on the ground. So, too, did the Los Angeles uprising of 1992. The riots *were* scary, and for people caught up in their midst, terrifying and dangerous. But even suburban whites living far from the violence appeared to feel at risk.[15]

A similar impression emerges from Jonathan Rieder's ethnographic exploration of Canarsie, a white ethnic community in Brooklyn undergoing racial change in the 1970s. Rieder argues that whites' perceptions of racial threat were rooted partly in social realities but were exaggerated by individual prejudice. "Racism," wrote Rieder, "primed whites to select fragments of reality that confirmed their prejudgments." The sense of threat was amplified further by the spread of what Rieder called "grotesque incidents," horrific stories that collectivized the experience of danger. Taken all around, then, the perception of racial threat is best understood as "an amalgam of fantasy, truth, and rumor."[16]

Black Americans aren't exactly clear-eyed on the subject of threat, either. According to recent surveys, imposing proportions of black Americans subscribe to the contention that black elected officials are harassed and persecuted by their own government, that crack cocaine is distributed in black communities in order to immobilize them, or that HIV was created in order to exterminate the black race.[17] One reason for the vitality of such "delusional" beliefs within the black community is history: the U.S. government has in fact harassed and persecuted black leaders, and has engaged in extremely dubious medical experiments with black subjects.[18] That even paranoids have enemies is not only a joke.

These various accounts are reminiscent of an older racial fear. In the period leading up to the Civil War, white dread of slave revolts reached epidemic proportions. The extent to which slaves actually erupted in violence remains controversial, but there is little controversial in the conclusion that white fear of slave rebellion was disproportionate to the actual incidence of violence.[19] Rebellion in the face of massive asymmetries in power and with the virtual certainty of violent retaliation seems, from our historical vantage point, foolhardy, and probably was recognized as such at the time by slaves themselves. Rather than violent rebellion, resistance ordinarily took the form of small acts of defiance, employing the "weapons of the weak" in James Scott's phrase.[20]

The prospect of black violence, however unlikely, nevertheless haunted the white southern imagination. Insurrection panics were frequent. Fear of a great bloodbath contributed to sentiment for secession. This apocalyptic frame of mind is captured well by Freehling, when he wrote that the prospect of emancipation "conjured up grotesque specters of plunder, rape, and murder. The slave, too barbaric and degraded to adjust to freedom, seemed certain to declare race war the moment he threw off his chains."[21] As the abolitionist movement gathered strength, racial fears multiplied. In New Orleans, when secession and war grew near:

> The papers continued to demand increased police vigilance; municipal officials sought wider powers and additional arms from state governments; vigilante committees stood ready to quash the colored rebels. Yet no insurrection occurred. The blood bath feared by so many was never drawn. "Christmas is passed and we are not yet annihilated," the *New Orleans Daily Crescent* noted with relief in 1856.[22]

Here again racial fear appears disproportionate to and largely disconnected from actual events. Winthrop Jordan argues that real threats were not irrelevant to such fears, but neither were they especially important. More significant were the anxieties and apprehensions entangled in the views whites held of themselves and their black slaves:

> Presumably the principal reason for the colonists' fear of slave insurrections was a pardonable distaste for having their throats cut. Plainly, however, their fears were exaggerated far beyond the proportions of the danger and were in part a response to more complicated anxieties. The specter of Negro rebellion presented an appalling world turned upside down, a crazy nonsense world of black over white, an anti-community which was the direct negation of the community as white men knew it.[23]

The specter of slave rebellions is an extreme case, but we suspect that racial conflict is *typically* accompanied by unrealistic and exaggerated threats, by fears of being overwhelmed or annihilated. Such threats can be detected in the anti-Semite's preoccupation with Jewish world domination; in the wild claims white

Americans attributed to the Black Power slogan of the 1960s; in the fears and apprehensions that race riots set off among suburban whites; in the current popularity of paranoid fears within black communities; and, reaching deeper into our past, both the panicky fear of black insurrection that haunted the white southern imagination before emancipation, and the nativist warnings of mongrelization that greeted immigrants to American shores in the 1910s and 1920s. Threat is both realistic and not, an incendiary mix of actual conflict, misinformation that amplifies and collectivizes the sense of danger, and private apprehensions displaced onto public objects.

Implications

The apparent unimportance of self-interest for public opinion is not necessarily cause for celebration.[24] Alternatives to self-interest are not necessarily good. For one thing, the disconnection between self-interest and opinion widens the possibilities for manipulation, since individual citizens no longer are special authorities on the foundations of their views. Democracy assumes that citizens are qualified to govern themselves, that they know best where their interests lie. But if interests matter little, and political views and choices become the province of group attachments and political principles, then citizens may be more susceptible to the alternative framings and rhetorical flourishes of those who compete for their support. When the anchor of private experience and personal interest is lost, power passes from citizens to leaders.

That citizens are not motivated by self-interest does not mean that they are motivated by altruism. Alternatives to self-interest are not always uplifting or inspiring or noble, nor do they necessarily produce a more just society. This point is central to Hirschman's analysis of eighteenth-century moral philosophy, where the hope was expressed that haggling over material interests might lead to a more peaceful politics than one based on the exaggerated sense of honor, which had left much of Europe ruined. Better calculations of interest than ethnic cleansing.[25] Better calculations of interest than the nativist impulse to turn away from strangers.[26] Better calculations of interest than the xenophobic backlash movements that have sporadically embarrassed American politics.[27] Better calculations of interest than the politics of fear and apprehension that seems to motivate outbursts of political intolerance.[28] As we have seen all too clearly, both in the United States and around the world, citizens are as apt to sink below self-interest as they are to rise above it.

Whether judged, in the end, as primarily good or evil for society and politics, the small part played by self-interest in opinion should at least be taken as cautionary to the theoretical rush so conspicuously on display in political analysis to reduce all motivation to the single-minded pursuit of self-interest. In an essay on *The Wealth of Nations*, George Stigler praises Adam Smith lavishly, as "widely read, widely traveled, superlatively observant" and characterizes the book itself as "stupendous palace erected upon the granite of self-interest." But Stigler chastises Smith for not seeing the role of self-interest as preeminent in political undertakings as it was in commercial transactions. Stigler wants Smith to say that *all* legislation with important economic effect is the "calculated achievement of interested economic classes"—and Smith does not. In Stigler's reading, Smith "gave a larger role to emotion, prejudice, and ignorance in political life than he ever allowed in ordinary economic affairs." This earns Stigler's disapproval, but not ours. We prefer Adam Smith's less parsimonious, but more realistic, account of public life to the one that Stigler imagines. Adam Smith, more than the modern-day practitioners of the economic approach to political analysis, would have appreciated the complexity of motives that give shape and meaning to contemporary American opinion.[29]

PREJUDICE (THAT WORD AGAIN) AND OPINION

The idea of black inferiority is a deeply ingrained habit in America, but its characteristic expression is fluid. In our century alone, the private meaning and public form of racial prejudice have undergone two important transformations, one reflected in the decline of the doctrine of biological racism, the other provoked by the sweeping changes and turbulent events set in motion by the civil rights movement and the urban riots of the 1960s. As a consequence of these developments, animosity toward blacks is expressed today less in the language of inherent, permanent inferiority and more in the language of American individualism. In this view, the virtues of diligence, hard work, and determination are conspicuous by their absence from black life; blacks are unwilling even to try to make it on their own and all too willing to take what they have not earned. Racial resentment, expressed in such terms, seems to be thriving and is far and away the single most important ingredient in whites' views on racial policies.

Remember what we have found here: racial resentment is a coherent and stable system of beliefs and feelings; whites express less of it in the presence of black Americans; racially resentful whites are much more likely to consider themselves and their families threatened by racial policies at work and school than are whites who express sympathetic views toward blacks—even though we can find virtually no evidence that they are in fact more threatened; white Americans who express racial resentment also subscribe to derogatory racial stereotypes (i.e., whites who say that blacks could be as well off as whites if they only tried are also inclined to believe that blacks are dangerous, lazy, and stupid); and, finally, racial resentment reveals a great deal about where white

Americans stand on matters of race. When it comes to school desegregation or federal assistance or affirmative action, nothing explains variation in white opinion as well as racial resentment.

Whitewashing Prejudice

Our results run against a recent turn in scholarship on American racial attitudes, which tends to be impressed with improvements in American race relations and skeptical about the present-day political power of racism. Here we have in mind such notable and in many ways admirable works as Carmine and Stimson's *Issue Evolution: Race and the Transformation of American Politics;* Huckfeldt and Kohfeld's *Race and the Decline of Class in American Politics;* the series of prominently placed reports by Sheatsley and his colleagues based on NORC's monitoring of white Americans' racial attitudes, beginning in the 1940s and continuing on up to the present; Schuman, Steeh, and Bobo's *Racial Attitudes in America;* Sniderman and Hagen's *Race and Inequality;* and Sniderman and Piazza's *Scar of Race.* In different ways, each of these works suggests that when it comes to understanding the political views of white Americans, race prejudice simply isn't that important.

In *Issue Evolution,* Carmines and Stimson argue persuasively that race has transformed modern American party politics.[30] They locate the turning point for this transformation, as we do, in Goldwater's capture of the Republican nomination in 1964. So far so good. The difficulty begins, as we see it, when Carmines and Stimson call Goldwater's opposition to federal intervention on civil rights, which was a centerpiece of his campaign for the presidency, "racial conservatism." And this racial conservatism, according to Carmines and Stimson, must not be confused with racial prejudice. Racial conservatism is not racism; rather, it is the application of conservative principles to the (new) issues of civil rights. Goldwater and his band of ideological followers were not racist, according to Carmines and Stimson; their opposition to the Civil Rights Act of 1964 was rooted in "racial policy conservatism, not racism."[31] Acknowledging that racial conservatism might appeal to bigots, Carmines and Stimson maintain that "its origin in western Republican doctrine of conservatism was altogether different in situation, culture, and ideology from southern white racism. It was a new species."[32]

Or consider Huckfeldt and Kohfeld's analysis of the emergence of race as the major social cleavage splitting American politics today. Huckfeldt and Kohfeld aim to understand racial polarization: the fact that black Americans give their support overwhelmingly to the Democratic party and its candidates, while decisive majorities of whites support the Republican party. As we have noted here, this racial divide dwarfs differences of class or religion or gender or indeed of any other social characteristic. Why? Huckfeldt and Kohfeld argue that racial polarization is a product of party competition. Polarization, they contend, is the natural culmination of the Democratic party's dependence on the electoral support of black Americans, which in turn compromises the party's ability to hold on to the support of working-class whites. Huckfeldt and Kohfeld concede that racism still exists, but in their political analysis it doesn't play much of a role. Citing Schelling's work on racial sorting, Huckfeldt and Kohfeld suggest that a little racism goes a long way; that "moderate levels of racial antagonism at the individual level are fully capable of fostering extreme levels of racial polarization at the corporate level." [33]

The withering away of prejudice is also the central theme running through the occasional reports based on the National Opinion Research Center's ongoing project on white Americans' racial attitudes. From the inaugural report in this series, issued in 1956, to the most recent, distributed in 1991, white Americans are portrayed as moving unswervingly toward enlightenment: early on in the series as repudiating "ancient beliefs about Negroes," and now, as embracing ever-more completely the doctrine of racial equality.[34] Inexorable progress is the main message of these bulletins, the "steady, massive growth in racial tolerance" their main result. Looking over the entire series, Smith and Sheatsley conclude that "a massive and wide-ranging liberalization of racial attitudes has swept America over the last forty years." [35]

We are impressed with these changes, too, but as Schuman, Steeh, and Bobo demonstrate in *Racial Attitudes in America*, the picture is actually more complex than Smith and Sheatsley's reading suggests. *Racial Attitudes* presents a more comprehensive description of the evolution of racial attitudes than the NORC series by itself can provide. Schuman and his colleagues show that white Americans have become much more sympathetic to racial equality *in principle*, just as the NORC reports concluded. That blacks have the right to go to the same schools as whites; that blacks should have an equal chance to compete for jobs and promotions; that segregation by race on buses and in restaurants is wrong; that blacks have the right to live wherever they like—on all such questions, white Americans have become dramatically more egalitarian, and all this in little more than a generation. At the same time, white support for racial *policy*, for steps the government might take to prohibit discrimination or diminish segregation or reduce racial inequalities, reveals an entirely different pattern. While white approval of the principles of equality and integration was steadily advancing over the last four decades, white support for the policies that might bring such principles to life was not—indeed, it was as likely to diminish as it was to increase.

While Schuman and his colleagues correct the overly optimistic reading of change in white racial attitudes suggested by the NORC series, they nevertheless participate in the demotion of prejudice as an explanation for political conflict. At the end of their book, after a meticulous and judicious presentation of the evidence on the transformation of attitudes on matters of race in the latter half of the twentieth century, Schuman and his colleagues (like the rest of us) are unable to resist a speculation or two. Given their findings, they were especially intrigued about why so many white Americans continue to oppose governmental efforts to reduce racial inequalities when they simultaneously favor equality and integration in principle. Prejudice, they suggest, provides no answer to this principle-policy gap. Schuman, Steeh, and Bobo are far more impressed with an explanation that portrays white Americans as responding realistically to the material threats that blacks pose to their collective interests—with group threat, as we would call it.

Perhaps the clearest example of this general scholarly turn toward disconnecting racial prejudice from white opposition to egalitarian racial policies is provided by Sniderman and Hagen's *Race and Inequality: A Study in American Values*. *Race and Inequality* argues that white Americans' views toward public policies designed to diminish racial inequalities are understood best in terms of the values (or, as we would prefer, principles) that the policies evoke. Underneath the surface squabbles over employment opportunity or school desegregation are deep differences over fundamental American values, especially individualism. According to Sniderman and Hagen, it is the American commitment to individualism, not any remnant of American racism, that erodes white support for egalitarian policies.

This theme is carried forward in *The Scar of Race*, our final example of the diminished place of prejudice in much contemporary political analysis. Sniderman and Piazza would contend that our analysis of present-day race relations is mired in the past, too ready to detect prejudice behind opposition to contemporary policies of affirmative action or federal assistance. Their claim is not that racism has disappeared, but that it no longer dominates, as it did a generation ago, the racial policy preferences of white Americans. It is "simply wrong," they conclude, "to suppose that the primary factor driving the contemporary arguments over the politics of race is white racism."[36]

Where does this confidence come from? We quite agree that the opinions of white Americans on racial issues are not reducible to racial resentment alone; that a comprehensive explanation of public opinion on racial questions must take into account principles and interests as well. And we agree that revolutionary changes have taken place in white Americans' racial attitudes: in contrast to a generation or two ago, most whites now reject the idea of permanent, biological inferiority, and they accept equal rights and opportunities as matters of principle. But we also believe that resentments rooted in racial difference continue to shape American opinion powerfully.

It is one thing to worry over, as we have done here, whether the current form of racial animosity is conceived of better as prejudice or resentment. It is quite another to conclude that conservative positions on issues of race these days are entirely a matter of realistic group threat or American values; that racial conservatism is merely conservative principles applied to questions that just happen to be about race; that prejudice is no longer important; that race itself has somehow been removed from the politics of equal opportunity and affirmative action. To this our results say, emphatically and unequivocally, think again.

Racial Resentment and Ethnocentrism

Perhaps our most striking result is the long reach of racial resentment into diverse aspects of American opinion. We found racial resentment to be implicated in whites' views not just on affirmative action or school desegregation, but on welfare, capital punishment, urban unrest, family leave, sexual harassment, gay rights, immigration, spending on defense, and more.

In part, this result is a reflection of how racially coded our political thinking has become. Consider welfare reform as an example. Simply raising the issue may invoke among many whites the assumption that most people on welfare are black and could make it on their own if they only tried. In fact, white Americans exaggerate the proportion of the poor who are black, and those whose picture of poverty is most distorted in this way are least supportive of federal spending on welfare.[37] White Americans may exaggerate the proportion of the poor who are black at least in part because the press does, too. Mainstream news magazines—*Time, Newsweek, US News and World Report*—portray the poor as substantially more black than is in fact the case.[38] Of course, black Americans are more likely to be poor than whites, just as they are more likely to be arrested and incarcerated, just as they are more likely to be on welfare. But the media pick up and amplify these differences. In telling their stories, news media rely, as Epstein once put it, on cultural icons with symbolic power and, in the process, both reinforce derogatory racial stereotypes and underwrite the racialization of public opinion.[39]

That racial resentment is implicated in white opinion across a wide range is in part a matter of racial coding, of the silent conversion of ostensibly nonracial issues into issues of race. But this line of interpretation can carry us only so far. Racial coding is no explanation for the role of racial resentment in defense spending, or in issues of gay rights, or in immigration policy. In assessing resentments directed specifically at black Americans, we seem to have tapped into a broader reaction to social difference, one that might be called "ethnocentric."

In this way, our results recall those reported by Adorno and his colleagues in *The Authoritarian Personality*, the famous and monumental study of anti-Semitism carried out in the United States in the 1940s. Its purpose was to explain the nature and origins of anti-Semitism, and to understand the implications of anti-Semitism for democratic society, tasks made urgent by the emergence of fascism and the ongoing extermination of Jews in Europe. We take the major discovery of *The Authoritarian Personality* to be that anti-Semitism was just one aspect of a person's broader outlook on society and politics. Fear and contempt for Jews, it turned out, were often accompanied by fear and contempt directed at blacks, criminals, Japanese-Americans, conscientious objectors, immigrants, and "foreign ideas"—in short, by an ethnocentrism of a very general sort. It is precisely this result that our findings on racial resentment's long reach call to mind.

When *The Authoritarian Personality* was published, it was greeted with widespread acclaim, and then, in the space of a few years, buried under an avalanche of criticisms.[40] The critics were right to point out the study's defects, and they were persuasive. But it is important to keep in mind that the powerful critical literature provoked by *The Authoritarian Personality* established only that the study failed to prove its conclusions, not that its conclusions were incorrect. This is an important distinction, one that seems to have been missed in the methodological battering the study received. And it seems to us that research over the last four decades, though it has come in a trickle, nevertheless sustains Adorno and company's insistence that there is an underlying coherence to the variety of ideas that make up an individual's outlook on society, economics, and politics.[41]

From the point of view of the psychodynamic theory that Adorno and his associates favored, attitudes like anti-Semitism and ethnocentrism are manifestations of a unitary personality and must be analyzed in that way. Prejudice reflects not direct experience with the outgroup, not the tangible threats the outgroup might realistically pose, but rather the twisted expression of largely unconscious and otherwise unresolved personal conflicts. In this style of explanation, anti-Semitism and ethnocentrism serve the authoritarian well. Jews, blacks, and other outgroups become convenient and safe psychological targets. Through displacement, Jews and blacks absorb the hostilities originally provoked by the authoritarian's parents; through projection, Jews and blacks take on forbidden qualities—unbridled power, liberation from the demands of work, free and easy sex—those things that the authoritarian secretly wants but cannot have.

We find this too psychological. People may well differ from one another in the tendency to see difference as threatening. Adorno and his associates were probably right to claim that "the prejudiced individual is prepared to reject groups with which he has never had contact; his approach to a new and strange person or culture is not one of curiosity, interest, and receptivity but rather one of doubt and rejection. The feeling of difference is transformed into a sense of threat and an attitude of hostility. The new group easily becomes an out-group."[42] Ethnocentrism is not the expression only of neurotic personality, however. To reduce ethnocentrism entirely to personality ignores the role played by elites and institutions in the creation and promotion of ethnocentric ideologies. It is oblivious to the economic, social, and political conditions that give rise to ethnocentrism. And it is blind to the part that leaders and parties play in the mobilization of ethnocentrism for political purposes.[43]

The Activation and Suppression of Racial Resentment

In our results, the power of racial resentment is far from uniform: often it is huge, but sometimes it is modest. Our purpose in this section is to suggest the conditions that determine the prominence of racial resentment in whites' political thinking. Conceding as we do that racial resentment is unlikely to disappear any day soon, how might its political consequences be diminished?

The prominence of racial resentment in white public opinion seems to depend in the first instance on the nature of the issue itself. Of the six race policy questions that we examined in greatest detail, the issue of quotas for black college students elicits racial resentment the most.[44] Why?

First of all, this does not appear to be something special about affirmative action. Giving blacks preferential treatment in hiring and promotion is an instance of affirmative action, too, but it does not evoke racial resentment to any unusual degree. We suspect instead the terminology of "quotas," present in this question uniquely. "Quotas" is a highly charged and contentious term, used often by the opponents of affirmative action policies and programs, and it appears three times in our question on college admissions. It calls up an odious history of discrimination, exclusion, and even genocide. "Quotas" is a rallying point, a powerful symbolic weapon in the rhetorical war against affirmative action, and it appears to work, by our analysis, at least in part by activating whites' racial resentments.

On the other end of the spectrum, school desegregation elicits racial resentment the least. This cannot be because school desegregation is a problem of the past, or because it evokes equality so powerfully, since it shares both of these features with fair employment policy, where racial resentment looms much larger. It certainly isn't anything special about the realm of education, because preferential admissions for black college students activates racial resentment most of all. Perhaps what is special about this policy, instead, is its concern for black children. The issue, remember, is whether the federal government "should see to it that white and black children go to the same schools." Perhaps many whites are inclined to regard black children as promising and full of potential, or as innocent victims of circumstance. Either construction diminishes the relevance of the individualistic form of racial hostility that plays such a prominent role in other racial policy questions.

Our account of these differences is speculative, not least because the policies that we have been discussing differ from one another in a variety of ways. Variation of this sort can be investigated with greater precision through experiments, as we did in Chapter 7. There we discovered, among other things, that the impact of racial resentment on white opinion depends importantly on how the issue is framed.

In Experiment I, when whites were reminded that government assistance to blacks could be thought about in terms of whether blacks deserved special assistance, the impact due to racial resentment increased. In Experiment II, framing opposition to affirmative action as unfair advantage brought racial resentment to center stage; framing it as reverse discrimination demoted racial resentment to a lesser role. In Experiment III, when we shifted from a race-neutral to a race-conscious frame, the effect of racial resentment on white opinion increased sharply. And in Experiment IV, white Americans were much more enthusiastic about policies that would benefit the poor than they were about the identical policies aimed at blacks alone, with the part played by racial resentment diminishing correspondingly. All these results suggest that in choosing how to formulate the public debate on issues of race, elites have some say over the extent to which white opinion is laced with racial resentment. The devil is in the details: the nature of the issue and how the issue is framed both matter a lot.

What also seems to matter is whether the issue comes up at all. This point is illustrated best by our analysis of the 1988 presidential campaign, a near-perfect example of what can happen when the political parties succumb to what we have called the electoral temptations of race. Who could have imagined, before the campaign got under way, that Bush and his advisers would choose to invest so much of their time and money in the story of Willie Horton?

This was a choice; there was nothing inevitable about it. Bush, Atwater, Ailes, Teeter, Baker, and company did not create racial resentment in 1988, but in deciding to exploit it for political purposes, they brought it to center stage. That they needn't have is strongly suggested by the experience of 1992. For a variety of reasons, perhaps most of all the Perot candidacy, the 1992 presidential campaign was much less preoccupied with matters of race than was its predecessor, and as a consequence, the decisions made by white voters were less a product of racial resentment. The contrast between 1992 and 1988 suggests, once more, that the prominence of racial resentment in the public realm depends on choices made by elites. Are racial tensions to be exploited or are they to be left alone?

PRINCIPLED OPINIONS

Public opinion in the affairs of race is also a matter of principle. White and black Americans derive their opinions on equal employment opportunity and federal assistance at least in part from broader views on equality and limited government. In this way, they reward Aristotle's insistence that politics and morality are inseparable.

Principles are thus part of the story of public opinion on race, but only a part, and sometimes a rather small one. The modesty of our results, and their contingency, don't fit very neatly the common portrayal of the American Creed as an unstoppable, triumphant force. Perhaps most surprising in this respect was the quite thoroughgoing failure of economic individualism. For whites as for blacks, faith that hard work brings success had very little to do with opinions on matters of race. This result moves against the common contention that contemporary debate over affirmative action and welfare reform is first and foremost a discussion about the virtues of hard work and individual responsibility. Much more, as we have seen here, it is a debate on the question of whether or not black Americans deserve help.

Of the three principles we examined, equality emerges from our results as the most impressive. We say this partly because differences of opinion on topical matters of race can often be traced to differences over the desirability of equality, but also because the strong connections we see in the domain of race appear to reflect an abstract commitment to equality in principle, for blacks and whites alike. We know this because views on equality turn out to be important for redistributive and rights policies generally, not just for policy questions in the realm of race. Thus equality appears to be more than just sympathy for a particular group; it seems to be a principle.

Even in the case of equality, however, we see evidence of contingency and specificity, and we see this even within the realm of racial policy itself. Equality is enormously important when it comes to the issues of school desegregation and fair employment, two issues at the vanguard of the struggle for equal rights and opportunities carried forward by the civil rights movement, but quite unimportant for the more contemporary issue of affirmative action, where, it would seem, both opponents and supporters can enlist equality as justification for their views.

Specificity is also the rule outside the racial realm. While various groups seem to be included in the American hope for a more egalitarian society—blacks, women, the elderly, the poor and working class, gays and lesbians, and perhaps children—this yearning does not extend to those who wish to become Americans. Egalitarians, black and white, are deaf to the "clamor at the gates." Those who favor equality most do not support easing immigration restrictions, nor are they more opposed to the establishment of English as an official language. For now at least, equality seems to mean equality for us, not for them.

Finally, the prominence of equality in public opinion on race depends partly on how the issue is framed. No doubt the most striking instance of this is supplied by Experiment II. Under the unfair advantage frame, whites who endorsed the principle of equality tended to support affirmative action; under the reverse discrimination frame, whites who supported equality tended to oppose affirmative action. Thus equality facilitated affirmative action in one case and stood in its way in the other. This result supports Gamson's contention that affirmative action's ideological battleground centers on the idea of equal opportunity and that partisans on both sides lay claim to it.[45] To its supporters, affirmative action is required to bring true equality of opportunity to life, whereas to its opponents, affirmative action, by treating some groups better than others, violates equal opportunity for individuals.

These results suggest that principles like equality are in fact bundles of complex ideas. Their complexity makes them malleable, available for more than one purpose, relevant at more than one time. If the modesty and contingency of our results disappoint those who yearn for a politics of ideas, others may be surprised that ideas count at all.

Origins of Principles

If principles are important—at least some principles, for some issues, on some occasions—where do they come from? How is it that some Americans attach higher priority to equality than others do? Why are certain Americans so much more suspicious of government authority than others are?

We know remarkably little about this. In the empirical study of political principles, the question of origins seldom comes up, and when it does, it is not taken very seriously. For example, Stanley Feldman, who has done splendid empirical work demonstrating the importance of principles for public opinion, suggests that there is little mystery about it, that ordinary people pick up principles simply by going about their business: "The public may easily absorb the major elements of the political culture through processes of socialization and continual reinforcement by the norms of society and the language of political debate." Feldman and Zaller make much the same point in their exploration of American opinion on social welfare policy. They argue that there exists in the United States a common, shared heritage of values to which all Americans have ready access. After demonstrating that Americans often justify their policy views by referring to one or another principle, Feldman and Zaller conclude that "most Americans can draw with apparent ease upon several elements of the American political tradition," that "nearly all Americans have absorbed the principal elements of their political culture."[46]

What these arguments overlook is this: whereas ideas of equality or limited government may be familiar, some Americans subscribe to them wholeheartedly, others are not so sure, and a few reject them altogether. That elements of the American Creed are readily available does not mean that everyone adopts them. Indeed, if this were true, principles would be of no use to us here. If everyone lined up with uniform inspiration behind the idea of equality, then equality could tell us nothing about why some Americans favor school desegregation while others oppose it. But everyone is not equally enthusiastic about equality, and the mystery is why?

We are of course as guilty as the rest. Up until now, we have ignored the question of origins, too. Like others, we have been much more interested in the consequences of political principles than their antecedents. At this late moment, we can remedy this imbalance a bit by reporting in summary fashion the results of our analysis of the origins of equality and limited government, based in the 1990–92 NES panel study. We must unfortunately restrict this analysis to whites alone, since too few blacks show up in the panel to warrant statistical analysis.[47]

When it comes to explaining variation in support for equality and limited government, we find that many standard variables matter not at all. Education, occupation, income, homeownership, employment status: each is completely irrelevant to white views on equality and limited government. These results contradict the contention that expressions of support for American values are a cover for class interests. According to our analysis, political principles and social class are completely disconnected.

Of the various considerations that we examined, just three showed up clearly for both principles. The first of these is political engagement: everything else equal, those most attentive to politics are both more egalitarian and more suspicious of government power. This result is consistent with the line of argument that the American Creed is expressed most clearly in an official political culture, and that citizens are most apt to subscribe to elements of the creed insofar as they are paying close attention to those expressions. Citizens who spend their time in politics are most likely to encounter arguments that celebrate American political pieties.[48]

We also found that how important equality seems, and how dangerous government appears, depend in part on change in economic welfare. Specifically, those whose family's economic position was deteriorating were more likely to support equality and less likely to worry about an intrusive government. These relationships suggest, again, that principles are not some eternal and permanent representations of the American political experience. In the context of an improving family economy, the demand for equality seems less pressing, and government intervention seems less necessary. When the family's economic condition suffers, equality and government intervention take on higher priority, perhaps because the experience of economic trouble close at hand induces sympathy for those suffering a similar misfortune in the nation at large.

Finally and most prominently, our analysis revealed connections between American principles, on the one hand, and sentiments toward various subordinate social and political groups, on the other. White Americans who provided favorable evaluations of the poor, of blacks, and of the women's movement were more egalitarian and less concerned about the dangers of government. By this analysis, principles arise out of sympathy for others' misfortunes. Those who expressed the most sympathy were simultaneously most concerned to ensure that opportunities really were equal, and most likely to see the federal government not as a dangerous leviathan but as a helpful instrument for social and political change. Principles are not merely expressions of social sympathy, of course, but these results suggest in still another way the importance of social groupings to public opinion.

The American Creed

Tocqueville's conclusion that America was fundamentally democratic, in firm possession of egalitarian values, required some artful dancing. He did not ignore the problem of race—indeed, he regarded the presence of blacks on American soil "the most formidable evil threatening the nation's future." Still, in the large sweep of his analysis, he relegated blacks (and Native American Indians) to a marginal place. He obscured the intellectual respectability of racism and thereby underestimated its power and persistence. To Tocqueville, the problem of race was an aberration in an otherwise successful experiment with democratic government.

A century later, Myrdal concluded his famous investigation of American race relations in an oddly optimistic frame of mind. Myrdal was far from blind to prejudice and discrimination, but in his view they would be no match for the inexorable onward march of the American Creed, where "the American thinks, talks, and acts under the influence of high national and Christian precepts."[49]

Myrdal's capacity to see blue sky among the threatening clouds is matched by many contemporary scholars on race relations, as we noted earlier in this chapter. There is conveyed in this body of work a sense of dramatic progress, of the withering away of racism and discrimination, of a new politics of race, one that is about "mere" interests and, especially, noble and lofty principles. In the rush to establish the importance of principles in public opinion, we must not deny a place to less savory considerations, racial resentment conspicuous among them. The American political tradition is both glorious and repulsive, a point that accounts of public opinion too often overlook.[50]

DEMOCRATIC DISCUSSION

Public opinion is not only a matter of individuals privately assembling their views; it is a political process as well. In this political aspect of public opinion, we have been especially interested in the interplay between elite constructions of political issues, on the one hand, and public understanding, on the other. Elites frame issues in particular ways, thereby providing citizens with recipes for how issues should be understood.

Framing is a likely feature of democratic politics—indeed, perhaps it is inevitable. Public issues are always complex and multifaceted; they can always be understood in more than one way. Verba and his colleagues make this point nicely, writing about issues of equality:

> In the real political world issues of equality do not emerge in neat analytical form. Any equality issue encompasses many dimensions and represents many analytical distinctions. The issue of government-mandated quotas in institutions of higher education for people of a disadvantaged ethnic background is many issues at once. It is about a particular valued good (education), the standards of access to that good (membership in a group rather than individual achievement), the equality criterion (opportunity or results), equality for a particular group in relation to the rest of society (the chosen disadvantaged group rather than some other disadvantaged group), as well as the extent to which the government ought to intervene to create conditions of equality.[51]

If, as we say, public issues are *always* "many issues at once," then there is always room for framing.

At the same time, citizens are generally capable of thinking about any issue in more than one way; they have interests and attitudes and principles all of which could be engaged. Which considerations turn out really to matter depends on what comes to mind. And this is what frames do: they spotlight some considerations and neglect others, thereby altering the mix of ingredients that citizens consider as they form their opinions.

Framing, then, is inescapable: public issues are complicated and political thinking is fluid.[52] Our purpose here is to consider the implications of our results on framing for the conversation that is or should be at the center of democratic politics.

Frames and Democratic Discussion

A persistent theme in democratic theory is the importance of cool and reasoned discussion.[53] John Stuart Mill, to take one prominent and influential example, placed debate over the common good at the heart of democracy.[54] Even majority rule, often thought to be the defining feature of democracy, faded into the background in his treatment. The majority's vote is important less because it has any right to rule, and more because it offers an effective way to discover the best policy:

> Unless opinions favourable to democracy and to aristocracy, to property and to equality, to co-operation and to competition, to luxury and to abstinence, to sociality and individuality, to liberty and discipline, and all the other standing antagonisms of practical life, are expressed with equal freedom, and enforced and defended with equal talent and energy, there is no chance of both elements obtaining their due; one scale is sure to go up, and the other down. Truth, in the great practical concerns of life, is so much a question of the reconciling and combining of opposites, that very few have minds sufficiently capacious and impartial to make the adjustment with an approach to correctness, and it has to be made by the rough process of a struggle between combatants fighting under hostile banners.

Critics of liberal democracy have often savaged it as mindless chatter, and celebrated instead the cult of action, the heroic leader who firmly grasps what needs to be done. Mill explains why we should want there to be endless talk, in and out of the legislature, and especially between legislators and citizens. Without it, we simply cannot grasp what might be worth doing, nor can we learn from our previous mistakes:

> There must be discussion, to show how experience is to be interpreted. Wrong opinions and practices gradually yield to fact and argument: but facts and arguments, to produce any effect on the mind, must be brought before it. Very few facts are able to tell their

own story, without comments to bring out their meaning. The whole strength and value, then, of human judgement, depending on the one property, that it can be set right when it is wrong, reliance can be placed on it only when the means of setting it right are kept constantly at hand.

Deliberation is also at the center of the distinction drawn by Hamilton in *The Federalist Papers*, between the public's "temporary delusions," on the one hand, and its more considered judgments following "cool and sedate reflection," on the other. In Hamilton's view, government should respond only to the "deliberate sense of the community," not "to every sudden breeze of passion or to every transient impulse which the public may receive from the arts of men who flatter their prejudices to betray their interests." [55]

The claim that democracy requires or should aspire to orderly and widespread discussion receives extensive attention in contemporary writing as well. Consider, as prominent cases in point, Robert Dahl's democratic criterion of "enlightened understanding," the requirement that democratic institutions provide citizens with adequate and equal opportunities for discovering their own interests; or the utopian proposal of Habermas on behalf of "ideal speech," where discussion is free and equal and practically endless, and where consensus emerges only as the result of the force of better arguments; or Manin's argument that a democratic regime achieves legitimacy insofar as its decisions result from full and open deliberation, where participants come to the discussion without definitive views, ready to modify their opinions in light of new information and persuasive arguments offered by others; or, finally, Fishkin's recent recommendation of the "deliberative opinion poll," a device for guaranteeing reasoned discussion a more prominent place in the American presidential selection process. [56] In short, deliberation is very widely embraced. Rational discourse over common problems supposedly enhances mutuality, builds a sense of community, and fosters individual autonomy. [57]

If democracy depends mightily upon conversation—if it is "government by discussion," as Bagehot once wrote—then issue frames take on special importance. For frames might offer at least a partial solution to the persistent complaint that democracy requires of citizens more than they can supply. Schumpeter argued against democracy on this ground: the average citizen, according to Schumpeter, "is impatient of long or complicated argument," is in possession of "weak rational processes," is "not 'all there.' " Because citizens are likely to succumb more readily to prejudice and manipulation than to rational argument, and indulge in crude excess when they assemble, Schumpeter concluded that the typical citizen "drops down to a lower level of mental performance as soon as he enters the political field. He argues and analyzes in a way which he would readily recognize as infantile within the sphere of his real interests. He becomes a primitive again."[58]

Schumpeter argued without systematic evidence in hand, but his complaint has been reinforced by empirical investigations, most notably by Converse's analysis of national surveys carried out from 1956 to 1960. Converse concluded that qualitative, perhaps unbridgeable differences distinguished the political thinking of elites from the political thinking of citizens. His results suggested that leaders and citizens think about public life in fundamentally different ways, and they questioned whether citizens are capable of participating in a political discussion at all. As Converse put it, the fragmentation and concretization of everyday political thinking "are not a pathology limited to a thin and disorganized bottom layer of the *lumpenproletariat;* they are immediately relevant in understanding the bulk of mass political behavior."[59]

Frames cut into this problem, though in a double-edged way. On the positive side, frames appear to provide a common vocabulary, one that enables elites and citizens to take part in the same conversation. Frames allow elites to speak clearly to citizens. Indeed, it would be odd if it were otherwise, since frames are created with this aim prominently in mind. Through frames, democratic discussion between leaders and citizens seems less intractable than where Converse's analysis left things.

The creation and dissemination of frames may be a mixed blessing for democratic conversation, however. One worry is that frames may actually discourage real deliberation. In *The Rhetoric of Reaction,* Albert O. Hirschman identifies a small set of formal arguments against progressive policies that have been trotted out, again and again, over the last 200 years. According to Hirschman, opponents of proposals to extend various civil, political, and economic rights have argued either that (1) however well-intentioned, such policies will actually make things worse (the perversity thesis), or (2) oblivious of some deep and powerful social force, such policies will have no chance of altering society (the futility thesis), or (3) while perhaps desirable in and of themselves, such policies would have disastrous consequences not foreseen by its supporters (the jeopardy thesis). The recurrent and stereotyped use of such arguments—and the progressive side to the various debates come off no better—Hirschman takes as evidence of precisely how *not* to argue in a democracy. Time worn, unamended for the special cases to which they are automatically applied, these arguments are, in Hirschman's judgment, "contraptions specifically designed to make dialogue and deliberation impossible"; their ritualistic invocation produces "a dialogue of the deaf."[60]

But perhaps the strongest apprehension set off by our results has to do with manipulation, the possibility that citizens may be led one way or another through artful appeals. We have suggested that by sponsoring and promoting rival opinion frames, political elites alter how issues are understood and, as a consequence, influence what opinion turns out to be. This is manipulation, but of a particular sort. It is not that frames induce citizens to act against their interests or principles. It is rather that frames define which of their interests and principles take precedence. If this is not manipulation in the classic sense, it is still both practically important and democratically unsettling.

The struggle among elites over whose frames shall prevail in public debate is an important part of a larger process that Riker calls the "political mobilization of tastes." Riker adroitly places this mobilization at the center of politics. In Riker's scheme, new issues arise because leaders are constantly preoccupied with assembling a winning coalition, and see in a new issue, or in a new way of framing an issue, a way to achieve it. Riker argues that

> leaders in voting bodies may be likened to entrepreneurs in a market. Entrepreneurs succeed by offering new products, and so it is with leaders. Of course, entrepreneurs often fail, offering products no one wants. So also with voting leaders: New alternatives, new issues, are like new products. Each one is sponsored as a test of the voting market, in the hope that the new alternative will render new issues salient, old issues irrelevant, and, above all, will be preferred by a majority to what went before.[61]

To Riker, this is the "art of politics." It is the restless and relentless search for winning issues and alternatives that lends democratic politics its dynamism. We see this clearly in the 1988 presidential contest and, more generally, in the electoral temptations organized around race. In 1988, having written off the votes of black Americans, the Bush campaign attempted to assemble a winning coalition by persuading racially conservative Democrats to vote their way. The work was done through coded racist appeals: an elaborate, well-orchestrated, and artful activation of racial resentment—and it succeeded handsomely.

It is the art of politics that our experiments on framing attempt to illuminate. In all four experiments, the prominence of racial resentment in white public opinion was shown to be contingent on how the issue was framed. Under certain frames—those that reminded whites that the issue in question was really a matter of whether or not blacks deserved help—the issue was converted into a referendum on black character. Then racial resentment became the dominant ingredient in public opinion; other considerations were shunted to one side. Under alternative frames, however—those that suggested that race policies should be thought of as conflicts of interest or as assistance to minorities in general or as help to the poor—the power of racial resentment was reduced, while principles, interests, and the claims of other groups all came more visibly into play. Under these frames, the interior debate that might be said to go on within the minds of individual citizens appeared to be richer, more complex, and perhaps healthier, for democratic deliberation and public opinion alike.

This general result is important for what it suggests about elite's ability to control the extent of racial resentment in public opinion, but it takes on additional significance within the context of democracy seen as discussion. Democratic discussion means that everyone talks, and everyone listens. But when racism is injected into campaigns, some voices are devalued, effectively silenced, and the mutual respect that real discussion requires is undermined. In the embrace of deliberation as a democratic ideal, it is striking that a basic issue has been overlooked: namely, that such conversations are routinely marked by vast differences in status, power, and privilege. How might more of the people who routinely speak less, because of impoverished resources or deep alienation from conventional politics, be encouraged to take part and be heard in democratic discussions? How might those who typically dominate such discussions be induced to attend to the views of others? Answers to these questions are far from obvious, but giving racial resentment a legitimate place in political debate is no way to start.[62]

Two Societies?

In the spring of 1967, as race riots were decimating the nation's cities, President Johnson appointed a commission headed by Governor Otto Kerner of Illinois to identify the causes of the violence and to suggest policies that might prevent its repetition. Published in March 1968, the Kerner Commission report interpreted the riots as a sign of a deep and perhaps permanent racial rift. It began with the famous and ominous warning that the United States was "moving toward two societies, one black, one white—separate and unequal."[63] To what extent does the evidence we have in hand today justify the Kerner Commission's pessimistic prophecy?

In some respects, the Kerner Commission's prediction of two societies, separate and unequal, seems all too real. Certainly economic and social inequalities continue to divide Americans along racial lines. Even with postwar progress taken into account, large racial differences in employment, income, and wealth remain. Blacks are twice as likely to be unemployed; they earn less when they are employed; the average black household commands less than one-tenth the financial assets of the average white household; black children are more likely than not to be born into poverty; and on it goes.[64] These inequalities seem suf-

ficiently glaring both to sustain the Kerner Commission's language of two unequal societies and to guarantee the persistence of political conflict over race
into the foreseeable future.

Johnson's presidential commission warned also of *separate* societies—one
black the other white—and on this point the evidence is, if anything, more discouraging. The persistence of racial segregation, the sheer fact of profound
physical isolation, is stunning. In neighborhoods across the country, blacks and
whites are separated more completely now than they were at the turn of the
century.[65] In the typical American city today, fully 80% of blacks would need to
settle in new neighborhoods in order to achieve racial balance in the city as a
whole.[66] Well-educated and affluent blacks are just as segregated from whites
as are impoverished and ill-educated blacks.[67] When blacks move to the suburbs, they move to black suburbs, or to black enclaves within predominantly
white suburbs adjacent to the central city.[68] Segregation by race declined modestly between 1970 and 1980, and again between 1980 and 1990. Even should
this trend continue, however, another *fifty years* would have to pass before the
level of black-white residential integration would match the levels already attained by Asian and Hispanic Americans. And if neighborhoods continue to
reflect the tenacious power of the color line, then so do schools, churches, work-
places, friendship circles, and marriages.[69] To a remarkable extent, white and
black Americans live physically separate lives.

It would be miraculous if racial segregation, as tenacious and complete as it
is, turned out to be a neutral fact, merely a description of how American society
happened to be organized. It is not: segregation has had pernicious consequences for the welfare and aspirations of black Americans, and it is arguably
a prime ingredient in the generation of a black urban underclass.[70]

Though less dramatic, segregation has political consequences as well.[71] For
one thing, segregation reduces incentives for coalition building. When political
jurisdictions are racially homogeneous, programs and services that benefit
blacks may benefit blacks alone; withholding programs and services harms the
interests of blacks and blacks alone. This arrangement diminishes the opportunities for blacks and whites to join together to press for common goals and
encourages the view of racial politics as competitive. In this way, segregation
of neighborhoods reinforces racial divisions in politics.[72]

Racial separation may also encourage whites to respond in a stereotyped
way to policy proposals on race. Segregation leaves whites without any
grounding in interpersonal experience, unable to accumulate information that
might challenge the racial stereotypes that were a likely part of their upbring-
ing. When asked about policies to provide assistance to blacks or to protect

blacks from discrimination, such whites have only their stereotypes to fall back on. Under these typical circumstances, the chances for compassion and sympathy seem slim.[73]

Racial segregation also encourages, or at least makes possible, the presentation of systematically different points of view to the two communities. A case in point is provided by the 1988 presidential campaign, where it could be said that black and white audiences witnessed different campaigns. Coverage of the campaign in the black press revolved around Jesse Jackson; in mainstream coverage, the dominant black figure instead was Willie Horton. Similar differences are apparent as well in coverage of the Los Angeles riot or uprising that followed the acquittal of the police officers who beat Rodney King. We say riot or uprising advisedly: it was a riot in the pages of the *Los Angeles Times,* and an uprising in the pages of the *Los Angeles Sentinel.*[74]

This point returns us to the observation that served as our empirical point of departure: to the racial divide in opinion. To us, the most arresting feature of public opinion on race remains how emphatically black and white Americans disagree with each other. On the obligation of government to ensure equal opportunity, on federal efforts to assist blacks, and on affirmative action in employment and schooling, a huge racial rift opens up. Blacks and whites also disagree sharply over policy questions that are racial only by implication. They differ over how generous the American welfare state should be and over the integrity of American political institutions. They differ enormously in their partisan loyalties: blacks are now the most loyal members of what remains of the New Deal coalition. Blacks and whites also differ on matters of principle: black Americans are much more attracted by the claims of equality and much less apprehensive over the intrusions of the federal government than are white Americans. And they differ fundamentally in their view of race and American society. Whites tend to think that racial discrimination is no longer a problem, that prejudice is withering away, that the real worry these days is reverse discrimination, penalizing innocent whites for the sins of the distant past. Meanwhile, blacks see racial discrimination as ubiquitous; they think of prejudice as a plague; they say that racial discrimination, not affirmative action, is still the rule in American society.

Political differences such as these are simply without peer: differences by class or gender or religion or any other social characteristic are diminutive by comparison. The racial divide is as apparent among ordinary citizens as it is among elites. It is not a mask for class differences: it is rooted in race itself, in differences of history. The racial divide in opinion widens when whites talk with whites and blacks talk with blacks, itself a sign of the tensions associated with race in American life. Divisions by race are nothing new to American politics, but if anything, they are more prominent now than they were a generation ago. Such differences reflect a deep and perhaps deepening racial alienation, one that seems completely in keeping with the Kerner Commission's warning.

IN THE SPRING OF 1989, a twenty-nine-year-old white woman who worked as an investment banker for Soloman Brothers in downtown Manhattan went for a run through Central Park after work. There in the dark she was set upon, viciously beaten, raped, and left for dead. By the time she awoke from coma, six black and Latino teenage boys had been charged with her assault and rape; eventually they would be convicted. In Joan Didion's analysis, reactions to the case exposed radically different points of view about contemporary society and racial conflict:

> What people said when they talked about the case of the Central Park jogger came to seem a kind of poetry, a way of expressing, without directly stating, different but equally volatile and similarly occult visions of the same disaster. One vision, shared by those who had seized upon the attack of the jogger as an exact representation of what was wrong with the city, was of a city systematically ruined, violated, raped by its underclass. The opposing vision, shared by those who had seized upon the arrest of the defendants as an exact representation of their own victimization, was of a city in which the powerless had been systematically ruined, violated, raped by the powerful.[75]

Differences like these admit no common ground. They suggest, if we can make use of an overworked term, that black and white Americans have taken possession of distinct *paradigms*. In the extreme, blacks and whites look upon the social and political world in fundamentally different and mutually unintelligible ways. As Thomas Kuhn emphasized the profound difficulties scientists encounter in attempting to speak across different theoretical paradigms, white and black citizens appear to have a terrible time talking to one another about race.[76]

Is democratic discussion across the racial divide impossible? No, not impossible, but it is hard. Given the tragic nature of our history—"Deep rooted prejudices entertained by whites; ten thousand recollections, by the blacks, of the injuries they have sustained," as Jefferson put it—it could hardly be otherwise.[77] But democratic debate need not sink to the covert and cunning mobilization of racial resentment among white Americans, on the one hand, or lapse into silence and evasion where black Americans are concerned, on the other.

Democratic politics could be the place where we learn a language of mutual respect and begin to work out our differences. We should insist on it, for the stakes are high. Race, Du Bois chastened us, is "merely a concrete test of the underlying principles of the great republic."[78] As it was in the beginning of the twentieth century, so it is now at the end.

More on the Meaning and Measurement
of Prejudice

Our concept of racial resentment is closely related to several contemporary notions of prejudice. Most conspicuously, it is indebted to the line of work by Sears, Kinder, and McConahay on "symbolic racism."[1] As this work has proven controversial, it is worth spending some time here rehearsing the controversy and clarifying the relationship between the two ideas.

The idea of symbolic racism originated in an analysis of the racially charged campaign for the mayor's office in Los Angeles in 1969. The contest matched a conservative white incumbent—Sam Yorty—against a liberal black city councilman—Tom Bradley. According to our analysis, the white suburban vote was dominated by racial animosity of a particular sort, one emphasizing abstract, moralistic racial resentments: blacks were too pushy, they were getting more than they were entitled to, blacks on welfare were lazy and didn't need the help, they were receiving attention from government that they didn't deserve. This collection of resentments formed an empirically coherent point of view, one that we chose to call "symbolic racism." Such racial resentment was symbolic, so we said, because on the one hand, it was sharply associated with complaints about society as a whole and with endorsement of traditional American values, while on the other, it was utterly unrelated to whatever personal dissatisfactions white suburbanites felt about their own communities, jobs, schools, or personal safety. Disconnected from the experiences of everyday life, symbolic racism appeared to be an expression of a moral code, a sense of how people should behave and society should work. Symbolic racism predicted the white vote powerfully—more powerfully than did partisanship, conservatism, the personal threats that blacks might pose to whites' private lives, or indeed anything else, and in the end, Yorty was returned to office.[2]

In 1973, Bradley challenged Yorty again, this time successfully, a circumstance that gave us not only the luxury of replication but also the obligation to define (and measure) symbolic racism more precisely. This time, we defined symbolic racism to be "a blend of antiblack affect and the kind of traditional American values embodied in the Protestant Ethic." It is based, we argued, not in direct and contemporary racial experiences of any sort—white suburbanites in Los Angeles and elsewhere had virtually no personal contact with blacks—but in "deep-seated feelings of social morality and propriety and in early-learned racial fears and stereotypes."[3] Symbolic racism dominated the white vote in 1973, as it had four years before. And as before, the threats that blacks might seem to pose to whites' private lives—to their jobs, their neighborhoods, to their children's schooling or to their family's safety—were unconnected to the vote and to symbolic racism itself.

In the meantime, working independently, McConahay developed an overlapping, but partially distinct, concept, which he called "modern racism." In McConahay's view, modern racism derives from "the feeling that blacks are violating cherished values or making illegitimate demands for changes in the racial status quo."[4] Its essential tenets, again according to McConahay, are that "discrimination is a thing of the past, blacks are pushing too hard, they are getting too much attention and sympathy from the nation's elites, and that blacks gains and demands are no longer justified."[5]

Closely related to both these formulations is Pettigrew and Meertens's notion of subtle racism—the subtle racism of today as against the blatant racism of yesteryear: "Blatant prejudice is hot, close, and direct. Subtle prejudice is cool, distant, and indirect."[6] According to Pettigrew and Meertens, subtle racism is composed of three elements: defense of traditional values, exaggeration of cultural—not genetic—differences, and denial or absence of positive emotional reactions, such as sympathy or admiration. The three are drawn together by a common thread, "the socially acceptable rejection of minorities for ostensibly non-prejudicial reasons."[7]

Defined and measured in these terms, symbolic or modern or subtle racism turns out to be a powerful ingredient in political conflicts over matters of race. In the United States, voting against black candidates, opposition to busing for the purposes of racial desegregation, rejection of affirmative action programs, opposition to the idea that the federal government has a special obligation to black citizens: all these are deeply marked by symbolic racism. And in Western Europe, support for punitive immigration policies and denial of benefits to immigrants already in residence also stem in important part from symbolic racism—directed at Turks or Asians or North Africans or West Indians, from one European nation to the next.[8]

If we looked hard enough, we could find differences among these three positions, but more important for our purposes is the commonalties they share.[9] Most important of all, the three insist that racism is the *conjunction* of prejudice and values. Symbolic (or modern or subtle) racism is neither prejudice, pure and simple, nor traditional values, pure and simple, but rather the combination of the two.

The point is worth emphasizing, because it is often misunderstood. For example, Sniderman and Tetlock argue that research on symbolic racism treats traditional values as if they were only a mask for underlying racism, a disguise that whites adopt after discovering that blatant racism is socially unacceptable. They write that "many white Americans, according to symbolic racism theory, oppose assistance to blacks, ostensibly out of a commitment to certain values—the work ethic, for example—but actually out of a dislike of blacks."[10] In this garbled reconstruction, traditional values are nothing more than "camouflage" for racism.[11]

Why this misunderstanding? We have said repeatedly that symbolic racism has its roots both in early-learned racial fears and stereotypes and in deep-seated feelings of social morality and propriety, that the secularized versions of the Protestant ethic which contribute to symbolic racism are not in themselves racist, that the rhetoric of conservatism that attends racially charged campaigns is not exclusively a rationalization for racial malice but in fact an expression of the blend of moral traditionalism and race prejudice that constitutes, we say, symbolic racism.[12]

Perhaps the trouble here should be traced to the phrase "symbolic racism" itself. In retrospect, it seems an unfortunate choice. By failing to mention values at all, it perhaps encourages the interpretation that symbolic racism is really just racism; that values are but a decorative mask, pretty rationalizations for what is not so pretty underneath.

What should we have called the moralistic resentments that Los Angeles suburbanites expressed toward blacks that figured so prominently in their votes in 1969? Not symbolic racism, but racial resentment. The new terminology acknowledges the point that as open expressions of biological racism have declined, prejudice has become more difficult to document.

In most other respects, we intend racial resentment to take on the characteristics normally attributed to symbolic racism. Like symbolic racism, racial resentment is proposed as a contemporary expression of racial discord, distinguishable from the biological racism that once dominated American institutions and white opinion. Like symbolic racism, racial resentment features indignation as a central emotional theme, one provoked by the sense that black Americans are getting and taking more than their fair share. Finally, like symbolic racism, racial resentment is thought to be the conjunction of whites' feelings toward blacks and their support for American values, especially secularized versions of the Protestant ethic.

If, as we say, racial resentment should take on these essential features of symbolic racism, then it is only fair that racial resentment should also inherit the criticism that has been directed symbolic racism's way. There has been more than a little of it, some of which we have already dealt with in the main text and some of which we have acknowledged here.[13] Two additional criticisms are worth taking seriously, both traceable to Lawrence Bobo.[14]

The first is that race prejudice is *always* a combination of race hostility and American values.[15] Bobo takes as one example the development of the doctrine in the American South following emancipation that blacks would not work without compulsion. Lazy, shiftless, and licentious by nature, the newly freed black worker required the kind of vigilant supervision that only white landowners and businessmen could provide, or so ran the argument. This view expresses racial hostility, and it takes a form defined by principal American values. The implication of this example and others that Bobo provides is this: what's new in symbolic racism (or racial resentment) is not the mixing together of negative sentiment and cherished values, but rather *the particular ingredients of the mix.* Today, we say, for reasons set out in Chapter 5, racial resentment takes primarily one form, a combination of racial anger and indignation, on the one hand, and secularized versions of the Protestant ethic, on the other.

A second and final criticism is that analysis informed by the concept of symbolic racism has been too psychological, insufficiently attentive to society, history, and culture. While acknowledging that symbolic racism captures something real in the changed character of white racial attitudes, Bobo goes on to say that "no sustained analysis of why this shift in attitudes has occurred is provided."[16] Instead, Bobo writes, "The image of blacks as permanently and categorically inferior to whites has been shorn of its economic, political, and social underpinnings."[17] In some ways this is an old complaint, often directed at studies of prejudice rooted in psychological frameworks. Blumer makes this point when he complains that "the preoccupation of students [of race relations] with the study of prejudice has turned their attention away from the actual association of races and led them into a detached and artificial world."[18] That the complaint is familiar does not reduce its relevance or power, of course, and we have tried to respond to it here. The first part of Chapter 5 pays considerable attention to the real world of race relations. There we attempt to spell out how racial hostility and American values have become fused in a particular way at a particular time in a particular society. If we have made an original theoretical contribution to the meaning of prejudice, it lies here, in our effort to specify how racial ideology is shaped by alterations in intellectual currents, changes in economic arrangements, and eruptions of political crisis.

Specifications and Results

THREE POLICY PACKAGES

To examine the structure of public opinion on race policy, we relied on confirmatory factor analysis, based on estimation routines developed by Jöreskog (1969). Because we wanted to compare the structure of public opinion on racial policy for blacks and whites, we analyzed the two samples separately, running the factor analysis on the variance-covariance matrix among the seven race policy items in each case.

We first specified a simple model, one that assumed a single latent factor. Under this specification, whites and blacks support or oppose race policy in a singleminded way, without regard to distinctions between general assistance and specific application, or between the equal opportunity agenda of the civil rights movement and the contemporary conflict over affirmative action. This specification is clearly wrong, for blacks and whites alike. The single factor model fits the variance-covariance matrix poorly in each case. For whites, Chi-square with 14 degrees of freedom = 163.31 (p < .01), adjusted goodness of fit = .888; for blacks, Chi-square with 14 degrees of freedom = 40.60 (p < .01), adjusted goodness of fit = .845. Opinion on race policy is evidently not singleminded.

Next we tested a slightly more elaborate model, one that assumes that Americans possess distinct, but correlated, views about particular aspects of policy on race. More precisely, the model specifies that Americans, black and white, distinguish among: (1) the general responsibility of the federal government to provide assistance to blacks (measured by two questions), (2) the obligation of the government in Washington to ensure equal opportunity, both as a matter of general principle and specifically in education and employment (measured by three questions), and (3) the appropriateness of affirmative action in the workplace and in college admissions. Notice that we are not claiming that these three constitute the only dimensions underlying public opinion on race issues in the 1980s. Our claim is more modest: that the 1986 NES survey covers a range of policies important to contemporary American racial politics, and that the policies we have put to respondents reflect three, somewhat different aspects of the current debate.

It turns out that the three-factor model fits the evidence quite well. Indeed, it fits the black data splendidly, and with a minor adjustment, fits the white data equally well. Tables B1 and B2 present these results. As shown there, the overall

| 295

Table B.1 White Opinion on Race Policy Reflects Three Related Themes
(maximum likelihood factor analysis estimates based on variance-covariance matrix)

	Federal Programs		Equal Opportunity		Affirmative Action	
	Coef.	SE	Coef.	SE	Coef.	SE
Federal spending	.183	(.012)				
Government effort	.166	(.010)				
Equal opportunity			.186	(.013)		
School desegregation			.136	(.021)	.081	(.020)
Fair employment			.236	(.017)		
Preferential hiring					.216	(.011)
College quotas					.273	(.014)

Chi-square with 10 degrees of freedom = 13.20 (prob. = .213)
Adjusted goodness of fit = .988

Factor Correlations		
	Federal Programs	Equal Opportunity
Equal opportunity	.690	
Affirmative action	.664	.503

Source: 1986 National Election Study.

Table B.2 Black Opinion on Race Policy Reflects Three Related Themes
(maximum likelihood factor analysis estimates based on variance-covariance matrix)

	Federal Programs		Equal Opportunity		Affirmative Action	
	Coef.	SE	Coef.	SE	Coef.	SE
Federal spending	.112	(.031)				
Government effort	.142	(.039)				
Equal opportunity			.140	(.036)		
School desegregation			.144	(.032)		
Fair employment			.190	(.031)		
Preferential hiring					.245	(.046)
College quotas					.329	(.053)

Chi-square with 11 degrees of freedom = 6.27 (prob. = .885)
Adjusted goodness of fit = .973

Factor Correlations		
	Federal Programs	Equal Opportunity
Equal opportunity	.709	
Affirmative action	.210	.461

Source: 1986 National Election Study.

fit of the model to the data is excellent, for blacks and whites alike. For whites, Chi-square with 10 degrees of freedom = 13.20 (p = .21), adjusted goodness of fit = .988; for blacks, Chi-square with 11 degrees of freedom = 6.27 (p = .86), adjusted goodness of fit = .973. These results imply, for both blacks and whites, three correlated, but distinct, packages of opinion on race policy. Federal assistance, equal opportunity, and affirmative action present different faces of the contemporary political debate over race.

For the most part, blacks and whites view these three aspects in much the same way. Such similarity may be surprising, in light of the evidence on the racial divide in opinion. Nevertheless, there is little in the results presented in tables B1 and B2 to distinguish blacks and whites: the structure of the model is virtually identical, the factor loadings are nearly the same, and (in evidence not shown) the estimated reliabilities of the individual variables are roughly equal. Two differences do come through, however, and each is of more than passing interest. The first concerns school integration. For blacks, the question of whether the federal government should ensure that black and white children go to the same schools is assimilated completely to the theme of equal opportunity. Whites see school integration in this way as well, but they also regard school integration as affirmative action. Thus for whites, but not for blacks, the integration of public schools raises the issue of preferential treatment. In table B1, for whites, under the affirmative action factor column, the estimated factor loading for school integration is .081 (se = .020). For blacks, the corresponding coefficient in table B2 was set to zero. When estimated directly, it is .010 (se = .036), or essentially zero. The second and related difference pertains to the relationship Americans see between the general role of the federal government in providing assistance to blacks and the desirability of affirmative action programs. Whites see the two as closely related; those who oppose federal assistance to blacks also tend to oppose affirmative action; those who favor government help also tend to favor affirmative action (or, more realistically, to oppose affirmative action policies less). In contrast, blacks draw a sharp distinction between the two; their opinions on federal assistance and affirmative action are bound together much less tightly. This contrast is indicated in the estimated correlations between the latent variables (or factors), displayed at the base of the tables. For whites, the correlation between opinions on federal assistance and affirmative action is .664; for blacks it is only .210. As in the first instance, the theme of preferential treatment appears more prominent in whites' thinking about public policy on matters of race than in blacks'.

These differences are intriguing, though we should not exaggerate their significance. In the end, they constitute minor deviations from the major theme of similarity. Despite huge differences between the races in their views about what public policy on race should be, blacks and whites nevertheless organize their thinking around racial issues in much the same way.

Table B.3 Effect of Race of Interviewer on Public Opinion on Race Policy

	White Americans		Black Americans	
	1986	1988	1986	1988
Fair employment	−.22	−.02	.21	.02
	(.11)	(.09)	(.09)	(.10)
School desegregation	−.11	—	.17	—
	(.10)		(.10)	
Federal spending	−.14	−.20	.05	.13
	(.06)	(.07)	(.05)	(.08)
Government effort	−.22	−.19	.17	.19
	(.08)	(.09)	(.13)	(.21)
Preferential hiring	−.08	−.33	.11	.06
	(.07)	(.06)	(.13)	(.13)
College quotas	−.34	−.16	.07	.01
	(.09)	(.08)	(.11)	(.12)

Source: 1986 and 1988 National Election Studies.

RACE OF INTERVIEWER EFFECTS

Race of interviewer effects are derived from OLS regression analysis. For each race policy, opinion was regressed on race of interviewer separately for black and white survey participants. Each equation also included a set of social background characteristics: age, gender, education, region, family income, and religion. All variables were coded onto the 0–1 interval. The resulting estimates of race of interviewer effects on opinion are shown in table B3, for whites and blacks, in 1986 and 1988. (The table presents the unstandardized version of the OLS regression coefficient, with standard errors in parentheses underneath.)

RACE, NOT CLASS

Perhaps the differences we see between black and white Americans on matters of race policy are really differences of class. To see whether this was so, we first needed a precise estimate of the size of the racial divide. To produce one, we regressed opinion on race policy on race alone. Then we reestimated the size of racial divide after adding in measures of social class: family income, level of education, and head of household occupational status. At issue is whether, in this second round of analysis, with class taken into account, the impact of race diminishes. It does not, as shown in table B4. Once again, all variables are coded onto the 0–1 interval; as before, the table presents the unstandardized version of the OLS regression coefficient.

THE RACIAL DIVIDE AMONG THE INFLUENTIAL

We defined politically influential citizens by their affluence, superior educational attainment, and deep engagement in public affairs. So defined, the influential take positions on race that are virtually indistinguishable from those expressed by the public as a whole. This means, as table B5 shows, that the racial divide is just as great among influential citizens as it is among ordinary people.

The estimates on display in table B5 were derived this way. First, for blacks and whites separately, we regressed the race policy index (scored 0–1) on family income, education, and several measures of policy engagement. Then, using the resulting regression weights, we generated a predicted score for politically influential whites and blacks. We took politically influential whites to be those who had completed college, with annual family incomes in excess of $75,000, and who reported that they followed public affairs most of the time, who were very interested in the last campaign, and who discussed politics with family or friends every day in the last week. Politically influential blacks were defined the same way, except that we lowered the income level to $50,000. In similar fashion, we generated estimates for average black and white citizens, assigning appropriately middling values to education, income, and the several measures of political engagement.

Table B.4 Race, Not Class
(estimated size of the racial divide with and without controls on social class)

	1986		1988	
	Without	With	Without	With
Fair employment	.36	.37	.32	.32
School desegregation	.33	.32	—	—
Federal spending	.36	.36	.36	.36
Government effort	.18	.17	.27	.26
Preferential hiring	.45	.43	.47	.44
College quotas	.44	.42	.45	.45

Source: 1986 and 1988 National Election Studies.

STEREOTYPING AND RESENTMENT

To what extent do our results depend on the particular ways we have measured racial resentment? One way to find out is to replace our measure of racial resentment with a measure of racial stereotyping, introduced earlier in Chapter 5 and included as part of the 1992 National Election Study. Do whites who believe blacks to be less intelligent, more violent, and less industrious also oppose policies formulated to diminish racial inequalities?

Table B.5 Racial Divide among the Influential (predicted score on race policy index)

	White Americans	Black Americans	Difference
Politically influential	.58	.12	.46
Average citizens	.65	.18	.47

Source: 1986 National Election Study.

We can supply answers to these questions from two sources. One is the 1992 NES, already noted. The other is the 1990 General Social Survey, which included a more comprehensive battery of racial stereotypes (from which the 1992 NES borrowed). As we said in Chapter 2, GSS is a national survey of high regard undertaken periodically by the National Opinion Research Center at the University of Chicago. As it happens, the 1990 GSS included two race policy questions in virtually the identical form to the pair of questions analyzed in great detail here. Whether federal support for programs that assist blacks should be increased or diminished, and whether the government in Washington is obligated to make special efforts to help blacks, are both parts of the 1990 GSS, as they have been a regular part of the NES studies. The 1990 GSS also includes measures of social background that are comparable in most respects to the NES collection, as well as measures of limited government and individualism. The simple empirical question then is whether eliciting racial hostility through stereotypes, which is theoretically and operationally quite different from the approach we have taken, leads to a similar conclusion about racial resentment's political power.

It does. As displayed in column 4 of table B6, our analysis of the 1990 GSS data produces virtually identical results. For the sake of comparison, the table also reproduces the results from the analysis of racial resentment in the 1986, 1988, and 1992 National Election Studies (corresponding to columns 1, 4, and 5 in table 5.5 in Chapter 5). On questions of federal responsibility for assistance to black Americans, white opinion turns heavily on racial hostility, and this is so regardless of whether it is measured by the expression of racial resentment (columns 1–3) or by the endorsement of racial stereotypes (column 4). (Kinder and Mendelberg [1995] show comparable results on matters of race policy that were part of the 1990 GSS but that have no close parallel in the NES studies.)

Our analysis of racial stereotyping in the 1992 NES is summarized in column 5 of table B6. As shown there, shifting to the measure of stereotypes occa-

Table B.6 Impact of Racial Hostility on White Americans' Opinions on Race Policy, Where Hostility Is Expressed through either Racial Resentments or Derogatory Stereotypes

	Racial Resentment			Derogatory Stereotypes	
	1986 NES	1988 NES	1992 NES	1990 GSS	1992 NES
Fair employment	.57	.63	.63	—	.61
School segregation	.30	—	.40	—	.49
Federal spending	.45	.41	.59	.55	.67
Government effort	.44	.53	.51	.45	.58
Preferential hiring	.40	.42	.47	—	.34
College quotas	.60	.63	.71	—	.61

Note: Table entry is B, the unstandardized regression coefficient representing the effect of racial resentment (columns 1–3) or racial stereotypes (columns 4, 5) on whites' views on race policy. All variables coded 0–1.

SPECIFICATIONS AND RESULTS

sionally produces a somewhat greater estimate of the impact of racial hostility (as on support for federal programs that go to blacks); occasionally it produces a somewhat smaller estimate (as on giving blacks preferential treatment at work). But on average, it makes little difference.

In short, our estimate of the role played by racial animosity in white opinion on racial policy is essentially unaffected by which measure we use—and in each case the role commands center stage. Whether by expressions of racial resentment or by endorsement of racial stereotypes, racial hostility is the primary ingredient in white opinion on racial affairs.

RACE OF INTERVIEWER AND RACE-CONSCIOUS FRAMES

In Chapter 2 we showed that liberal views on race were expressed more often in the presence of black interviewers, and less often in the presence of white interviewers, for both black and white citizens. Now we see that same pattern repeated for views on government assistance to blacks, but only when the issue frame singles out blacks as the sole beneficiary. When framed in a more race-neutral way, the issue of government assistance elicits opinions that are unaffected by race of interviewer. Only when the issue is framed in a race-conscious way does the familiar result appear: then both blacks and whites express more support for government assistance when questioned by a black interviewer than when questioned by a white—roughly fifteen to twenty percentage points more support.

These results are shown in table B7. They are derived from regression estimates of the following equation (separately for white and for black citizens):

$$\text{Opinion on government help} = a_0 + B_1 \text{ Question Frame}$$
$$+ B_2 \text{ Race of Interviewer}$$
$$+ B_3 \text{ [Race of Interviewer} * \text{Frame]}$$

where Question Frame is a binary variable, coded 0 if the question is asked with reference to blacks and other minorities and 1 if asked with reference to blacks alone; and Race of Interviewer is a binary variable, coded 1 if the interviewer is black and 0 if not.

ORIGINS OF POLITICAL PRINCIPLES

How is it that some Americans attach higher priority to equality than others do? Why are certain Americans so much more suspicious of government authority than others are? Our answer to these questions is based on a rudimentary analysis of the 1990–92 NES panel study. We predict equality and limited government, as expressed in 1992, on the basis of variables assessed in 1990. We restrict our analysis to whites alone, since too few blacks show up in the panel to warrant statistical analysis. The regression results are on display in table B8.

Table B.7 Effect of Race of Interviewer on White and Black Americans' Support for Government Assistance, by Issue Frame

	Whites				Blacks			
	1986		1988		1986		1988	
	Blacks Only Frame	Blacks and Minorities Frame	Blacks Only Frame	Blacks and Minorities Frame	Blacks Only Frame	Blacks and Minorities Frame	Blacks Only Frame	Blacks and Minorities Frame
Race of interviewer	-.21 (.08)	-.11 (.07)	-.15 (.09)	-.04 (.08)	-.17 (.13)	.09 (.12)	-.16 (.17)	.02 (.09)
Number of cases	1122		1472		178		220	

Source: 1986 and 1988 National Election Studies.

Note: Table entry is *B*, the unstandardized regression coefficient indexing the effect of race of interviewer (coded 0, 1) on white and black Americans' views on government assistance (also coded 0–1).

Table B.8 Sources of Political Principles among White Americans

	Equality		Limited Government	
Gender	.02	(.02)	−.09	(.04)
Age				
17–29	.02	(.03)	−.06	(.06)
30–39	−.02	(.03)	.02	(.05)
40–49	—	—	—	—
50–59	−.05	(.03)	.12	(.06)
60–69	−.04	(.03)	.01	(.07)
70+	−.10	(.03)	−.01	(.07)
Religion				
Catholic	−.01	(.02)	−.01	(.04)
Jewish	.10	(.07)	.02	(.13)
Fundamentalist	−.03	(.02)	.10	(.04)
Head of household occupation				
Farmer	.04	(.04)	.05	(.08)
Unskilled	.01	(.03)	.00	(.07)
Service	.02	(.03)	.02	(.06)
Sales/clerical	−.02	(.03)	.05	(.05)
Manager	.04	(.03)	.04	(.06)
Professional	.06	(.03)	.01	(.01)
Education				
8 years or less	−.04	(.04)	.04	(.08)
Some high school	.02	(.03)	−.03	(.06)
High school	—	—	—	—
Some college	.02	(.02)	.02	(.05)
BA	.05	(.03)	.01	(.06)
BA+	.05	(.04)	.05	(.08)
Homeowner	−.03	(.04)	.04	(.04)
Family income ($)				
< 10K	.02	(.03)	−.07	(.07)
10–17K	.05	(.03)	−.07	(.06)
17–25K	.01	(.03)	−.05	(.06)
25–35K	—	—	—	—
35–50K	−.00	(.03)	−.02	(.06)
50–75K	.00	(.03)	−.13	(.07)
75K+	−.02	(.04)	−.03	(.08)
Change in economic situation	.07	(.03)	−.12	(.05)
Bouts of unemployment	.02	(.03)	−.02	(.04)
Political engagement	.05	(.05)	.26	(.10)
Evaluation of social groups				
Poor	.08	(.05)	−.20	(.10)
Blacks	.04	(.04)	.01	(.08)
Women's movement	.14	(.04)	−.12	(.07)
Constant	.39	(.06)	.57	(.11)
R-squared	.20		.18	
Standard error	.18		.35	
Number of cases	474		474	

Source: 1990–92 National Election Study.
Note: Table entry is *B*, the unstandardized regression coefficient, with standard error in parentheses to the side. All variables coded 0–1.

Chapter One

1. Our account of this famous incident is taken from Branch 1988. On the importance of the Montgomery bus boycott, see Morris 1984.

2. Bob Herbert's Op-Ed column in the Sunday *New York Times*, September 4, 1994.

3. In a recent essay, Cornel West (1993, p. 12) refers to "the murky waters of despair and dread that now flood the streets of black America . . . the monumental eclipse of hope, the unprecedented collapse of meaning, the incredible disregard for human (mostly black) life and property."

4. Farley and Allen 1987; Lieberson 1980; Taeuber and Taeuber 1965; Massey and Denton 1993.

5. Jaynes and Williams 1989; Farley 1977, 1984; Orfield 1978, 1983, 1993.

6. Farley and Allen 1987, pp. 155–157; Massey 1991; Massey and Denton 1993, pp. 149–153.

7. See, e.g., Barber 1984; Fishkin 1991; and Mansbridge 1980.

8. See Sigelman and Welch 1991; Blauner 1989; and Kluegel and Smith 1986.

9. Former black *male* slaves, that is.

10. Apart from the most backward counties of Alabama and Mississippi, where violence ran free (Kousser 1974).

11. Kousser 1974, 1992.

12. Key 1949, p. 555. Key regarded the poll tax, literacy tests, and the rest primarily as vivid reflections of the extent to which whites dominated southern society, but without much independent effect. For Key, the job of disfranchisement was already accomplished by economic threats, violence, and intimidation. Without denying the importance of these forms of control, Morgan Kousser (1974) and Jerrold Rusk (1974; Rusk and Stucker 1978) contend that the laws governing elections instituted by southern legislatures in the latter stages of the nineteenth century did independently suppress black participation—and we believe they are right (for additional corroborating evidence, see Rosenstone and Hansen 1993). Regardless of how it was accomplished, the effort to banish blacks from voting was stunningly successful.

13. Shklar 1991, pp. 56, 3.

14. See Rosenstone and Hansen 1993.

15. Such positions are concentrated mostly and disproportionately in municipal offices. See the report issued by the Joint Center for Political and Economic Studies 1994.

16. On this and other forms of representation, see Pitkin 1972.

17. According to Grofman and Handley 1989a, 1989b.

18. Jaynes and Williams 1989; Farley and Allen 1987; and Landry 1987.

19. Jencks 1992. Much of this evidence is summarized and presented in Jaynes and Williams 1989 and in Farley and Allen 1987. Also see Donohue and Heckman 1990 and Wilson 1987.

20. Smith and Sheatsley 1984, p. 50.

21. Rae et al. 1981, p. 4.

22. Schuman, Steeh, and Bobo 1985.

23. Myrdal 1944.

24. Quoted in Fredrickson 1971, p. 23; Tocqueville 1945, 1:370–372, 390–392, 397.

25. *Notes on Virginia.* Passage quoted in Jordan 1968, p. 436.

26. From the Lincoln-Douglas debates in 1858. See Fredrickson 1971, pp. 149–151, and 1988, pp. 54–72.

27. Race is a controversial idea, with an often disgraceful history (Jordan 1968; Gould 1981; Banton 1977; and Stevens 1993). In the nineteenth century, biologists and naturalists used the term to refer to separate and immutable species. Their empirical research was devoted to establishing a natural hierarchy of races, with the "Caucasian" at the top and the African at the bottom, just above the chimpanzee. They did so by measuring heads: the superiority of Caucasians supposedly certified by their imposing cranial capacities. Gould (1981) exposed how misguided was this "science" or, rather, how guided it was by ethnocentric presumptions.

Modern biology, beginning with Darwin and Mendel, effectively demolished the notion of race as separate species, though the idea persists among the lay public, as we will see in Chapter 5. Many biological and social scientists now argue that the idea of race has no scientific integrity and should therefore be abandoned (e.g., Webster 1992; Zimmerman 1990). This would be a mistake, as our evidence (and much other evidence besides) will show. If done in by biology, the idea of race is very much alive in contemporary commerce and conversation (Yinger 1976).

Race is a socially constructed category. In this light, when we say we are going to examine the opinions of black and white Americans, we refer not to biological types, as some genetic analysis of blood samples might confirm, but black and white as society defines them. As a practical matter, we rely on the judgment of interviewers to identify survey participants as black or white. In the 1988 NES, 1,698 whites and 269 blacks participated. That is, 1,698 participants were identified by interviewers as white; 269 were identified as black. How did interviewers arrive at their judgments? We have no way to know for sure, but they probably relied on a configuration of cues: skin color, hair texture, facial features, style of speaking, the apparent racial identity of family and neighbors, and perhaps more. That is, interviewers do what we Americans all do: make quick (and mostly confident) assignments of individuals to racial categories. We may wish it were otherwise, and we can certainly dispute the biological foundations of racial categories, but their power and habitual use are difficult to deny. In the contemporary United States, the distinction between black and white is salient and emotionally charged. As part of a general discussion of ethnic difference, Yinger argues that it is "important to distinguish a sociologically and psychologically important ethnicity from one that is only administratively or classificatory . . . [categories concerned merely] with naming and counting (1976, p. 200). In our society, race goes much deeper than naming and counting.

CHAPTER TWO

1. Key 1961, p. 14.

2. Ibid.

3. Converse 1964, 1970. On the same point, see Key 1961; McClosky 1964; and Prothro and Grigg 1960.

4. For general reviews of this enormous and contentious literature, see Kinder 1983; Luskin 1987; and Smith 1989.

5. See esp. Achen 1975, and for a review of the evidence on nonattitudes, Smith 1984.

6. See, e.g., Aberbach and Walker 1973; Carmines and Stimson 1982; Kinder and Rhodebeck 1982; Nie, Verba, and Petrocik 1979; and Sniderman and Hagen 1985.

7. See Piazza, Sniderman, and Tetlock (1989) for a demonstration that on some racial issues, sizable fractions of white Americans can apparently be talked at least partway out of their opinions.

8. For a defense of this claim, see Rosenstone, Kinder, and Miller 1993, esp. pp. 9–13. Converse and Traugott (1986) provide a more general comparison between academic surveys and commercial polls.

9. By comparison with census data, our samples underrepresent both young men and the poorly educated, among blacks and whites alike. These differences are regrettable, but they are small, and they fade away entirely on other aspects of social background. A more detailed description of NES sampling procedures can be found in the codebooks associated with each study published and distributed by the Inter-University Consortium for Political and Social Research.

10. Jackman 1981, p. 162.

11. A detailed account of the research and development effort leading up to the 1986 NES can be found in two technical reports available from the Center for Political Studies, Institute for Social Research, University of Michigan (Kinder and Sanders 1985, 1986).

12. That equal opportunity, federal assistance, and affirmative action represent three correlated, but distinct, packages of opinion, for blacks and whites in equal measure, is documented in Appendix B (tables B1–B2), in a pair of confirmatory factor analysis.

13. Table 2.1 excludes those (relatively few) respondents who said that they had no opinion. Forty-six percent of our white sample answered all six questions; 75% answered all but one. In a reversal of the usual finding (Iyengar 1990; Krosnick and Milburn 1990), blacks were even more likely to express an opinion; 56% of the black sample answered all six questions; 83% answered all but one. That most Americans seem quite willing to hazard an opinion on racial policy does not guarantee that the opinions they express are well considered and deeply felt, of course; the expression of opinion is an undeniably weak test. Still, most Americans pass it.

14. Rae et al. 1981, p. 64.

15. Burstein 1985. Although the evidence is not overwhelming, Title VII appears in fact to have improved employment opportunities for black Americans (Donohue and Heckman 1990).

16. Schuman, Steeh, and Bobo 1985.

17. Quoted in Kluger 1975.

18. C. Vann Woodward 1974, p. 161.

19. Jaynes and Williams 1989; Orfield 1993.

20. Schuman, Steeh, and Bobo 1985.

21. Ibid.

22. Downs 1972, p. 38.

23. On the persistence of segregation in the public schools, see Jaynes and Williams 1989; Orfield 1978, 1983, 1993; and Massey and Denton 1993. On the persistence of discrimination at work, see Jaynes and Williams 1989; and Kirschenman and Neckerman 1991.

24. Converse and Presser 1986, p. 47.

25. This point is made stylishly, if a bit dramatically, by Mueller (1994, esp. Chapter 1).

26. Glazer 1987, p. vii.

27. As part of his argument against affirmative action, Glazer (1987) claims that a national consensus supported policies of equal opportunity as expressed in the 1964 Civil Rights Act, and that this consensus was violated as affirmative action was transformed into preferential treatment and race-conscious programs. Glazer is certainly correct to point to the tensions between equal opportunity and preferential treatment, but he is dead wrong on the existence of a national consensus. In 1964 (as in 1986), a majority of whites *opposed* the idea of the federal government implementing equal opportunity.

28. See, e.g., Gamson 1992; Gamson and Modigliani 1987; Kinder and Sanders 1990; and Rieder 1985.

29. At least as we have formulated affirmative action here. For additional and corroborating evidence see Kluegel and Smith 1986, Lipset and Schneider 1978, Sigelman and Welch 1991, and any number of *Washington Post* or CBS/*New York Times* polls from the middle 1980s to the present.

30. To create the composite index, we first coded each of the six race policy opinion variables to a zero–one continuum. Respondents who answered fewer than three of the six questions were set aside (19 of 887 whites; 0 of 163 blacks). We then computed, for each remaining respondent, an average score in which each opinion is equally weighted. Finally, for purposes of display in figure 2.2, we divided the composite index into ten equal intervals: 0–0.1, 0.1–0.2, . . . 0.9–1.0.

31. It is worth remembering that figure 2.2 includes Hispanics among the white public. The racial gap is diminished by this move compared with what it would be otherwise, since Hispanics are notably sympathetic to policies intended to benefit blacks.

32. In the 1986 NES, 76 blacks were questioned by white interviewers (24.9% of the total); 40 whites were questioned by black interviewers (3.2% of the total). Two of the interviewers designated as "nonwhite" in the 1986 NES Codebook were Native Americans. Our analysis sets them aside.

33. These estimates are based on ordinary least squares regression analysis. For each race policy, opinion was regressed on race of interviewer, separately for black and white respondents. Each equation also included a full set of social background characteristics: age, education, region, income, religion, and more. Thus our estimates of race of interviewer effects control for the possibility that black and white interviewers might be assigned to different kinds of respondents, and it is those differences that account for the differences in opinion we observe. We find race of interviewer effects in both the 1986 and 1988 NES, reported in detail in table B3 of Appendix B. Findings similar to our own are reported by Anderson, Silver, and Abramson 1988; Schaeffer 1980; Hatchett and Schuman 1975; and Schuman and Converse 1971.

In social science parlance, the race of interviewer effects we report are statistically significant. Statistical significance refers to the certainty that the effects we estimate are real. A statistically significant effect is one that we would expect to find over and over were we to replicate our procedures exactly. According to table B3 of Appendix B, for example, in 1988, whites interviewed by blacks were less supportive of school desegregation than were whites interviewed by whites, with the difference given by −.16, the unstandardized regression coefficient. This means that net of the effects of other variables included in the regression equation, whites interviewed by blacks were, on average, .16 less supportive than whites interviewed by whites on school integration (measured on a 0–1 scale). Can we be confident that this effect is real? We can. According to a two-tailed t-test, the probability that the two groups do not differ, that the effect of race of interviewer is really zero, is less than five in one hundred, written as p < .05. We will use this standard notation throughout, as a precise way of indicating the confidence that should be placed in our results.

34. Brehm (1990) finds that race of interviewer can also affect compliance with surveys: whites approached by blacks, and blacks approached by whites, are typically less likely to agree to be interviewed than are those approached by members of their own race. So there appears to be a cascade of effects here: race of interviewer influences who participates, as well as what they say.

35. Dahrendorf 1959; and Wright 1979.

36. To carry this analysis out, we first needed a precise estimate of the size of the racial divide. To produce one, we regressed opinion on race policy on race alone. We actually generated six estimates, one for each of our measures of contemporary opinion on race policy. Then we reestimated each of the six after adding in measures of social class: family income, level of education, and head of household occupational status. At issue is whether, in this second round of analysis, with class taken into account, the impact of race diminishes. It does not, not even a trace. See table B4 of Appendix B for this result, which holds for 1988 and 1986 alike.

37. On the general point, consult Key 1961; Miller and Stokes 1966a; Verba and Nie 1972; Page and Shapiro 1983. On civil rights in particular, see Burstein 1985.

38. Key 1961, p. 428.

39. These results are presented in table B5 of Appendix B.

40. Sheatsley 1966.

41. Bryce 1921, p. 153.

42. The evidence we present here comes entirely from National Election Studies and is confined for the most part to opinions on public policy, the target of our investigation. But we should hasten to say that the racial divide is not a product of the special way that the National Election Studies have put questions to citizens, nor is it restricted to matters of policy alone. It is just as apparent, for example, in what black and white Americans have to say about prejudice and discrimination, as recorded in a series of ABC/*Washington Post* national surveys in the 1980s (reported in Sigelman and Welch 1991). This evidence indicates that most white Americans believe that racism against blacks is an anachronism, to be found today only in a small and shrinking corner of society; that discrimination is mostly an historical curiosity; and that blacks have taken huge strides forward in recent years. In the meantime, according to the same surveys, black Americans see things quite differently: they believe that most whites harbor strong prejudices against them; they regard discrimination as an utterly familiar feature of everyday life; and although remaining reasonably optimistic about their own lives, are much less impressed with how far their racial group has come than whites are.

42. See, e.g., Barber 1984; Mansbridge 1988; and Reich 1988.

43. Glazer and Moynihan 1975, p. 7.

44. Horowitz 1985.

45. Dahl 1956, 1961; Polsby 1980.

46. Jackman and Jackman 1983, p. 3.

CHAPTER THREE

1. McClosky 1964. As noted in the preceding chapter, the most influential presentation of the ideological innocence argument is provided by Converse 1964. For reviews of and commentary on the huge literature that Converse's paper set off, see Converse (1975), Kinder (1983), Kinder and Herzog (1993), and Sniderman (1993).

2. That ideological ideas are foreign to most Americans serves to remind us, first of all, that we should not expect great sophistication from ordinary citizens as they contemplate public policy on questions of race. The conclusion of ideological innocence also leads us to be skeptical about claims that the American public is swerving to the left or moving to the right. Such claims are commonplace, but they are usually wrong: most often, public opinion travels in various ideological directions all at once. See, e.g., Gold 1992; Schuman, Steeh, and Bobo 1985; Page and Shapiro 1992.

3. At this general level, our framework resembles several influential theoretical treatments of political motivation. In his well-known analysis of political organizations, for example, James Q. Wilson (1973) distinguished among three types of incentives that draw citizens to political parties and interest groups: *material* incentives, by which Wilson meant such tangible rewards as reductions in taxes, changes in tariff levels, improvements in property values and so on; *solidary* incentives, reflecting the enjoyment and conviviality of group membership; and *purposive* incentives, which derive from the satisfaction of having contributed to the attainment of a noble goal. Our framework also brings to mind Amartya Sen's analysis of motivation, presented as a stinging rebuke to his fellow economists. In "Rational Fools," Sen (1977) insists that citizens are motivated by more than sheer egoism, that their choices also reflect sympathy for others and commitment to moral principles. Still another notable and comparable scheme is David Hume's (1985) analysis of the diverse motives that give rise to political factions, where he distinguishes among interests, affections, and principles.

4. Barry 1978.

5. Stigler 1975.

6. Quoted in A. O. Hirschman 1977, p. 54.

7. Sen 1977, p. 336.

8. Converse 1964, pp. 234–238. To illustrate his argument, Converse chose public policy on race. Converse's sketch of an argument is developed in Nelson and Kinder 1996.

9. Lane 1973, p. 97.

10. Notable exceptions include Feldman 1988; McClosky and Zaller 1984; Rokeach 1973; and Verba and Orren 1985.

11. We have drawn heavily on the writings of Tocqueville 1945; Hofstadter 1948; Huntington 1981; Lipset 1963; Myrdal 1944; and Pole 1993.

12. There are a few exceptions to our complaint (e.g., Sniderman, Brody, and Kuklinski 1984; Kinder and Sears 1981; and esp. Kluegel and Smith 1986). But even these are technical or partial exceptions in the sense that none takes up and tests among a comprehensive set of alternative claims, as we try to do here.

13. Ashmore (1970) registered essentially this same complaint more than twenty years ago, in his fine review of the social science literature on racial prejudice. As he put it then, most reviewers, when faced with this sprawling literature, "have tended to simply construct a long list of 'causes' and to treat them all somewhat uncritically, assuming that each theory is valid under certain circumstances or to a certain extent. They have made

little effort to set priorities among the explanations, or to categorize the explanations so that we can ascertain how they fit together" (p. 256).

14. E.g., Schuman and Presser 1981; Tanur 1991.

15. One major exception is provided by the work of William Gamson, which we will take up in Chapter 7.

16. Kramer 1986, p. 18. For complaints and exhortations along the same lines, see Achen 1983; Blalock 1979; and Duncan 1984.

17. Kelley 1983, p. 10.

18. Abelson 1976, p. 79.

19. We take this approach to be similar in spirit to Achen's (1982) treatment of the specification problem in political analysis, though we absolve him of any responsibility for what we have done here. Also see Bartels 1985, 1990; and King 1991.

20. There are exceptions: Converse 1964; Kinder and Mebane 1983; Rivers 1988; Stimson 1975; and Zaller 1992.

21. Rivers 1988, p. 750.

CHAPTER FOUR

1. The quotation is from Thomas Macaulay, himself no friend to the effort to place self-interest at the center of human motivation. In a critical commentary on James Mill's essay on government, Macaulay (1978, p. 125) suggests that to discover self-interest behind an action is little different than to claim that "a man had rather do what he had rather do."

2. According to David Hume, the desire for gain is "perpetual," "a universal passion," "which operates at all times, in all places, and upon all persons" (1898, p. 176).

3. Hobbes 1968, p. 161.

4. Hirschman 1977, p. 32.

5. Madison, Hamilton, and Jay 1987, p. 20.

6. See esp. Dahl 1961, 1971, 1978; and Truman 1951.

7. The most important works in this tradition are Downs 1957; Olson 1971; and Riker 1963. Downs's formulation permits voters to take into account considerations other than their own economic welfare (1957, p. 37): "It is possible for a citizen to receive utility from events that are only remotely connected to his own material income. . . . There can be no simple identification of 'acting for one's greatest benefit' with selfishness in the narrow sense because self-denying charity is often a great source of benefits to oneself. Thus our model leaves room for altruism in spite of its basic reliance upon the self-interest axiom." This is little more than a gesture, however: at the center of Downs's stylized analysis of democratic government is the calculation of self-interest.

8. Kramer 1971.

9. E.g., Tufte 1978, Rosenstone 1983, and Hibbs, Rivers, and Vasilatos 1982.

10. Campbell, Converse, Miller, and Stokes 1960, p. 205.

11. A critical literature is now emerging. See, e.g., Sen 1977; Mansbridge 1990; and Stoker 1992. The criticism is spreading, though Mansbridge's claim of a paradigm in crisis seems exaggerated. We will return to this point in our final chapter.

12. Barry 1990, p. 183.

13. Holmes 1990.

14. Not everyone thinks so. David Sears has argued forcefully against the use of

demographic characteristics to measure self-interest. According to Sears, demographic characteristics are "excessively crude." They fail because they are too distant from any particular policy dispute: they do not measure interests precisely enough. Demographic characteristics fail also because they reflect not only the citizens' current material interests but also, often, their past. Thus when indexed by demographic characteristics, interests are confounded with "the residues of much earlier socialization" (Sears and Funk 1991, pp. 19–20).

Indiscriminate use of demographic characteristics to identify self-interest is a mistake, of course, and Sears is right to say that empirical demonstrations of this sort should not be taken seriously, either as evidence for or against self-interest. That is not what we do here.

15. The two questions appeared toward the end of the 1986 interview, separated from each other by a half-dozen intervening questions.

16. Bonacich 1972, 1976.

17. Rieder 1985.

18. Orfield 1978, p. 2.

19. Data on racial composition come from the 1986 Current Population Survey, disaggregated to the level of the census "segment." These data were provided to us by the NES staff, in a form that scrupulously protected the identities of individual respondents after our formal request was approved by the NES board. We welcome this opportunity to thank the staff for their customary efficiency and good cheer.

These measures are admittedly indirect. They were supplemented in our analysis of the 1985 NES survey with a question included there, which asked respondents for their views regarding the likelihood that busing would come to their own school district. We found the same effect in the 1985 NES as we did with the 1986 data—namely, no effect of self-interest. (The 1985 analysis was restricted to whites alone, owing to small sample size.)

20. Our analysis set aside the handful of students that make their way into NES samples, on grounds that their status is intermediate: they have not yet entered, but presumably will soon enter, the labor market.

21. Written in equation form:

$$\text{(4.1) Opinion on Race Policy} = a_0$$
$$+ B_1 \text{ Perceived Advantage/Threat in Workplace}$$
$$+ B_2 \text{ Perceived Advantage/Threat in Schools}$$
$$+ B_3 \text{ Class} + B_4 \text{ Family Economic Well-Being}$$
$$+ B_5 \text{ [Young Children} * \text{ Racially Mixed Community]}$$
$$+ B_6 \text{ [Older Children} * \text{ Middle Class Resources]}$$
$$+ B_7 \text{ Employment Status} + B_{8-8+k} \text{ } Z^*$$

The presentation here is somewhat stylized, since several items in equation 4.1 represent sets of variables, as indicated in the earlier discussion. The term Employment Status, for example, actually stands for three specific measures: in versus out of the labor market, self-employed, and employed by the government. Likewise, Z^* is a vector of k social background characteristics, included for purposes of statistical control. Here $Z^* = $ Age, Region, Religion, Marital Status, Gender, Union Household, Ethnicity (present only in the analysis of whites), and Race of Interviewer.

22. This conclusion is reached by calculating, for each variable, the ratio of the un-

standardized coefficient, B, to its standard error. With ratios exceeding two, we can be quite certain that the effect is in fact greater than zero; more precisely, that the probability that the effect is zero, given by a two-tailed t-test, is less than 5 in 100, written as $p < .05$.

23. We tried alternative specifications in searching for self-interest effects. First of all, we represented each perception-of-threat variable as a set of dummy variables, to take into account the possibility of nonlinear effects, hinted at by preliminary rounds of bivariate analysis. And we also represented each of the continuous class variables—family income, occupation, and education—as a set of dummy variables, in the hopes of identifying specific classes that might be specially opposed to changes in the racial status quo. Both of these alterations in specification enhanced the chances of uncovering evidence supporting self-interest. But as things turned out, these changes produced results that differed immaterially from those presented in table 4.2.

24. Nisbett and Ross 1980, p. 18.

25. On cognitive heuristics, see Tversky and Kahneman 1974; and Kahneman, Tversky, and Slovic 1982. Fiske and Taylor (1992) provide a general overview of the field.

26. Because racial resentment is plausibly both a cause and a consequence of the perception of threat, estimating its impact with ordinary least squares regression would risk simultaneity bias. Thus we estimate the effect of racial resentment with two-stage least squares. We will have much more to say about the meaning and measurement of racial resentment in the next chapter.

27. These results resemble those reported by Tyler (1977) and Bobo (1988b).

28. On racial group identification and racial group interest, see esp. Gurin, Jackson, and Hatchett 1989; Tate 1993; and Dawson 1995. There has been a good bit of research on the relationship between class and opinion among black Americans, which certainly can be interpreted as relevant to self-interest. See, e.g., Welch and Foster 1987; Parent and Stekler 1983; and Cohen and Dawson 1993.

29. We cannot take this very far, given the small sample size. In bivariate analysis, we find that blacks who see little likelihood that affirmative action policies in school admissions will benefit themselves or their families are also unimpressed with racial progress generally (v562 in the 1986 NES codebook, Pearson $r = .18$), more taken with the idea that whites deliberately attempt to hold blacks down (v577, $r = .15$), more apt to identify with their racial group (measured weakly, by a single item, the so-called thermometer-score rating of blacks, v149, $r = .08$), and more apt to say that institutions are unresponsive to blacks (government officials pay less attention to blacks than to whites, v567, $r = .05$). When we include these measures as right-hand-side variables in equation 4.1, we find that the effect due to the perception of personal advantage in schooling is reduced by about one-third to one-half its original value. This pattern is consistent with the idea that the perception of family advantage has less to do with self-interest and more to do with views on race relations generally.

30. In equation form:

$$(4.2)\ \text{Support for Government Help} = a_0$$
$$+ B_1\ \text{Family Economic Well-Being}$$
$$+ B_2\ \text{R Employment Status} + B_3\ \text{Class}$$
$$+ B_{4-4+k}\ Z^*$$

where Family Economic Well-Being is the familiar single retrospective item; R Employment Status indicates whether the respondent is currently out of work or temporarily laid off; Class consists of family income, head of household occupation, respondent education, and home ownership; and Z^* = Age, Region, Religion, Marital Status, Gender, and Union Household. All variables coded 0–1. Results estimated with ordinary least squares regression, using the NES Cumulative Data File from 1970 to 1990.

31. For purposes of this analysis, we relied on a simplified form of equation 4.2. It includes, on the right-hand side, only the family economic situation variable. Across the eleven NES surveys, the black sample size ranges from 87 to 287. For the pooled sample, for this simpler model, $B = -.055$, not all that different from the estimate shown in table 4.5, drawn from the more elaborate specification (there, $B = -.043$).

32. $B = -.14$, as against an average effect over the entire series of $-.04$.

33. In the first-stage equation, change in family economic well-being is regressed on employment status, home ownership, gender, union membership, education, and change in real disposable income over the previous twelve-month period. The results show that black Americans are more likely to report that their family's economic condition has deteriorated especially when their head of household has been out of work recently and when the national economy is in decline. The second-stage equation, estimated with two-stage least squares, regresses opinion against family income, occupation, and change in family economic well-being (the last treated endogenously).

34. For a full account of the development of these questions and a detailed assessment of their reliability and validity, see Rosenstone, Hansen, and Kinder 1986; for their application to an analysis of the 1984 American presidential election, see Kinder, Adams, and Gronke 1989. In the course of these investigations, we discovered that the standard question on change in family economic well-being does in fact measure what it is intended to—it is a valid measure of change in family economic well-being—but that it suffers from unreliability or imprecision, which is what we correct here.

35. Details on measurement can be found in Kinder, Adams, and Gronke 1989. Cronbach's *alpha* for the scale = .76. The analysis summarized in table 4.6 also included Family Economic Experiences, a composite scale representing the behavioral dimension to change in family economic well-being, based on equally weighted answers to six separate questions. Results indicated that, of the two new measures used in this analysis, the political power of self-interest was carried entirely by the cognitive one: the estimated direct effect of self-interest was essentially zero for behavioral aspects of family economic well-being in each of the two equations, consistent with earlier results (Rosenstone, Hansen, and Kinder 1986; Kinder, Adams, and Gronke 1989). Thus, for simplicity's sake, we present only the results for retrospective assessments in table 4.6.

36. This argument is made, with different purposes in mind, by Kinder and Mebane 1983; and Kramer 1983.

37. Palmer and Sawhill 1984, p. 1.

38. Sawhill and Stone 1984.

39. Our analysis is based on a simple equation, a concession to small sample size. In equation form:

(4.3) Support for Government Help = a_0
  $+ B_1$ Retrospective Assessment of Family Economic Well-Being
  $+ B_2$ Currently Receiving Govt Benefits $+ B_3$ Govt Benefits Cut
  $+ B_4$ Expect Govt Benefits to be cut

where Support for Government Help = government aid to blacks (and other minorities); and government services versus cuts in government spending; Retrospective Assessment of Family Economic Well-Being = single retrospective item; Currently Receiving Govt Benefits = 1 if currently receiving AFDC or Food Stamps (not quite 30% of the full black sample), 0 otherwise; Govt Benefits Cut = 1 if reported cuts in AFDC or Food Stamps in the past year, 0 otherwise; and Expect Govt Benefits to be Cut = 1 if expects AFDC or Food Stamps to be cut in the next year, 0 otherwise. Results are virtually identical to those presented in table 4.8 if we take up each of the three measures of benefits one at a time, excluding the other two.

On the broader question of whether the federal government should provide more services or cut spending, we find no effects of dependence on government programs. Being a current recipient of Food Stamps or AFDC, or experiencing reductions in such benefits over the past year, or the threat of further cuts to come, has nothing to do with blacks' general views on government spending. The B coefficients are, respectively, .06 (.08), .03 (.09), and −.13 (.09).

40. Achen 1985. This analysis treats receipt of AFDC and Food Stamps as endogenous, and estimates its effect with two-stage least squares. In the first-stage equation, receipt of AFDC or Food Stamps is regressed on family income, marital status, gender, age, and change in family economic well-being. The first-round results show, as one would expect, a huge effect of income.

41. The standard error presented in table 4.8 is corrected for heteroskedasticity.

42. Unfortunately, not before then. We would have loved to make use of such a question in our analysis of the 1982 NES, reported in the immediately preceding section, which was an effort to assess the consequences for opinion of receiving government benefits, Food Stamps notably among them.

43. Blacks are much less willing to support increases in federal dollars for Food Stamps than they are increases in federal dollars for the generic "programs that assist blacks." From 1984 to 1990, nearly three-quarters of black Americans (71.4%) said that federal spending on programs that assist blacks should be increased, 26.2% believed that spending should remain the same, and just 2.4% favored reductions in such programs.

44. The estimates summarized in table 4.9 are derived from the following equation:

(4.4) Support for Food Stamps $= a_0$
$$+ B_1 \text{ Family Economic Well-Being}$$
$$+ B_2 \text{ R Employment Status}$$
$$+ B_3 \text{ Class} + B_{4-4+k} \text{ } Z^*$$

where Family Economic Well-Being is the familiar single retrospective item; R Employment Status indicates whether the respondent is currently out of work or temporarily laid off; Class consists of family income, head of household occupation, respondent education, and home ownership; and Z^* = Age, Region, Religion, Marital Status, Gender, and Union Household. All variables coded 0–1. Results estimated with ordinary least squares regression, using the NES Cumulative Data File from 1984 to 1990.

Additional analysis supports the conclusion as well. Following procedures described in previous sections, improving the measurement of change in family economic well-being is amply rewarded in the case of predicting opinion on Food Stamps. When we apply the statistical correction, we find that the estimated impact of change in family economic well-being on support for Food Stamps increases from −.04 (.03) to −.46 (.19). Likewise, when we replace the single item with the multiple-item scale measuring assessments of change in family economic well-being, the estimated effect on support for Food

Stamps increases from −.10 (.06) to −.30 (.14). Both these results support the conclusion that self-interest is an important ingredient in black opinion toward the Food Stamps program.

45. Sumner's (1906) confidence in the universality of an ethnocentric syndrome has generally been rewarded (Brewer 1979; Kinder 1995) and his theoretical beginnings have been elaborated upon by, among others, Coser (1956), Blumer (1958a), Sherif and Sherif (1953), and Campbell (1965). The theory has been applied to American race relations by Blalock (1967), van den Berghe (1967), and Bobo (1988a). Our presentation here draws heavily on LeVine and Campbell (1972).

46. Giles and Evans 1986, pp. 470, 471.

47. Key 1949, p. 5.

48. Ibid., p. 10.

49. In addition to Key 1949, see Kousser 1974; Mathews and Prothro 1966; Woodward 1974; and Black and Black 1987.

50. In the South in 1968, George Wallace did best in black belt counties, just as Thurmond and the Dixiecrats had done 20 years before him (Heard 1952; Wright 1977; Sundquist 1973). Some twenty years after Wallace, Jesse Jackson, in his bid to capture the Democratic presidential nomination, did best among whites in states with relatively low proportions of blacks (Groffman and Handley 1989c). Likewise for matters of opinion: white support for fair housing or school integration or federal assistance to blacks declines as the proportion of blacks nearby increases (e.g., Wright 1976; Giles and Evans 1986; Glaser 1994; Blalock 1967).

51. With few exceptions: Jessor and Sears (1986), on whose work we draw later; Kinder and Sanders (1987, 1990), our own preliminary empirical efforts; and Bobo (1988b), who treats the civil rights and black power movements as manifestations of group threat.

52. Campbell 1965, p. 292.

53. In line with our conception of self-interest developed earlier in this chapter, we require collective interests to be rooted in material conditions. For group interest to be at stake, conflict between groups must be over wealth and power—or over ways to secure wealth and power.

54. For a related conclusion, derived from an argument rooted in the special historical experiences and current circumstance of black Americans, see Dawson 1995.

55. The questions were developed by David Sears and Thomas Jessor and included in both the 1985 and 1986 NES surveys. For a recounting of the research and development effort that produced these questions, see Jessor and Sears (1986).

56. If interpreted literally, this question seems quite impossible to disagree with; it is surprising, perhaps, that the proportion in agreement was not greater. Perhaps those who disagreed were really saying that *few* whites have been harmed by affirmative action; or that affirmative action *seldom* works against the interests of whites.

57. The Pearson correlations range from .42 to .64. The perception of group threat, represented as a scale based on equally weighted responses to each of the three questions, is quite reliable—or as we would say, too reliable: here Cronbach's *alpha* = .76.

58. Our analysis of the sources of the perception of racial group threat follows in most respects our earlier analysis of the sources of personal racial threat. Once again we estimate the sources of perceived threat with two-stage least squares, treating racial resentment, measured as before, as endogenous. One change is that we treat the perception

of racial group threat as a linear scale, based on equally weighted responses to the three questions. Respondents must be present on at least two of the three questions to be present on the scale, which runs 0–1. The reliability of the scale, assessed by Cronbach's *alpha*, is .76. In the prediction of racial group threat, the impact due to racial resentment is given by $B = -.57$, se $= .21$.

59. In equation form:

(4.5) Opinion on Race Policy $= a_0$

$+ B_1$ Perception of Group Threat

$+ B_2$ Racial Resentment $+ B_{3-3+k} Z^*$

where Z^* includes racial composition of the workplace, racial composition of the neighborhood, age, region, religion, union household, Hispanic ethnicity, marital status, and race of interviewer.

60. These findings are described in detail in Kinder and Sanders 1987.

61. This point is expressed directly by black Americans participating in group discussions organized by William Gamson and reported in *Talking Politics* (1992; see esp. pp. 43–51).

62. These correlations are diminished in part because responses to the questions are skewed in opposite directions, which places limits on the magnitude of the resulting correlations. But nothing in the marginal distributions requires that the correlations fade all the way to zero.

63. In equation form:

(4.6) Opinion on Race Policy $= a_0$

$+ B_1$ Perception of Group Advantage

$+ B_2$ Perception of Group Barriers

$+ B_3$ Perceived Personal Advantage in Schools

$+ B_{4-4+k} Z^*$

where Z^* includes age, region, religion, gender, union household, marital status, and race of interviewer.

64. The results also hold up well with additional controls for what we call, rather loosely, "racial ideology." By racial ideology, we mean blacks' views on change in race relations, on the responsiveness of institutions to black claims, on whether white elites conspire to oppress blacks, and their feelings of solidarity with their racial group. When we reestimated the equation summarized in table 4.13 adding in measures of racial ideology (each treated separately), the effects of group advantage are completely unaffected; the effects of group discrimination are diminished, but only slightly (on average, by less than 20%). As for the effects of racial ideology, there are some. Most notable is racial group solidarity, which shows up consistently in each of the six equations, ranging from $-.12$ to $-.27$. In four of six equations, this one, rather pathetic measure of a complex concept produces a bigger effect than both group-interest measures.

65. Campbell 1965, p. 285.

66. Citrin and Green 1990, p. 16.

67. Coser 1956.

68. Lipset 1981, p. 234.

69. Alford 1963; Converse 1958; Campbell et al. 1960; Centers 1949; Knoke 1979; Hamilton 1972; and Inglehart 1977.

70. The phrase belongs to Robert Lane (1978), who argues that as individuals make

their way politically in modern society, they rely less and less on such traditional sources as family, group, class, party, and community.

CHAPTER FIVE

1. Smith's remarks are quoted in Michie and Ryhlick, *Dixie Demagogues* (1939, pp. 266, 281). According to V. O. Key, Smith was "unrivaled as a critic of the New Deal, unmatched as an exponent of white supremacy, and without peer as a defender of southern woman-hood" (1949, p. 139). Such qualities earned Smith the enthusiastic support of his South Carolina constituents. Only ill health brought Smith's career to a close, and not until 1944.

2. Much of the relevant evidence regarding change in public opinion on racial matters has been carefully assembled and presented by Schuman, Steeh, and Bobo in *Racial Attitudes in America* (1985). Also see Page and Shapiro (1992), who have examined trends over the past fifty years in American public opinion of all sorts.

3. See, e.g., Feagin and Sikes 1994; Jaynes and Williams 1989; Kirschenman and Neckerman 1991; Yinger 1986; Sigelman and Welch 1991.

4. Jordan 1968, p. 6.

5. Richard Hakluyt, "The Second Voyage to Guinea . . ." (1554, p. 167). Quote appears in Jordan 1968, p. 24.

6. Ibid., p. 97. The profound ethnocentrism with which the English greeted the African is a familiar, if discouraging, story. In *Folkways*, William Graham Sumner defined ethnocentrism as "the view of things in which one's own group is the center of everything. . . . Each group nourishes its own pride and vanity, boasts itself superior, exalts its own divinities, and looks with contempt on outsiders. Each group thinks its own folkways the only right ones, and if it observes that other groups have other folkways, these excite its scorn" (1906, p. 12). Defined in this way, ethnocentrism is a ubiquitous fact of social life, not only in the United States but around the world. Sumner provided abundant examples of ethnocentrism in operation in his day; more recent and systematic surveys merely fortify the point (Brewer 1979; Levine and Campbell 1972; Horowitz 1985).

7. Fredrickson 1971.

8. According to James Oakes, "The slaveholders' chief defense of bondage focused on the profitability of slavery and the white man's right to make money and accumulate property" (1982, p. 134).

9. As South Carolina Governor George McDuffie put it, in a speech delivered to his state's General Assembly in 1835. To McDuffie the black race was "unfit for self-government of any kind" and "in all respects, physical, moral, and political, inferior to millions of the human race." Mindful of the abolitionist agitation to the north, McDuffie expressed astonishment that anyone might "suppose it possible to reclaim the African race from their destiny" as slaves. Quoted in Fredrickson 1971, pp. 46–47.

10. On these several points see Fredrickson 1971 and Gould 1981. The quoted material is from John C. Calhoun, in Fredrickson 1971, p. 51.

11. Litwak 1961, p. vii.

12. Quoted in Sitkof 1978, p. 27. On the more general point of elite racism, see Degler 1991; Woodward 1974; Fredrickson 1971; Myrdal 1944; and Gould 1981.

13. Indeed, for reasons set out later in the chapter, we are not completely persuaded that the term "prejudice" should still be used; we prefer "racial resentment" to describe contemporary expressions of racial hostility.

14. Not dramatic new ideas, or fundamental changes in economic relations, or politi-

cal crises are everyday occurrences, of course. In ordinary times, racial doctrines change imperceptibly. But in extraordinary times, the form and substance of prejudice may change quite rapidly. Such change probably takes place first and most completely among elites rather than ordinary citizens. Few citizens have the time and resources required to follow carefully the flow of events and ideas that later historians claim defined their time. Even the momentous debate over slavery was probably carried out before a relatively small audience (Converse 1964). This guarantees that change in whites' attitudes toward blacks will typically proceed slowly, fitfully, and incompletely. Not only that, but change may be accomplished primarily through generational replacement, whereby older generations, with more traditional ideas about race, are gradually replaced by younger generations more in tune with modern ideas. Thus, our insistence that prejudice is socially constructed and always evolving is compatible with the claim that we make later on that most white adults cling to their racial beliefs tenaciously.

15. Fredrickson 1971, p. 330.

16. Gould 1981.

17. Horace Bushnell, *A Discourse on the Slavery Question, Delivered in the North Church, Hartford, Conn., January 10, 1839* (quoted in Fredrickson 1971, p. 155). The studies are summarized in Myrdal 1944.

18. Benedict 1934; Mead 1930, 1935.

19. Myrdal 1944; Klineberg 1935; Gould 1981.

20. According to Carl Degler, the shift from biology to culture was driven primarily by "a philosophical belief that the world could be a freer and more just place. . . . Science, or at least certain scientific principles or innovative scholarship also played a role in the transformation, but only a limited one. The main impetus came from the wish to establish a social order in which innate and immutable forces of biology played no role in accounting for the behavior of social groups" (1991, p. viii).

21. The quoted passage comes from Fredrickson 1971, p. 330. Woodward (1974), among others, suggests that segregation and discrimination in the American South hindered American foreign policy.

22. Apostle et al. 1983, pp. 24–25. On the other hand, the figures reported in the text probably underestimate the real proportion subscribing to genetic explanations: some people who in fact saw biology as responsible for differences in achievement between blacks and whites may have been reluctant to say so.

23. The 1972 and 1986 question formats are not identical: the 1986 version included a response option for those who neither agreed nor disagreed with the assertion; the 1972 question did not. Thus the 1986 percentages reported in the text are among those who either agreed or disagreed; those respondents (12.2%) who neither agreed nor disagreed with the claim of genetic inferiority were set aside and the figures repercentaged on the smaller base.

24. The increase in the proportion of whites who say they believe in racial equality in intelligence is impressive, but the figure still falls well short of unanimity. Moreover, since 1956, the proportion of whites subscribing to racial equality in intelligence has leveled off. The question made its last appearance on national surveys in 1968, perhaps because some respondents, and probably some interviewers, found it too offensive to bring up.

25. We are not much interested here in understanding why the civil rights movement and the eruption of urban violence that shortly followed happened when they did, as

important as such scholarly endeavors are (McAdam 1982; Morris 1984). Our purpose is rather to suggest how this remarkable cascade of public events may have altered the black image in the white mind.

26. Morris 1984, p. 51.

27. Woodward 1974, pp. 165–166.

28. Pole 1993, p. 325. Passage of the 1964 Civil Rights Bill led to rapid and dramatic declines in racial segregation in public accommodations and facilities, laid the ground-work for enforcement of the Supreme Court's decision on school desegregation, reduced the use of terror as a routine means of social and political control in the South, and en-hanced employment opportunities for black Americans (Jaynes and Williams 1989; Piven and Cloward 1977; Heckman and Payner 1989; Donohue and Heckman 1990).

29. For example, on the front page of the *New York Times* appeared this story, filed by Roy Reed, present at the scene:

> The troopers rushed forward, their blue uniforms and white helmets blur-ring into a flying wedge as they moved. The wedge moved with such force that it seemed almost to pass over the waiting column instead of through it. The first 10 or 20 Negroes were swept to the ground screaming, arms and legs flying, and packs and bags went skittering across the grassy di-vider strip and on to the pavement on both sides. Those still on their feet retreated. The troopers continued pushing, using both the force of their bodies and the prodding of their nightsticks. A cheer went up from the white spectators lining the south side of the highway. The mounted posse-men spurred their horses and rode at a run into the retreating mass. The Negroes cried out as they crowded together for protection, and the whites on the sidelines whooped and cheered. The Negroes paused in their retreat for perhaps a minute, still screaming and huddling together. Suddenly there was a report like a gunshot and a gray cloud spewed over the troopers and the Negroes. "Tear gas!" someone yelled. The cloud began covering the highway. Newsmen, who were confined by four troopers to a corner 100 yards away, began to lose sight of the action. But before the cloud finally hid it all, there were several seconds of unobstructed view. Fifteen or twenty nightsticks could be seen through the gas, flailing at the heads of the march-ers. The Negroes broke and ran. Scores of them streamed across the parking lot of the Selma Tractor Company. Troopers and possemen, mounted and unmounted, went after them. (March 8, 1965)

30. Quotation from Garrow 1978, p. 107.

31. Woodward 1974, p. 186.

32. Before the mid-1960s, it was primarily southerners who expressed concern over civil rights (Smith 1980).

33. This embrace of equality fits harmoniously with another ongoing change in white attitudes mentioned earlier: the gradual demise of biological racism. As whites continued to abandon the idea that blacks originated from an inferior race, they also came to em-brace the ideal of equality.

Others have been well impressed by these changes. See, for the most important pres-entations and interpretations, Sheatsley 1966; Hyman and Sheatsley 1956, 1964; Greeley and Sheatsley 1974; Taylor, Sheatsley, and Greeley 1978; Smith and Sheatsley 1984; Page and Shapiro 1992; and Schuman, Steeh, and Bobo 1985.

34. Quotation from Kluger 1975, p. 756.

35. Quotation from Garrow 1978, p. 107.

36. Race riots were nothing new to America: they had occurred sporadically through the twentieth century, most taking place between the two world wars. What was new was their intensity and their form: instead of white mobs rampaging through black neighborhoods, the race riots of the 1960s featured angry blacks taking to the streets (Lieberson and Silverman 1965).

37. For an attempt to understand the outbreak of violence in Watts, see Sears and McConahay (1973).

38. Smith (1980) calls this a concern over "social control." From the mid-1960s on, this meant crime, violence, and riots, on the campus and especially in the cities. The spike of concern visible during the early 1950s in figure 5.2 reflects Americans' apprehensions about domestic subversion, fed by the Army-McCarthy hearings.

39. In national surveys carried out in 1968, for example, 62% of whites declared that looters should be *shot*, 72% said that civil rights leaders were trying to push too fast, and 79% agreed that blacks shouldn't push themselves where they're not wanted.

40. Aberbach and Walker 1973; Rieder 1985. Differences between blacks and whites extended even to how the disorders should be named. In Los Angeles, city officials referred to the events of August 1965 as a riot (as we have), but upward of 40% of black citizens preferred "revolt," "insurrection," "rebellion," "uprising," or some comparable term (Sears and McConahay 1973). Just the same difference shows up in black and white interpretations of the Los Angeles disturbance of 1992 (Bobo et al. 1994).

41. Orfield 1988, p. 330.

42. Our conception of racial resentment and the questions we use to measure it are both indebted to a controversial line of work by Sears, Kinder, and McConahay on "symbolic racism" (Sears and Kinder 1971; Kinder and Sears 1981; McConahay and Hough 1976; McConahay 1982; and Sears 1988). In Appendix A, we recount the development of the idea of symbolic racism, review the controversy it has touched off, and spell out the relationship between it and racial resentment.

43. Brown 1965, p. 483. The subtlety of our questions provides at least one real advantage. Such questions diminish the problem posed by "social desirability": the tendency for people to put themselves in a favorable light, to present themselves as "well adjusted, unprejudiced, rational, open minded, and democratic" (Cook and Seltiz 1964, p. 39). If we were to ask white Americans to say whether they thought blacks were as smart as whites, we would be placing some of them in an uncomfortable position. Knowing on the one hand that the socially desirable answer is to say that there are no differences between blacks and whites in intelligence but, on the other hand, privately believing that whites are smarter on average, what in fact do they say? Presumably some will present themselves as freer of racial prejudice than they really are. Our questions are designed to finesse this problem. Because each possesses "a kind of fair-minded and reasonable veneer," the conflict between private attitudes and democratic norms is reduced.

44. The table percentages exclude those who declined to answer—about 2%, on average, of the white sample as a whole.

45. Allport 1979, p. 9.

46. Dagger 1986, pp. 270–271.

47. For a detailed discussion on the difficulty of assessing the accuracy of social stereotypes, see Judd and Park 1993.

48. Allport 1979, p. 9.

49. The Pearson correlation coefficient measures strength of linear association between two variables. It ranges from −1.0, which reflects a perfect negative relationship, through 0.0, which reflects no linear relationship at all, to +1.0, which reflects a perfect positive relationship.

50. The consistency displayed in table 5.2 shows up not only in the 1986 NES, but in every national study undertaken by the Center for Political Studies between 1985 and 1992, and in the Detroit Area Survey carried out in 1989. The questions are reliable whether they are asked face-to-face or over the telephone, and whether the questions appear consecutively or are scattered across the interview.

Such consistency makes it possible to create an overall scale based on answers to the individual questions, a great convenience for later analysis. Scales are always preferred over single items for their greater precision and reliability, and for their capacity to represent complex concepts. Our scale is a linear composite, based on the person's average response to the six individual questions. Before averaging, we coded each question onto the 0–1 range, where 0 stands for a racially sympathetic answer and 1 stands for a racially resentful answer (this means that the scale itself also ranges from 0 to 1). When we created the scale, each of the six questions was weighted equally. More complicated weighting schemes are available, but they typically produce small or negligible increases in scale reliability (McIver and Carmines 1981). With all six items included, the reliability of the overall scale, as indicated by Cronbach's *alpha* coefficient, is a respectable .77. Because *alpha* systematically underestimates the reliability of scales formed from Likert questions (Bollen 1989), the figure of .77 is actually even more respectable than it seems. The racial resentment scale is centered on .61, where 0 = racial sympathy and 1 = racial resentment. Scores are distributed more or less normally: most whites end up in the middle, with decreasing numbers at either extreme. But the bell shape is asymmetric: the numbers decline more precipitously in the direction of sympathy than they do in the direction of resentment.

Perhaps an even more primitive empirical implication of our insistence that our questions really measure racial resentment than consistency is that blacks and whites should differ sharply in their answers. They do. The differences are sizable on all six questions included in the 1986 NES. Across the six questions, hardly any whites chose the most sympathetic category: the percentages were 6.5, 3.3, 3.9, 4.7, 8.2, and 17.0 (average = 7.3). In contrast, significant fractions of blacks did so, more than four times the number of whites: the corresponding percentages were 16.0, 35.9, 39.9, 25.0, 34.6, and 44.6 (average 32.7). Comparable differences show up on the four racial resentment questions that were repeated in the 1988 and the 1992 NES studies.

51. The literature on these points is enormous. Classic studies include Clark and Clark 1947; and Porter 1971. Brown 1986 provides a useful summary.

52. On this point see Campbell 1967; Katz 1976; and Tajfel 1969.

53. Allport 1979, p. 9.

54. Views on equality are assessed by a series of six questions present in both the 1990 and 1992 NES, and so perhaps presents the closest and best comparison for racial resentment. For more evidence on the stability of political attitudes indexed by Pearson correlations, see Converse 1964 and Converse and Markus 1979.

55. See, e.g., Nunnally 1978.

56. We estimate the reliabilities of the racial resentment scale to be .77 in 1990 and .76

in 1992, each expressed in terms of Cronbach's *alpha*. Applying the same correction for attenuation, this time to continuities in views on equality between 1990 and 1992, produces a corrected Pearson correlation of .75, up from the raw correlation of .49.

57. The statistical foundations for the confirmatory factor analysis model are spelled out in Jöreskog (1969). Our model specifies autocorrelated error terms, which turn out to be positive, as expected, in all four cases. For the "blacks gotten less than they deserved" question, the correlation between error terms is .19 (se = .03); for "blacks should work their way up," .04 (.03); for "blacks need only to work harder," .06 (.03); and for the "slavery and discrimination" question, .23 (.03). The model that is summarized in table 5.3 and that takes correlated errors into account fits the data much better than does a model that is otherwise identical but that specifies uncorrelated errors. The improvement in fit is given by Chi-square = 112.52, df = 4, p < .001.

When we altered the model to require that the factor loadings be identical in the two years, the overall fit declined insignificantly: Chi-square = 5.40, df = 4, p = .25. This is additional evidence for the stability of racial resentment.

Finally, further tinkering with the factor analysis model took the form of taking into account acquiescence response set. When we did so (by allowing certain error terms to be correlated), the overall fit of the model significantly improved, but without altering the estimate of the correlation between resentment in 1990 and resentment in 1992. Over various specifications, the stability coefficient remained within .03 of either side of .80.

58. Our analysis regresses racial resentment on interviewer's race and respondent's social background. We wanted to be sure that any difference we observed in resentment associated with white and black interviewers was due to that fact and not to the possibility that black and white interviewers might have been assigned to different kinds of respondents. As measures of politically significant social background, we included age, education, occupational status (of the respondent's head of household), family income, union household, employment status, region, religion, and ethnicity. The effect of race of interviewer on racial resentment is given by the unstandardized regression coefficient, B. In 1986, $B = -.04$, se = .036, t = 1.15 (p = .13); in 1988, $B = -.14$, se = .05, t = 2.65 (p < .01); in 1992, $B = -.14$, se = .04, t = 3.54 (p < .01).

59. The GSS questions were developed by a team headed by Lawrence Bobo as part of a larger effort to assess contemporary racial attitudes. This research and development project is described in Bobo et al. (1988).

60. The percentage disagreeing strongly was 51.6; 23.5% disagreed somewhat; 2.3% strongly agreed; 10.4% agreed somewhat; while the remainder—12.2%—neither accepted nor rejected the proposition that blacks come from an inferior race.

61. We grant that this is not a decisive test: we have only a single item to assess old-fashioned bigotry, and responses to the item are skewed, which tends to suppress strength of relationships. Still, we have some confidence that our conclusion is correct, in large part because of a line of research undertaken by McConahay (1982, 1986). McConahay has pursued the question of the empirical relationship between old-fashioned bigotry and what he calls "modern racism," which bears more than a passing resemblance to our concept of racial resentment (see Appendix A). To assess old-fashioned racism, McConahay employs questions that touch on opposition to racial integration as a general principle, the endorsement of offensive racial stereotypes, and objections to interracial contact. McConahay's evidence is drawn from two surveys of the adult population of Louisville, Kentucky, a community then in the midst of a controversial busing pro-

gram, and from a number of informal samplings of white college student opinion over more than a decade. In a series of analyses, modern racism and old-fashioned racism emerge as correlated, but clearly distinct, components of racial antagonism. Also in support of this distinction, various studies have shown that the two forms of racial animosity have separate and distinctive effects on political judgment, with modern forms dominating the old-fashioned expressions of racism (McConahay 1982; Bobo 1983; McClendon 1985; Sniderman and Piazza 1993).

62. Written in equation form:

(5.1) Opinion on Race Policy $= a_0 + B_1$ Racial Resentment

$+ B_2$ Perceived Threat in Workplace

$+ B_3$ Perceived Threat in Schools

$+ B_4$ Limited Government $+ B_{5-5+k} Z^*$

where Z^* is a vector of k social background characteristics, included for purposes of statistical control. $Z^* =$ Age, Region, Gender, Hispanic Ethnicity, Family Income, Respondent Education, Head of Household Occupational Status, and Race of Interviewer. Limited government is one of three political principles that we take up in detail in the next chapter.

63. Here Individualism is a linear scale, consisting of an averaged response to six equally weighted questions, coded 0–1. The six individualism items were developed by Stanley Feldman (1985, 1988). They appear as v508–v513 in the 1986 NES Codebook (we will have more to say about individualism in the next chapter). Thus in equation form:

(5.2) Opinion on Race Policy $= a_0 + B_1$ Racial Resentment

$+ B_2$ Perceived Threat in Workplace

$+ B_3$ Perceived Threat in Schools

$+ B_4$ Limited Government

$+ B_5$ Individualism $+ B_{6-6+k} Z^*$

where all the other variables are defined as before.

64. What if we reverse this experiment, eliminating racial resentment from the equation? Then the estimated influence of individualism increases a bit but becomes reliably different from flat zero in just two of six cases, and is modest even then.

65. These results contradict Sniderman and Hagen's argument, spelled out in *Race and Inequality* (1985), that opposition to changes in racial status quo among white Americans stems from their overriding commitment to the "master idea" of individualism, and has little or nothing to do with the ill-will they might feel toward blacks. According to Sniderman and Hagen, whites reject policies designed to move the country toward racial equality not out of any aversion to blacks, but out of commitment to a transcendent individualism.

A close reading of *Race and Inequality* shows that Sniderman and Hagen are twice mistaken (details provided in Kinder and Mendelberg 1994). First, they provide no evidence that opposition to racial equality among white Americans stems from commitment to individualism. Second, their claim that opposition to racial equality has nothing to do with race is simply wrong: contradicted by their own results, by evidence available to them had they pursued their analysis a bit further, and by the results we are presenting now, based on better and more decisive evidence provided by the 1986 NES.

66. A more precise comparison can be had by reestimating the effects of racial resentment on opinion in 1986, this time using just the four-item version of the resentment

scale. When we did this, we found effects every bit as large as those on display in table 5.5. From the top (fair employment) to the bottom (college quotas), the coefficients are: .60, .40, .45, .43, .38, and .56.

67. The six equal opportunity items are v364–v369 in the 1986 NES Codebook. The reliability of the linear composite scale, as given by Cronbach's *alpha*, is .63. We will have much more to say on the measurement and meaning of equality in the next chapter. In equation form:

$$(5.3) \text{ Opinion on Race Policy} = a_0 + B_1 \text{ Racial Resentment}$$
$$+ B_2 \text{ Personal Threat} + B_3 \text{ Conservatism}$$
$$+ B_4 \text{ Individualism} + B_5 \text{ Equality} + B_{6-6+k} \, Z^*$$

68. Written in equation form:

$$(5.4) \text{ Opinion on Race Policy}_{92} = a_0$$
$$+ T_1 \text{ Racial Resentment}_{92} + T_2 \text{ Equality}_{92}$$
$$+ B_{1-1+k} \, Z^*_{90}$$

where Racial Resentment and Equality are treated as endogenous, and estimates are provided with two-stage least squares. The panel design allows us to use Racial Resentment$_{90}$ as the principal instrument for Racial Resentment$_{92}$, and Equality$_{90}$ as the principal instrument for Equality$_{92}$. The first-round equations indicate that views on equality are in an important way a reflection of racial resentment ($B = -.33$, se = .05), *and* that racial resentment is a reflection of general views on equality ($B = -.25$, se = .10). Both earlier arguments appear to be correct, then.

69. The results shown in table 5.6 come entirely from the 1992 NES, with three exceptions. For reasons that are not difficult to see, the 1992 NES did not include questions on whether the United States should cooperate with the Soviet Union, whether we should become more involved in the internal affairs of Central American countries, and whether the United States should tighten economic sanctions against South Africa. By 1992, these issues were no longer matters of national urgency. In 1986, however, they were, and in an effort to fill out our empirical test of the range of racial resentment in white opinion, we make use of them as well.

70. See Higham 1988.

71. We can push this analysis one step further by examining the relationship between racial resentment and whites' evaluations of various social groups prominent in American life. The 1988 NES asked respondents to report how warmly or coolly they felt toward a wide array of groups: Catholics, the elderly, feminists, the moral majority, and many more. To estimate the impact of racial resentment on evaluations of these various groups, we repeated our now-familiar analysis, taking up each group one at a time. The results come roughly in three varieties. The first is made up of groups implicated in the political struggles pushed by the religious right: born-again Christians, the moral majority, women, prochoice activists, and Catholics. Racial resentment was completely unrelated to the evaluations whites made of these groups. In the second set of social groups we find statistically significant, but tiny, effects. The racially resentful tend to feel slightly more warmly toward whites and slightly more coolly toward Jews and the poor. Third and last are the groups where racial resentment makes a real difference. Such groups notably include, it should surprise no one, blacks and civil rights leaders. But racial resentment also has a large impact on how white Americans feel toward gays, people on welfare, communists, illegal aliens, Palestinians, Hispanics, and feminists. Across these groups, the

unstandardized regression coefficient indexing the impact of racial resentment ranges from .14 to .31 (median = .23).

72. This verdict is also unaffected if we rely on alternative measures of racial resentment. In Appendix B, we report the results of a series of regressions, comparable in all important respects to those we have presented here, except that the scale of racial resentment is replaced by a scale of racial stereotyping, available in both the 1992 NES and the 1990 GSS. The results are virtually indistinguishable. Whether by expressions of racial resentment or by endorsement of derogatory stereotypes, racial animosity is the principal ingredient in white opinion on racial affairs (see table B6).

73. Hyman and Sheatsley 1956.

74. Smith and Sheatsley 1984.

75. Sheatsley (1966, p. 237).

76. *GSS News* 1991, p. 4.

77. Farley 1984, pp. 203–204.

78. Herrnstein 1990, p. 6.

79. Ibid., p. 7.

80. Degler 1991.

81. Herrnstein and Murray 1994. Publication of *The Bell Curve* was clearly an event: it has already produced two full-length anthologies of debate; no doubt more are on the way (Fraser 1995; Jacoby and Glauberman 1995).

CHAPTER SIX

1. Williams 1968, p. 283.

2. Principles, or *values*. We will use the terms interchangeably, mostly for aesthetic variety.

3. That is, each of the three principles seems to occupy the space between "a string of high abstractions and a list of 'planks' in a platform" (Barry 1990, p. 36).

4. Notice that we are forgoing the study of deep cultural beliefs, or dominant ideologies, those matters on which there is no real disagreement and no public discussion (Abercrombie, Hill, and Turner 1980).

5. For a more extended treatment of this point, and examples, see Sanders 1995. Principles (or values) are very prominent in the analysis of contemporary American politics. At present, we have in hand thick and learned books on the American ethos (McClosky and Zaller 1984), the politics of postmaterialism (Inglehart 1977, 1990), American individualism run rampant (Bellah et al. 1985), and fundamental political change driven by the gulf between ideals and practice (Huntington 1981). Indeed, the examination of American principles is on display in virtually all corners of political science: philosophical essays (Walzer 1983), analytical dissections (Rae et al. 1981), sweeping historical narratives (Pole 1993), studies of American political development (Weir, Orloff, and Skocpol 1988), investigations of elite attitudes (Verba and Orren 1985), and, less often, detailed examinations of mass opinion of the sort we are offering here (Feldman 1988).

6. Myrdal 1944, p. 3.

7. Ibid., p. lxix.

8. Additional examples of portraying principles or values as essentially unstoppable include Hartz 1955; Pole 1993; and Wills 1992.

9. Lipset 1963.

10. Tocqueville 1945, 2:271. On the same point, the stability of American values, also see Kluckhohn 1958; McClosky and Zaller 1984; Hartz 1955; and Huntington 1981.

11. Rodgers 1987, p. 3.

12. Lane 1973, p. 102.

13. Tocqueville 1945, p. 3.

14. Pole 1993 and Verba and Orren 1985.

15. Smith 1993.

16. See, e.g., Huber and Form 1973; Hyman 1953; Schlozman, Lehman, and Verba 1979; Sennet and Cobb 1972; Feagin 1975; Katz and Haas 1988; Sniderman and Brody 1977; Feldman 1983, 1988; McClosky and Zaller 1984; Rokeach 1973; Sears, Huddy, and Schaffer 1986; and Feldman and Zaller 1992.

17. Rae et al. 1981, p. 3.

18. According to Rae et al.'s analysis, the concrete world throws up five structural impediments to the smooth application of the formal idea of equality: societies are not indivisible, they can be divided along many lines at once (black and white, rich and poor, men and women); the allocation of goods is embedded in history and is decentralized across many agencies, so that the question of equality is interdependently complex and is never finally settled; goods are typically lumpy, and so cannot be divided simply and evenly; people differ enormously in value and need, thereby defying a simple definition of equality of condition; and because equality is regarded as a relative term (some inequalities are more extreme than others), there exist various and mutually inconsistent ways to calculate equality. Taken together and analyzed systematically, these five obstacles amount to a "grammar" of equality, producing some 720 specific varieties (1981, pp. 133, 189).

19. See, e.g., McClosky and Zaller 1984; Verba and Orren 1985; Hochschild 1981; and Walzer 1983.

20. Or what Rae and his associates call the problem of the domain of reference (Rae et al. 1981, p. 3).

21. What may count in these questions isn't only the substantive definition of equality, but who seems to be arguing for it, and how loudly. Arguments and statements about equality also betray views about politics and political actors. Because of the political or social character embedded in conceptions of egalitarianism, discussions or statements about equality evoke more or less obtrusive pictures of the state or the political community, the enforcers of or the adherents to claims about equality. This abstract social or political entity, which may be more or less well defined, is certainly present in all six of the equality items carried by the 1986 NES, taking the form of "our society," "we," and, most popularly, "this country." The questions also contain varying levels of activism; the social entity in the questions does things with more ("pushing" equal rights) or less vehemence ("our society should do whatever is necessary"). Finally, note that the six questions taken together are balanced against the intrusions of acquiescence: three of the items are worded so that agreement means support for equality; the other three are worded so that agreement means opposition to equality.

22. Pole 1993, p. ix. On race differences on equality, see Sanders and Stoker 1989; Rokeach 1973; and Feldman 1988.

The racial divide on equality appears to be a difference rooted in *racial* experiences. In particular, the differences between whites and blacks shown in detail in table 6.1 are not attributable to class. On average, black Americans enjoy less income, education, and occupational status, and fewer blacks by far own their own homes, but these differences cannot explain the large differences we see on equality.

To show that this is so, we first created an equality scale, based on a simple linear combination of answers to all six equality questions. Such a composite measure is justified empirically because whites and blacks respond to these questions quite consistently, as if they had one thing primarily in mind. For white Americans, the average interitem Pearson r = .22 in 1986 and .28 in 1992; the item-total correlations (corrected) are reasonably homogeneous (they range from .33 to .39 in 1986 and from .30 to .51 in 1992); and Cronbach's *alpha* for the linear composite scale is .63 in 1986 and .71 in 1992. The pattern is similar, though somewhat attenuated, for black Americans: the average interitem Pearson r = .15 in 1986 and .24 in 1992; the item-total correlations (corrected) are less homogeneous (they range from .11 to .42 in 1986 and from .23 to .51 in 1992); and Cronbach's *alpha* for the overall scale = .52 in 1986 and .67 in 1992.

To provide a precise estimate of the racial divide on equality, we first regressed the composite measure of equality, coded on the 0–1 interval, on race of respondent (with black = 1, white = 0). The magnitude of the racial divide is then given by B, the unstandardized regression coefficient on the race variable. As expected, the divide is sizable in both years: in 1986, B = .20 (se = .01); in 1992, B = .16 (se = .01). Then we added to this simple equation measures of class (Family Income, Respondent Education, Head of Household Occupational Status, and Home Ownership), social position (Age, Region, and Gender), and race of interviewer. The empirical question is: how much of the original racial divide on equality can be explained by differences in class and social position? And the answer is: hardly any. Taking into account the effects due to class, social position, and race of interviewer, the regression coefficient on the race variable now is .18 (se = .01) in 1986, and .15 (se = .02) in 1992, down ever so slightly from their original values.

23. Bryce 1900, 3:270; Hofstadter 1948, p. viii; Bellah et al. 1985, p. 142.

24. Weber 1971, p. 222.

25. Pierre Leroux 1833 (quoted in Arieli 1964, p. 233); Edmund Burke 1910, p. 94.

26. Arieli 1964.

27. According to Rodgers 1978.

28. All quotations are from ibid., pp. 231, 217, 220, and 212.

29. McClosky and Zaller (1984) summarize their survey evidence this way: "Long after the strictly theological tenets of Puritanism have lost their status as behavioral imperatives, many Americans continued to view work and wealth through the moral prism of the Calvinist creed" (p. 107).

30. These results are presented in Feldman and Zaller 1992.

31. Feldman 1988.

32. See Feldman 1983; and Sniderman and Brody 1977.

33. One major effort has wrestled with just this question, but, we think, not successfully. In *Race and Inequality: A Study in American Values* (1985), Sniderman and Hagen argue that opposition to racial equality, in principle and in practice, is rooted primarily in white Americans' commitment to individualism. Whites oppose racial integration as a general matter and resist federal efforts to desegregate public schools in particular because they are individualists, committed to the idea that individuals must take care of themselves.

We believe that *Race and Inequality* provides no justification for the claim that individualism stands behind opposition to racial inequality. The details of our disagreement are set out in Kinder and Mendelberg (1994). Other efforts, which seem to us to be better tests of the hold of individualism on the American imagination, find a small or negligible role for individualism in white opinion on racial matters (see, e.g., Bobo 1991; Feldman 1988; Kluegel and Smith 1986; Markus 1989; and Sears 1988).

34. Note also that, as in the case of equality, the economic individualism items are balanced against the intrusions of acquiescence: three of the items are worded so that agreement means support for economic individualism; the other three are worded so that agreement means opposition to economic individualism.

35. On the overall scale coded 0–1, the mean score for whites = .58; for blacks = .54. This tiny difference is statistically significant but substantively unimportant. The structure of response to the individualism questions is also virtually identical for blacks and whites. The correlation matrix for one is interchangeable with the other. For white Americans, the average interitem Pearson r = .20; the item-total correlations (corrected) are relatively homogeneous (they range from .22 to .43); and Cronbach's *alpha* for the linear composite scale = .59. For black Americans, the average interitem Pearson r = .21; the item-total correlations (corrected) are also reasonably homogeneous (they range from .26 to .45); and Cronbach's *alpha* for the scale = .62.

36. Huntington 1981, p. 33.

37. Quoted phrase is from Held 1987, p. 69.

38. Arieli 1964; Hofstadter 1955.

39. Sumner, quoted in Hofstadter 1955, p. 59.

40. Spencer, quoted in ibid., p. 41.

41. Fredrickson 1971, p. 253.

42. Huntington 1981, p. 36.

43. Of the perversity argument Hirschman (1991) writes: "The attempt to push society in a certain direction will result in its moving all right, but in the opposite direction. Attempts to reach for liberty will make society sink into slavery, the quest for democracy will produce oligarchy and tyranny, and social welfare programs will create more, rather than less, poverty. *Everything backfires.*"

44. Free and Cantril 1968; Lipset and Schneider 1978; and McClosky and Zaller 1984.

45. See, e.g., Feldman and Zaller 1992; Jackman 1981a; Kessel 1972; Markus 1989; Nie, Verba, and Petrocik 1979; and Schuman and Bobo 1988.

46. In the 1986 NES, Pearson r = .20 for whites, .25 for blacks. In 1992, r = .31 for whites, .05 for blacks.

47. These questions were developed by Gregory Markus. See his technical report (Markus 1989), available from the Center for Political Studies at the University of Michigan.

48. This is truer of whites than of blacks. For white Americans, the average interitem Pearson r = .46; the item-total correlations (corrected) are homogeneous (they range from .47 to .59); and Cronbach's *alpha* for a linear composite scale = .72. For black Americans: the average interitem Pearson r = .13; the item-total correlations (corrected) range from .08 to .22; and Cronbach's *alpha* for an overall scale = .29.

49. As in the case of equality, this racial divide appears to be rooted in *racial* experience. Differences between whites and blacks on limited government that are presented in table 6.3 are not, for the most part, due to differences in class or social position. Here we follow the same procedures we did in our analysis of racial differences

in equality, set out in n. 22. The magnitude of the racial divide on limited government in 1986 is −.20 (se = .02); in 1992, it is −.15 (se = .01); and in 1992 with limited government defined in terms of abstract opposition, it is −.23 (se = .03). As before, all variables are coded onto the 0–1 interval. When we take into account the effects due to class, social position, and race of interviewer, the regression coefficient on the race variable modestly declines in all three cases: to −.15 (se = .02), −.11 (se = .02), and −.18 (se = .03), respectively.

50. If we repeat the simple calculations presented in table 6.4, but first partition the sample by level of political information, then we begin to see intimations of systematic and coherent thinking among the best informed. When we cut the 1986 white sample into thirds by level of information, for example, the correlations between the principles are noticeably enhanced among the best informed, and they essentially dissolve among the least informed. For the best-informed third, the Pearson r's range from .26 to .50 (absolute values), and average .39; for the least-informed third, the Pearson r's range from .02 to .23 (absolute values), and average just .12. No such pattern is apparent for black Americans, perhaps because once we partition the sample by information, we begin to run out of cases.

51. More formally, the base equation is written this way:

$$(6.1) \quad \text{Opinion} = a_0 + B_1 \text{ Racial Resentment}$$
$$+ B_2 \text{ Equal Opportunity}$$
$$+ B_3 \text{ Economic Individualism}$$
$$+ B_4 \text{ Limited Government} + B_{5-5+k} \text{ } Z^*$$

where Z^* is our familiar vector of k social background characteristics, included for purposes of statistical control. Z^* = Age, Region, Gender, Hispanic Ethnicity, Family Income, Respondent Education, Head of Household Occupational Status, and Race of Interviewer. The results we report in table 6.5 actually come from a second equation. After estimating equation 6.1, we trimmed variables from the k vector whose coefficients were indistinguishable from zero and then reestimated the modified equation (call it 6.1*). Equation 6.1* supplies the parameter estimates presented in table 6.5. We follow this procedure throughout.

52. In table 6.5 fewer cases appear for the fair employment and integrated schools questions; this is so because these two include strong filters; roughly one-third of whites say they have no opinion on each, and in the analysis presented in table 6.5, these people are set aside. One alternative is to include them, coding them to the middle of the scale. When we did this, we found essentially the same results.

53. Adding a measure of group threat into the equation has no effect on any of the estimates shown in table 6.5. This is a convenient result, since we want to extend our analysis of the impact of principles to the 1992 NES, which does not include measures of group threat. Deleting the measure of racial resentment, however, does have consequences. For equality, the estimated effect increases sharply on all six policy issues, in roughly equal fashion. On average, the impact of equality goes from .23 to .43, a substantial gain. For economic individualism, there are also real consequences: the picture now looks brighter—though not too bright. In the absence of racial resentment, all six coefficients take the right sign, they range from .07 (government provide special assistance) to .21 (government ensure same schools), they average .15, they all at least approach statistical significance by conventional standards, and two clearly surpass conventional

significance. All in all, under this specification, we see a modest effect of economic individualism on race policy. Finally, whether racial resentment is in or out of the equation makes no difference whatever to the estimated effect of limited government.

54. See Kinder and Sanders (1986, 1987) for the details.

55. These results on the importance of equality in 1992 hold whichever version of limited government is included in the equation.

56. Virtually the identical set of results emerges from our analysis of the 1985 NES pilot study as well. Three independent tries, three sets of converging results, give us confidence that equality matters, and matters in a issue-specific way. The 1985 NES findings are reported in Kinder and Sanders (1986, 1987).

57. Pearson r, uncorrected for unreliability, = .44.

58. In the new analysis, where limited government is assessed through opposition to big government in the abstract, the estimated effects, given by B, in the same left-to-right order in which they appear in table 6.6, are: .04 (se = .02), .09 (.02), .24 (.04), .16 (.04), .04 (.02), and .05 (.02). We find the one conspicuous discrepancy between the two analyses suspicious on two grounds. First, the policy version of limited government is based on consistent reactions to a pair of policy items that share an *identical* format with just one of the six race policy questions—the one under examination here, on whether the government should make special efforts for blacks. Second, one of the policy items that goes into the limited government scale poses the question of whether government is responsible for the economic welfare of citizens or whether citizens should get ahead under their own steam. Formulated this way, the question bears an obvious—and, for present purposes, uncomfortable—resemblance to the "government provide special help to blacks" question. Similarity in format and substance can perhaps explain our one clear failure to replicate. More important, similarity in format and substance suggests that the estimated effect of limited government on opposition to government making special efforts on behalf of blacks shown in table 6.6 exaggerates the real effect.

59. In equation form:

$$(6.2)\ \text{Opinion} = a_0 + B_1 \text{ Perception of Personal Advantage at School}$$
$$+ B_2 \text{ Group Advantage} + B_3 \text{ Group Discrimination}$$
$$+ B_4 \text{ Equal Opportunity} + B_5 \text{ Economic Individualism}$$
$$+ B_6 \text{ Limited Government} + B_{7-7+k} Z^*$$

where Z^* is an abbreviated version of our vector of k social background characteristics—the abbreviation a concession to small sample size.

60. All these results—the strong effect of equality, the modest but consistent effect of limited government, and the weak effect due to economic individualism—are robust across alternative specifications of equation 6.2. In particular, the results presented in table 6.7 are essentially unaffected when the various measures of interest were deleted from the estimating equation. This is convenient, since we will momentarily be presenting results from the 1992 NES on the power of equality and limited government, and the 1992 NES did not carry any of the interest variables. Evidently, this omission will not damage our replication. Nor were the results presented in table 6.7 affected when we expanded our analysis to include measures of what we have been calling "racial ideology." This term encompasses blacks' views on change in race relations, on the responsiveness of institutions to black claims and requests, on the extent to which white elites conspire to keep blacks down, and on feelings of racial solidarity. When all of these are

added to equation 6.2, the estimates of the effects due to equality, economic individualism, and limited government generally diminish but microscopically. In material terms, nothing changes at all.

61. As was true for whites, the results on the impact of equality on black opinion in 1992 are unchanged if we replace the measure of limited government with the measure based on consistent reactions to particular government interventions.

62. See n. 58 for our suspicions about this peculiarly large effect.

63. For black Americans, the average interitem Pearson $r = .13$; the item-total correlations (corrected) range from .08 to .22; and the Cronbach's *alpha* for the scale as a whole is a miserable .29. The association between the two versions of limited government, given by Pearson r, is just .11.

64. Results come from our analysis of the 1992 NES, with one exception. A question on whether the United States should apply stricter sanctions against South Africa appeared in the 1986 NES, but not in 1992. Because this question raises issues of equality in an especially dramatic way, and does so outside the domain of American domestic politics, we decided to include it here. In a few instances, the identical policy question appeared in both the 1986 and 1992 NES. When we estimated comparable models in the two years, for identical policy questions, we found essentially the same results. Rather than clutter already full tables, we chose to present only the results from 1992.

65. The specificity of effects associated with limited government for black Americans on display in table 6.12 is consistent with the empirical difficulties we encountered earlier in trying to develop adequate measures.

66. Rae et al. 1981, p. 64.

67. Huntington 1981, p. 33.

68. Pole 1993, p. 1.

69. Perhaps—but there is another way to interpret our results. The zero effect of individualism might testify not to the failure of the theoretical claim, but to the way we carried out the test: perhaps we measured individualism wretchedly. Other results argue against this, however. For one thing, economic individualism *is* important in one case of black opinion on race policy, on the question of whether the government should make special efforts for black Americans. For another, economic individualism does appear to influence black and white opinion elsewhere, in particular, in the domain of social welfare policy. On opposition to the Food Stamps program and assistance to the unemployed, economic individualism made a noticeable difference, to whites and blacks alike. For whites: Food Stamps program, $B = .19$, se $= .07$, p $< .01$; assistance to the unemployed, $B = .19$, se $= .07$, p $< .01$. For blacks: Food Stamps program, $B = .15$, se $= .17$, one-tailed p $< .20$; assistance to the unemployed, $B = .37$, se $= .14$, one-tailed p $< .01$. Economic individualism does have a role to play in public opinion, then, but not, for the most part, on matters of race.

70. Stoker 1992, p. 370.

Chapter Seven

1. After much debate and a few minor adjustments in the legislation, Congress passed and President Bush signed the bill (it was now the Civil Rights Act of 1991).

2. Gamson 1992; Gamson and Lasch 1983; and Gamson and Modigliani 1987, 1989. On other uses of frame, see, e.g., Minsky's (1977) development of an architecture for cognition; Goffman's (1974) account of how individuals construct meaning out of their social

experience; and Tversky and Kahneman's (1981) celebrated experimental demonstrations that, contrary to expected utility theory, decision outcomes can be systematically and decisively influenced by altering how the options are framed.

3. Gamson and Modigliani 1987, p. 143.

4. William James 1890, p. 488.

5. Converse makes a congenial point in his discussion of the diffusion of ideological systems through mass society. "The shaping of belief systems of any range into apparently logical wholes that are credible to large numbers of people," he wrote, "is an act of creative synthesis characteristic of only a minuscule proportion of any population" "To the extent that multiple idea elements of a belief system tend to be diffused from such creative sources, they tend to be diffused in 'packages,' which consumers come to see as 'natural' wholes, for they are presented in such terms" (Converse 1964, p. 211).

6. Our interest in reenacting the elite debate sets us apart from most other experimental research on question wording, form, and placement. Such work is often motivated by an interest in designing better questions. On the assumption that systematic evidence and intuition trump intuition alone, such research has an obvious and valuable payoff, even if an agreed-upon recipe for writing survey questions is still some distance off (see, e.g., Schuman and Presser 1981; Bradburn et al. 1979; Krosnick and Berent 1993; Krosnick and Fabrigar 1995; Converse and Presser 1986). Such experiments are also used to test predictions drawn from psychological theories of human cognition. This research is valuable, too, as it clarifies the nature of fundamental concepts (e.g., attitude) and processes (e.g., long-term memory) that are implicated in the meaning and measurement of public opinion (see, e.g., Tourangeau and Rasinski 1988 and Tanur 1991).

7. For a book-length argument on behalf of experimentation as a mode of political inquiry, see Kinder and Palfrey 1993.

8. For a detailed account of this famous early experiment, see Gosnell 1927.

9. Cook and Campbell 1979 p. 5.

10. Hovland (1959), it seems, was right: Sears (1986) demonstrated that, compared with the adult American population as a whole, American college students typically possess less-crystallized opinions about public life, less secure senses of self, stronger cognitive skills, greater tendencies to comply with authority, and less stable relations with peers. Sears concluded that all these qualities have crept insidiously into social psychology's portrait of "human nature."

11. This sounds good, and it is. Notice, however, that while inserting experiments into probability sample surveys provides a powerful reply to the standard complaint directed at experimentation, it has little to say about other aspects of generalizability: apprehensions about the representativeness of settings (after all, our surveys take place in a specialized setting, typically the respondent's living room) or of treatments (our question-wording experiments are for the most part limited to the manipulation of semantic material).

12. Dahl 1989, p. 100.

13. Quote comes from Dennis Thompson 1970, p. 15.

14. Mencken 1956.

15. Hochschild 1981. Lane's (1962) famous interviews make the same point, and Feldman and Zaller (1992) place ambivalence among competing considerations at the center of their theory of public opinion.

16. Gamson and Modigliani 1987.

17. The story is a bit more complicated than we suggest in the text. For reasons that need not concern us here, the 1989 NES survey was actually divided into four forms of roughly equal numbers. Some of our analyses compare Forms A and B versus C and D; others compare A and C versus B and D. (See the 1989 American National Election Pilot Study Codebook for details.) As a general matter, respondents assigned to the four forms were indeed comparable: we found no differences on age, gender, education, race, income, turnout in 1988, ideological identification, or political information (all these variables came from the 1988 NES interview with 1989 NES study respondents). One clear difference did emerge, however. By chance, Form C includes too many Democrats. Combining strong, weak, and leaning identifiers, the Form C group was 56% Democratic; in the other three groups, the comparable percentages were 37% (A), 46% (B), and 48% (D). This difference is annoying not only because it is statistically and substantively significant but also because partisanship is central to other key political variables. Sure enough, Form C respondents were also more critical of President Reagan's performance (p < .01); sure enough, had the 1988 presidential election been confined to Form C respondents, Dukakis would have won in a landslide (57% of Form C respondents reported voting for Dukakis, compared with roughly 45% in the other three groups). The importance of this difference for our analysis is mitigated by the fact that none of our comparisons rests on Form C respondents alone. All our comparisons combine the four conditions into two: some compare Forms A and B versus C and D; others compare A and C versus B and D. This diminishes the importance of Form C respondents' unusual affinity for the Democrats, but we must keep the difference in mind. Where appropriate, our analysis will include partisanship as a control variable.

18. This difference surpasses conventional levels of statistical significance: Chi-square = 7.09, p < .01. Roughly the same size difference, in the same direction, shows up among black respondents, but the number of cases is so small that the observed difference does not even approach significance (53.8% versus 43.8%, Chi-square = .25, p = .61).

19. Right-hand side variables in each of the regression equations included, in addition to opinion on government assistance to blacks, measures of age, region (South), education, sex (male), level of political information, ideological identification, and party identification, all taken from the 1988 NES (from which the 1989 NES pilot study was drawn). Evaluations of Bush, Dukakis, Jackson, and Reagan were measured by 101-point thermometer ratings given in the preelection wave of the 1988 NES. As usual, all variables are coded onto the 0–1 scale.

For each of the four leaders, we estimated a single equation based on the framed and stripped conditions pooled together:

$$(7.1) \quad \text{Evaluation of Bush} = a_0$$
$$+ B_1 \text{ Government Assistance to Blacks}$$
$$+ B_2 \text{ Question Frame}$$
$$+ B_3 \text{ [Question Frame * Government Assistance to Blacks]}$$
$$+ B_{4-k} Z^*$$

where Question Frame is a binary variable, coded 0 if the question is asked in stripped form and 1 if in framed form, and Z^* is the vector of control variables noted above. The impact of white opinion on government assistance to blacks in the stripped condition is then given by B_1; the impact of white opinion on government assistance to blacks in the framed condition is given by $B_1 + B_3$; and the statistical difference between conditions is tested by B_3 and its associated standard error.

20. The findings in table 7.2 are derived from regression estimates of equation 7.2:

(7.2) Opinion on Government Help to Blacks $= a_0$
$+ B_1$ Question Frame $+ B_2$ Racial Resentment
$+ B_3$ Equal Opportunity $+ B_4$ Limited Government
$+ B_5$ Attitude toward the Poor
$+ B_6$ [Question Frame * Racial Resentment]
$+ B_7$ [Question Frame * Equal Opportunity]
$+ B_8$ [Question Frame * Limited Government]
$+ B_9$ [Question Frame * Attitude toward the Poor]
$+ B_{10}$ Republican $+ B_{11}$ Democrat

where Question Frame is a binary variable, coded 0 if the question is asked in stripped form and 1 if in framed form, and all the other variables are as described earlier. All the right-hand-side variables are taken from the 1988 NES interview, some twelve months before the 1989 study. For our purposes, the coefficients of special interest in equation 7.2 are B_6, B_7, B_8, and B_9, which together disclose whether the effects of key opinion ingredients are enhanced or diminished when the question on government assistance is framed.

21. For racial resentment, $B = .20$, se $= .15$, t $= 1.34$, p $< .10$ (one-tailed); for equality, $B = .29$, se $= .19$, t $= 1.50$, p $< .10$ (one-tailed).

22. Only the latter difference reaches statistical significance: $B = .22$, se $= .13$, t $= 1.68$, p $< .05$ (one-tailed).

23. Gamson and Modigliani 1987.

24. The 1985 NES study completed interviews with just twenty-eight black Americans.

25. Apart from the affirmative action questions, the interview schedules administered to the two samples were virtually identical. The questions appeared in the first wave of the survey, back to back, toward the middle of the interview, following some of the questions on race policy and preceding others.

26. We compared the two samples on more than one hundred variables (means and, where appropriate, variances), searching for some difference, apart from the experimental manipulation itself, that could account for any framing effects we might observe. Our search yielded only a handful of cases where differences between the samples were statistically reliable; none was sizable or important.

27. The findings in table 7.3 are derived from regression estimates of the following equation:

(7.3) Opinion on Affirmative Action $= a_0$
$+ B_1$ Question Frame $+ B_2$ Perceived Threat in Schools
$+ B_3$ Racial Resentment $+ B_4$ Equal Opportunity
$+ B_5$ Economic Individualism $+ B_6$ Limited Government
$+ B_7$ [Frame * Perceived Threat in Schools]
$+ B_8$ [Frame * Racial Resentment]
$+ B_9$ [Frame * Equal Opportunity]
$+ B_{10}$ [Frame * Economic Individualism]
$+ B_{11}$ [Frame * Limited Government]

where Question Frame is a binary variable, coded 0 if the question is asked framed as reverse discrimination and 1 if framed as unfair advantage, and all the other variables are as described earlier. The coefficients of special interest are the multiplicative terms—B_7 through B_{11}—which reveal whether the effects of key opinion ingredients are altered under alternative frames.

28. Our analysis is based on Jöreskog's maximum likelihood model available in LISREL VI (Jöreskog 1969). Because we want to compare parameter estimates for the reverse discrimination and undeserved advantage frames, we analyzed the two samples separately, estimating the coefficients from the variance-covariance matrix in each case. For convenience, we coded all race policy opinion variables on a 0–1 interval, with 1 representing the conservative end of the continuum in all instances.

29. The three-factor model fits the data well in absolute terms, as the goodness of fit statistics provided in table 7.4 indicate, and it also fits the data much better than does the alternative model that specifies a single latent factor. Under this assumption, whites support or oppose racial policy in a single-minded way, without regard to distinctions between the equal opportunity agenda of the civil rights movement and the contemporary demand for affirmative action. This specification is clearly wrong. The single factor model fits the variance-covariance matrix poorly, and equally poorly for the two alternative frames: under the reverse discrimination frame, Chi-square with 20 degree of freedom = 80.75 (p < .001), adjusted goodness of fit = .792; under the unfair advantage frame, Chi-square with 20 degrees of freedom = 76.69 (p < .001), adjusted goodness of fit = .772.

30. The differences are significant in both cases at p < .05. To provide the most direct test of these differences, we reestimated the model summarized in table 7.4, this time making use of the multiple group option to Jöreskog's maximum likelihood model. We specified that the structure of the model be identical across the two frames, that the factor loadings be the same, and that the correlation between the federal assistance latent variable and the equal opportunity latent variable also be the same. With these constraints, only the correlations involving the affirmative action latent variable are permitted to vary across the frames. This specification fits the data well. For the overall model, Chi-square with 51 degrees of freedom is 63.34 (p = .115). The goodness of fit is .951 under the reverse discrimination frame and .947 under the unfair advantage frame. Consistent with the results from the separate sample analysis, affirmative action opinions are correlated much more strongly with federal assistance and equal opportunity opinions in this analysis when opposition to affirmative action is framed in terms of giving unearned advantages to blacks than when framed in terms of reverse discrimination. Under the undeserved advantage frame, the correlations between the latent variables are .705 (affirmative action with federal assistance) and .569 (affirmative action with equal opportunity); under the reverse discrimination frame, the correlations are .512 (affirmative action with federal assistance) and .319 (affirmative action with equal opportunity). Both differences are statistically significant (p < .01).

31. The differences reach statistical significance in two of three comparisons: federal support for cities, p = .06; support for welfare, p = .06.

32. In statistical terms, the differences are significant for disgust (p < .01) and for infuriated (p < .10), but not for angry (p = .38). Respondents were asked about their positive emotional reactions to affirmative action, too: specifically whether preferential treatment of blacks had ever made them feel hopeful, proud, or sympathetic. In contrast to the results on negative emotions, correlations between positive emotional reactions and affirmative action opinions were independent of frame. See Kinder and Sanders 1990 for details.

33. Wilson 1991, pp. 477–478. *The Declining Significance of Race* appeared in 1978; *The Truly Disadvantaged* in 1987.

34. In addition to Wilson, see Skocpol 1988, 1991; and Orfield 1988.

35. As always, we made sure that the two groups of respondents—one randomly assigned the first version of the question, the other assigned the second version—are in fact comparable. We looked for differences between samples on age, race, gender, region, education, party identification, ideological identification, political knowledge, and race of interviewer. We found none.

36. Survey participants were encouraged to consult a "showcard" in selecting their answer, which provided a visual display of the response options. The extreme points were labeled, and labeled differently in the two frame conditions. In the first, the two extremes were "Government should help blacks" versus "Blacks should help themselves." In the second, the two extremes were "Government should help minorities" versus "Minorities should help themselves."

37. Rae et al. 1981.

38. Chi-square = 17.82, df = 6, p < .01.

39. Because of the much smaller sample, this difference does not reach statistical significance: Chi-square = 7.39, df = 6, p = .29. Fortunately for our purposes, the 1986 NES carried virtually the identical question-wording experiment, and exactly the same pattern of results appears there, for blacks and whites. Thus the race-neutral frame appears to have the same effect on blacks and whites. We tested this by estimating the following equation:

$$(7.4) \text{ Opinion on Government Help} = a_0$$
$$+ B_1 \text{ Question Frame} + B_2 \text{ Race} + B_3 \text{ [Race } * \text{ Frame]}$$

Here the interaction term—[Race * Frame]—tests whether the effect of the frame is different for blacks and whites. It is not: B_3 = .038, se = .042.

40. Our first two experiments were not designed with shifts in the overall distribution of opinion in mind. In Experiment I, we expected that the distinction between a framed presentation and a stripped presentation would have less to do with inducing citizens to adopt a particular position than with altering the volume and quality of thought devoted to the issue (which might, but might not, have implications for opinion change). In fact, as things turned out, opinion was a bit stronger against government assistance to blacks under the framed condition than under the stripped presentation, but the difference did not reach statistical significance (Chi-square = 5.55, p = .24).

Likewise, in Experiment II, we found that whites rejected affirmative action in employment decisions and in college admissions pretty much independently of which oppositional frame we employed. When opposition to preferential hiring and promotion was formulated in terms of reverse discrimination, 67.3% strongly opposed the policy; when formulated in terms of handing to blacks advantages they haven't earned, 62.5% strongly opposed the policy. Similarly, 53.9% of whites strongly opposed setting aside places for blacks in college admissions when framed in terms of reverse discrimination; 52.9% did so when framed in terms of undeserved advantage. Neither difference approaches statistical significance: on hiring and promotion, Chi-square with 3 degrees of freedom = .82 (p = .85); on college admissions, Chi-square with 3 degrees of freedom = .68 (p = .88). In the 1986 NES, which provides an exact replication, the differences run in the same direction and are roughly the same size. Thanks primarily to the larger sample size of the 1986 study (roughly three times the size of the 1985 NES), the differences attributable to question frame in 1986 reach statistical significance: in the case of hiring and promotion, Chi-square = 8.39, p = .04; in the case of quotas in college admissions, Chi-square = 10.62, p = .01. And, from the 1989 NES, white opinion ran a bit more strongly against affirmative action when the issue was framed as reverse discrimination rather than unfair advantage (the relevant figures are 79.5% and 75.3%). The difference is not large, and it does not reach statistical significance (and the questions are not quite the same as those used in 1985 and 1986), but it is virtually identical in size to the differences previously observed. In all cases, then, opposition to affirmative action is a bit stronger when the issue is framed as reverse discrimination.

In Experiment III, by contrast, shifts in opinion induced by alternative frames are precisely what we are looking for, first and foremost. And, as table 7.6 shows, we find them.

41. These results come from regression estimates of the following equation, separately for white and for black respondents:

$$(7.5) \text{ Opinion on government help} = a_0$$
$$+ B_1 \text{ Question Frame} + B_2 \text{ Race of Interviewer}$$
$$+ B_3 [\text{Race of Interviewer} * \text{Frame}]$$

where Question Frame is a binary variable, coded 0 if the question is asked with reference to blacks and other minorities and 1 if asked with reference to blacks alone; and Race of Interviewer is a binary variable, coded 1 if the interviewer is black and 0 if not. B_2 gives the effect due to race of interviewer on opinion toward government assistance when the issue is framed in a race-neutral way; $(B_2 + B_3)$ gives the effect due to race of interviewer on opinion toward government assistance when the issue is framed in a race-conscious way. The magnitude of the difference of the race of interviewer effect across frames, given by B_3, is statistically significant in both instances (at $p < .10$). These results are presented in Appendix B (table B7); they are replicated in a fine-grained way by an identical analysis of the same comparison available in the 1986 NES, also displayed in table B7 of Appendix B.

An additional replication of sorts is possible using a different patch of the 1986 NES data. There we find race of interviewer effects on affirmative action opinions only when the issue is framed in terms of unfair advantage: then, B is $-.27$ (.07) on the issue of college quotas for blacks and $-.08$ (.06) on the issue of preferential hiring; the race of interviewer effect evaporates when the issue is framed as reverse discrimination ($-.03$ and $-.00$ on the two issues).

42. In equation form:

$$(7.6) \text{ Opinion on government help} = a_0$$
$$+ B_1 \text{ Question Frame} + B_2 \text{ Racial Resentment}$$
$$+ B_3 \text{ Equal Opportunity} + B_4 \text{ Limited Government}$$
$$+ B_5 \text{ Hispanic} + B_6 \text{ Attitude toward Hispanics}$$
$$+ B_7 [\text{Question Frame} * \text{Racial Resentment}]$$
$$+ B_8 [\text{Question Frame} * \text{Equal Opportunity}]$$
$$+ B_9 [\text{Question Frame} * \text{Limited Government}]$$
$$+ B_{10} [\text{Question Frame} * \text{Hispanic}]$$
$$+ B_{11} [\text{Question Frame} * \text{Attitude toward Hispanics}]$$

where Hispanic is a binary measure of whether or not the respondent claims Hispanic origins; Attitude toward Hispanics is measured by the 101-point thermometer rating scale, rescaled to 0–1; and Racial Resentment, Equal Opportunity, and Limited Government are linear composites, scaled 0–1, put together in the usual way. The interaction terms test whether the effect of each ingredient differs across the two frames. Our results are unaffected by whether or not the estimating equation also includes terms for race of interviewer and race of interviewer * frame. For the sake of simplicity and aesthetics, we present results here that ignore race of interviewer.

43. The decline of roughly 15% in the effect of racial resentment does not quite reach statistical significance: one-tailed p = .18. Across a variety of other specifications, however, the effect of frame on the impact of racial resentment is at least as large as that shown in table 7.7 and often surpasses conventional levels of statistical significance. For example, when we replace the composite scale of racial resentment with a single item, that based on the thermometer rating of blacks, the effect attributed to racial sentiments nearly doubles in the race-conscious frame: B is .15 under the race-neutral frame and .29 under the race-conscious frame, with the difference being statistically significant at p < .10. The sharp increase in the impact of equal opportunity shown in table 7.7 associated with the race-neutral frame is statistically significant (p < .01).

44. p = .27, by two-tailed test.

45. $B = -.04$, se = .06, t = .62, p = .54.

46. The experiment was designed by Bobo and Kluegel, and we are grateful to them for it; their analysis, motivated by purposes similar to our own, is reported in Bobo and Kluegel (1993).

47. The findings in table 7.9 are derived from regression estimates of the following equation:

$$(7.7) \text{ Opinion on poverty policy} = a_0 + B_1 \text{ Question Frame}$$
$$+ B_2 \text{ Racial Stereotyping}$$
$$+ B_3 \text{ [Question Frame * Racial Stereotyping]}$$
$$+ B_{4-4+k} Z^*$$

where Z^* = measures of Social Background, Limited Government, Equality, and Individualism.

48. Our analysis of opinion on government assistance to blacks was just one of several such experiments carried out in the 1989 NES, the only one that dealt explicitly with race. We planned and analyzed two others: one on relations with the (then) Soviet Union, the other on abortion. Meanwhile, working independently, John Zaller carried out a set of five similar experiments, again comparing the quality of opinion elicited by framed versus stripped questions. Zaller's experimental tests focused on public opinion toward federal spending on the B2 bomber, oil drilling in Alaska, aid to the Contras, the death penalty for convicted murderers, and drug testing. In general, the results from these experiments replicate the findings presented here on government assistance to blacks, and the findings are generally stronger on the point that framing produces more stable opinions. For details on these experiments, see Kinder and Nelson 1995 and Zaller 1990.

49. Gamson and Modigliani (1987). The replications are reported in Nelson and Kinder 1996.

50. Gamson 1992, p. 149.

51. Eastland and Bennett 1978, p. 34.

52. Rae et al. 1981, p. 5.

53. One might say that the difference we explore in Experiment IV goes beyond framing. On the surface, what is altered in our final experiment is not so much the policy's

justification as the policy itself. Spending more money on schools in black neighborhoods is simply different, one could say, from spending more money on schools in poor neighborhoods. Of course this is right, though it may be a distinction without a difference. For one thing, defining the beneficiaries differently is one way to imply different kinds of justifications. For another, black neighborhoods are much more likely to be poor than are others, and black schools are therefore likely to profit disproportionately from a policy that is on its face neutral with respect to race. Indeed, this is precisely William Wilson's point. Thus whether or not Experiment IV fits altogether neatly within our analysis of elite frames, it surely is responsive to the practical political question of building coalitions in support of egalitarian policies. And on this point, the results are clear: whites are much more apt to support redistributive policies when the benefits and programs go to the poor and the disadvantaged regardless of color.

54. These results can be read off figure 2.2 in Schuman, Steeh, and Bobo 1985, p. 60.

55. Stoker 1996.

56. Ibid., p. 20.

CHAPTER EIGHT

1. Quoted in Gillette 1979, p. 23.

2. Dahl 1956, p. 125; Miller 1983, p. 133; and Riker 1982, p. 5.

3. On retrospective voting, see Fiorina 1981. For the argument that increasingly in American national politics, things get done that have nothing to do with elections, see Ginsberg and Shefter 1990.

4. See, e.g., Barber 1984, Dahl 1989, and Fishkin 1991.

5. Converse, Eulau, and Miller 1982, pp. 33–34.

6. For evidence that elections perform this service, if incompletely and imperfectly, see esp. Key 1961; Hibbs 1987; Cameron 1978; Bunce 1981; and Verba and Nie 1972.

7. Myrdal 1944, p. 449.

8. Quoted in Foner 1955, 4:159–160. Much the same theme surfaces in Stokely Carmichael and Charles Hamilton's *Black Power*, widely regarded at the time of its appearance as a radical attack upon the nonviolent tactics and gradualism of the established civil rights leadership. *Black Power* nevertheless emphasized the importance of the vote. Carmichael and Hamilton argued (1967, pp. 103–105) that by demanding and then exercising the franchise, southern blacks took their first step of resistance to racial oppression:

> The black man who goes to register is saying to the white man, "No." He is saying: "You have said that I cannot vote. You have said that this is my place. This is where I should remain. You have contained me and I am saying 'No' to your containment. I am stepping out of bounds. I am saying 'No' to you and thereby creating a better life for myself. I am resisting someone who has contained me." That is what the first act does. The black person begins to live.

9. Shklar 1991, p. 3.

10. U.S. President's Committee on Civil Rights 1947, p. 139.

11. Quoted in Key 1949, p. 330. Fielding's speech was excerpted in the *Times-Picayune* (New Orleans), January 21, 1948.

12. Quoted in Sundquist 1983, p. 274.

13. Clifford commissioned this now famous memorandum on political strategy in

1948; James Rowe wrote it, and Clifford presented it to the president (Clifford and Hol-
broke 1991; McCullough 1992; Sundquist 1983).

14. Simkins and Roland 1972, p. 590.

15. *The State* (Columbia, S.C.), May 11, 1948. Quoted by Lamis 1990, p. 9.

16. Quoted in Black and Black 1992, pp. 143–144.

17. In these four states—South Carolina and Louisiana as well as Mississippi and
Alabama—the Dixiecrats succeeded in taking over the Democratic party, enabling them
to list Thurmond (not Truman) as the regular Democratic candidate (Key 1949).

18. On the formidable obstacles to third-party voting in the United States, see Rosenstone, Behr, and Lazarus 1984.

19. Key 1949, p. 666.

20. Sundquist 1983, p. 283. On the same point, also see Key 1949 and Heard 1952.

21. Sitkoff 1978.

22. See, e.g., Carmines and Stimson 1989; Pomper 1972.

23. Kelley 1966, p. 48.

24. Ibid.

25. Republican National Committee press release, transcript of a speech at Pikesville,
Maryland, October 21, 1964.

26. Kelley 1966, p. 55.

27. Campbell 1966b, pp 269–270.

28. Quoted in Kelley 1966, pp. 52, 53. The Republican platform conceded nothing to
the moderates; indeed, it repudiated past Republican policies. Amendments to the platform, including one that would endorse and continue the party's moderately progressive
position on civil rights, were crushed.

29. See, e.g., Converse, Clausen, and Miller 1965, p. 328.

30. Kessel provides the best defense of Goldwater and his campaign against the
charge of intentional racism (Kessel 1968, pp. 103–104; 188–189; 208–209; but also see
p. 216).

31. As Converse, Clausen, and Miller put it: "White supremacists in the South had
so long paraded under the states' rights banner as to leave little room for fear lest the
Goldwater gesture go unappreciated" (1965, p. 328; also see Hofstadter 1965).

32. Rovere 1965, p. 140. Rovere describes one such carnival in detail. It took place in
Cramton Bowl, just outside Montgomery, Alabama, on Goldwater's second night in the
black belt of the Old South:

> Some unsung Alabama Republican had hit upon an idea of breathtaking
> simplicity—to show the country the "lily-white" character of Republican-
> ism in Dixie by planting, for the Goldwater rally in the bowl, a great field of
> white lilies—living lilies, in perfect bloom, gorgeously arrayed. The night
> was soft; the stars and moon were bright; the grass in the bowl was impos-
> sibly green, as if it grew out of something far richer than dirt; the stadium
> lights did not destroy the colors and shadows of evening, but they lighted
> the turf so individual blades of grass could be seen. And sown on the turf
> were seven hundred Alabama girls in long white gowns, all of a whiteness
> as impossible as the greenness of the green. The girls came, we were told,
> from every one of Alabama's sixty-seven counties—from Tallapoosa and
> Bibb and Etowah and Coffee—as well as from Montgomery, Birmingham,

and Mobile. Their dresses were uniform only in color and length; taken all and all it was a triumph, among other things, of Alabama couture. ·

The sowing of lilies had been done about a half hour before the proceedings were to begin. The girls stood on the turf, each waving a small American flag, while the bands played and the arrangers made and announced last-minute arrangements. Then, right on schedule, an especially powerful light played on a stadium gate at about the fifty-yard line, and the candidate of the Republican Party rode in as slowly as a car can be made to go, first down past fifty or so yards of choice Southern womanhood, and then, after a sharp left at the goal line, past more girls to the gorgeously draped stand. It was all as solemn and as stylized as a review of troops by some such master of the art as General de Gaulle. The girls did not behave as troops—they swayed a bit as Goldwater passed, and sounds came from them—not squeals or shrieks, but pleasing and ladylike murmurs. And in a sense, of course, they *were* Goldwater's troops, as well as representatives of what the rest of his Southern troops—the thousands in the packed stands, the tens of thousands in Memphis and New Orleans and Atlanta and Shreveport and Greenville—passionately believed they were defending. (Pp. 141–142)

33. Black and Black 1992, p. 153.

34. With one famous exception: in the final days of the 1960 campaign, Kennedy placed a telephone call to Coretta King, whose husband was in jail, to offer his sympathy. Kennedy himself said almost nothing of this publicly, though according to Taylor Branch (1988), two million (!) copies of a pamphlet describing the incident were distributed outside black churches on the Sunday before election day.

35. Kennedy did instruct the Justice Department to place a higher priority on civil rights, and more litigation did indeed ensue, especially on school desegregation and voting rights cases—but with little or no effect. Schools in the South remained virtually as segregated early in the Kennedy administration as they had been before the *Brown* decision in 1954. In the case of voting-rights abuses, the strategy of litigation proved tedious, costly, and ineffective (Thernstrom 1987). Though he issued an executive order against discrimination in federal employment and strengthened federal efforts to reduce discrimination in the private sector, Kennedy also, under pressure from the southern congressional delegation, appointed several notorious racists to the federal bench. The president, to be sure, provided assistance and financial aid to voter registration efforts aimed at southern blacks. This effort was aimed at least in part at managing the civil rights movement, at redirecting activities away from the unruly and politically unpredictable business of boycotts, sit-ins, and marches, toward what was assumed to be (quite erroneously as things turned out) the more innocuous endeavor of voter registration (Piven and Cloward 1977; Meir and Rudwick 1975). In the spring of 1963, Kennedy submitted a civil rights bill to Congress but did little to secure its passage.

36. Woodward 1974, p. 175.

37. Kelley 1966, p. 63.

38. Ibid., p. 67.

39. White 1965.

40. Kelley 1966, p. 61.

41. Kessel 1968, pp. 295–296; Black and Black 1992, p. 155.

42. On the decisive nature of the 1964 outcome, see Kelley 1983.

43. See RePass 1971; Pomper 1972; Carmines and Stimson 1989; Campbell 1966b; and Converse, Clausen, and Miller 1965.

44. On this point of change in the politics of race in Congress, see the figures prepared by Carmines and Stimson 1989, pp. 63, 64.

45. Shafer 1983, p. 524. Shafer provides a highly detailed account of this period of party reform. Polsby (1983) covers some of the same ground, but with an eye more on the consequences of reform.

46. Jaynes and Williams 1989, p. 217, table 5-6.

47. Kousser 1974, 1992.

48. Myrdal 1944; Sitkoff 1978; Jaynes and Williams 1989.

49. Weiss 1983, p. 23.

50. Recollection of Clarence Mitchell, as disclosed in an interview with Nancy Weiss (1983, pp. 4–5).

51. Weiss 1983; Andersen 1979; Ladd and Hadley 1978.

52. Weiss 1983, pp. xiv, xvi.

53. Weiss 1983; Sitkoff 1978.

54. Weiss 1983, p. 211. Also see Myrdal 1944, p. 74.

55. In 1936, the colored division "provided speakers and publicity, sponsored rallies, secured endorsements . . . from well-known blacks, and encouraged voter registration" (Weiss 1983, p. 192).

56. Quoted in ibid., p. 200. On the New Deal and race, see, in addition, Skocpol 1988 and Sitkoff 1978.

57. See, e.g., Barton Bernstein (1968), who concludes that the New Deal was a less radical intrusion upon American politics than it seemed at the time, and that blacks in particular were excluded from the new order that Roosevelt's programs sought to create.

58. Sitkoff 1978, pp. 106–107.

59. Key 1949, pp. 560–576. The Twenty-fourth Amendment applied to federal elections exclusively. Two years later, the Supreme Court abolished poll taxes altogether, in *Harper* v. *Virginia State Board of Elections*, U.S. 663 (1966).

60. Mathews and Prothro 1966; Lawson 1976; and Rosenstone and Hansen 1993. At the same time, these activities provoked an intense and often violent counterreaction. The ironic consequence was that the civil rights movement increased electoral participation of blacks and white voters, and in roughly equal measure (Rosenstone and Hansen 1993; Stanley 1987).

61. Rosenstone and Hansen 1993.

62. Stanley 1987; Watters and Cleghorn 1967. The quotation comes from Attorney General Patterson of Mississippi in August 1965, cited in Stanley 1987, p. 95.

63. Rosenstone and Hansen 1993, p. 203.

64. Chandler Davidson 1992, p. 7. In response to the obvious success of the Voting Rights Act, the forces of southern reaction were not idle. They promptly began to convert single-member districts to at-large electoral systems (so that, under the at-large arrangement, black minorities would be unable to overcome bloc voting by white majorities against black candidates); to re-draw district lines in creative ways so as to divide black electoral strength; to annex areas where whites were numerically dominant in order to reduce black electoral strength in the original district; and to remake elected positions into appointed ones. All these contrivances were intended to have the effect of diminish-

ing—or *diluting*—the power of blacks in electoral politics without ostentatiously interfering in the constitutionally protected right to register and to vote.

In part to cope with such diluting maneuvers, the Voting Rights Act has evolved over the years. Its several extensions and the case law built up around it have grown increasingly controversial. The major bone of contention is the extent to which the Voting Rights Act now mandates proportional representation—or as the critics would say, the extent to which it has been subverted from the intentions of its original framers to become a vehicle for racial quotas in public office. For a history of the evolution of the Voting Rights Act, and for sharply contrasting views on the meaning and wisdom of voting rights law today, see Thernstrom 1987; Karlan and McCrary 1988; and Kousser 1992.

65. Black and Black 1987, p. 260.

66. Quoted in Tindall 1967, p. 166. On the Solid South following Reconstruction, see Kousser 1974, 1992; and Foner 1988.

67. Black and Black 1992, p. 141. Key introduced his classic analysis of southern politics, issued at the midpoint of the twentieth century, with the claim that, "In its grand outlines, the politics of the South revolves around the position of the Negro" (p. 5)—and then proceeded over the next 700 pages to make the case convincingly. On this point also see Kousser 1974, 1992; Van Woodward 1951; and Foner 1988.

68. Converse 1966, p. 212.

69. Ibid., p. 220.

70. Converse knew full well the dangers of such predictions; he offered the linear prediction to make the "snail's pace" change he observed concrete. The best single account of the sweeping changes that have transformed the American South since midcentury is Black and Black (1987).

71. The sharp decline in Democratic partisanship we see in figure 8.5 holds for southern whites alone. Outside the South, whites were becoming slightly more Democratic (Miller 1992). And among southern whites, both generational and period effects are apparent. In particular, the postwar cohort of southern whites, those who came of age politically from 1946 (as Thurmond was about to lead the Dixiecrat revolt) and 1964 (the turning point), moved sharply away from the Democratic party in the middle to late 1960s (Beck 1977; Black and Black 1987). Another change evident in figure 8.5 is the gradual decline, among southern whites, in Democratic loyalty during the Reagan years, interrupted momentarily by the 1982 recession. Finally, although the evidence isn't all that reliable, based as it is on small samples, it would appear that the change among blacks seen in figure 8.5 is a national movement, occurring among blacks inside and outside the South in roughly equal measure. The movement is perhaps a bit sharper and more rapid among southern blacks, whose partisanship was less developed heading into the critical period of 1964–68, though it is hard to say with confidence (Converse 1972).

72. Migration is entirely invisible in figure 8.5, since it presents the partisanship of *native* southern whites.

73. Fiorina 1981; Hibbs 1987; and MacKuen, Erickson, and Stimson 1989.

74. Key 1955, p. 16.

75. The most important work on realignment theory can be found in Campbell 1966a; Burnham 1970; Sundquist 1973; Beck 1974; and Clubb, Flanigan, and Zingale 1980. An excellent guide to the now-vast literature on realignment is provided by the essays collected in Shafer 1991.

76. See, e.g., Silbey 1991.

77. McAdam 1982.
78. Stanley 1987; Jaynes and Williams 1989.
79. Converse 1972, pp. 305–306; 312–313.
80. For accounts of this change sympathetic to our own, see Sundquist (1983) and, to a lesser extent, Black and Black (1992). Surprisingly, many analysts who have tried to explain the decline of the solid Democratic South have concluded that race figures rather little in it (e.g, Beck 1977; Ladd and Hadley 1978; Campbell 1977; Wolfinger and Arseneau 1978).
81. With this in mind, Paul Beck has referred to the changes we have been discussing as a *de*-alignment (Beck 1977).
82. Key 1949.
83. Sundquist 1983.
84. Black and Black 1987, p. 281.
85. Campaign speeches as quoted in the Jackson *Clarion-Ledger*, June 14; July 2; July 15; July 16, 1959. Passages appear in Black 1971.
86. Black 1976, p. 13. The famous quotation is taken from Phillips 1928, p. 31.
87. Black 1976, p. 14.
88. Ibid., p. 304.
89. Himelstein 1983, p. 156.
90. Ibid.
91. Wolfinger and Greenstein 1968, p. 764. Proposition 14 was declared unconstitutional by the U.S. Supreme Court in the spring of 1967.
92. Rovere 1965, p. 143. Rovere's point is restated in essentially the same form by Converse, Clausen, and Miller 1965; Kelley 1966; and Hofstadter 1965.
93. Page 1978, p. 82.
94. Ibid., pp. 200–202.
95. Ambrose 1987, pp. 144–145.
96. Axelrod 1972. As president, Nixon delivered on the implicit promises of his 1968 campaign. During his first term, he nominated three southern conservatives to the Supreme Court, forced the liberal chairman of the Civil Rights Commission to resign, opposed the extension of the Voting Rights Act of 1965, delayed the Johnson administration's fall 1969 school desegregation deadline, watered down desegregation plans for twenty-one South Carolina school districts, ordered cabinet departments to slow down desegregation of Mississippi's public schools, and directed the Justice Department to file a brief with the Supreme Court arguing against desegregation, the first time the government had done so on a major civil rights case since *Brown v. Board of Education*.
97. Speech quoted in Frady 1968, pp. 141–142.
98. *Newsweek*, June 1, 1964.
99. See, e.g., Page 1978; Lipset and Raab 1970. A report prepared for the American Jewish Committee in 1968 (cited in Lipset and Raab 1970, p. 355) concluded that "local and state headquarters were devoid of any material even faintly suggesting an aroma of bigotry. Indeed not only was there no distribution of anti-Semitic material, there was surprisingly no national circulation of anti-Negro material; this despite enthusiastic support given to Wallace by the racist White Citizens Councils and the Klan."
100. Quoted in Frady 1968, pp. 6–7. For a description of Wallace's campaign for the presidency in 1968, see Page 1978; Wills 1971; and Lipset and Raab 1970.
101. Duke's several campaigns are described in a front-page article in the *New York*

Times, June 18, 1990, and summarized in essays by Moore 1992 and Esolen 1992. On prejudice as the foundation of Duke's appeal, see Howell and Warren 1992 and Rose 1992.

For more on racial codewords, see Luebke (1990) and Edsall and Edsall (1992, Chapter 10 and Afterword), who argue that during the Reagan years, the various terms "taxes," "special interests," and "liberalism" have taken on racial connotations. We should keep in mind that even Strom Thurmond, way back in 1948, watched what he said, according to Black and Black's recapitulation of the Dixiecrat campaign (1992, pp. 143, 144).

CHAPTER NINE

1. See, e.g., Burnham 1989; Pomper 1989a; and McWilliams 1989.

2. Michael Dawson and Tali Mendelberg contributed to our reconstruction of the 1988 campaign, which draws on a variety of sources: Black and Oliphant 1989; Drew 1989; Edsall and Edsall 1992; Jamieson 1992; Pomper 1989b; numerous conversations with reporters covering the campaign; and our own clipping file of stories that first appeared in the *New York Times, Washington Post, Newsweek,* and several large-circulation periodicals that cater primarily to black audiences.

3. Cain, Lewis, and Rivers 1989.

4. The quotation appears in Drew 1989, p. 346.

5. For public opinion evidence on this point, see Sigelman and Welch 1991; Dawson 1995.

6. Williams (1987) estimated that the Republican National Committee spent twenty times the money on outreach to Hispanic Americans that it did on black Americans.

7. Drew 1989, p. 266.

8. Ibid., p. 304.

9. As the controversy over "Weekend Passes" grew, Americans for Bush announced that it would pull the commercial off the air if so requested by the Bush campaign. And the Bush campaign then did so—but the request came nearly three weeks after the Americans for Bush announcement, twenty-five days after the commercial had begun to run, and just three days before its scheduled expiration.

10. According to the evidence presented by West 1993.

11. Runkel 1989, p. 117.

12. According to Drew (1989), Dukakis meant to declare himself a *Democrat* in the tradition of Harry Truman and John Kennedy, and said liberal by mistake. After a vigorous private discussion, the Dukakis campaign decided to continue saying liberal rather than endure the embarrassment of admitting the error.

13. According to exit polls, just 4% of black votes in Democratic primaries went to Dukakis (Pomper 1989c, p. 47).

14. Dukakis then proceeded to do it (Drew 1989, p. 333).

15. "CBS Evening News," October 27.

16. The notion of priming is developed and tested in Iyengar and Kinder (1987).

17. Simon 1979, p. 3.

18. For reviews of the evidence on accessibility, see Fischhoff, Slovic, and Lichtenstein 1980; and Fiske and Taylor 1992.

19. For evidence on priming in political settings, see Iyengar and Kinder 1987 and Krosnick and Kinder 1990.

20. *Congressional Quarterly Weekly Report,* January 21, 1989. The NES estimate is based

on the postelection reports of those respondents who were subsequently determined, in an independent study, to have voted (*validated* voters, in NES terminology).

21. As elsewhere in our analysis, "white" includes nonblacks of Hispanic origin. In the NES survey, 35% of Hispanics reported voting for Bush.

22. 22.0%, to be exact. For the purpose of this analysis, we coded responses to the open-ended questions into two categories: hard line on crime, including support for the death penalty (Master Code nos. 974–978, 1042); and soft line on crime, including opposition to the death penalty (969–973, 1041).

23. Jencks 1991.

24. On who would make the "best" president, the difference among white voters is fourteen percentage points; on effectiveness on the drug problem, also fourteen points; and on cares about the environment, no difference at all.

25. These results are summarized in Farah and Klein 1989.

26. The four are:

Irish, Italian, Jewish and many other minorities overcame prejudice and worked their way up. Blacks should do the same without any special favors.

Over the past few years, blacks have gotten less than they deserve.

It's really a matter of some people not trying hard enough; if blacks would only try harder they could be just as well off as whites.

Generations of slavery and discrimination have created conditions that make it difficult for blacks to work their way out of the lower class.

Note that two of the questions were written so that agreement represents a racially resentful answer, while in the other two, a resentful response requires disagreement. Thus, when answers are averaged together, the four questions together effectively cancel whatever acquiescence bias might be operating.

27. In figure 9.1 and in all the analysis that follows, racial resentment is represented by a linear composite scale, based on answers to the individual questions. In creating the scale, as before, we weighted each of the four questions equally. With all four items included, the reliability of the overall scale, as indicated by Cronbach's *alpha* coefficient, is .74. The scale is centered at .61 (where 0 = racially sympathetic and 1 = racially resentful), with standard deviation of .22.

In one form of the 1988 NES postelection survey, the four questions were asked in consecutive order; in a second form, presented to the other half of the sample, they were scattered in different, widely spaced sections of the questionnaire. Form was utterly unrelated to mean response to the four questions, but it was slightly associated with the strength of relationship between responses to the four questions. When they were asked consecutively, the average interitem Pearson *r* was .45 (and the corresponding Cronbach's *alpha*, .77); when they were asked apart, the average Pearson *r* was .39 (and the corresponding Cronbach's *alpha*, .71). These differences are sufficiently anemic to be reassuring that the questions are really measuring a settled view (not a nonattitude). Moreover, as a practical matter, the results allow us in the analyses that follow to ignore whether the questions appeared together or apart.

28. A statistical test confirms what the eye can see in figure 9.1: that the association between vote and resentment is linear. F-test for deviation from linearity: $F_{1,8} = 1.17$ (p > .3).

29. On party loyalty and the vote, see Campbell et al. 1960 and Fiorina 1981; on policy

voting, Key 1966 and Page and Brody 1972; on the electoral effects of retrospective assessments of personal and national conditions, Kramer 1971, Fiorina 1981, and Kinder and Kiewiet 1981; and on the effect of the retiring incumbent's reputation, Converse et al. 1966 and Converse et al. 1969. For general reviews of the vast literature on voters and elections, see Converse 1975, Kinder and Sears 1985, and Dalton and Wattenberg 1993.

30. In equation form, these various claims can be written as:

$$(9.1) \text{ Vote} = a_0 + B_1 \text{ Party Identification}$$
$$+ B_2 \text{ Social Welfare Policy}$$
$$+ B_3 \text{ Foreign Policy}$$
$$+ B_4 \text{ Assessment of National Economy}$$
$$+ B_5 \text{ Evaluation of Reagan}$$
$$+ B_6 \text{ Evaluation of Jackson}$$

31. In a recent paper, Abramowitz (1994) concludes that "racial attitudes had a negligible impact on whites' candidate preference in the 1988 presidential election" (p. 1). But Abramowitz looks only at views on racial issues and only at direct effects. We examine racial resentments, take into account direct and indirect effects, and come to a very different conclusion.

32. On the general point, see Edelman 1964; and on the 1988 campaign in particular, Pomper 1989a.

33. Under this specification, the estimated effect of racial resentment diminished slightly and insignificantly, by about 10%. More generally, our estimate of the effect of racial resentment on the vote in 1988 of course depends upon the particular assumptions we make—but as things turned out, not too much. When we reestimated the reduced-form equation, this time setting whites of Hispanic origins aside, the estimated effect of racial resentment was completely unaffected. If views on social welfare policy were included in the equation (a move we oppose, since it rules out the highly plausible possibility that racial resentment affects the vote partly by affecting views on social welfare policy), then the impact of racial resentment declined somewhat. It was diminished further when we also included in the reduced-form equation views on foreign policy (a move that we also think is wrong-headed, and for the same reason). Still, when both views on social welfare and foreign policy were included, the impact on racial resentment remained significant and sizable (probit coefficient = .61, se = .32). As a final alternative, we entertained the possibility that racial resentment influenced the vote through its effect on partisanship. This is hardly wild-eyed, in view of claims about the racial reorientation of the American party system (e.g., Carmines and Stimson 1989; Huckfeldt and Kohfeld 1989). When we removed partisanship from the reduced-form equation of the vote, the estimated impact of racial resentment increased noticeably (probit coefficient = 1.43, se = .26). In short, results from these various "specification experiments" give us confidence that racial resentment made a real difference in 1988.

34. See the account offered by Elizabeth Drew 1989, p. 304.

35. We also replaced reported vote taken from the postelection survey with intended vote as expressed in the preelection survey. The object of this analysis is to estimate the impact of racial resentment on vote, conditioned on how large a "dose" of the Horton story voters had likely absorbed. For this purpose, we examine vote intention as expressed at the time of the preelection interview.

36. This result is not a consequence of the election's drawing near. If that were true, then considerations in addition to racial resentment should be increasing their impact on

the vote as well. But we see no evidence of this. We added a series of multiplicative terms to the reduced form equation, one to see whether the impact of national economic assessments on the vote was increasing as the Horton initiative grew more prominent (E * Assessment of national economy), another for Democratic identification (E * Democrat), and still a third for Republican identification (E * Republican). Not one of the three coefficients was statistically significant, nor was the estimate of the impact of racial resentment disturbed by the addition of these terms. In short, the increasing impact of racial resentment on the vote in 1988 seems to be attributable to the racial content of the Republican campaign.

37. It failed to show up in one other place: on cooperation with the Soviet Union, where black voters saw Bush and Reagan as equally conservative. This exception can perhaps be attributed to the president's successful pursuit of a nuclear arms treaty.

38. Landry 1987; Jaynes and Williams 1989; Farley and Allen 1987.

39. As in Dahl 1961.

40. In each instance, $p > .25$. Comparably weak results are also found in our analysis of the 1988 National Black Election Study (Kinder, Mendelberg, and Dawson 1994). It could be that the slight negative association we find in 1988 between class and Republican vote is declining, that a shift in the direction of the kind of class voting that Wilson and others imagined is in fact under way. Because our cross-sectional analysis, limited to 1988 alone, is blind to this possibility, we undertook an analysis of the relationship between indicators of class and the vote among blacks in each of the National Election Studies conducted between 1964 and 1984. We found no hint in this evidence that class-based voting among blacks is beginning to emerge.

41. See, e.g., McAdam 1982; Sears and McConahay 1973; Gurin, Hatchett, and Jackson 1989; Tate 1993; Rhodebeck 1986; and Dawson 1995.

42. Pearson $r = .14$. We coded the scale to range from 0 to 1, where 0 means that the respondent failed to select blacks as a group that they felt close to and rated blacks coolly, and 1 is given to those who claimed to feel close to blacks and who evaluated blacks warmly. The distribution of responses on this scale is tilted toward the racial group identification end. Slightly more than one-half of the blacks questioned by NES in 1988 ended up with a perfect score of 1 (54.1% to be precise), and the overall mean lies well to the positive side of the neutral point (mean = .65).

43. The "vote" equation includes as right-hand-side variables, in addition to racial group identification, measures of class (family income, head of household occupational status, education, and employment status), social background (region, gender), change in family economic well-being, assessments of change in the economic well-being of the country, and race of interviewer.

44. Reported in Kinder, Mendelberg, and Dawson 1994.

45. Farah and Klein 1989; Hershey 1989; Quirk 1989.

46. For corroborating results on the power of the Horton issue to activate prejudice, based on experimental research, see Mendelberg 1992.

47. Rosenstone and Hansen 1993.

48. Schudson 1978, p. 185.

49. Woodward 1988, p. 14.

50. Quoted in Runkel 1989, p. 115.

51. Brunvard 1984, p. ix. For a description of the modern legend of the "mutilated boy," see pp. 78–92.

52. Estrich 1989, p. 10.

53. As the aging civil-rights activist is described in *Civil Wars,* Rosellen Brown's 1984 novel.

54. For an overview of the 1992 campaign, and the results of our side-by-side analysis of the white vote in 1988 and 1992, see Kinder and Tamerius 1994.

55. That the 1992 campaign was comparatively free of the racism that plagued the 1988 contest, and consequently that white voters were less preoccupied with racial resentment, are all to the good. But there is another and more discouraging way to read the 1992 campaign. As racial resentment was fading away in 1992, moral conservatism was gaining ground. Gay rights and abortion on demand replaced crime and capital punishment as the central social issues of the campaign. As a consequence, anxieties and apprehensions over changes in moral standards, centered especially on matters of sexuality and challenges to traditional family arrangements, were more important to the white vote in 1992 than in 1988 (these results are also presented in Kinder and Tamerius 1994). If the 1992 campaign merely exchanged sexual apprehensions and hostilities for the racial ones prominent four years before, then the apparent improvement for democratic process— for government by discussion—is far less than first meets the eye.

CHAPTER TEN

1. Du Bois 1990, p. 3. Several pages later (at p. 16), Du Bois repeats and elaborates his prediction: "The problem of the twentieth century is the problem of the color-line,—the relation of the darker to the lighter races of men in Asia and Africa, in America and the islands of the sea."

2. Campbell et al. 1960, p. 205.

3. For useful surveys of the empirical literature, see Citrin and Green 1990; and Sears and Funk 1991.

4. See Verba and Orren 1985, p. 248.

5. All three of these conditions were clearly in place during the battle over Proposition 13 in California in 1978. Thanks to massive publicity, Californians came to understand that if 13 passed, homeowners would receive very substantial reductions in their property tax bills, while an assortment of public services—schools, libraries, police and fire departments, and more—would be drastically cut. In this particular and special case, then, the benefits and harms at stake were unusually large, well advertised, and, because they were written into the referendum, virtually certain to take effect. Sure enough, under these conditions, self-interest emerged as a powerful force in public opinion. Support for Proposition 13 was disproportionate among homeowners, the more so as their anticipated savings grew and as their feeling of tax burden increased. Meanwhile, opposition was strongest among public employees, those whose livelihoods appeared to be on the line (Sears and Citrin 1982). For similar findings, on public support for tax cuts embodied in the 1978 Tax Revenue Act, see Hawthorne and Jackson 1987.

6. For comparable results, see Young et al. (1987, 1991), where citizens are more likely to express views consistent with their interests after overhearing an ostensibly unrelated conversation that prominently featured self-interest arguments as against one that featured political arguments framed in terms of moral principles; and Sears and Lau (1983), who demonstrate how self-interest can be primed by artful arrangement of survey questions.

7. Real effects in real campaigns are reported by Sears and Citrin (1982) on California

Proposition 13; Courant, Gramlich, and Rubinfield (1980) on a set of Michigan tax-cutting proposals; and Hawthorne and Jackson (1987) on the 1978 Federal Tax Revenue Act. Zero effects of self-interest on tax preferences in hypothetical settings are reported by Beck and Dye (1982) and Lowrey and Sigelman (1981), among others.

8. Why the links between self-interest and public opinion are typically so tenuous is unclear: the literature is more persuasive on the empirical demonstration that self-interest matters little than it is in testing among various arguments about why that might be so. The unexpectedly low profile of self-interest in public opinion has become a playground for interesting speculation.

For instance, the disjuncture between interests and opinions might reflect a deeper truth that people don't know what their interests really are. And even if citizens know what they want, they may not see a way to get it: they may lack the information and intellectual skills required for instrumental behavior, perhaps especially in the realm of politics. Such skepticism runs deep in psychology, from Freud's analysis of the unconscious to Simon's accounts of bounded rationality. Or perhaps the limited role of self-interest in public opinion is a reflection of a distinctive culture of politics, which socializes citizens "to behave in the general interest and to justify their choice in ethical terms" (Citrin and Green 1990, p. 20; also see Wilson and Banfield 1964 on "public-regardingness" in political life). Or perhaps interests are disengaged because the political realm is utterly unimportant: citizens believe whatever they want because no discernible consequences follow. This view is most often associated with Schumpeter's (1942) scathing attack on "classical democracy"; also see Edelman (1964) for a different but related variation on this theme. Or perhaps interests are overwhelmed by emotionally powerful predispositions acquired early in life that are triggered by contemporary conflicts, as Sears (1988) has argued. Or, finally, perhaps the faint impression left by self-interest on public opinion is a reflection of the disjuncture between symbol-laden communication from journalists and politicians, on the one hand, and the messy, atomized world of private experience, on the other (Sniderman and Brody 1977; Kinder and Mebane 1983).

9. Stouffer et al. 1949; Runciman 1966.

10. Geschwender and Geschwender 1973. For additional examples that make the same point, see Orbell 1967; Kinder, Adams, and Gronke 1989; Vannemann and Pettigrew 1972; Abeles 1976; and Useem 1980.

11. In Converse's (1964) original classification, some 42% of the American public did so.

12. Campbell et al. 1960, p. 234.

13. Converse's (1964) original findings seem quite representative of other times and places. Many things have changed since 1956, but references to groups continue to occupy a central place in citizens' appraisals of parties and candidates—and not only in the United States. See Kagy and Caldeira 1980; Key 1961; Klingemann 1979; and Rhodebeck 1986.

14. Most notably, Bobo 1988a; Coser 1956; and Sherif et al. 1961.

15. Sears and McConahay 1973; Aberbach and Walker 1973.

16. Rieder 1985, pp. 69, 111. Gordon Allport (1979) makes a similar point in his discussion of the application of realistic group conflict theory to American race relations.

17. These results come from a June 1990 *New York Times*/WCBS poll, reported in the national edition of the *Times* on October 29, 1990. On the possibility that black elected officials are harassed and persecuted by their own government, 77% of black New Yorkers

said that such a thing was true or might possibly be true, compared with 34% of whites. Nearly as many blacks agreed that crack cocaine is distributed in black communities in order to immobilize them: 60% of blacks, compared with just 16% of whites, said that such a thing was true or might possibly be true. And nearly one-third of black New Yorkers agreed with the proposition that HIV was created in order to exterminate the black race: 29% of blacks versus 5% of whites. For an analysis and classification of such "delusions," see Turner 1993.

18. As in the Justice Department's infiltration of the civil rights movement (Garrow 1983) and the notorious Tuskegee syphilis study (Jones 1993).

19. See, e.g., Jordan 1968; Fredrickson 1971; van den Berghe 1967; and Wilson 1973.

20. According to Scott (1986, p. 34), the history of American plantation slavery is replete with accounts of "foot dragging, false compliance, flight, feigned ignorance, sabotage, theft, and, not least, cultural resistance."

21. Freehling 1966, p. 51; also see Channing 1970; Wade 1964.

22. Quote from Mendelberg 1994.

23. Jordan 1968, pp. 114–115.

24. If self-interest plays a small and often invisible role in opinion, it appears to loom larger when it comes to behavior. Thus parents of school-age children are more likely to take an active part in the affairs of the local school board, and white parents of school-age children are more likely to participate in antibusing organizations (Jennings 1979; Green and Cowden 1992). Self-interest predicts not the positions people take on public issues, then, but whether or not they act on their opinions, whatever their opinions might be.

Public opinion is one of several forces that contribute to the formation of government policy. It seems reasonable to suppose that the contribution of opinion to policy is carried primarily by those members of the public who take an active part in politics. Opinion backed by interest is more likely to be given voice and therefore more likely to have an impact. Insofar as self-interest motivates political action, its political importance is at least partially redeemed.

Finally, that self-interest predicts behavior so consistently, using the same measures of self-interest that predict opinion so poorly, moves against the idea that self-interest's problem in predicting public opinion is one of measurement. Were that true, self-interest would fail to predict behavior, too.

25. Horowitz 1985.

26. Higham 1988.

27. Lipset and Raab 1970.

28. Sullivan, Piereson, and Marcus 1982; Gibson 1988.

29. Stigler 1975, pp. 238, 241.

30. Abramowitz (1994) disagrees, arguing that "white voters have been moving toward the Republican party out of disillusionment with the welfare state, rather than hostility to civil rights" (p. 23), but the evidence he presents is generally irrelevant to the major claims that Carmines and Stimson advance.

31. Carmines and Stimson 1989, p. 191.

32. Ibid., p. 190.

33. Schelling 1978; Huckfeldt and Kohfeld 1989, p. 16.

34. Hyman and Sheatsley 1956, 1964; Greeley and Sheatsley 1974; Taylor, Sheatsley, and Greeley 1978; Smith and Sheatsley 1984; and GSS News 1991.

35. Smith and Sheatsley 1984, p. 50.

36. Sniderman and Piazza 1993, p. 5.

37. Gilens 1993.

38. Ibid.

39. Epstein 1973. On racial coding and crime, see Edsall and Edsall 1992; and Gross 1993.

40. Especially devastating were the essays collected in Christie and Jahoda 1954.

41. The most important studies are Martin and Westie 1959; Williams 1964; Selznick and Steinberg 1969; and esp. Altemeyer 1981, 1988. Roger Brown's essay (1965), written as a chapter for the first edition of his textbook on social psychology, remains the most judicious presentation of *The Authoritarian Personality*, the methodological hue and cry that it provoked, and what remained after the dust settled.

42. Adorno et al. 1950, p. 149.

43. To be fair, Levinson and his associates initiated their investigation hoping to illuminate the nature and origins of anti-Semitism and its implications for democratic society. They deliberately restricted their attention to why it was some were more ready than others to accept anti-Semitic ideology. Their object was to develop a psychology of prejudice, to understand why some people accept prejudice while others reject it. They never intended their study, massive as it was, to provide a comprehensive account of prejudice.

44. This contrast holds across different model specifications and political periods, and so we are inclined to take it seriously.

45. Gamson 1992, p. 149.

46. Feldman 1988, p. 418; Feldman and Zaller 1992, pp. 292, 272.

47. Specification and results are presented in Appendix B, table B8.

48. This argument is made, in somewhat different form, by Sniderman 1975; Mc-Closky and Zaller 1984; McClosky and Brill 1983; and Zaller 1992.

49. Myrdal 1944, p. lxix.

50. Du Bois 1990; Smith 1993.

51. Verba et al. 1987, p. 94.

52. Also see Popkin 1991, pp. 81–91.

53. This section draws in part on Kinder and Herzog 1993.

54. For Mill's view of deliberation, we draw primarily on *Considerations on Representative Government* (1951a) and *On Liberty* (1951b). Quotes are from Mill 1951b, pp. 28, 27.

55. *The Federalist Papers No. 71* (Madison, Hamilton, and Jay 1987, p. 432).

56. Dahl 1989; Habermas 1982; and Fishkin 1991.

57. E.g., Mansbridge 1991; Barber 1984; Dewey 1927.

58. Schumpeter 1942, pp. 257, 262.

59. Converse 1964, p. 213.

60. Hirschman 1991, p. 170.

61. Riker 1982, p. 209.

62. Our research on framing gives but a glimpse of democratic discussion. For one thing, we have had little to say about the origins of frames, and about why some succeed while others fail. How much latitude do elites enjoy in defining issues? How constrained are they by their expectations of what the public will find acceptable? Another limitation of our analysis is that we have examined just one form of deliberation or discussion: elite talk aimed at the general public. But conversation goes on in a multitude of places, between and among a variety of participants. We know much less about this than we should, about how ideas and arguments and frames circulate through society, being en-

riched and simplified and in other ways transformed as they move (for an excellent start on this problem, see Page and Shapiro 1992). Our picture is incomplete, finally, because elites do more than promote and endorse frames. Among other things, they take and advertise specific positions: they support or oppose the Civil Rights Act, they vote for or against war in the Persian Gulf, they endorse or ridicule the Crime Bill. How loud and clear this signaling of positions is, and how closely citizens follow it, have powerful consequences for public opinion, as Zaller (1992) has recently demonstrated.

63. U.S. National Advisory Commission on Civil Disorders 1968, p. 1.

64. This evidence and more is ably summarized by Jaynes and Williams 1989; and Farley and Allen 1987.

65. Farley and Allen 1987; Lieberson 1980; Massey and Denton 1993.

66. For Asian and Hispanic Americans, by contrast, the comparable figure is roughly 40–50% (Farley and Allen 1987; Massey and Denton 1993).

67. Again, this pattern can be contrasted with that for Hispanics and Asians, where money and education *are* tickets to a more integrated world (Farley and Allen 1987; Massey and Denton 1993).

68. Massey and Denton 1988.

69. After massive resistance and then some significant progress, school desegregation has ground to a halt (Orfield 1993). On the racial homogeneity of friendship circles, see Jackman and Crane 1986. On racial segregation of churches and places of employment, see Jaynes and Williams 1989. And on the astonishing power of the color line in marriage, consult Lieberson and Waters 1988.

70. Farley and Allen 1987, pp. 155–157; Massey and Denton 1993, pp. 149–153. On the underclass, see Massey and Denton (1993), who argue that racial segregation, in combination with the economic dislocations that visited rustbelt cities in the 1970s, produced explosive concentrations of poverty. Spatial concentrations of poverty, in turn, produced dilapidated neighborhoods, inadequate schools, broken families, welfare dependence, epidemics of idleness, theft, violence, and drugs.

71. By no means are all of segregation's political consequences negative. Segregation offers opportunities for building group solidarity. It encourages the articulation of political interests held in common. It fosters the development of organizations to advance political objectives. It creates incentives for the emergence of local leadership. And it may eventually yield a bloc vote of sufficient size to catch the attention and interest of national parties and campaigns. On these various points, see, e.g., Kilson 1971.

72. On this point, see Pinderhughes's analysis of ethnic and racial politics in Chicago (1987).

73. For evidence consistent with this argument, see Kinder and Mendelberg 1995.

74. See Gross 1995.

75. Didion 1992, pp. 299–300.

76. Research on the linguistic aspects of segregation takes the racial divide one step further and suggests that our invocation of paradigms is not that far-fetched. Over the last twenty years, Labov and his associates have been studying Black English Vernacular (BEV), the dialect learned first by most blacks in the United States. BEV is highly consistent in grammar, pronunciation, and lexicon, and, according to Labov's studies, it is drifting further and further away from Standard American English. Whereas whites and blacks share a large part of the general English language, differences between them in grammar and pronunciation are growing and are already sufficient to warrant the claim

that their languages constitute separate systems. The differences are most pronounced for black Americans whose lives are most circumscribed by the ghetto, who have least contact with whites. Labov concludes that Philadelphia, where he has done most of his empirical work, but by clear implication the nation as a whole, is "separating into two distinct speech communities: white and black." See esp. Labov 1972, 1975; and Labov and Harris 1986.

77. *Notes on Virginia.* Passage quoted in Jordan 1968, p. 436.

78. Du Bois 1990, p. 14.

APPENDIX A

1. The term was introduced in Sears and Kinder (1971), and defined and elaborated upon in Kinder and Sears (1981); McConahay and Hough (1976); McConahay (1982); and Sears (1988).

2. Sears and Kinder 1971.

3. Kinder and Sears 1981, p. 416.

4. McConahay and Hough 1976, p. 38.

5. McConahay 1982, p. 707.

6. Pettigrew and Meertens 1995, p. 58.

7. Ibid., p. 71.

8. On symbolic racism and voting against black candidates, see Kinder and Sears 1981; McConahay and Hough 1976; and Sears and Kinder 1971; on symbolic racism and white opposition to various government policies, see McConahay 1982; Sears and Allen 1984; Kluegel and Smith 1983; Mendelberg 1994; and on racism and immigration in Western Europe, Pettigrew and Meertens 1995; and Jackson and Kirby 1991.

9. E.g., McConahay's conception is a bit different from that offered by Kinder and Sears in that it includes the conviction that American society has successfully rid itself of discrimination and that opportunities for blacks are now abundant.

10. Sniderman and Tetlock 1986a, pp. 24–25.

11. Sniderman and Hagen 1985, p. 110. On this point, also see Katz, Wackenhut, and Hass 1986; Brewer and Kramer 1985; Schuman, Steeh, and Bobo 1985.

12. Sears and Kinder 1985, p. 1141; McConahay and Hough 1976, p. 41; and Sears and McConahay 1973, p. 140.

13. See, e.g., the exchange of views between Kinder 1986 and Sniderman and Tetlock 1986a, 1986b in the *Journal of Social Issues;* between Sniderman and Hagen 1985 and Kinder and Mendelberg 1994; and between Bobo 1983 and Sears and Kinder 1985. Also Bobo 1988a; Sears 1988; Sidanius 1989; Weigel and Howes 1985.

14. See Bobo 1983; Sears and Kinder 1985; and Bobo again 1988a.

15. Bobo 1988a.

16. Ibid., p. 107.

17. Ibid., p. 106.

18. Blumer 1958b, p. 434.

Abeles, Ronald P. 1976. "Relative Deprivation, Rising Expectations, and Black Militancy." *Journal of Social Issues* 32:119–137.

Abelson, Robert P. 1976. "Social Psychology's Rational Man." In *Rationality and the Social Sciences*, ed. S. I. Benn and G. W. Mortimore. London: Routledge and Kegan Paul.

Aberbach, Joel D., and Jack L. Walker. 1973. *Race in the City*. Boston: Little, Brown.

Abercrombie, Nicholas, Stephen Hill, and Bryan S. Turner. 1980. *The Dominant Ideology Thesis*. London: George Allen and Unwin.

Abramowitz, Alan I. 1994. "Issue Evolution Reconsidered: Racial Attitudes and Partisanship in the U.S. Electorate." *American Journal of Political Science* 38: 1–24.

Achen, Christopher H. 1975. "Mass Political Attitudes and the Survey Response." *American Political Science Review* 69:1218–1231.

———. 1982. *Interpreting and Using Regression*. Sage University Paper series on Quantitative Applications in the Social Sciences, No. 29. Beverly Hills: Sage.

———. 1983. "Toward Theories of Data: The State of Political Methodology." In *Political Science: The State of the Discipline*, ed. Ada F. Finifter. Washington, DC: American Political Science Association.

———. 1985. *The Statistical Analysis of Quasi-Experiments*. Berkeley: University of California Press.

Adorno, Theodore W., Else Frenkel-Brunswick, Daniel J. Levinson, and R. Nevitt Sanford. 1950. *The Authoritarian Personality*. New York: Harper and Row.

Alford, Robert R. 1963. *Party and Society: The Anglo-American Democracies*. Chicago: Rand McNally.

Allport, Gordon W. [1954] 1979. *The Nature of Prejudice*. Reading, MA: Addison-Wesley.

Altemeyer, Bob. 1981. *Right-Wing Authoritarianism*. Winnipeg: University of Manitoba Press.

———. 1988. *Enemies of Freedom: Understanding Right-Wing Authoritarianism*. San Francisco: Jossey-Bass.

Ambrose, Stephen E. 1987. *Nixon*. New York: Simon and Schuster.

Andersen, Kristi. 1979. *The Creation of a Democratic Majority 1928–1936*. Chicago: University of Chicago Press.

Anderson, Barbara A., Brian D. Silver, and Paul R. Abramson. 1988. "The Effects of the Race of Interviewer on Race-Related Attitudes of Black Respondents in SRC/CPS National Election Studies." *Public Opinion Quarterly* 52:289–324.

Apostle, Richard A., Charles Y. Glock, Thomas Piazza, and Marijean Suelzle. 1983. *The Anatomy of Racial Attitudes*. Berkeley: University of California Press.

Arieli, Yehoshua. 1964. *Individualism and Nationalism in American Ideology*. Baltimore: Penguin.

Ashmore, Richard D. 1970. "Prejudice: Causes and Cures." In *Social Psychology*, ed. Barry Collins. Reading, MA: Addison-Wesley.

Axelrod, Robert. 1972. "Where the Votes Come From: An Analysis of Electoral Coalitions, 1952–1968." *American Political Science Review* 66:11–20.

———. 1986. "Presidential Election Coalitions in 1984." *American Political Science Review* 80:281–284.

Banton, Michael. 1977. *The Idea of Race*. London: Tavistock.

Barber, Benjamin, R. 1984. *Strong Democracy*. Berkeley: University of California Press.

Barry, Brian M. [1970] 1978. *Sociologists, Economists, and Democracy*. Chicago: University of Chicago Press.

———. [1965] 1990. *Political Argument*. Berkeley: University of California Press.

Bartels, Larry M. 1985. "Alternative Misspecifications in Simultaneous-Equation Models." *Political Methodology* 11:181–199.

———. 1990. "Five Approaches to Model Specification." *Political Methodologist* 3:2–6.

Beck, Paul Allen. 1974. "A Socialization Theory of Partisan Realignment." In *The Politics of Future Citizens*, ed. Richard Niemi et al. San Francisco: Jossey-Bass.

———. 1977. "Partisan Dealignment in the Postwar South." *American Political Science Review* 71:477–498.

Beck, Paul Allen, and T. R. Dye. 1982. "Sources of Public Opinion on Taxes: The Florida Case." *Journal of Politics* 44:172–182.

Bellah, Robert N., Richard Madsen, William N. Sullivan, Ann Swidler, and Steven M. Tipton. 1985. *Habits of the Heart: Individualism and Commitment in American Life*. Berkeley: University of California Press.

Benedict, Ruth. 1934. *Patterns of Culture*. Boston: Houghton, Mifflin.

Bernstein, Barton. 1968. *Towards a New Past*. New York: Pantheon.

Black, Christine M., and Thomas Oliphant. 1989. *All by Myself: The Unmaking of a Presidential Campaign*. Chester, CT: Globe Pequot Press.

Black, Earl. 1971. "Southern Governors and Political Change: Campaign Stances on Racial Segregation and Economic Development, 1950–1969." *Journal of Politics* 33:719–726.

———. 1976. *Southern Governors and Civil Rights*. Cambridge, MA: Harvard University Press.

Black, Earl, and Merle Black. 1987. *Politics and Society in the South*. Cambridge, MA: Harvard University Press.

———. 1992. *The Vital South*. Cambridge, MA: Harvard University Press.

Blalock, Herbert M., Jr. 1967. *Toward a Theory of Minority-Group Relations*. New York: Wiley.

————. 1979. "Measurement and Conceptualization Problems: The Major Obstacle to Integrating Theory and Research." *American Sociological Review* 44:881–894.

Blauner, Bob. 1989. *Black Lives, White Lives.* Berkeley: University of California Press.

Blumer, Herbert. 1958a. "Race Prejudice as a Sense of Group Position." *Pacific Sociological Review* 1:3–7.

————. 1958b. "Recent Research on Race Relations: United States of America." *International Social Science Bulletin* 10:403–477.

Bobo, Lawrence. 1983. "Whites' Opposition to Busing: Symbolic Racism or Realistic Group Conflict?" *Journal of Personality and Social Psychology* 45:1196–1210.

————. 1988a. "Group Conflict, Prejudice, and the Paradox of Contemporary Racial Attitudes." In *Eliminating Racism: Profiles in Controversy,* ed. Phylis Katz and Dalmas A. Taylor. New York: Plenum.

————. 1988b. "Attitudes toward the Black Political Movement: Trends, Meaning, and the Effects on Racial Policy Attitudes." *Social Psychology Quarterly* 51:287–302.

————. 1991. "Social Responsibility, Individualism, and Redistributive Policies." *Sociological Forum* 6:71–92.

Bobo, Lawrence, Mary R. Jackman, James R. Kluegel, J. S. Reed, Howard Schuman, and A. W. Smith. 1988. "A Module Proposal on Intergroup Tolerance." Department of Sociology, University of California, Los Angeles. Typescript.

Bobo, Lawrence, and James R. Kleugel. 1993. "Opposition to Race Targeting: Self-Interest, Stratification Ideology, or Racial Attitudes?" *American Sociological Review* 58:443–464.

Bobo, Lawrence, Camille L. Zubrinsky, James H. Johnson, Jr., and Melvin L. Oliver. 1994. "Public Opinion before and after a Spring of Discontent." In *The Los Angeles Riots: Lessons for the Urban Future,* ed. Mark Baldassare. Boulder, CO: Westview.

Bollen, Kenneth A. 1989. *Structural Equations with Latent Variables.* New York: Wiley.

Bonacich, Edna. 1972. "A Theory of Ethnic Antagonism: The Split Labor Market." *American Sociological Review* 37:547–559.

————. 1976. "Advanced Capitalism and Black/White Relations in the United States." *American Sociological Review* 41:34–51.

Bradburn, Norman M., et. al. 1979. *Improving Interview Method and Questionnaire Design.* San Francisco: Jossey-Bass.

Branch, Taylor. 1988. *Parting the Waters.* New York: Simon and Schuster.

Brehm, John. 1990. "Opinion Surveys and Political Representation." Ph.D. diss., Department of Political Science, University of Michigan.

Brewer, Marilyn B. 1979. "The Role of Ethnocentrism in Intergroup Conflict." In *The Social Psychology of Intergroup Relations,* ed. William G. Austin and Stephen Worchel. Monterey, CA: Brooks/Cole.

Brewer, Marilyn B., and Roderick M. Kramer. 1985. "The Psychology of Intergroup Relations and Behavior." *Annual Review of Psychology* 36:219–244.

Brown, Roger. 1965. *Social Psychology*. New York: Free Press.

——. 1986. *Social Psychology: The Second Edition*. New York: Free Press.

Brown, Rosellen. 1984. *Civil Wars*. New York: Penguin.

Brunvard, Jan H. 1984. *The Choking Doberman*. New York: Norton.

Bryce, James B. 1900. *The American Commonwealth*, vol. 3. London: Macmillan.

——. 1921. *Modern Democracies*. London: Macmillan.

Bunce, Valerie. 1981. *Do New Leaders Make a Difference?* Princeton, NJ: Princeton University Press.

Burke, Edmund. [1790] 1910. *Reflections on the Revolution in France*. London: Everyman's Library.

Burnham, Walter D. 1970. *Critical Elections and the Mainsprings of American Politics*. New York: Norton.

——. 1989. "The Reagan Heritage." In *The Election of 1988: Reports and Interpretations*, ed. Gerald Pomper. Chatham, NJ: Chatham House.

Burstein, Paul. 1985. *Discrimination, Jobs, and Politics*. Chicago: University of Chicago Press.

Cain, Bruce E., I. Lewis, and Douglas R. Rivers. 1989. "Strategy and Choice in the 1988 Presidential Primaries." Division of the Humanities and Social Sciences, California Institute of Technology, Pasadena. Social Science Working Paper 686.

Cameron, David. 1978. "The Expansion of the Public Economy: A Comparative Analysis. *American Political Science Review* 72:1243–1261.

Campbell, Angus. 1966a. "A Classification of the Presidential Elections." In *Elections and the Political Order*, ed. Angus Campbell, Philip E. Converse, Warren E. Miller, and Donald Stokes. New York: Wiley.

——. 1966b. "Interpreting the Presidential Victory." In *The National Election of 1964*, ed. Milton C. Cummings. Washington, DC: Brookings.

Campbell, Angus, Philip E. Converse, Warren E. Miller, and Donald Stokes. 1960. *The American Voter*. New York: Wiley.

Campbell, Bruce A. 1977. "Patterns of Change in the Partisan Loyalties of Native Southerners." *Journal of Politics* 39:730–761.

Campbell, Donald T. 1965. "Ethnocentric and Other Altruistic Motives." *Nebraska Symposium on Motivation* 13:283–312.

——. 1967. "Stereotypes and the Perception of Group Differences." *American Psychologist* 22:812–829.

Carmichael, Stokely, and Charles Hamilton. 1967. *Black Power*. New York: Vintage.

Carmines, Edward G., and James A. Stimson. 1982. "Racial Issues and the Structure of Mass Belief Systems." *Journal of Politics* 44:2–20.

——. 1989. *Issue Evolution: Race and the Transformation of American Politics*. Princeton, NJ: Princeton University Press.

Centers, Richard. 1949. *The Psychology of Social Classes*. Princeton, NJ: Princeton University Press.

Channing, Steven A. 1970. *Crisis of Fear: Secession in South Carolina*. New York: Simon and Schuster.

Christie, Richard, and M. Jahoda, eds. 1954. *Studies in the Scope and Method of "The Authoritarian Personality."* New York: Free Press.

Citrin, Jack, and Donald Philip Green. 1990. "The Self-Interest Motive in American Public Opinion." *Research in Micropolitics* 3:1–28.

Clark, Kenneth B., and M. P. Clark. 1947. "Racial Identification and Preference in Negro Children." In *Readings in Social Psychology*, ed. T. Newcomb and E. L. Hartley. New York: Holt.

Clifford, Clarke, and R. Holbrooke. 1991. "Annals of Government. The Truman Years—Part II." *New Yorker*, April.

Clubb, Jerome M., William H. Flanigan, and Nancy H. Zingale. 1980. *Partisan Realignment*. Beverly Hills: Sage.

Congressional Quarterly Weekly Report, 1989. "Official 1988 Presidential Election Results." 139 (January 21).

Cohen, Cathy J., and Michael C. Dawson. 1993. "Neighborhood Poverty and African American Politics." *American Political Science Review* 87:286–302.

Converse, Jean M., and Stanley Presser. 1986. *Survey Questions: Handcrafting the Standardized Questionnaire*. Beverly Hills: Sage.

Converse, Philip E. 1958. "The Shifting Role of Class in Political Attitudes and Behavior." In *Readings in Social Psychology*, 3d ed., ed. E. E. Maccoby, T. M. Newcomb, and E. L. Hartley. New York: Holt, Rinehart, and Winston.

———. 1964. "The Nature of Belief Systems in Mass Publics." In *Ideology and Discontent*, ed. David E. Apter. New York: Free Press.

———. [1963] 1966. "On the Possibility of Major Political Realignment in the South." In *Elections and the Political Order*, ed. Angus Campbell, Philip E. Converse, Warren E. Miller, and Donald Stokes. New York: Wiley.

———. 1970. "Attitudes and Non-Attitudes: Continuation of a Dialogue." In *The Quantitative Analysis of Social Problems*, ed. Edward Tufte. Reading, MA: Addison-Wesley.

———. 1972. "Change in the American Electorate." In *The Human Meaning of Social Change*, ed. Angus Campbell and Philip E. Converse. New York: Russell Sage.

———. 1975. "Public Opinion and Voting Behavior." In *Handbook of Political Science*, vol. 4, ed. Fred Greenstein and Nelson Polsby. Reading, MA: Addison-Wesley.

Converse, Philip E., Angus Campbell, Warren E. Miller, and Donald E. Stokes. [1961] 1966. "Stability and Change in 1960: A Reinstating Election." In *Elections and the Political Order*, ed. Angus Campbell, Philip E. Converse, Warren E. Miller, and Donald Stokes. New York: Wiley.

Converse, Philip E., Aage R. Clausen, and Warren E. Miller. 1965. "Electoral Myth and Reality: The 1964 Election." *American Political Science Review* 59:321–336.

Converse, Philip E., Heinz Eulau, and Warren E. Miller. 1982. "The Study of Voting." In *Behavioral and Social Science Research: A National Resource*, pt. 2, ed. Robert McAdams, Neil J. Smelser, and Donald Treiman. Washington, DC: National Academy Press.

Converse, Philip E., and Gregory B. Markus. 1979. "Plus ça change . . . The New CPS Election Study Panel." *American Political Science Review* 73:32–49.

Converse, Philip E., Warren E. Miller, Jerold G. Rusk, and Alan C. Wolfe. 1969.

"Continuity and Change in American Politics: Parties and Issues in the 1968 Election." *American Political Science Review* 63:1083–1105.

Converse, Philip E., and Michael W. Traugott. 1986. "Assessing the Accuracy of Polls and Surveys." *Science* 234:1094–1098.

Cook, Stuart W., and Claire E. Seltiz. 1964. "A Muliti-Indicator Approach to Attitude Measurement." *Psychological Bulletin* 62:36–55.

Cook, Thomas, and Donald T. Campbell. 1979. *Quasi-Experimentation.* Chicago: Rand McNally.

Coser, Lewis A. 1956. *The Functions of Social Conflict.* Glencoe, IL: Free Press.

Courant, Paul N., Edward M. Gramlich, and Daniel L. Rubinfield. 1980. "Why Voters Support Tax Limitation Amendments: The Michigan Case." *National Tax Journal* 32:147–158.

Dagger, Richard. 1986. "Politics and the Pursuit of Autonomy." In *NOMOS XXVIII: Justification,* ed. J. Roland Pennock and John W. Chapman. New York: New York University Press.

Dahl, Robert A. 1956. *A Preface to Democratic Theory.* Chicago: University of Chicago Press.

———. 1961. *Who Governs? Democracy and Power in an American City.* New Haven, CT: Yale University Press.

———. 1971. *Polyarchy: Participation and Opposition.* New Haven, CT: Yale University Press.

———. 1978. "Pluralism Revisited." *Comparative Politics* 10:191–204.

———. 1989. *Democracy and Its Critics.* New Haven, CT: Yale University Press.

Dahrendorf, Ralf. 1959. *Class and Class Conflict in Industrial Society.* Stanford: Stanford University Press.

Dalton Russel J., and Martin P. Wattenberg. 1993. "The Not So Simple Act of Voting." In *Political Science: The State of the Discipline II,* ed. Ada F. Finifter. Washington, DC: American Political Science Association.

Davidson, Chandler. 1992. "The Voting Rights Act: A Brief History." In *Controversies in Minority Voting,* ed. Bernard Grofman and Chandler Davidson. Washington, DC: Brookings.

Dawson, Michael C. 1995. *Behind the Mule.* Princeton, NJ: Princeton University Press.

Degler, Carl N. 1991. *In Search of Human Nature.* New York: Oxford University Press.

Dewey, John. 1927. *The Public and Its Problems.* New York: Holt.

Didion, Joan. 1992. *After Henry.* New York: Simon and Schuster.

Donohue, J. J., and James Heckman. 1990. "Continuous versus Episodic Change: The Impact of Civil Rights Policy on the Economic Status of Blacks." Northwestern University Law School. Typescript.

Downs, Anthony. 1957. *An Economic Theory of Democracy.* New York: Harper.

———. 1972. "Up and Down with Ecology—the 'Issue-Attention Cycle.' " *Public Interest* 28:38–50.

Drew, Elizabeth. 1989. *Election Journal: Political Events of 1987–1988.* New York: William Morrow.

Du Bois, W. E. B. [1903] 1990. *The Souls of Black Folk.* New York: Vintage.

Duncan, Otis Dudley. 1984. *Notes on Social Measurement*. New York: Russell Sage.

Eastland, Terry, and William J. Bennett. 1978. *Counting by Race: Equality from the Founding Fathers to Bakke and Weber*. New York: Basic.

Edelman, Marian Wright. 1992. *The Measure of Our Success: A Letter to My Children and Yours*. Boston: Beacon.

Edelman, Murray. 1964. *The Symbolic Uses of Politics*. Urbana: University of Illinois Press.

Edsall, Thomas B., and Mary D. Edsall. 1992. *Chain Reaction: The Impact of Race, Rights, and Taxes on American Politics*. New York: Norton.

Epstein, Edward J. 1973. *News from Nowhere*. New York: Random House.

Erbring, Lutz, Edie M. Goldenberg, and Arthur H. Miller. 1980. "Front Page News and Real World Cues: A New Look at Agenda-Setting." *American Journal of Political Science* 24:16–49.

Esolen, Gary. 1992. "More than a Pretty Face: David Duke's Use of Television as a Political Tool." In *The Emergence of David Duke and the Politics of Race*, ed. Douglas Rose. Chapel Hill: University of North Carolina Press.

Estrich, Susan. 1989. "Willie Horton, Racism, and Our Campaign." *Washington Post* (National Edition), May 17.

Farah, Barbara G., and Ethel Klein. 1989. "Public Opinion Trends." In *The Election of 1988: Reports and Interpretations*, ed. Gerald M. Pomper. Chatham, NJ: Chatham House.

Farley, Reynolds. 1977. "Residential Segregation in Urbanized Areas of the United States, 1970: An Analysis of Social Class and Racial Differences." *Demography* 14: 497–518.

———. 1984. *Blacks and Whites: Narrowing the Gap?* Cambridge, MA.: Harvard University Press.

Farley, Reynolds, and Walter R. Allen. 1987. *The Color Line and the Quality of Life in America*. New York: Russell Sage.

Farley, Reynolds, and William H. Frey. 1992. "Changes in the Segregation of Whites from Blacks during the 1980s: Small Steps toward a More Racially Integrated Society." Population Studies Center, University of Michigan, Ann Arbor. Research Report #92-257.

Feagin, Joe R. 1975. *Subordinating the Poor*. New York: Prentice-Hall.

Feagin, Joe R., and Melvin P. Sikes. 1994. *Living with Racism: The Black Middle-Class Experience*. Boston: Beacon.

Feldman, Stanley 1983. "Economic Individualism and Mass Belief Systems." *American Politics Quarterly* 11:3–29.

———. 1985. "Report on Values in the 1984 Pilot Study." Center for Political Studies, University of Michigan. Technical Report to the National Election Studies Board.

———. 1988. "Structure and Consistency in Public Opinion: The Role of Core Beliefs and Values." *American Journal of Political Science* 32:416–440.

Feldman, Stanley, and John Zaller. 1992. "The Political Culture of Ambivalence: Ideological Responses to the Welfare State. *American Journal of Political Science* 36:268–307.

Fiorina, Morris P. 1981. *Retrospective Voting in American National Elections.* New Haven, CT: Yale University Press.

Fischhoff, Baruch, Paul Slovic, and Sara L. Lichtenstein. 1980. "Knowing What You Want: Measuring Labile Values." In *Cognitive Processes in Choice and Decision Behavior,* ed. T. Wallsten. Hillsdale, NJ: Erlbaum.

Fishkin, James S. 1991. *Democracy and Deliberation: New Directions for Democratic Reform.* New Haven, CT: Yale University Press.

Fiske, Susan T., and Shelley E. Taylor. 1992. *Social Cognition,* 2d ed. Reading, MA: Addison-Wesley.

Foner, Eric. 1988. *Reconstruction: America's Unfinished Revolution, 1863–1877.* New York: Harper and Row.

Foner, Philip S., ed. 1955. *The Life and Writings of Frederick Douglass.* New York: International.

Frady, Marshall. 1968. *Wallace.* New York: World Publishing.

Fraser, Steven, ed. 1995. *The Bell Curve Wars: Race, Intelligence, and the Future of America.* New York: Basic.

Fredrickson, George M. 1971. *The Black Image in the White Mind: The Debate on Afro-American Character and Destiny, 1817–1914.* New York: Harper and Row.

———. 1988. *The Arrogance of Race.* Middletown, CT.: Wesleyan University Press.

Free, Lloyd A., and Hadley Cantril. 1968. *The Political Beliefs of Americans: A Study of Public Opinion.* New York: Simon and Schuster.

Freehling, William W. 1966. *The Road to Disunion.* New York: Oxford University Press.

Gamson, William A. 1992. *Talking Politics.* New York: Cambridge University Press.

Gamson, William A., and K. E. Lasch. 1983. "The Political Culture of Social Welfare Policy." In *Evaluating the Welfare State,* ed. S. E. Spiro and E. Yuchtman-Yaar. New York: Academic Press.

Gamson, William A., and A. Modigliani. 1987. "The Changing Culture of Affirmative Action." In *Research in Political Sociology,* vol. 3, ed. Richard D. Braungart. Greenwich, CT: JAI Press.

———. 1989. "Media Discourse and Public Opinion on Nuclear Power: A Constructionist Approach." *American Journal of Sociology* 95:1–37.

Garrow, David J. 1978. *Protest at Selma: Martin Luther King, Jr., and the Voting Rights Act of 1965.* New Haven, CT: Yale University Press.

———. 1983. *The FBI and Martin Luther King, Jr.* New York: Penguin.

Gates, Henry Louis, Jr. 1995. "Why Now?" In *The Bell Curve Wars: Race, Intelligence, and the Future of America,* ed. Steven Fraser. New York: Basic.

Geschwender, B. N., and J. A. Geschwender. 1973. "Relative Deprivation and Participation in the Civil Rights Movement." *Social Science Quarterly* 54: 403–411.

Gibson, James L. 1988. "Political Intolerance and Political Repression during the McCarthy Red Scare." *American Political Science Review* 82:511–530.

Gilens, Martin. 1996. "Race and Poverty in America: Public Misperceptions and the American News Media." *Journal of Politics*, forthcoming.

Giles, Michael W., and Arthur Evans. 1986. "The Power Approach to Intergroup Hostility." *Journal of Conflict Resolution* 30:469–486.

Gillette, William. 1979. *Retreat from Reconstruction, 1869–1879*. Baton Rouge: Louisiana State University Press.

Ginsberg, Benjamin, and Martin Shefter. 1990. *Politics by Other Means: The Declining Importance of Elections in America*. New York: Basic.

Glaser, James M. 1994. "Back to the Black Belt: Racial Environment and White Racial Attitudes in the South." *Journal of Politics* 56:21–41.

Glazer, Nathan. [1975] 1987. *Affirmative Discrimination: Ethnic Inequality and Public Policy*. Cambridge, MA: Harvard University Press.

Glazer, Nathan, and David P. Moynihan, eds. 1975. *Ethnicity: Theory and Experience*. Cambridge, MA: Harvard University Press.

Goffman, Erving. 1974. *Frame Analysis: An Essay on the Organization of Experience*. New York: Harper and Row.

Gold, Howard J. 1992. *Hollow Mandates: American Public Opinion and the Conservative Shift*. Boulder, CO: Westview Press.

Gosnell, Harold F. 1927. *Getting out the Vote: An Experiment in the Stimulation of Voting*. Chicago: University of Chicago Press.

Gould, Steven J. 1981. *The Mismeasure of Man*. New York: Norton.

Greeley, Andrew M., and Paul B. Sheatsley. 1974. "Attitudes toward Racial Integration." In *Inequality and Justice*, ed. Lee Rainwater. Chicago: Aldine.

Green, Donald P., and Jonathan Cowden. 1992. "Who Protests: Self-Interest and White Opposition to Busing." *Journal of Politics* 54:471–496.

Grofman, Bernard, and Chandler Davidson. 1992. *Controversies in Minority Voting: The Voting Rights Act in Perspective*. Washington, DC: Brookings.

Grofman, Bernard, and Lisa Handley. 1989a. "Black Representation: Making Sense of Electoral Geography at Different Levels of Government." *Legislative Studies Quarterly* 14:265–279.

———. 1989b. "Minority Population Proportion and Black and Hispanic Congressional Success in the 1970s and 1980s." *American Politics Quarterly* 17:436–445.

———. 1989c. "In the Footsteps of George Wallace: Race and Politics—or the Republican Majority Has Already Emerged, Color It White." Presented at the annual meeting of the American Political Science Association, Washington, DC.

Gross, Kimberly A. 1995. "Images of 'Others': Media Portrayals of the 1992 Los Angeles Rebellion." Presented at the annual meeting of the Midwest Political Science Association, Chicago.

Gross, Samuel R. 1993. "The Romance of Revenge: Capital Punishment in America." *Studies in Law, Politics, and Society* 13:71–104.

GSS News. 1991. "Growing Acceptance, Enduring Stereotypes: Race Relations in America." Chicago: National Opinion Research Center.

Guimond, S., and L. Dube-Simard. 1983. "Relative Deprivation Theory and the Quebec Nationalist Movement." *Journal of Personality and Social Psychology* 44:526–535.

Gurin, Patricia, Shirely Hatchett, and James S. Jackson. 1989. *Hope and Independence.* New York: Russell Sage.

Habermas, Jürgen. 1982. "A Reply to My Critics." In *Habermas: Critical Debates,* ed. John B. Thompson and David Held. Cambridge, MA: MIT Press.

Hamilton, Richard F. 1972. *Class and Politics in the United States.* New York: Wiley.

Hartz, Louis. 1955. *The Liberal Tradition in America.* San Diego: Harcourt, Brace.

Hatchett, Shirley, and Howard Schuman. 1975. "White Respondents and Race of Interviewer Effects." *Public Opinion Quarterly* 39:523–528.

Hawthorne, Michael R., and John E. Jackson. 1987. "The Individual Political Economy of Tax Policy." *American Political Science Review* 81:757–774.

Heard, A. 1952. *A Two-Party South?* Chapel Hill: University of North Carolina Press.

Heckman, J. J., and B. S. Payner. 1989. "Determining the Impact of Federal Antidiscrimination Policy on the Economic Status of Blacks: A Study of South Carolina." *American Economic Review* 79:138–177.

Held, David. 1987. *Models of Democracy.* Stanford: Stanford University Press.

Herrnstein, Richard J. 1990. "Still an American Dilemma." *Public Interest* (winter), 3–17.

Herrnstein, Richard J., and Charles Murray. 1994. *The Bell Curve: Intelligence and Class Structure in American Life.* New York: Free Press.

Hershey, Marjorie Randon. 1989. "The Campaign and the Media." In *The Election of 1988: Reports and Interpretations,* ed. Gerald Pomper. Chatham, NJ: Chatham House.

Hibbs, Douglas, A., Jr. 1987. *The American Political Economy.* Cambridge, MA.: Harvard University Press.

Hibbs, Douglas A. Jr., R. Douglas Rivers, and Nicholas Vasilotos. 1982. "The Dynamics of Political Support for American Presidents Among Occupational and Partisan Groups." *American Journal of Political Science* 26: 312–332.

Higham, John. [1955] 1988. *Strangers in the Land: Patterns of American Nativism, 1860–1925.* New Brunswick, NJ: Rutgers University Press.

Himelstein, J. 1983. "Rhetorical Continuities in the Politics of Race: The Closed Society Revisited." *Southern Speech Communication Journal* 48:153–166.

Hirschman, Albert O. 1977. *The Passions and the Interests.* Princeton, NJ: Princeton University Press.

———. 1991. *The Rhetoric of Reaction.* Cambridge, MA: Belknap Press.

Hobbes, Thomas. [1651] 1968. *Leviathan.* Ed. C. B. Macpherson. Harmondsworth: Penguin.

Hochschild, J. L. 1981. *What's Fair? American Beliefs about Distributive Justice.* Cambridge, MA: Harvard University Press.

Hofstadter, Richard. 1948. *The American Political Tradition.* New York: Vintage.

———. [1944] 1955. *Social Darwinism in American Thought.* Philadelphia: University of Pennsylvania Press.

———. 1965. *The Paranoid Style in American Politics.* New York: Knopf.

Holmes, Stephen. 1990. "The Secret History of Self-Interest." In *Beyond Self-Interest,* ed. Jayne J. Mansbridge. Chicago: University of Chicago Press.

Horowitz, Donald L. 1985. *Ethnic Groups in Conflict*. Berkeley: University of California Press.

Hovland, Carl I. 1959. "Reconciling Conflicting Results from Experimental and Survey Studies of Attitude Change." *American Psychologist* 14:8–17.

Howell, Susan E., and Sylvia Warren. 1992. "Public Opinion and David Duke." In *The Emergence of David Duke and the Politics of Race*, ed. Douglas Rose. Chapel Hill: University of North Carolina Press.

Huber, J., and William. H. Form. 1973. *Income and Ideology*. New York: Free Press.

Huckfeldt, Robert, and Carol Weitzel Kohfeld. 1989. *Race and the Decline of Class in American Politics*. Urbana: University of Illinois Press.

Hume, David. [1741] 1898. *Essays: Moral, Political, and Literary*, vol. 1, ed. T. H. Green and T. H. Grose. London: Longmans.

———. [1741] 1985. "Of Parties in General." In *Essays: Moral, Political, and Literary*. Indianapolis: Liberty Classics.

Huntington, Samuel E. 1981. *American Politics: The Promise of Disharmony*. Cam-·bridge, MA: Belknap Press.

Hyman, Herbert H. 1953. "The Value Systems of Different Classes." In *Class, Status, and Power*, ed. R. Bendix and Seymour Martin Lipset. Glencoe, IL: Free Press.

Hyman, Herbert H., and Paul B. Sheatsley. 1956. "Attitudes toward Desegregation." *Scientific American* 195 (December): 35–39.

———. 1964. "Attitudes toward Desegregation." *Scientific American* 211:16–23.

Inglehart, Ronald. 1977. *The Silent Revolution*. Princeton, NJ: Princeton University Press.

———. 1990. *Culture Shift in Advanced Industrial Society*. Princeton, NJ: Princeton University Press.

Iyengar, Shanto. 1990. "Shortcuts to Political Knowledge: The Role of Selective Attention and Accessibility." In *Information and Democratic Processes*, ed. John A. Ferejohn and James H. Kuklinski. Urbana: University of Illinois Press.

Iyengar, Shanto, and Donald R. Kinder. 1987. *News That Matters*. Chicago: University of Chicago Press.

Jackman, Mary R. 1981a. "Reply: Issues in the Measurement of Commitment to Racial Integration." *Political Methodology* 8:160–172.

———. 1981b. "Education and Policy Commitment to Racial Integration." *American Journal of Political Science* 25:256–269.

Jackman, Mary R., and M. Crane. 1986. "'Some of My Best Friends Are Black. . . .' Interracial Friendship and Whites' Racial Attitudes." *Public Opinion Quarterly* 50:459–486.

Jackman, Mary R., and Robert W. Jackman. 1983. *Class Awareness in the United States*. Berkeley: University of California Press.

Jackson, James S., and Daria Kirby. 1991. "Models of Individual Outgroup Rejection: Cross-National Western Europe—United States Comparisons." Presented at the annual meeting of the American Sociological Association, Cincinnati.

Jacoby, Russell, and Naomi Glauberman, eds. 1995. *The Bell Curve Debate: History, Documents, Opinions.* New York: Random House.

James, William. 1890. *The Principles of Psychology.* New York: Holt.

Jamieson, Kathleen Hall. 1992. *Dirty Politics: Deception, Distraction, and Democracy.* New York: Oxford University Press.

Jaynes, Gerald David, and Robin M. Williams, Jr. 1989. *A Common Destiny: Blacks and American Society.* Washington, DC: National Academy Press.

Jencks, Christopher. 1991. "Is Violent Crime Increasing?" *American Prospect* 1: 98–109.

———. 1992. *Rethinking Social Policy: Race, Poverty, and the Underclass.* Cambridge, MA: Harvard University Press.

Jencks, Christopher, and Paul E. Peterson. 1991. *The Urban Underclass.* Washington, DC: Brookings.

Jennings, M. Kent. 1979. "Another Look at the Life Cycle and Political Participation." *American Journal of Political Science* 23:755–771.

Jessor, Thomas, and David O. Sears. 1986. "Racial Conflict in the 1985 NES Pilot Study." Center for Political Studies, University of Michigan. Report prepared for the National Election Studies Board.

Joint Center for Political Studies. 1994. *Black Elected Officials.* Washington, DC: Joint Center for Political and Economic Studies Press.

Jones, J. H. [1981] 1993. *Bad Blood: The Tuskegee Syphilis Experiment.* New York: Free Press.

Jordan, Winthrop D. 1968. *White over Black.* Chapel Hill: University of North Carolina Press.

Jöreskog, Karl G. 1969. "A General Approach to Confirmatory Maximum Likelihood Factor Analysis." *Psychometrika* 32:443–482.

Judd, Charles M., and Bernadette Park. 1993. "Definition and Assessment of Accuracy in Social Stereotypes." *Psychological Review* 100:109–128.

Kagy, Michael, and Gregory A. Caldiera. 1980. "A 'Reformed' Electorate? Well, At Least a Changed Electorate, 1952–1976." In *Paths to Political Reform,* ed. William J. Crotty. Lexington, MA: Heath.

Kahneman, Daniel, Amos Tversky, and Paul Slovic, eds. 1982. *Judgment under Uncertainty.* Cambridge: Cambridge University Press.

Karlan, Pamela S., and Peyton McCrary. 1988. "Without Fear and without Research: Abigal Thornstrom on the Voting Rights Act." *Journal of Law and Politics* 4:751–757.

Katz, Irwin, and R. Glen Hass. 1988. "Racial Ambivalence and American Value Conflict: Correlational and Priming Studies of Dual Cognitive Structures." *Journal of Personality and Social Psychology* 55:893–905.

Katz, Irwin, Joyce Wackenhut, and R. Glen Hass. 1986. "Racial Ambivalence, Value Duality, and Behavior." In *Prejudice, Discrimination, and Racism: Theory and Research,* ed. John Dovidio and S. L. Gaertner. New York: Academic Press.

Katz, Phylis A. 1976. "The Acquisition of Racial Attitudes in Children." In *Towards the Elimination of Racism,* ed. Phylis A. Katz. Elmsford, NY: Pergamon Press.

Kelley, Stanley, Jr. 1966. "The Presidential Campaign." In *The National Election of 1964*, ed. Milton C. Cummings. Washington, DC: Brookings.

———. 1983. *Interpreting Elections.* Princeton, NJ: Princeton University Press.

Kessel, John H. 1968. *The Goldwater Coalition.* Indianapolis, IN: Bobbs-Merrill.

———. 1972. "Comment: The Issues in Issue Voting." *American Political Science Review* 66:459–465.

Key, V. O., Jr. 1949. *Southern Politics in State and Nation.* New York: Knopf.

———. 1955. "A Theory of Critical Elections." *Journal of Politics* 17:3–18.

———. 1961. *Public Opinion and American Democracy.* New York: Knopf.

———. 1966. *The Responsible Electorate.* Cambridge, MA: Harvard University Press.

Kilson, Martin. 1971. *Key Issues in the Afro-American Experience.* New York: Harcourt, Brace, Jovanovich.

Kinder, Donald R. 1983. "Diversity and Complexity in American Public Opinion." In *Political Science: The State of the Discipline*, ed. Ada F. Finifter. Washington, DC: American Political Science Association.

———. 1986. "The Continuing American Dilemma: White Resistance to Racial Change Forty Years after Myrdal." *Journal of Social Issues* 42:151–172.

———. 1995. *Aliens and Enemies: The Resurgence of Ethnocentrism in American Political Life.* Department of Political Science, University of Michigan. Typescript.

Kinder, Donald R., Gordon S. Adams, and Paul W. Gronke. 1989. "Economics and Politics in the 1984 American Presidential Election." *American Journal of Political Science* 33:491–512.

Kinder, Donald R., and Don Herzog. 1993. "Democratic Discussion." In *Reconsidering the Democratic Public*, ed. George E. Marcus and Russell L. Hanson. University Park: Pennsylvania State University Press.

Kinder, Donald R., and D. Roderick Kiewiet. 1979. "Economic Discontent and Political Behavior: The Role of Personal Grievances and Collective Economic Judgments in Congressional Voting." *American Journal of Political Science* 23:495–527.

———. 1981. "Sociotropic Politics: The American Case." *British Journal of Political Science* 11:129–161.

Kinder, Donald R., and Walter R. Mebane, Jr. 1983. "Politics and Economics in Everyday Life." In *The Political Process and Economic Change*, ed. Kristen Monroe. New York: Agathon.

Kinder, Donald R., and Tali Mendelberg. 1994. "Prejudice and Principles in American Public Opinion." Department of Political Science, University of Michigan, Ann Arbor. Typescript.

———. 1995. "Cracks in Apartheid? The Political Impact of Prejudice among Desegregated Whites." *Journal of Politics* 57: 402–424.

Kinder, Donald R., Tali Mendelberg, and Michael C. Dawson. 1994. "Benign Neglect, Racial Codewords, and the 1988 American Presidential Campaign." Department of Political Science, University of Michigan. Typescript.

Kinder, Donald R., and Thomas E. Nelson. 1995. "Democratic Debate and Real Opinions." Department of Political Science, University of Michigan. Typescript.

Kinder, Donald R., and Thomas R. Palfrey, eds. 1993. *Experimental Foundations of Political Science.* Ann Arbor: University of Michigan Press.

Kinder, Donald R., and Laurie A. Rhodebeck. 1982. "Continuities in Support for Racial Equality, 1972 to 1976." *Public Opinion Quarterly* 46:195–215.

Kinder, Donald R., and Lynn M. Sanders. 1985. "Righting Benign Neglect." Proposal to the National Election Studies Planning Committee and Board. Center for Political Studies, University of Michigan.

———. 1986. "Revitalizing the Measurement of White Americans' Racial Attitudes." Technical report prepared for the National Election Studies Board. Center for Political Studies, University of Michigan.

———. 1987. "Pluralistic Foundations of American Opinion on Race." Presented at the annual meeting of the American Political Science Association, Chicago.

———. 1990. "Mimicking Political Debate with Survey Questions: The Case of White Opinion on Affirmative Action for Blacks." *Social Cognition* 8: 73–103.

Kinder, Donald R., and David O. Sears. 1981. "Prejudice and Politics: Symbolic Racism versus Racial Threats to the Good Life." *Journal of Personality and Social Psychology* 40:414–431.

———. 1985. "Public Opinion and Political Action." In *The Handbook of Social Psychology,* 3d ed., ed. G. Lindzey and E. Aronson. New York: Random House.

Kinder, Donald R., and Karin Tamerius. 1994. "Racism and the Electoral Connection." Presented at the annual meeting of the American Political Science Association, Washington, DC.

King, Gary. 1991. "'Truth' Is Stranger than Prediction, More Questionable than Causal Inference." *American Journal of Political Science* 35:1047–1053.

Kirschenman, Joleen, and Kathryn M. Neckerman. 1991. "'We'd Love to Hire Them, but . . .': The Meaning of Race for Employers." In *The Urban Underclass,* ed. Christopher Jencks and Paul E. Peterson. Washington, DC: Brookings.

Klineberg, Otto. 1935. *Race Differences.* New York: Harper.

Klingeman, Hans. 1979. "Measuring Ideological Conceptualizations." In *Political Action: Mass Participation in Five Western Democracies,* ed. Samuel H. Barnes et al. Beverly Hills: Sage.

Kluckhohn, Clyde. 1958. "Have There Been Discernible Shifts in American Values during the Last Generation?" In *The American Style: Essays in Value and Performance,* ed. Elting Elmore Morrison. New York: Harper.

Kluegel, James R. 1990. "Trends in Whites' Explanations of the Black-White Gap in Socioeconomic Status, 1977–1989." *American Sociological Review* 55:512–525.

Kluegel, James R., and Elliot R. Smith. 1983. "Affirmative Action Attitudes: Effects of Self-Interest, Racial Affect, and Stratification Beliefs on Whites' Views." *Social Forces* 61:797–824.

———. 1986. *Beliefs about Inequality: Americans' Views of What Is and What Ought to Be.* Hawthorne, NY: Aldine de Gruyter.

Kluger, Richard. 1975. *Simple Justice.* New York: Vintage.

Knoke, David. 1979. "Stratification and the Dimensions of American Political Orientations." *American Journal of Political Science* 23:772–791.

Kousser, J. Morgan. 1974. *The Shaping of Southern Politics.* New Haven, CT: Yale University Press.

———. 1992. "The Voting Rights Act and the Two Reconstructions." In *Controversies in Minority Voting,* ed. Bernard Grofman and Chandler Davidson. Washington, DC: Brookings.

Kramer, Gerald H. 1971. "Short-Term Fluctuations in U.S. Voting Behavior, 1896–1964." *American Political Science Review* 65:131–143.

———. 1983. "The Ecological Fallacy Revisited: Aggregate versus Individual-Level Findings on Economics and Elections and Sociotropic Voting." *American Political Science Review* 77:92–111.

———. 1986. "Political Science as Science." In *Political Science: The Science of Politics,* ed. Herbert F. Weisberg. New York: Agathon Press.

Krosnick, Jon A., and Mathew K. Berent. 1993. "Comparisons of Party Identification and Policy Preferences: The Impact of Survey Question Format." *American Journal of Political Science* 37:941–964.

Krosnick, Jon A., and Leandre R. Fabrigar. 1995. "Questionnaire Design for Attitude Measurement in Social and Psychological Research." Department of Psychology, Ohio State University. Typescript.

Krosnick, Jon A., and Donald R. Kinder. 1990. "Altering the Foundations of Support for the President through Priming." *American Political Science Review* 84:497–512.

Krosnick, Jon A., and Michael Milburn. 1990. "Psychological Determinants of Political Opinionation." *Social Cognition* 8:49–72.

Labov, William. 1972. *Language in the Inner City: Studies in the Black English Vernacular.* Philadelphia: University of Pennsylvania Press.

———. 1975. "The Logic of Nonstandard English." In *Black American English: Its Background and Usage in the Schools and in Literature,* ed. P. Stoller. New York: Dell.

Labov, William, and Wendell A. Harris. 1986. "De Facto Segregation of Black and White Vernaculars." In *Current Issues in Linguistic Theory 53: Diversity and Diachrony.* Amsterdam: Benjamins.

Ladd, Everett C., and C. D. Hadley. [1975] 1978. *Transformations of the American Party System.* New York: Norton.

Lamis, Alexander P. 1990. *The Two-Party South.* New York: Oxford University Press.

Landry, Bart. 1987. *The New Black Middle Class.* Berkeley: University of California Press.

Lane, Robert E. 1962. *Political Ideology.* New York: Free Press.

———. 1973. "Patterns of Political Belief." In *Handbook of Political Psychology,* ed. Jeanne Knutson. San Francisco: Jossey-Bass.

———. 1978. "Interpersonal Relations and Leadership in a 'Cold Society.'" *Comparative Politics* 10:443–459.

Lawson, Steven F. 1976. *Black Ballots: Voting Rights in the South, 1944–1969.* New York: Columbia University Press.

LeVine, Robert A., and Donald T. Campbell. 1972. *Ethnocentrism: Theories of Conflict, Ethnic Attitudes, and Group Behavior.* New York: Wiley.

Lieberson, Stanley. 1980. *A Piece of the Pie: Black and White Immigrants since 1880.* Berkeley: University of California Press.

Lieberson, Stanley, and A. R. Silverman. 1965. "The Precipitants and Underlying Conditions of Race Riots." *American Sociological Review* 30:887–898.

Lieberson, Stanley, and Mary C. Waters. 1988. *From Many Strands.* New York: Russell Sage.

Lipset, Seymour Martin. 1963. *The First New Nation.* New York: Norton.

———. [1960] 1981. *Political Man: The Social Bases of Politics.* Baltimore: Johns Hopkins University Press.

Lipset, Seymour Martin, and Earl Raab. 1970. *The Politics of Unreason: Right-Wing Extremism in America, 1790–1970.* New York: Harper and Row.

Lipset, Seymour Martin, and William Schneider. 1978. "The Bakke Case: How Would It Be Decided at the Bar of Public Opinion?" *Public Opinion* 1: 38–44.

Litwack, Leon. 1961. *North of Slavery: The Negro in the Free States, 1790–1860.* Chicago: University of Chicago Press.

Lowery, David, and Lee Sigelman. 1981. "Understanding the Tax Revolt: Eight Explanations." *American Political Science Review* 75:963–974.

Luebke, P. 1990. *Tar Heel Politics: Myths and Realities.* Chapel Hill: University of North Carolina Press.

Luskin, Robert C. 1987. "Measuring Political Sophistication." *American Journal of Political Science* 31:856–899.

McAdam, Doug. 1982. *Political Process and the Development of Black Insurgency, 1930–1970.* Chicago: University of Chicago Press.

Macauley, Thomas. 1978. "Mill's Essay on Government: Utilitarian Logic and Politics." In *Utilitarian Logic and Politics,* ed. J. Lively and J. Rees. Oxford: Clarendon Press.

McClendon, M. J. 1985. "Racism, Rational Choice, and White Opposition to Racial Change: A Case Study of Busing." *Public Opinion Quarterly* 49: 214–233.

McClosky, H. 1964. "Consensus and Ideology in American Politics." *American Political Science Review* 58:316–382.

McClosky, Herbert, and Alida Brill. 1983. *Dimensions of Tolerance.* New York: Russell Sage.

McClosky, Herbert, and John Zaller. 1984. *The American Ethos: Public Attitudes toward Capitalism and Democracy.* Cambridge, MA: Harvard University Press.

McCombs, M. E., and D. L. Shaw. 1972. "The Agenda-Setting Function of the Media." *Public Opinion Quarterly* 36:176–187.

McConahay, John B. 1982. "Self-Interest versus Racial Attitudes as Correlates of Anti-Busing Attitudes in Louisville." *Journal of Politics* 44:692–720.

———. 1986. "Modern Racism, Ambivalence, and the Modern Racism Scale."

In *Prejudice, Discrimination, and Racism: Theory and Research*, ed. John F. Dovidio and Samuel L. Gaertner. New York: Academic Press.

McConahay, John B., and J. C. Hough. 1976. "Symbolic Racism." *Journal of Social Issues* 32:23–46.

McCullough, David. 1992. *Truman*. New York: Simon and Schuster.

McIver, John P., and Edward G. Carmines. 1981. *Unidimensional Scaling*. Sage University Paper series on Quantitative Applications in the Social Sciences, No. 07-024. Beverly Hills: Sage.

MacKuen, Michael, Robert S. Erickson, and James S. Stimson. 1989. "Macropartisanship." *American Political Science Review* 83:1125–1142.

McWilliams, Wilson Carey. 1989. "The Meaning of the Election." In *The Election of 1988: Reports and Interpretations*, ed. Gerald Pomper. Chatham, NJ: Chatham House.

Madison, James, Alexander Hamilton, and John Jay. [1788] 1987. *The Federalist Papers*. London: Penguin.

Mansbridge, Jayne J. 1980. *Beyond Adversary Democracy*. Chicago: University of Chicago Press.

———. 1988. "Motivating Deliberation in Congress." In *Constitutionalism in America*, vol. 2, ed. Sarah Baumgartner Thurow. New York: University Press of America.

———. 1991. "A Deliberative Theory of Interest Representation." Presented at the annual meeting of the Midwest Political Science Association.

———, ed. 1990. *Beyond Self Interest*. Chicago: University of Chicago Press.

Markus, Gregory B. 1989. "American Individualism." Technical report prepared for the National Election Studies. Center for Political Studies, Institute for Social Research.

Martin, J. G., and F. R. Westie. 1959. "The Tolerant Personality." *American Sociological Review* 24:521–528.

Massey, Douglas S. 1990. "American Apartheid: Segregation and the Making of the Underclass." *American Journal of Sociology* 96:329–357.

Massey, Douglas S., and Nancy A. Denton. 1988. "Suburbanization and Segregation in U.S. Metropolitan Areas." *American Journal of Sociology* 94:592–626.

———. 1993. *American Apartheid: Segregation and the Making of the Underclass*. Cambridge, MA: Harvard University Press.

Mathews, Donald R., and James W. Prothro. 1966. *Negroes and the New Southern Politics*. New York: Harcourt, Brace, and World.

Mead, Margaret. 1930. *Growing Up in New Guinea*. New York: William Morrow.

———. 1935. *Sex and Temperament in Three Primitive Societies*. New York: Morrow.

Meir, August, and Elliot Rudwick. 1975. *CORE: A Study in the Civil Rights Movement, 1942–1968*. Urbana: University of Illinois Press.

Mencken, H. L. [1949] 1956. *A Mencken Chrestomathy*. New York: Knopf.

Mendelberg, Tali. 1992. "The Politics of Racial Resentment: An Experimental Investigation." Presented at the annual meeting of the Midwest Political Science Association, Chicago.

———. 1994. "The Politics of Racial Ambiguity: Origin and Consequences of Implicitly Racial Appeals." Ph.D. diss., Department of Political Science, University of Michigan.

Michie, Allan A., and Frank Ryhlick. 1939. *Dixie Demagogues*. New York: Vanguard.

Mill, John Stuart. [1861] 1951a. "Considerations on Representative Government." In *Three Essays*. Oxford: Oxford University Press.

Mill, John Stuart. [1859] 1951b. "On Liberty." In *Three Essays*. Oxford: Oxford University Press.

Miller, David. 1983. *The Nature of Political Theory*. Oxford: Clarendon Press.

Miller, Warren E. 1992. "Generational Changes and Party Identification." *Political Behavior* 14:333–352.

Miller, Warren E., and Donald E. Stokes. 1966a. "Constituency Influence in Congress." In *Elections and the Political Order*, ed. Angus Campbell, Philip E. Converse, Warren E. Miller, and Donald E. Stokes. New York: Wiley.

Minsky, Marvin. [1975] 1977. "Frame-System Theory." In *Thinking: Readings in Cognitive Science*, ed. P. N. Johnson-Laird and P. C. Wason. Cambridge: Cambridge University Press.

Moore, William V. 1992. "David Duke: The White Knight." In *The Emergence of David Duke and the Politics of Race*, ed. Douglas Rose. Chapel Hill: University of North Carolina Press.

Morris, Aldon D. 1984. *The Origins of the Civil Rights Movement: Black Communities Organizing for Change*. New York: Free Press.

Mueller, John. 1994. *Policy and Opinion in the Gulf War*. Chicago: University of Chicago Press.

Myrdal, Gunnar 1944. *An American Dilemma: The Negro Problem and Modern Democracy*. New York: Harper and Row.

Nelson, Thomas E., and Donald R. Kinder. 1996. "Issue Frames and Group-Centrism in American Public Opinion." *Journal of Politics*, forthcoming.

Nie, Horman H., Sidney Verba, and John R. Petrocik. 1979. *The Changing American Voter*. Cambridge, MA: Harvard University Press.

Nisbett, Richard E., and Lee Ross. 1980. *Human Inference: Strategies and Shortcomings in Social Judgment*. Englewood Cliffs, NJ: Prentice-Hall.

Nunnally, J. C. 1978. *Psychometric Theory*. New York: McGraw-Hill.

Oakes, James. 1982. *The Ruling Race*. New York: Knopf.

Olson, Mancur, Jr. [1965] 1971. *The Logic of Collective Action*. Cambridge, MA: Harvard University Press.

Orbell, J. M. 1967. "Protest Participation among Southern Negro College Students." *American Political Science Review* 61:446–456.

Orfield, Gary. 1978. *Must We Bus? Segregated Schools and National Policy*. Washington, DC: Brookings.

———. 1983. *Public School Desegregation in the United States, 1968–1980*. Washington, DC: Joint Center for Political Studies.

———. 1988. "Race and the Liberal Agenda: The Loss of the Integrationist Dream, 1965–1974." In *The Politics of Social Policy in the United States*, ed.

Margaret Weir, Ann Shola Orloff, and Theda Skocpol. Princeton, NJ: Princeton University Press.

———. 1993. *The Growth of Segregation in American Schools: Changing Patterns of Separation and Poverty since 1968.* Alexandria, VA: NSBA Council of Urban Boards of Education.

Page, Benjamin I. 1978. *Choices and Echoes in Presidential Elections: Rational Man and Electoral Democracy.* Chicago: University of Chicago Press.

Page, Benjamin I. and Richard A. Brody. 1972. "Policy Voting and the Electoral Process: The Vietnam War Issue." *American Political Science Review* 66: 979–995.

Page, Benjamin I., and Robert Y. Shapiro. 1983. "Effects of Public Opinion on Policy." *American Political Science Review* 77: 175–190.

———. 1992. *The Rational Public.* Chicago: University of Chicago Press.

Palmer, John L., and Isabel V. Sawhill, eds. 1984. *The Reagan Record: An Assessment of America's Changing Domestic Priorities.* Cambridge, MA: Ballinger.

Parent, Wayne, and Paul Stekler. 1983. "The Political Implications of Economic Stratification in the Black Community." *Western Political Quarterly* 38: 521–537.

Pettigrew, Thomas F., and R. W. Meertens. 1995. "Subtle and Blatant Prejudice in Western Europe." *European Journal of Social Psychology* 25: 57–75.

Phillips, U. B. 1928. "The Central Theme of Southern History." *American Historical Review* 34: 31.

Piazza, Thomas, Paul M. Sniderman, and Philip E. Tetlock. 1989. "Analysis of the Dynamics of Political Reasoning: A General Purpose Computer-Assisted Methodology." In *Political Methodology,* ed. James Stimson. Ann Arbor: University of Michigan Press.

Pinderhuges, Dianne M. 1987. *Race and Ethnicity in Chicago Politics.* Urbana: University of Illinois Press.

Pitkin, Hanna Fenichel. 1972. *The Concept of Representation.* Berkeley: University of California Press.

Piven, Frances Fox, and Richard A. Cloward. 1977. *Poor People's Movements: Why They Succeed, How They Fail.* New York: Vintage.

Pole, J. R. [1978] 1993. *The Pursuit of Equality.* Berkeley: University of California Press.

Polsby, Nelson W. [1963] 1980. *Community Power and Political Theory.* New Haven, CT: Yale University Press.

———. 1983. *Consequences of Party Reform.* New York: Oxford University Press.

Pomper, Gerald M. 1972. "From Confusion to Clarity: Issues and American Voters, 1956–1968." *American Political Science Review* 66: 415–428.

———. 1989a. "The Presidential Election." In *The Election of 1988: Reports and Interpretations,* ed. Gerald Pomper. Chatham, NJ: Chatham House.

———, ed. 1989b. *The Election of 1988: Reports and Interpretations.* Chatham, NJ: Chatham House.

Pomper, Gerald M. 1989c. "The Presidential Nominations." In *The Election of 1988: Reports and Interpretations,* ed. Gerald M. Pomper. Chatham, NJ: Chatham House.

Popkin, Samuel. 1991. *The Reasoning Voter.* Chicago: University of Chicago Press.

Porter, Judith D. 1971. *Black Child, White Child: The Development of Racial Attitudes.* Cambridge, MA: Harvard University Press.

Prothro, James W., and Charles M. Grigg. 1960. "Fundamental Principles of Democracy; Bases of Agreement and Disagreement. *Journal of Politics* 22: 276–294.

Quirk, Paul J. 1989. "The Election." In *The Elections of 1988,* ed. Michael Nelson. Washington, DC: CQ Press.

Rae, Douglas, Doug Yates, Jennifer Hochschild, Joseph Morone, and Carol Fessler. 1981. *Equalities.* Cambridge, MA: Harvard University Press.

Reich, Robert B., ed. 1988. *The Power of Public Ideas.* Cambridge, MA: Ballinger.

RePass, David. 1971. "Issue Salience and Party Choice." *American Political Science Review* 65:389–400.

Rhodebeck, L. A. 1986. "The Influence of Group Identification on Political Preferences." Ph.D. diss., Department of Political Science, Yale University.

Rieder, Jonathan. 1985. *Canarsie: The Jews and Italians of Brooklyn against Liberalism.* Cambridge, MA: Harvard University Press.

Riker, William H. 1963. *The Theory of Political Coalitions.* New Haven, CT: Yale University Press.

———. 1982. *Liberalism against Populism.* San Francisco: Freeman.

Rivers, Douglas. 1988. "Heterogeneity in Models of Electoral Choice." *American Journal of Political Science* 32:737–757.

Rodgers, Daniel T. 1978. *The Work Ethic in Industrial America, 1850–1920.* Chicago: University of Chicago Press.

———. 1987. *Contested Truths: Keywords in American Politics since Independence.* New York: Basic.

Rokeach, Milton. 1973. *The Nature of Human Values.* New York: Free Press.

Rose, Douglas, ed. 1992. *The Emergence of David Duke and the Politics of Race.* Chapel Hill: University of North Carolina Press.

Rosenstone, Steven J. 1983. *Forecasting Presidential Elections.* New Haven, CT: Yale University Press.

Rosenstone, Steven J., Roy L. Behr, and Edward H. Lazarus. 1984. *Third Parties in America: Citizen Response to Major Party Failure.* Princeton, NJ: Princeton University Press.

Rosenstone, Steven J., and Mark J. Hansen. 1993. *Mobilization, Participation, and Democracy in America.* New York: Macmillan.

Rosenstone, Steven J., Mark J. Hansen, and Donald R. Kinder. 1986. "Measuring Change in Personal Economic Well-Being." *Public Opinion Quarterly* 50: 176–192.

Rosenstone, Steven J., Donald R. Kinder, and Warren E. Miller. 1993. Proposal to the National Science Foundation: Long-Term Support for the National Election Studies, 1994–1998. Center for Political Studies, University of Michigan.

Rovere, Richard R. 1965. *The Goldwater Caper.* New York: Harcourt, Brace, and World.

Runciman, W. G. 1966. *Relative Deprivation and Social Justice: A Study of Attitudes to Social Inequality in Twentieth-Century England*. London: Routledge and Kegan Paul.

Runkel, David R. 1989. *Campaign for the President: The Managers Look at '88*. Cambridge MA: Institute of Politics, Harvard University.

Rusk, Jerrold G. 1974. "Comment: The American Electoral Universe: Speculation and Evidence." *American Political Science Review* 68: 1028–1049.

Rusk, Jerrold G., and John J. Stucker. 1978. "The Effect of the Southern System of Election Laws on Voting Participation." In *The History of American Electoral Behavior*, ed. Joel H. Silbey, Allan G. Bogue, and William H. Flanigan. Princeton, NJ: Princeton University Press.

Sanders, Lynn M. 1995. "The Racial Legacy of American Values." Ph.D. diss., Department of Political Science, University of Michigan.

Sanders, Lynn M., and Laura L. Stoker. 1989. "Competing Meanings of American Values." Presented at the annual meeting of the Midwest Political Science Association, Chicago.

Sawhill, Isabel V., and Charles F. Stone. 1984. "The Economy: The Key to Success." In *The Reagan Record: An Assessment of America's Changing Domestic Priorities*, ed. John L. Palmer, and I. V. Sawhill. Cambridge, MA: Ballinger.

Schaeffer, Nora C. 1980. "Evaluating Race-of-Interviewer Effects in a National Survey." *Sociological Methods and Research* 8 : 400–419.

Schelling, Thomas C. 1978. *Micromotives and Macrobehavior*. New York: Norton.

Schlozman, Kay Lehman, and Sidney Verba. 1979. *Injury to Insult*. Cambridge, MA: Harvard University Press.

Schudson, Michael. 1978. *Discovering the News*. New York: Basic.

Schuman, Howard, and Lawrence Bobo. 1988. "Survey-Based Experiments on White Racial Attitudes toward Residential Integration." *American Journal of Sociology* 94 : 273–299.

Schuman, Howard, and Jean M. Converse. 1971. "The Effects of Black and White Interviewers on Black Responses in 1968." *Public Opinion Quarterly* 35 : 44–68.

Schuman, Howard, and Stanley Presser. 1981. *Questions and Answers in Attitude Surveys: Experiments in Question Form, Wording, and Context*. New York: Academic Press.

Schuman, Howard, Charlotte Steeh, and Lawrence Bobo. 1985. *Racial Attitudes in America: Trends and Interpretations*. Cambridge: Harvard University Press.

Schumpeter, Joseph A. 1942. *Capitalism, Socialism, and Democracy*. New York: Harper and Row.

Scott, James C. 1986. *Weapons of the Weak: Everyday Forms of Peasant Resistance*. New Haven, CT: Yale University Press.

Sears, David O. 1986. "College Sophomores in the Laboratory: Influence of a Narrow Data Base on Social Psychology's View of Human Nature." *Journal of Personality and Social Psychology* 51 : 515–530.

———. 1988. "Symbolic Racism." In *Eliminating Racism: Profiles in Controversy*, ed. Phylis Katz and Dalmas A. Taylor. New York: Plenum.

Sears, David O., and Harris M. Allen, Jr. 1984. "The Trajectory of Local Desegregation Controversies and Whites' Opposition to Busing." In *Groups in*

Contact: The Psychology of Desegregation, ed. Norman Miller and Marilyn Brewer. New York: Academic Press.

Sears, David O., and Jack Citrin. 1982. *Tax Revolt: Something for Nothing in California*. Cambridge, MA: Harvard University Press.

Sears, David O., and Carolyn L. Funk. 1991. "The Role of Self-Interest in Social and Political Attitudes." In *Advances in Experimental Social Psychology* 24: 1–91.

Sears, David O., Leonie Huddie, and L. G. Schaffer. 1986. "A Schematic Variant of Symbolic Politics Theory, as Applied to Racial and Gender Equality." In *Political Cognition*, ed. Richard R. Lau and David O. Sears. Hillsdale, NJ: Erlbaum.

Sears, David O., and Donald R. Kinder. 1971. "Racial Tensions and Voting in Los Angeles." In *Los Angeles: Viability and Prospects for Metropolitan Leadership*, ed. Werner Z. Hirsch. New York: Praeger.

———. 1985. "Whites' Opposition to Busing: On Conceptualizing and Operationalizing 'Group Conflict.'" *Journal of Personality and Social Psychology* 48:1141–1147.

Sears, David O., and Richard R. Lau. 1983. "Inducing Apparently Self-Interested Political Preferences." *American Journal of Political Science* 27: 223–252.

Sears, David O., and John B. McConahay. 1973. *The Politics of Violence: The New Urban Blacks and the Watts Riot*. Boston: Houghton Mifflin.

Selznick, G. J., and S. Steinberg. 1969. *The Tenacity of Prejudice*. New York: Harper and Row.

Sen, Amartya. 1977. "Rational Fools: A Critique of the Behavioral Foundations of Economic Theory." *Philosophy and Public Affairs* 6:317–344.

Sennet, R., and J. Cobb. 1972. *The Hidden Injuries of Class*. New York: Vintage.

Shafer, Byron E. 1983. *Quiet Revolution*. New York: Russell Sage.

———. 1991. *The End of Realignment?* Madison: University of Wisconsin Press.

Sheatsley, Paul B. 1966. "White Attitudes toward the Negro." *Daedalus* 95:217–238.

Sherif, Muzafer, O. J. Harvey, B. J. White, W. R. Hood, and Carolyn W. Sherif. 1961. *Intergroup Conflict and Cooperation: The Robber Cave Experiment*. Norman: Institute of Group Relations, University of Oklahoma.

Sherif, Muzafer, and Carolyn W. Sherif. 1953. *Groups in Harmony and Tension*. New York: Harper.

Shklar, Judith N. 1991. *American Citizenship. The Quest for Inclusion*. Cambridge, MA: Harvard University Press.

Sidanius, Jim. 1989. "Symbolic Racism and Social Dominance Theory." Presented at the annual meeting of the Society for Experimental Social Psychology, Los Angeles.

Sigelman, Lee and Susan Welch. 1991. *Black Americans' Views of Racial Inequality: The Dream Deferred*. Cambridge, MA: Cambridge University Press.

Silbey, Joel H. 1991. "Beyond Realignment and Realignment Theory: American Political Eras, 1789–1989." In *The End of Realignment?* ed. Byron E. Shafer. Madison: University of Wisconsin Press.

Simkins, Francis B., and Charles P. Roland. 1972. *A History of the South*, 4th ed. New York: Knopf.

Simon, Herbert A. 1979. *Models of Thought*. New Haven, CT: Yale University Press.

Sitkoff, Harvard. 1978. *A New Deal for Blacks: The Emergence of Civil Rights as a National Issue: The Depression Decade*. New York: Oxford University Press.

Skocpol, Theda. 1988. "The Limits of the New Deal System and the Roots of Contemporary Welfare Dilemmas." In *The Politics of Social Policy in the United States*, eds. Margaret Weir, Ann Shola Orloff, and Theda Skocpol. Princeton, NJ: Princeton University Press.

———. 1991. "Targeting within Universalism: Politically Viable Policies to Combat Poverty in the United States." In *The Urban Underclass*, ed. Christopher Jencks and Paul E. Peterson. Washington, DC: Brookings.

Smith, Eric R. A. N. 1989. *The Unchanging American Voter*. Berkeley: University of California Press.

Smith, Rogers M. 1993. "Beyond Tocqueville, Myrdal, and Hartz: The Multiple Tradition of America." *American Political Science Review* 87:549–566.

Smith, Tom W. 1980. "America's Most Important Problem: A Trend Analysis, 1946–1976." *Public Opinion Quarterly* 44:164–180.

———. 1984. "Non-Attitudes: A Review and Evaluation." In *Surveying Subjective Phenomena*, vol. 2, ed. Charles Turner and Elizabeth Martin. New York: Russell Sage.

Smith, Tom W., and Paul B. Sheatsley. 1984. "American Attitudes toward Race Relations." *Public Opinion* 14–15 (October/November), 50–53.

Sniderman, Paul M. 1975. *Personality and Democratic Politics*. Berkeley: University of California Press.

———. 1993. "The New Look in Public Opinion Research." In *Political Science: The State of the Discipline II*, ed. Ada F. Finifter. Washington, DC: American Political Science Association.

Sniderman, Paul M., and Richard A. Brody. 1977. "Coping: The Ethic of Self-Reliance." *American Journal of Political Science* 21:501–522.

Sniderman, Paul M., Richard A. Brody, and James H. Kuklinski. 1984. "Policy Reasoning and Political Values: The Problem of Racial Equality." *American Journal of Political Science* 28:75–94.

Sniderman, Paul M., with Michael G. Hagen. 1985. *Race and Inequality: A Study in American Values*. Chatham, NJ: Chatham House.

Sniderman, Paul M., and Thomas Piazza. 1993. *The Scar of Race*. Cambridge, MA: Harvard University Press.

Sniderman, Paul M., and Philip E. Tetlock. 1986a. "Symbolic Racism: Problems of Motive Attribution in Political Analysis." *Journal of Social Issues* 42:129–150.

Sniderman, Paul M., and Philip E. Tetlock. 1986b. "Reflections on American Racism." *Journal of Social Issues* 42:173–187.

Stanley, Harold W. 1987. *Voter Mobilization and the Politics of Race: The South and Universal Suffrage, 1952–1984*. New York: Praeger.

Stanley, Harold W., William T. Bianco, and Richard G. Niemi. 1986. "The Demise of the New Deal Coalition: Partisanship and Group Support over Time, a Multivariate Analysis." In *Democracy's Feast: Elections in America,* ed. Herbert F. Weisberg. Chatham, NJ: Chatham Press.

Stevens, Jacqueline. 1993. "The Politics of Identity." Ph.D. diss., Department of Political Science, University of California, Berkeley.

Stigler, George J. 1975. "Smith's Travels on the Ship of State." In *Essays on Adam Smith,* ed. A. Skinner and T. Wilson. Oxford: Clarendon Press.

Stimson, James A. 1975. "Belief Systems: Constraint, Complexity, and the 1972 Election." *American Journal of Political Science* 19:383–418.

Stoker, Laura. 1992. "Interests and Ethics in Politics. *American Political Science Review* 86:369–380.

———. 1996. "Political Value Judgments." In *Political Values and Political Psychology,* ed. James Kuklinski. Cambridge: Cambridge University Press. Forthcoming.

Stouffer, Samuel A. 1955. *Communism, Conformity, and Civil Liberties.* New York: Doubleday.

Stouffer, Samuel A., E. A. Suchman, L. C. DeVinney, S. A. Star, and R. M. Williams, Jr. 1949. *The American Soldier.* Princeton, NJ: Princeton University Press.

Sullivan, John L., J. E. Piereson, and George E. Marcus. 1982. *Political Tolerance and American Democracy.* Chicago: University of Chicago Press.

Sumner, William Graham. 1906. *Folkways: A Study of the Sociological Importance of Usages, Manners, Customs, Mores, and Morals.* Boston: Athenaeum Press.

Sundquist, James L. [1973] 1983. *Dynamics of the Party System: Alignment and Realignment of Political Parties in the United States.* Washington, DC: Brookings.

Taeuber, Karl E., and Alma F. Taeuber. 1965. *Negroes in Cities.* Chicago: Aldine.

Tajfel, Henri. 1969. "Cognitive Aspects of Prejudice." *Journal of Social Issues* 25: 79–97.

Tanur, Judith M., ed. 1991. *Questions about Questions: Inquiries into the Cognitive Bases of Surveys.* New York: Russell Sage.

Tate, Katherine. 1993. *From Protest to Politics: The New Black Voters in American Elections.* Cambridge, MA: Harvard University Press.

Taylor, D. Garth, Paul B. Sheatsley, and Andrew M. Greeley. 1978. "Attitudes toward Racial Integration." *Scientific American* 238 (June): 42–51.

Thernstrom, Abigal M. 1987. *Whose Votes Count? Affirmative Action and Minority Voting Rights.* Cambridge, MA: Harvard University Press.

Thompson, Dennis F. 1970. *The Democratic Citizen.* Cambridge: Cambridge University Press.

Tindall, George B. 1967. *The Emergence of the New South, 1913–1945.* Baton Rouge: Louisiana State University Press.

Tocqueville, Alexis de. [1848] 1945. *Democracy in America.* New York: Knopf.

Tourangeau, Roger, and Kenneth A. Rasinski. 1988. Cognitive Processes Underlying Context Effects in Attitude Measurement. *Psychological Bulletin* 103: 299–314.

Truman, David B. 1951. *The Governmental Process.* New York: Knopf.

Tufte, Edward R. 1978. *Political Control of the Economy*. Princeton, NJ: Princeton University Press.

Turner, Patricia A. 1993. *I Heard It through the Grapevine*. Berkeley: University of California Press.

Tversky, Amos, and Daniel Kahneman. 1974. "Judgment under Uncertainty: Heuristics and Biases." *Science* 185:1124–1131.

———. 1981. "The Framing of Decisions and the Psychology of Choice." *Science* 211:453–458.

Tyler, Tom R. 1977. "Drawing Inferences from Behavior: The Effect of Crime Victimization Experiences upon Crime-Related Attitudes and Behavior." Ph.D. diss., Department of Psychology, University of California, Los Angeles.

U.S. Commission on Civil Rights. 1968. *Political Participation*. Washington, DC: Government Printing Office.

U.S. National Advisory Committee on Civil Disorders. 1968. *Report of the National Advisory Committee on Civil Disorders*. Washington, DC: Government Printing Office.

U.S. President's Committee on Civil Rights. 1947. *To Secure These Rights*. New York: Simon and Schuster.

Useem, Bert. 1980. "Solidarity Model, Breakdown Model, and the Boston Anti-Busing Movement." *American Sociological Review* 45:357–369.

Van den Berghe, Pierre L. 1967. *Race and Racism: A Comparative Perspective*. New York: Wiley.

Vanneman, R. D., and Thomas F. Pettigrew. 1972. "Race and Relative Deprivation in the Urban United States." *Race* 13:461–486.

Verba, Sidney, and Norman H. Nie. 1972. *Participation in America: Political Democracy and Social Equality*. New York: Harper and Row.

Verba, Sidney, and Gary R. Orren. 1985. *Equality in America: The View from the Top*. Cambridge, MA: Harvard University Press.

Verba, Sidney, et al. 1987. *Elites and the Idea of Equality: A Comparison of Japan, Sweden, and the United States*. Cambridge, MA: Harvard University Press.

Wade, Richard C. 1964. *Slavery in the Cities: The South 1820–1860*. New York: Oxford University Press.

Walzer, Michael. 1983. *Spheres of Justice: A Defense of Pluralism and Equality*. New York: Basic.

Watters, Pat, and Reese Cleghorn. 1967. *Climbing Jacob's Ladder: The Arrival of Negroes in Southern Politics*. New York: Harcourt, Brace, and World.

Weber, Max. [1930] 1971. *The Protestant Ethic and the Spirit of Capitalism*. London: Allen and Unwin.

Webster, Yehudi. 1992. *Racialization of America*. New York: St. Martin's.

Weigel, R. H., and P. W. Howes. 1985. "Conceptions of Racial Prejudice: Symbolic Racism Reconsidered." *Journal of Social Issues* 41:117–138.

Weir, Margaret, Ann Shola Orloff, and Theda Skocpol. 1988. *The Politics of Social Policy in the United States*. Princeton, NJ: Princeton University Press.

Weiss, Nancy J. 1983. *Farewell to the Party of Lincoln*. Princeton, NJ: Princeton University Press.

Welch, Susan, and Lorn Foster. 1987. "Class and Conservatism in the Black Community." *American Politics Quarterly* 15:445–470.

West, Cornel. 1993. *Race Matters*. Boston: Beacon Press.

West, Darrell. 1993. *Airwars, TV Advertising, and Election Campaigns, 1952–1992*. Washington, DC: CQ Press.

White, Theodore H. 1965. *The Making of the President, 1964*. New York: Atheneum.

Williams, Linda. 1987. "Black Political Progress in the 1980s: The Electoral Arena." In *The New Black Politics: The Search for Political Power*, 2d ed., ed. M. B. Preston, L. J. Henderson, Jr., and P. L. Puryear. New York: Longman.

Williams, Robin M., Jr. 1964. *Strangers Next Door: Ethnic Relations in American Communities*. Englewood Cliffs, NJ: Prentice-Hall.

———. 1968. "Values." In *International Encyclopedia of the Social Sciences*, ed. David L. Sills. New York: Macmillan and Free Press.

Wills, Gary. 1971. *Nixon Agonistes*. New York: Knopf.

———. 1992. *Lincoln at Gettysburg*. New York: Simon and Schuster.

Wilson, James Q. 1973. *Political Organizations*. New York: Basic.

Wilson, James Q., and Edward C. Banfield. 1964. "Public-Regardingness as a Value Premise in Voting Behavior." *American Political Science Review* 58: 876–887.

Wilson, William J. 1973. *Power, Racism, and Privilege: Race Relations in Theoretical and Sociohistorical Perspective*. New York: Free Press.

———. 1978. *The Declining Significance of Race: Blacks and Changing American Institutions*. Chicago: University of Chicago Press.

———. 1987. *The Truly Disadvantaged: The Inner City, the Underclass, and Public Policy*. Chicago: University of Chicago Press.

———. 1991. "Public Policy Research and *The Truly Disadvantaged*." In *The Urban Underclass*, ed. Christopher Jencks and Paul E. Peterson. Washington, DC: Brookings.

Wolfinger, Raymond E., and R. B. Arseneau. 1978. "Partisan Changes in the South, 1952–1976." In *Political Parties: Development and Decay*, ed. L. Maisel and J. Cooper. Beverly Hills: Sage.

Wolfinger, Raymond E., and Fred I. Greenstein. 1968. "The Repeal of Fair Housing in California: An Analysis of Referendum Voting." *American Political Science Review* 62:753–769.

Woodward, C. Vann. 1951. *Reunion and Reaction*. Boston: Little, Brown.

———. [1955] 1974. *The Strange Career of Jim Crow*. New York: Oxford University Press.

———. 1988. "Referendum on Reagan." *New York Review of Books*, 22 December.

Wright, Erik Olin. 1979. *Class Structure and Income Determination*. New York: Academic Press.

Wright, Gerald C., Jr. 1976. "Community Structure and Voting in the South." *Public Opinion Quarterly* 40:201–215.

———. 1977. "Contextual Models of Electoral Behavior: The Southern Wallace Vote." *American Political Science Review* 71:497–508.

Yinger, J. Milton. 1976. "Ethnicity in Complex Societies." In *The Uses of Contro-*

versy in Sociology, ed. Lewis A. Coser and Otto N. Larsen. New York: Free Press.

Yinger, John. 1986. "Measuring Racial Discrimination with Fair Housing Audits: Caught in the Act." *American Economic Review* 76:881–893.

Young, Jason, Eugene Borgida, John L. Sullivan, and John J. Aldrich. 1987. "Personal Agendas and the Relationship between Self-Interest and Voting Behavior." *Social Psychology Quarterly* 50:64–71.

Young, Jason, Cynthia J. Thomsen, Eugene Borgida, John L. Sullivan, and John H. Aldrich. 1991. "When Self-Interest Makes a Difference: The Role of Construct Accessibility in Political Reasoning." *Journal of Experimental Social Psychology* 27:271-96.

Zaller, John A. 1990. "Experimental Tests of the Question-Answering Model of the Mass Survey Response." Center for Political Studies, Institute for Social Research, University of Michigan. Technical Report to the National Election Studies Board.

———. 1992. *The Nature and Origins of Mass Opinion.* Cambridge: Cambridge University Press.

Zaller, John A., and Feldman, Stanley. 1992. "A Simple Theory of the Survey Response: Answering Questions versus Revealing Preferences. *American Journal of Political Science* 36:579–616.

Zimmerman, Marvin. 1990. "Some Dubious Premises in Research and Theory on Racial Differences." *American Psychologist* 45:1297-1303.

INDEX

The letter *t* after a page number indicates a table.

Abelson, Robert, 43
abolitionists, 93–94
Adorno, Theodore W., 106, 125, 273–74
AFDC (Aid to Families with Dependent
    Children), 76–78
affirmative action, 8, 9, 17t, 263, 308 n.27;
    frames and, 174–82, 192; group inter-
    est of blacks and, 85–88; group in-
    terest of whites and, 83–85; public
    opinion toward, 194; racial attitudes
    toward, 25–27; self-interest and, 53–
    56, 59–60
Agnew, Spiro T., 225
Ailes, Roger, 234, 235–36, 254, 255
Alexander v. Holmes, 20
alienation, racial divide on, 30t, 31
Allport, Gordon, 108–9, 111
Almond, J. Lindsay, 222
American conservatism, 245–46
American Creed, 38, 129–30, 278–80
American Dilemma, An (Myrdal), 8
American Solder, The (Stouffer), 264
American Voter, The (Campbell), 51
Anatomy of Racial Attitudes, The (Apostle),
    97
Anderson, Marian, 96
anti-Semitism, 273–74
Apostle, Richard A., 97
Aristotle, 128
Armstrong, Louis, 96
Atwater, Lee, 234, 236, 254–56, 257
Authoritarian Personality, The (Adorno),
    106, 125, 273–74

Barnes, Clifford, 234
Barnett, Ross, 221, 222
Barry, Brian, 36, 51
Bellah, Robert, 135–36
Bell Curve, The (Murray), 127
Benedict, Ruth, 96

Bennett, William, 163
Bentsen, Lloyd, 237–38
Biden, Joesph, 229
biological racism, 105, 126–27, 319 n.20;
    decline of, 95–98; origins of, 92–95;
    racial resentment and, 115
Black, Earl, 221–22, 223
Black Cabinet, 211
black enfranchisement, 340 n.8
Black English Vernacular (BEV), 354 n.76
black opinion: principle of economic
    individualism and, 151; principle
    of equality and, 151, 152; principle of
    limited government and, 151–52; self-
    interest and, 68–81
Black Power, 103
black representation, 5
black voters: Democratic party and, 209–
    12; increase in, 213–16; 1988 presi-
    dential campaign and, 247–51;
    Republican party and, 208–9
Blake, J. P., 3
Blease, Cole, 216
Bobo, Lawrence, 269, 270–71, 293–94
Bradley, Tom, 291
Brown, Pat, 224
Brown, Willie, 233
Brown v. Board of Education, 19, 20, 98–99,
    100, 222
Bryce, James B., 33, 135
Bush, George, 257; black voters and, 247–
    48, 249, 250–51; and Civil Rights Bill
    of 1990, 163; presidential campaign
    of, 231–36

Campbell, Angus, 51, 264
Campbell, Donald, 88, 166
Carmine, Edward G., 269
Carter, Jimmy, 221
Chaney, James, 237

385

Protestant Ethic and the Spirit of Capitalism
(Weber), 136–37
public opinion, 12–14; government policy
and, 352 n.24; measurement of, 41–44;
opinion frames and, 38–39; principles
and, 38, 128–31, 145–58
public opinion structure: race policy and,
295–97; self-interest and, 36; social
groups and, 37–38; theoretical determinants of, 36–38

Quayle, Dan, 238
quotas, 163, 274

race: approaches to, 11; as idea, 306 n.27
*Race and Inequality: A Study in American
Values* (Sniderman and Hagen), 269,
271
*Race and the Decline of Class in American
Politics* (Huckfeldt and Kohfeld), 269
race-conscious frames: government assistance and, 182–87; interviewer's race
and, 301
race policy: racial divide on, 27–31; racial
resentment, 116–17; structure of public opinion on, 295–97
race relations, 4, 6
race riots, 102–6, 321 n.36
Racial Attitudes in America (Schuman,
Steeh, and Bobo), 269
racial codewords, 198, 223–28, 345 n.101
racial conservatism, 269
racial divide, 17–34, 309 n.42; class and,
31; elections and, 198; equality principle and, 327 n.22; equal opportunity
and, 18–27; foreign policy and, 29–
31; influential citizens and, 298–99;
Medicare and, 29, 30t; race policy
and, 27–31; social issues and, 29, 30t;
Social Security and, 29, 30t; social
spending and, 29–30
racial environmentalism, 95–98
racial equality, 6–7
racial fear, 264–67
racial ideology, 317 n.64
racial prejudice, 310 n.13
racial resentment, 321 n.42; American conservatism and, 245–46; characteristics
of, 108–15; class frames and, 190–91,
192; conditions for, 274–76; empirical
evidence of, 268–76; frames and, 177t,

177–78; toward Jesse Jackson, 242–
43; measurement of, 106–8; 1988
presidential campaign and, 240–47;
1992 campaign and, 257–58; public
policy and, 115–24; racial prejudice
and, 108–9; racial stereotyping and,
299–301; role in white opinion, 124–
26; and Willie Horton, 246–47. *See
also* prejudice, racial
racial threat: class and, 90–91; group-
conflict theory and, 90; group interest
and, 89–90; self-interest and, 88–89;
white opinion and, 60–68
racism: biological, 92–98, 105, 115, 126–
27, 319 n.20; modern, 292; subtle, 292;
symbolic, 291–94; theory of, 93–95
Rae, Douglas, 6, 132, 159, 183
Reagan, Ronald, 76, 104–5, 208, 231
Reagan Democrats, 228
realignment theory, 218–19, 344 n.75
Reconstruction, 5
relative deprivation, 264
Republican party: black voters and,
208–9; campaign strategy in 1964,
201–4; effect of 1964 election on, 208;
1988 presidential nomination and,
230–36; 1964 realignment, 206; racial
predicament of, 198; rise of in South,
216–21; role of race in 1988 cam-
paign, 252–56
reverse discrimination, 227
reverse discrimination frames, 175–82,
192–93
Rhetoric of Reaction, The (Hirschman), 283
Rieder, Jonathan, 265
Riker, William H., 196, 284
riots, 102–6, 265
Rivers, Douglas, 44
Robertson, Pat, 231
Robeson, Paul, 96
Rodgers, Daniel T., 130
Roosevelt, Eleanor, 211–12
Roosevelt, Franklin D., 92, 209–11
Ross, Lee, 64–65
Rovere, Richard, 224–25
Rumford Act, 224
Runciman, W. G., 264

Sawhill, Isabel V., 76
Scar of Race, The (Sniderman and Piazza),
271